WHO'S WHO IN FICTION?

Who's Who in Fiction?

A DICTIONARY OF NOTED NAMES IN NOVELS, TALES, ROMANCES, POETRY, AND DRAMA

BY

H. SWAN

LONDON :
GEORGE ROUTLEDGE & SONS, LIM.
NEW YORK : E. P. DUTTON & CO.

Republished by Gale Research Company,
Book Tower, Detroit, Michigan 1975

Library of Congress Cataloging in Publication Data

Swan, Helena, comp.
  Who's who in fiction?

  Reprint of the 1906 ed. published by Routledge, London,
and Dutton, New York, in series: Routledge's miniature
reference library.
  1. English literature--Dictionaries. 2. Characters
and characteristics in literature--Dictionaries.
I. Title. II. Series: Routledge's miniature reference
library.
PR19.S9 1975   820'.8'027   73-167218
ISBN 0-8103-4114-X

PREFACE

THIS little book aims at supplying information frequently sought for in larger works of reference without success. Its scope is limited to *standard* works within the sphere of English Fiction, both prose and verse, whether novel, poem, or play. Exceptions have been made in the cases of a few books, chiefly of Oriental origin, such as *The Arabian Nights'*, which have been rendered familiar by English translations, and of the great medieval romances of chivalry, with which we have become acquainted through Middle-English versions.

H. S.

WHO'S WHO IN FICTION

Aaron : a Moor with whom Tamora, Queen of the Goths, was in love [Shakespeare, *Titus Andronicus*].

Abberville, Lord : a young nobleman whose career of dissipation is arrested by means of a faithful bailiff. He is the hero of the play [Cumberland, *Fashionable Lover*].

Abdael : is intended for General Monk, afterwards Duke of Albemarle, who was a strong partizan of Charles II [Dryden, *Absalom and Achitophel*].

Abdalazis : a Moor who became Governor of Spain after the fall of Roderick [Southey, *Roderick*].

Abdaldar : a magician chosen as the destroyer of Thalaba, but who died just as he was about to stab his victim [Southey, *Thalaba*].

Abdalla : a slave belonging to Sir Brian de Bois Gilbert [Scott, *Ivanhoe*].

Abdallah : a brother of Giaffer, and murdered by him [Byron, *Bride of Abydos*].

——— el Hadgi : an envoy employed by Saladin [Scott, *Talisman*].

Abdiel : a seraph, who, though urged by Satan to revolt, remained 'unmoved, unshaken, unseduced' [Milton, *Paradise Lost*].

Abelard : *see* Eloisa.

Abellino : a beggar and a bandit who ultimately marries a niece of the Doge of Venice [M.G. Lewis, *Bravo of Venice*]

Aben-Ezra, Raphael : a friend of the Prefect of Alexandria [Charles Kingsley, *Hypatia*].

Abessa : the personification of Abbeys and Convents and the paramour of Kirkrapine [Spenser, *Faëry Queene*].

Abhorson : the executioner [Shakespeare, *Measure for Measure*].

Abigail : a servant [Beaumont and Fletcher, *Scornful Lady*].

Abney : Albert Lee's friend [Scott, *Woodstock*].

Abou Ben Adhem : the hero of the poem of that title [Leigh Hunt, *Abou Ben Adhem*].

—————— **Hassam :** the hero of the story called the *Sleeper Awakened* [*Arabian Nights*].

Absalom : intended by the author for Charles II's son, the Duke of Monmouth [Dryden, *Absalom and Achitophel*].

Absolon : the parish clerk and a suitor for the hand of Alison [Chaucer. *Canterbury Tales : The Miller's Tale*].

Absolute, Captain : a suitor for the hand of Lydia Languish under the name of Ensign Beverley.

—————— *Sir Anthony :* a warm-hearted old gentleman of irascible temper. The father of Captain Absolute [Sheridan, *Rivals*].

Abudah : a merchant of Bagdad who meets with many wonderful adventures [Ridley, *Tales of the Genii*].

—————— the Second in Command of an Arabian Army investing Damascus [John Hughes, *Siege of Damascus*].

Acasto, Lord : an unfortunate noble who survives all his children [Otway, *The Orphan*].

Achilles : the chief character in the opera of that name [Gay, *Achilles*].

Achitophel : is intended for the Earl of Shaftesbury, who aided the Duke of Monmouth (Absalom) in his designs on the Crown [Dryden, *Absalom and Achitophel*].

Achthar, Lord Anophel : an idiotic and scoundrelly young man [Peacock, *Melincourt*].

Ackland, Sir Thomas : one of the royalist party [Scott, *Woodstock*].

Acrasia : an enchantress living in ' The Bower of Bliss,' and personifying Intemperance [Spenser, *Faëry Queene*].

Acrates : the personification of Incontinence and the father of Gluttony and Drunkenness [Phineas Fletcher, *Purple Island*].

Acres, Bob : a coward and swearer, the rival of Ensign Beverley as a suitor for the hand of Lydia Languish [Sheridan, *Rivals*].

Adam : a college tutor ' white-tied, clerical, silent ' [Clough, *Bothie of Toberna-Vuolich*].

—————— the aged servant of Oliver. A part supposed to have been acted by the author [Shakespeare, *As You Like It*].

—————— **Bede :** *see* Bede, Adam.

—————— **Bell :** *see* Bell, Adam.

Adams, Parson Abraham : a learned, sweet-natured country clergyman, noted for his unworldliness [Fielding, *Joseph Andrews*].

Adelaide : killed, in error, by her own father [Jephson, *Count of Narbonne*].

Adeline : ' Faintly smiling Adeline ' [Alfred Tennyson, *Adeline*].

Adhem, Abou Ben : a man who loved his fellow-men [Leigh Hunt, *Abou Ben Adhem*].

Adicia : wife of the soldan, who after sundry misdeeds is changed into a tigress [Spenser, *Faëry Queen*].

Adicus : the personification of Unrighteousness [Phineas Fletcher, *Purple Island*].

Adie of Aikenshaw : a neighbour of the Glendinnning family [Scott, *The Monastery*].

Admetus : King of Thessaly and husband of Alcestis [Lowell, *Shepherd of King Admetus*].

Adolpha : daughter of the Governor of Prague, married to Idenstein [Knowles, *Maid of Mariendorpt*].

Adonais : the name under which the poet Keats was immortalized by his friend [Shelley, *Adonais*].

Adonbec el Hakim : the name which Saladin assumed when he visited Sir Kenneth's Squire as a doctor [Scott, *Talisman*].

Adosinda : the daughter of the Gothic Governor of Auria [Southey, *Roderick*].

Adramelech : a fallen angel, vanquished by Uriel and Raphael [Milton, *Paradise Lost*].

Adriana : the wife of Antipholus of Ephesus [Shakespeare, *Comedy of Errors*].

Adriano de Armado, Don : a pompous, poor, and boastful Spaniard [Shakespeare, *Love's Labour's Lost*].

Adriel : represents the royalist Earl of Mulgrave [Dryden, *Absalom and Achitophel*].

Aegeon : a merchant of Syracuse [Shakespeare, *Comedy of Errors*].

Aella : the hero of the tragedy ' [Chatterton, *Aella*].

Aemelia : a noble lady in love with Amias, whom she is enabled to marry through the good offices of Prince Arthur [Spenser, *Faëry Queene*].

Aemilia : an abbess, the wife of Aegeon, and mother of the twin Antipholus [Shakespeare, *Comedy of Errors*].

Aetion : a character supposed to be intended for Shakespeare [Spenser, *Colin Clout's Come Home Again*].

Agag : intended for Sir E. Godfrey, a magistrate murdered on Primrose Hill [Dryden, *Absalom and Achitophel*].

Agamemnon : the hero of an unsuccessful play [James Thomson, *Agamemnon*].

Agatha : the saintly heroine of a story of rural life in Germany [George Eliot, *Agatha*].

Agathocles : the leading character in the play, and intended for Oliver Cromwell [Perrinchief, *Agathocles ; or, The Sicilian Tyrant*].

Aged, The : the name by which Wemmick's father was known [Dickens, *Great Expectations*].

Agelastes, Michael : the philosopher and cynic [Scott, *Count Robert of Paris*].

Ager, Captain : a soldier and noble gentleman who makes a fine distinction between physical and moral courage [Middleton and Rowley, *A Fair Quarrel*].

Agil : the third Calendar in the story of *The Three Calendars* [*Arabian Nights*].

Aglaura : the heroine in a tragi-comedy [Sir John Suckling, *Aglaura*].

Agneia : Wifely Chastity personified [Phineas Fletcher, *Purple Island*].

Agnes of Sorrento : the heroine of the tale [Harriet Beecher Stowe, *Agnes of Sorrento*].

Agravaine, Sir : a Knight of the Round Table, the son of Lot, King of Orkney, and a nephew of King Arthur [Malory, *History of Prince Arthur*].

Agrios : the personification of Sullenness [Phineas Fletcher, *Purple Island*].

Aguecheek, Sir Andrew : a silly country squire, the butt of the witty, and a fop [Shakespeare, *Twelfth Night*].

Ahaback : an enchanter who was crushed to death by a stone being let down on him, that had formed the head of his bed [Ridley, *Tales of the Genii*].

Ahmed, Prince : the owner of a tent, given him by a fairy, that could shelter a whole army, yet fold up so closely that he could carry it in his pocket [*Arabian Nights*].

Aholibamah : the granddaughter of Cain [Byron, *Heaven and Earth*].

Aikwood, Ringan : a forester in the service of Sir Arthur Wardour [Scott, *Antiquary*].

Aimwell, Thomas, Viscount : a man who having fallen on evil days, tries to retrieve his position by marrying an heiress [Farquhar, *Beaux' Stratagem*].

Aircastle : a discursive talker after the fashion of Mrs. Nickleby, said to have been drawn from life [Foote, *Cozeners*].

Airlie, The Earl of : a royalist follower of Charles I [Scott, *Legend of Montrose*].

Airy, Sir George : a gentleman of wealth, in love with Miranda [Mrs. Centlivre, *Busybody*].

Aladdin : the owner of a wonderful lamp that, upon being rubbed, gave him all he longed for, but which he lost, and with it all his wealth [*Arabian Nights*].

Aladine : a lusty knight [Spenser, *Faëry Queene*].

Alasco : the alias of Dr. Doboobie, an astrologer [Scott, *Kenilworth*].

Alasnam : the possessor of eight priceless statues, but who, craving for a ninth, found one still more precious, in the form of a woman, and her he married [*Arabian Nights*].

Alastor : 'a youth of uncorrupted feelings and adventurous genius' [Shelley, *Alastor ; or, The Spirit of Solitude*].

Alberick : the squire of Richard, son of Henry II of England [Scott, *Betrothed*].

—— of Mortemar : an exiled nobleman also known as Theodorick, the hermit of Engaddi [Scott, *Talisman*].

Albert : the judge of Wyoming, and father of Gertrude [Campbell, *Gertrude of Wyoming*].

—— = Lord Wilfrid, who assumes the character of the 'Blind Beggar' [Knowles, *Beggar of Bethnal Green*].

—— of Geierstein : president of the Secret Tribunal [Scott, *Anne of Geierstein*].

Albovine : King of Lombardy, married to Rosamonde [Davenant, *Albovine, King of Lombardy*].

Albumazar : the chief character in the play [Tomkis, *Albumazar the Astronomer*].

Alciphron ; a freethinker who debates [Bp. Berkeley, *Alciphron ; or, the Minute Philosopher*].

—— the hero of the story [Thomas Moore, *Epicurean*].

Alcolomb : the daughter of Abou Aibou, who marries the caliph Haroun-al-Raschid [*Arabian Nights*].

Alcyon : once a jolly shepherd but afterwards 'the wofullest man alive' [Spenser, *Daphnaïdi*].

Aldabella : a beautiful Florentine admired by the ill-fated Fazio, and condemned to end her days in a nunnery [Milman, *Fazio*].

Alden, John : the lover of Priscilla, whom he marries in the end, though he first woos her for his friend [Longfellow, *Courtship of Miles Standish*].

Aldiborontephoscophornio : a courtier in a burlesque [Carey, *Chrononhotonthologos*].

Aldingar, Sir : the steward of Queen Eleanor, who accused her of infidelity to Henry II, but whose innocence was established through a child-angel [Percy, *Reliques*].

Aldoi : elopes with Lorna, King Erragon's wife, and is slain in single combat by the injured husband [Ossian, *Battle of Lora*].

Aldovrand : chaplain to Sir Raymond Berenger [Scott, *The Betrothed*].

Aldrick : the Jesuit Confessor to the Countess of Derby [Scott, *Peveril of the Peak*].

Alexander : [Lyly, *Alexander and Campaspe*].

Alexas : an unworthy member of Cleopatra's household—a eunuch [Dryden, *All for Love*].

Alfonso, Don : the jealous husband of Donna Julia [Byron, *Don Juan*].

Ali Baba : a poor wood-carrier who learnt the magic phrases 'open sesamê' and 'shut sesamê'—the hero of the story of '*The Forty Thieves*' [*Arabian Nights*].

———— **Mahbub :** a man in the employ of the Indian secret service [Kipling, *Kim*].

Alice : the central figure in two fairy stories [Lewis Carroll (C. L. Dodgson), *Alice in Wonderland ; Alice Through the Looking-Glass*].

———— the sister of Valentine [J.Fletcher, *Monsieur Thomas*].

———— the heroine in a book which is the sequel to *Ernest Maltravers* [Lytton, *Alice ; or, The Mysteries*].

———— the heroine of a poem in three parts—a merry child in the first, and dying in the last [Alfred Tennyson, *May Queen*].

———— the heroine of a tale of village love [Alfred Tennyson, *Miller's Daughter*].

———— **du Clos :** the heroine of a ballad [S. T. Coleridge, *Alice du Clos*].

———— **Fell :** *see* Fell, Alice.

———— **Gray, Old :** *see* Gray, Old Alice.

———— **Mistress :** heroine of the story told by Magog to Gog [Dickens, *Master Humphrey's Clock*].

———— **The Lady :** *see* Avenal, White Lady of.

Alicia : the treacherous wife of Arden [Lillo, *Arden of Feversham*].

———— the mistress of Lord Hastings, whose affections she alienated by her jealousy. She afterwards went mad [Rowe, *Jane Shore*].

Alinda : daughter of Alphonso of Segovia [J. Fletcher, *The Pilgrim*].

———— the name taken by Archas when he disguises himself as a woman [J. Fletcher, *Loyal Subject*].

———— the original of 'Celia' in Shakespeare's play of *As You Like It* [Lodge, *Rosalynde*].

Aliris : the Sultan of Bucharia, who, in the guise of an escort won the love of Lalla Rookh [Thomas Moore, *Lalla Rookh*].

Alisaunder, Sir : the son of Prince Boudwine and nephew of Mark, King of Cornwall, who slew him treacherously [Malory, *History of Prince Arthur*].

Alison : wife of John, the carpenter, and in love with the poor scholar Nicholas [Chaucer, *Canterbury Tales : The Miller's Tale*].

Alison: an old servant of the Earl of Leicester's at Cumnor Place [Scott, *Kenilworth*].

Alithea: a brilliant woman of the world [Wycherley, *Country Wife*].

Alken: an old shepherd, learned in the ways of witches [Ben Jonson, *Sad Shepherd*].

All-All, Sir Positive: a boastful character, 'pretending to all manner of arts and sciences' [Evelyn, *Diary*, Routledge's 1906 edn., p. 424]. Said both by Pepys [*Diary*, Routledge's 1906 edn., p. 646], and by Evelyn, *loc. cit.*, to be intended for Sir Robert Howard, Dryden's brother-in-law and auditor of the Exchequer [Thomas Shadwell, *Sullen Lover*].

Allan: a poverty-stricken Scottish nobleman [Scott, *Bride of Lammermoor*].

—— **Mrs.**: housekeeper to Colonel Mannering [Scott, *Guy Mannering*].

Allegre: the faithful servant of Philip Chabot [Chapman and Shirley, *Tragedy of Philip Chabot*].

Allen, Arabella: sister of Benjamin Allen, and afterwards married to Mr. Winkle.

—— *Benjamin*: a medical student and the friend of Bob Sawyer, for whom he destines his sister Arabella [Dickens, *Pickwick Papers*].

—— **Barbara**: the subject of a ballad [Allan Ramsey, *Barbara Allen's Cruelty*].

—— **Major**: one of Monmouth's officers [Scott, *Old Mortality*].

—— **Mr. and Mrs.**: the friends with whom Catharine Morland stays at Bath [Jane Austen, *Northanger Abbey*].

Allen-a-Dale: one of Robin Hood's archers in Sherwood Forest [*Old Ballad*].

Allnut, Noll: landlord of the *Swan*, Lambythe Ferry, where he dwelt with his wife Grace and his son Oliver [Sterling, *John Felton*].

Allworth, Lady: the step-mother of Tom.

—— *Tom*: the lover, and, in the end, the husband of Margaret Overreach [Massinger, *New Way to Pay Old Debts*].

Allworthy, Mr.: a man of great honesty, charity, independence, and modesty [Fielding, *Tom Jones*].

Alma: the Queen of 'Body Castle': meant to impersonate the human soul [Spenser, *Faëry Queene*].

Almanzor: one of the characters in the tragedy [Dryden, *Conquest of Granada*].

—— the hero of an old romance [attrib. Sir P. Sidney, *Almanzor and Almanzaida*].

Almeria : daughter of Manuel, King of Granada, and the wife of Alphonso, Prince of Valentia [Congreve, *Mourning Bride*].

Alnaschar : the dreamy brother of the barbar, who, having invested all his money in glass, broke it all [*Arabian Nights*].

Aloadin : a sorcerer who dwelt in an ' Earthly Paradise ' in Arabia, but was slain by Thalaba [Southey, *Thalaba*].

Alonso : King of Naples, the father of Ferdinand, and brother of Sebastian [Shakespeare, *Tempest*].

Alonzo : the hero of a bailad [M. G. Lewis, *Alonzo the Brave and the Fair Imogine*].

—— a Portuguese, the great enemy of Duarte [Beaumont and Fletcher, *Custom of the Country*].

—— **Don :** friend of Don Carlos and husband of Leonora [Young, *The Revenge*].

—— a valiant knight, the friend of Rolla and husband of Cora. He fights Pizarro and kills him [Sheridan, *Pizarro*].

Alp : the hero of the play ; a Venetian renegade in command of the Turish army [Byron, *Siege of Corinth*].

Alphonse : Mrs. Wititterly's diminutive page [Dickens, *Nicholas Nickleby*].

Alphonso : King of Naples, deposed by his brother and nearly poisoned by Sorano. He regains his crown in the end [J. Fletcher, *Wife for a Month*].

—— an irritable old nobleman [J. Fletcher, *The Pilgrim*].

—— **Don :** in love with Don Scipio's daughter Victoria, who, however, marries another [O'Keefe, *Castle of Andalusia*].

—— son of Pedro, of Cantabria ; he becomes King of Spain [Southey, *Roderick*].

Alpiew : Lady Reveller's waiting-woman [Mrs. Centlivre, *Basset-Table*].

Alscrip, Miss : an illiterate and vulgar *parvenue* who apes the manners of the great.

—— *Mr. :* the father of the heiress, who finds it an intolerable nuisance to live up to his new position [Burgoyne, *The Heiress*].

Altamont : a Genoese noble who marries Calista and then discovers she has been betrayed by Lothario whom he kills in a duel [Rowe, *Fair Penitent*].

—— **Col. :** an escaped convict, and Lady Clavering's first husband [Thackeray, *Pendennis*].

—— **Duke of :** the vulgar-minded and precise nobleman to whom Adelaide Douglas was married [Susan E. Ferrier, *Marriage*].

Alton, Miss : companion to Miss Alscrip, ' the heiress', and beloved by Lord Gayville [Burgoyne, *The Heiress*].

——— **Locke :** *see* Locke, Alton.

Alvan : a character founded on that of Ferdinand Lasalle. A brilliant, impetuous Democrat, who is uniformly successful, till he falls in love with Clotilde von Rüdiger, who has not his strength and fails him. Maddened, he challenges her other suitor to a duel and is killed. [George Meredith, *The Tragic Comedians*].

Alyface, Annot : servant to Dame Christian Custance [Udall, *Ralph Roister Doister*].

Amadis de Gaul : the son of King Perion and Princess Elizena, and the hero of many Spanish and Portuguese romances.

Amalahta : the son of Erillyab, sometime Queen of the Hoamen ; he was wily and cruel [Southey, *Madoc*].

Amanda : the heroine [Cibber, *Love's Last Shift* ; continued by Vanbrugh in *The Relapse*, and adapted by Sheridan in *Trip to Scarborough*].

——— the girl whom Peregrine Pickle ruins [Smollett, *Peregrine Pickle*].

——— really intended for a Miss Young, afterwards married to Admiral Campbell [James Thomson, *The Seasons : Spring*].

Amarant : a cruel giant who was slain by Guy, Earl of Warwick [*Guy and Amarant*].

Amaranta : wife of Bartolus and beloved by Leandro [J. Fletcher, *The Spanish Curate*].

Amaranth, Lady : a character at one time acted by Mrs. Pope [O'Keefe, *Wild Oats*].

Amarillis : a shepherdess who loved Perigot and got herself magically transformed into the likeness of his real love. Her trick was, however, discovered in time [J. Fletcher, *Faithful Shepherd*].

Amaryllis : intended for the Countess Dowager of Derby [Spenser, *Colin Clout's Come Home Again*].

Amavia : the personification of Intemperate Grief [Spenser, *Faëry Queene*].

Ambree, Mary : the heroine of a ballad often referred to by the older dramatists. Sometimes called the ' English Joan of Arc '.

Ambrose : the servant of the Miss Arthurets [Scott, *Redgauntlet*].

——— **Brother :** a monk in attendance on the Prior at Jorvaulx Abbey [Scott, *Ivanhoe*].

——— **Father :** is really Edward Glendinning, the brother of Sir Halbert Glendinning [Scott, *The Abbot*].

Ambrosio : Abbot of the Capucins at Madrid, called the Man of Holiness because of his sanctity. He falls from his high ideals, tempted by Matilda [M. G. Lewis, *The Monk*].

Amelia : a character supposed to have been drawn from the author's own wife. She is the spotless wife of Will Booth [Fielding, *Amelia*].

———— a country beauty, who is killed by lightning whilst walking with her lover Celadon [James Thomson, *The Seasons : Summer*].

———— **Sedley :** *see* Sedley, Amelia.

Amelot : the page in attendance on Sir Darian de Lacy [Scott, *Betrothed*].

Amgiad : the son of Camaralzaman and Badoura [*Arabian Nights*].

Amias : the lover of Aemilia, whose suit is favoured by Prince Arthur [Spenser, *Faëry Queene*].

Amidas : the lover of Lucy, who jilted her and married Philtra for her wealth [Spenser, *Faëry Queene*].

Amiel : intended for Sir Edward Seymour, Speaker of the House of Commons [Dryden, *Absalom and Achitophel*].

Amin, Prince : son of Haroun-al-Raschid [*Arabian Nights*].

Amine : half-sister of Zobeide and wife of Amin [*Arabian Nights*].

———— the fair wife of Lidi Nouman, who was discovered to be a ghoul who fed on the newly-buried dead [*Arabian Nights*].

Amintor : betrothed to Aspatia, but compelled by the king to marry Evadue [Beaumont and Fletcher, *Maid's Tragedy*].

Amlet, Richard : a gamester, the son of a tradesman ; he retrieves his fortunes by marrying the daughter of a wealthy scrivener, Corinna Gripe [Vanbrugh, *Confederacy*].

Ammiani, Carlo : a noble Italian youth who joins wholeheartedly in the Revolution for freedom. He marries Vittoria and is finally killed [George Meredith, *Vittoria*].

Amoret : a modest, constant shepherdess betrothed to Perigot, whom she marries after much tribulation [J. Fletcher, *Faithful Shepherdess*].

———— twin sister to Belphoebe, discovered in a wood by Venus and Diana. The personification of Womanly Charm [Spenser, *Faëry Queene*].

Amory, Blanche : one of the author's less happy efforts to draw a woman. She is selfish and insipid [Thackeray, *Pendennis*].

Amoury, Sir Giles: the Grand Master of the Knights Templars, whose head Saladin cut off whilst he was raising a cup of wine to his lips [Scott, *Talisman*].

Amphialus: the son of Cecropia, in love with Philoclea, but at last wedded to Helen of Corinth [Sidney, *Arcadia*].

Amphion: the son of Jupiter and Antiope, who played the lyre with such skill that stones and trees moved about at his ordering [Alfred Tennyson, *Amphion*].

Amri: intended for Heneage Finch, the Lord Chancellor [Dryden and Tate, *Absalom and Achitophel*, pt. ii.].

Amundeville, The Lady Adeline: one of the female characters in the poem [Byron, *Don Juan*].

Amynta: the subject of a pastoral poem [Elliott, *Amynta*].

Amyntas: the subject of a dramatic pastoral [Randolph, *Amyntas; or, The Impossible Dowry*].

Amys and Amylion two of Charlemagne's knights supposed to have lived in the reign of Pepin, the Damon and Pythias of mediaeval fiction.

Anah: a granddaughter of Cain, loved by Japhet but herself loving the seraph Azaziel [Byron, *Heaven and Earth*].

Anastasius: a Greek who, to escape the effects of his own crimes, becomes a renegade [Hope, *Memoirs of Anastasius*].

Ancient Mariner: the man who shot an albatross and was therefore doomed to perpetual wanderings from land to land [S. T. Coleridge, *Ancient Mariner*].

Anderson, Eppie: the maid at the inn at St. Ronan's Well [Scott, *St. Ronan's Well*].

────── **John:** the hero of a Scottish song [Percy, *Reliques; John Anderson my Jo*].

André: one of Louis XI's executioners [Scott, *Quentin Durward*].

Andrea del Sarto: the faultless painter [R. Browning, *Men and Women*].

Andreos: the personification of Fortitude [Phineas Fletcher, *Purple Island*].

Andrew: Godfrey Bertram's gardener [Scott, *Guy Mannering*].

Andrews, Joseph: a footman who marries a maidservant—the hero of the story—which was written to ridicule Richardson's *Pamela* [Fielding, *Joseph Andrews*].

Andromache: the widow of Hector, courted by Pyrrhus, who, in his last moments, placed the crown of Epirus on her head [Ambrose Phillips, *Distressed Mother*].

Andromeda: the subject of a poem based on the classical story [Charles Kingsley, *Andromeda*].

Androphilus : Philanthropy personified [Phineas Fletcher, *Purple Island*].

Andrugio : the Duke of Genoa—noble but fiery [Marston, *Antonio and Mellida*].

Aneal : the daughter of Maäni, by whom Djabal was beloved [R. Browning, *Return of the Druses*].

Anemolius : the Poet Laureate of Utopia [Sir Thomas More, *Utopia*].

Angela Pisani : *see* Pisani, Angela.

Angelica : betrothed to Valere, the gamester, whom she cures of his folly [Mrs. Centlivre, *The Gamester*].

———— ward of Sir Sampson Legend in love with Valentine, for whom she jilts her guardian [Congreve, *Love for Love*].

———— the heroine [Farquhar, *Constant Couple*].

———— the heroine [Farquhar, *Sir Harry Wildair*].

———— a princess, and the ' Lady of the Golden Tower " with whom Parismenos is in love [Foorde, *History of Parismus*, pt. ii.].

Angelina : the daughter of Charino ; she elopes with Carlos, a bookworm [Cibber, *Love Makes a Man*].

———— sister of Don Rhodorigo, and in love with Gonsalvo. Disguising herself as a man, she assumes the name of Amides [Dryden, *Rival Ladies*].

———— the daughter of Lord Lewis [J. Fletcher, *The Elder Brother*].

———— the heroine, beloved of Edwin [Goldsmith, *The Hermit : a ballad*].

Angelo : a friend of Julio's [Beaumont and Fletcher, *The Captain*].

———— a Goldsmith [Shakespeare, *Comedy of Errors*].

———— Lord-Deputy of Vienna, and betrothed to Mariana [Shakespeare, *Measure for Measure*].

Angiolina : daughter of Loredano and wedded to the Doge of Venice, Marino Faliero [Byron, *Marino Faliero*].

Anglides : wife of Prince Boudwine, and mother of Alisaunder [Malory, *History of Prince Arthur*].

Anguisant : King of Erin and ally of Leodogran, King of Cameliard [Alfred Tennyson, *Coming of Arthur*].

Ann, The Princess : the lady of Beaujeu [Scott, *Quentin Durward*].

Anna, Princess : daughter of the Emperor Alexius and the Empress Irene [Scott, *Count Robert of Paris*].

———— one of the leading women's characters in the play [Home, *Douglas*].

Annabel : intended for the Duchess of Marlborough [Dryden, *Absalom and Achitophel*].

———— **Lee :** *see* Lee, Annabel.

Anne : daughter of King Uther and Ygerne, and sister of King Arthur. She married Lot, who became King of Norway. Called by Tennyson, Bellicent [*Arthurian Cycle*].

—— **Hereford :** *see* Hereford, Anne.

—— **of Geierstein :** Baroness of Arnheim and daughter of Count Albert of Geierstein, ' The Black Monk ' ; she falls in love with and marries Sir Arthur de Vere [Scott, *Anne of Geierstein*].

—— **Sister :** the sister of Bluebeard's seventh wife, Fatima. She watches from the tower for the brothers that are to rescue Fatima from death [*Bluebeard*, a nursery tale, originally derived from Scandinavia].

Annesley : a man who goes through many thrilling adventures amongst the Indians [Mackenzie, *Man of the World*].

—— **Charles :** the name of the hero [Reade, *Wandering Heir*].

Annette : daughter of Matthias the Miller, and the bride of Christian [Ware, *Polish Jew*].

Annie, Fair : the heroine of an old ballad.

—— **Laurie :** *see* Laurie, Annie.

—— **of Lochroyan, Fair :** [*Lord Gregory* : a ballad].

—— **Winnie :** *see* Winnie, Annie.

Annir : the King of Inisthona [Ossian, *War of Inisthona*].

Annophel : she was the daughter of Cassilane, the General of Candy [Beaumont and Fletcher, *Laws of Candy*].

Anselm : Prior of St. Dominic and the Confessor of King Henry IV of Scotland [Scott, *Fair Maid of Perth*].

Antenor : a Trojan prince, related to Priam [Shakespeare, *Troilus and Cressida*].

Anthony : an English archer living with Farmer Dickson [Scott, *Castle Dangerous*].

—— the postillion at the inn at St. Ronan's Well [Scott, *St. Ronan's Well*].

Antigonus : entrusted by King Leontes to carry his baby to some desert shore that it might perish [Shakespeare, *Winter's Tale*].

—— **King :** an aged king, still subject to the passions of youth [Beaumont and Fletcher, *Humorous Lieutenant*].

Antinous : the son of General Cassilane and brother of Annophel [Beaumont and Fletcher, *Laws of Candy*].

Antiochus : Emperor of Greece and would-be assassin of Pericles [Shakespeare, *Pericles, Prince of Tyre*].

Antipholus of Ephesus and **Antipholus of Syracuse :** the twin sons of Aegeon and Emilia [Shakespeare, *Comedy of Errors*].

Anton, Sir : he to whom Merlin gave King Arthur, when an infant, to bring up [Alfred Tennyson, *Coming of Arthur*].

Antonio : a kinsman of Petruccio and Governor of Bologna [J. Fletcher, *The Chances*].

—— **Don :** the father of Carlos and Clodis, the two leading characters [Cibber, *Love Makes a Man*].

—— and **Mellida :** the leading characters [Marston, *History of Antonio and Mellida*].

—— a minor character [Shakespeare, *Much Ado About Nothing*].

—— the merchant from whom Bassanio borrows 3,000 ducats, and whose life is nearly forfeited in consequence [Shakespeare, *Merchant of Venice*].

—— the sea-captain who saved the life of Sebastian, [Shakespeare, *Twelfth Night*].

—— the usurper of the dukedom of Milan and uncle of Miranda [Shakespeare, *Tempest*].

—— the father of Proteus, and a suitor for the hand of Julia [Shakespeare, *Two Gentlemen of Verona*].

—— **Don :** a poor nobleman in love with Louisa, the daughter of Don Jerome of Seville [Sheridan, *The Duenna*].

Antony : the great Roman Triumvir, who wrecked his whole career for the sake of his love for Cleopatra, Queen of Egypt [Shakespeare, *Antony and Cleopatra*].

—— **Mark :** the same as above [Dryden, *All For Love*].

Aodh : the last of a primitive priesthood, known as the Culdees. The Danes invaded Iona where they dwelt, and then Aodh gathered his few remaining followers together and migrated to Ireland [Campbell, *Reullura*].

Apemantus : a cynical misanthrope [Shakespeare, *Timon of Athens*].

Apicata : the wife of Sejanus, who deserted her for Livia [Ben Jonson, *Fall of Sejanus*].

Apollodoros : the chief character in this 'spasmodic tragedy' [Aytoun, *Firmilian*].

Apollyon : an evil spirit with whom Christian has a terrible encounter [Bunyan, *Pilgrim's Progress*].

Appius : intended to represent John Dennis, the literary critic [Pope, *Essay on Criticism*].

—— and **Virginia :** the two leading figures in an old morality play where many of the other characters are personifications of virtues, etc. [R. B., *Appius and Virginia*].

—— —— this play, like that above, is founded on an episode in early Roman history [Webster, *The Roman Virgin; or, The Unjust Judge*].

Arabella : the ward of Justice Day and wooed by his son. She however marries Captain Manly [Knight, *Honest Thieves*].

Aragnol : the son of Arachne [Spenser, *Muiopotmos; or, The Butterfly's Fate*].

Aram, Eugene : a schoolmaster of Knaresborough, who committed a murder and afterwards committed suicide [Lytton, *Eugene Aram*]. This true history has been chosen also by Thomas Hood for the subject of a poem and by W. G. Wills for a drama.

Aramnita : the friend of Clarissa and the wife of Moneytrap [Vanbrugh, *Confederacy*].

Aranza, The Duke of : husband of the haughty Juliana, whom he forces to do menial labour until her spirit is tamed, and then reveals to her what his real position in life is [Tobin, *Honeymoon*].

Arbaces : King of Iberia, a vain voluptuary [Beaumont and Fletcher, *King and No King*].

——— a satrap of Media and Syria, founder of the Empire of Media [Byron, *Sardanapalus*].

——— a priest of Isis [Lytton, *Last Days of Pompeii*].

Arbasto : the leading character in the play [Greene, *History of Arbasto, King of Denmarke*].

Arcanes : a soldier and the friend of Cassilane [Beaumont and Fletcher, *Laws of Candy*].

Archas : the hero of the play [J. Fletcher, *Loyal Subject*].

Archer, Francis : a gentleman who has come down in the world, and acts as confidential servant to Aimwell [Farquhar, *Beaux' Stratagem*].

Archimago *or* **Archimage :** an enchanter typifying the Evil Principle in opposition to the Red Cross Knight, who represents Holiness [Spenser, *Faëry Queene*].

Arcite : a Theban knight, taken captive by Duke Theseus [Chaucer, *Canterbury Tales : Knight's Tale*].

——— friend of Palamon [Fletcher, *Two Noble Kinsmen*].

Arden : a noble man, wedded to a faithless wife, who plots his death with her paramour [Lillo, *Arden of Feversham*].

——— **Enoch :** a shipwrecked sailor, who returns after many years to find his wife has married his dearest friend, and leaves again without revealing himself [Alfred Tennyson, *Enoch Arden*].

Aresby, Captain : an affected captain in the Militia, 'a most petrifying wretch' [Fanny Burney, *Cecilia*].

Arethusa : the daughter of King Messina [J. Fletcher, *Philaster ; or, Love Lies Bleeding*].

Argalus : the unfortunate lover of Parthenia [Sidney, *Arcadia*].

Argante : a giantess who was 'the very monster and miracle of lust' [Spenser, *Faëry Queene*].

Argenis : the heroine of a political romance written in Latin, but often translated [Barclay, *Argenis ; or, Loves of Poliarchus and Argenis*].

Argentile : the daughter of King Adelbright, wooed by Prince Curan, the Dane [Warner, *Albion's England*].

Argentin : an officer in the army of the Duke of Burgundy [Scott, *Anne of Geierstein*].

Argon and **Ruro :** the sons of Annir, King of Inisthona [Ossian, *War of Inisthona*].

Aribert : King of Lombardy and father of Rhodalind [Davenant, *Gondibert*].

Ariel : one of the fallen angels [Milton, *Paradise Lost*].

———— the most important of the sylphs [Pope, *Rape of the Lock*].

———— a spirit of the air whom Prospero forces into his service [Shakespeare, *Tempest*].

Arioch : one of the fallen angels conquered by Abdiel [Milton, *Paradise Lost*].

Ariodante : the hero of a play performed by children before Queen Elizabeth [*History of Ariodante and Ginevra*].

Armado, Don Adriano de : an affected military bully [Shakespeare, *Love's Labour's Lost*].

Armgart : the subject of the poem [George Eliot, *Armgart*].

Armine, Ferdinand : Henrietta Temple's lover [Beaconsfield, *Henrietta Temple*].

Armstrong, Archie : James I of England's Court Jester [Scott, *Fortunes of Nigel*].

———— **Grace :** the betrothed of Hobbie Elliot [Scott, *Black Dwarf*].

———— **John :** an aged warrior known as 'The Laird's Jock' [Scott, *Laird's Jock*].

———— **Johnny :** a freebooter of the days of James V of Scotland [*Scottish ballad*].

———— **Robert :** comes to Farmer Fleming to learn farming and wins confidence by his steadiness. Formerly addicted to drinking. He finally marries Rhoda Fleming [George Meredith, *Rhoda Fleming*].

Armusia : the lover of Quisara [J. Fletcher, *Island Princess*].

Arnheim, Baron Herman von : Anne's father, and known as 'The Black Monk' [Scott, *Anne of Geierstein*].

Arnold : the misshapen son of Bertha [Byron, *Deformed Transformed*].

———— disguises himself as a beggar, and goes by the name of 'Ginks' [J. Fletcher, *Beggar's Bush*].

———— the torchbearer at Rotherwood [Scott, *Ivanhoe*].

Arnoldo : betrothed to Zenocia [Beaumont and Fletcher, *Custom of the Country*].

Arod : is intended for Sir William Waller [Dryden and Tate, *Absalom and Achitophel*, pt. ii.].

Aroundight : the sword of Lancelot of the Lake.

Arpasia : betrothed to Moneses, but forced into marriage with Bajazet, Sultan of Turkey [Rowe, *Tamerlane*].

Arrowpoint, Catharine : a sensible girl, educated and accomplished [George Eliot, *Daniel Deronda*].

Artaxaminous : King of Utopia and married to Griskinissa, whom he wishes to divorce in favour of Distaffina [Rhodes, *Bombastes Furioso*].

Artegal : known as the 'Salvage Knight', the allegorical representative of Justice [Spenser, *Faëry Queene*].

Artemis : one of the ladies of the Court [Dryden, *Marriage A-la-Mode*].

Artevelde, Clara Van : the sister of Philip and beloved by Walter d'Arlon.

——— *Philip Van :* the heroes of this historical romance are the father and son who figure so prominently in the history of Flanders [Sir Henry Taylor, *Philip Van Artevelde*].

Artful Dodger : *see* Dawkins, John.

Arthegal : *see* Artegal.

Arthur, King of Great Britain and founder of the Round Table, occurs so frequently in English literature that it is not possible to name every instance here. Some of the more important are: Lord Berners, *History of the most noble and valiant knight, Arthur of Lytel Breytagne* ; Thomas Hughes, *The Misfortunes of Arthur* ; Hathaway, *Arthur, King of England* ; Alfred Tennyson, *Idylls of the King* ; Lytton, *King Arthur*, an old romance of *Morte d' Arthur* ; and an old ballad, *King Arthur's Death*.

Arthuret, Miss Angelica and **Miss Serephina :** two sisters who nurse Alan Fairford through an illness [Scott, *Redgauntlet*].

Arundel : the favourite steed of Sir Bevis of Southampton, a gift from his wife Josian [Drayton, *Polyolbion*].

——— **Percy :** Lord Ashdale, who has to divide his property with his half-brother, Norman [Lytton, *Sea-Captain*].

Arvalan : the son of Kehama, a reprobate, who attempts the honour of Kailyal, the daughter of Ladurlad [Southey, *Curse of Kehama*].

Arvida, Prince : a friend of Gustavus Vasa, and, like him, in love with Christina, daughter of Christian II of Scandinavia [Brooke, *Gustavus Vasa*].

Arviragus : son of Cymbeline, kidnapped in infancy by
Belarius [Shakespeare, *Cymbeline*].

——— husband of Dorigen, a true gentleman wedded to
a pure and noble wife [Chaucer, *Canterbury Tales : The
Franklin's Tale*.

Ascanio : son of Henrique and hero of the play [J. Fletcher,
Spanish Curate].

Ascapart : a giant who tucked Sir Bevis, his wife Josian
and his steed Arundel under his arm, and carried them
off [Drayton, *Polyolbion*, pt. ii.].

Asebie : the personification of Irreligion [Phineas Fletcher,
Purple Island].

Aselges : the personification of Lasciviousness [Phineas
Fletcher, *Purple Island*].

Ashburton, Mary : the girl with whom Paul Flemming
falls in love [Longfellow, *Hyperion*].

Ashfield, Dame : a woman dreadfully afraid of what her
neighbour, Mrs. Grundy, will think. Hence the phrase.

——— *Farmer :* a tender-hearted, hot-headed man, the
father of Susan Ashfield.

——— *Susan :* daughter of Farmer and Dame Ashfield,
who marries the son of Sir Abel Handy [J. M. Morton,
Speed the Plough].

Ashford, Isaac : one of Nature's gentlemen, a peasant
' contented to be poor ' [Crabbe, *Parish Register*].

Ashton, Lady Eleanor and **Col. Sholto :** the mother and
brother of Lucy.

——— *Lucy :* daughter of Sir William, betrothed to Edgar
of Ravenswood, but forced into a marriage with the
Laird of Bucklaw.

——— *Sir William :* Lord Keeper of Scotland and father
of Lucy [Scott, *Bride of Lammermoor*].

Asmadai : a rebellious angel, overthrown by Uriel and
Raphael [Milton, *Paradise Lost*].

Asotus : the personification of Prodigality [Phineas
Fletcher, *Purple Island*].

Aspasia : an unhappy maid, betrothed to Amintor, who
forsakes her for Evadne [Beaumont and Fletcher,
Maid's Tragedy].

——— the most cultured woman of her time, and the
friend of Pericles [Landor, *Pericles and Aspasia*].

Asper : intended by the poet as a portrait of himse'? [Ben
Jonson, *Every Man Out of His Humour*].

Aspramonte, Brenhilda of : becomes the wife of Count
Robert [Scott, *Count Robert of Paris*].

Assad : son of Camaralzaman and Haiatalnfous and half-
brother of Amgiad [*Arabian Nights*].

Astarte : the heroine, beloved by Manfred [Byron, *Manfred*].

Astery : a nymph turned into a butterfly by Venus [Spenser,
Muiopotmos ; or, The Butterfly's Fate].

Aston, Sir Jacob : an old Cavalier [Scott, *Woodstock*].

Astragon : physician and philosopher, whose daughter
Bertha was betrothed to Gondibert[Davenant,*Gondibert*].

Astrophel : intended for Sir Philip Sidney and meaning
' star-lover '. The ' star ' he loved was Penelope
Devereux [Spenser, *Shepherd's Calendar*].

Aswad : the son of Shedad, King of Ad [Southey, *Thalaba*].

Ate : the friend of Duessa and mother of ' all dissension '
[Spenser, *Faëry Queene*].

Athanasia : the heroine of the story [Lockhart, *Valerius*].

Athelstane : ' the Unready ', thane of Coningsburgh [Scott,
Ivanhoe].

Atimus : ' A careless, idle swain ', the personification of
Baseness of Mind [Phineas Fletcher, *Purple Island*].

Atin : representing Strife, the Squire of Pyrochles [Spenser,
Faëry Queene].

Atkinson, Sergeant : a sterling and devoted friend to Amelia
and Booth [Fielding, *Amelia*].

Atossa : supposed to have been intended for the Duchess
of Buckingham [Pope, *Moral Essays*, Epistle ii.].

Atticus : intended for Joseph Addison [Pope, *Epistle to
Dr. Arbuthnot*].

Aubrey, Augusta : a motherless girl, insulted during her
father's absence by her guardian, whose nephew,
Francis Tyrrel, she ultimately marries.

—— *Mr. :* a widower, and the father of Augusta Aubrey
[Cumberland, *Fashionable Lover*].

—— **Mr. :** the chief character, who afterwards becomes
Lord Drelincourt [Warren, *Ten Thousand a Year*].

Audrey : an awkward country lass, who jilts William for
Touchstone [Shakespeare, *As You Like It*].

Augusta : the mother of Gustavus Vasa [Brooke, *Gustavus
Vasa*].

Auld Robin Gray : *see* Gray, Auld Robin.

Aullay : an enormous horse [Southey, *Curse of Kehama*].

Aurelia : a dissipated, proud woman [Marston, *The Mal-
content*].

—— pretty, impertinent, and a flirt [Dryden, *An
Evening's Love ; or, The Mock Astrologer*].

—— **Darnel :** *see* Darnel, Aurelia.

Aurelius : elder brother of Uther and uncle of King Arthur
[*Arthurian Cycle*].

Aurora Leigh : *see* Leigh, Aurora.

—— **Raby :** *see* Raby, Aurora.

Austin : the name by which the lord of Clarinsal was known
[Jephson, *Count of Narbonne*].

Autolycus : the pedlar and 'snapper up of unconsidered trifles' [Shakespeare, *Winter's Tale*].

Automathes : the hero, a youth left in his infancy on a solitary island, where he remained for nineteen years [Kirkby, *History of Automathes*].

Avenel, Dick : a warm-hearted, noisy Yankee [Lytton, *My Novel*].

—— **White Lady of :** the guardian spirit of the Avenel family [Scott, *Monastery*].

Averanche, Lionel : a politician, thinker and man of pleasure combined [G. S. Smythe, *Angela Pisani*].

Avery, Captain : the hero of the story [Defoe, *King of Pirates*].

Aveugle : the son of Erebus and Nox [Spenser, *Faëry Queene*].

Ayesha : the daughter of Sir Edward Wortley and the bride of Lord Osmond [J. Morier, *Ayesha, the Maid of Kars*].

Aylmer, Colonel : saves Hilary Lorraine's life at Waterloo and afterwards marries Alice Lorraine [Blackmore, *Alice Lorraine*].

—— **Rose :** the subject of a lyrical poem [Landor, *Rose Aylmer*].

—— **Mrs. :** a friend and neighbour of Sir Henry Lee [Scott, *Woodstock*].

Aymer, Prior : a jovial Benedictine monk, Prior of Jorvaulx Abbey [Scott, *Ivanhoe*].

Ayresleigh, Mr. : a prisoner for debt, met by Mr. Pickwick in the Coffee-room in Coleman Street [Dickens, *Pickwick Papers*].

Azaria : intended for the Duke of Monmouth [Pordage, *Azaria and Hushai*].

Azazel : a ginn made of 'smokeless fire' created before man, but driven forth from the earth by angels [Milton, *Paradise Lost*].

Azaziel : a seraph who fell in love with Anah, a grand-daughter of Cain [Byron, *Heaven and Earth*].

Azazil : the standard-bearer of the Infernal Host [Milton, *Paradise Lost*].

Azim : first a convert to, afterwards an opponent of, the Veiled Prophet [Thomas Moore, *Lalla Rookh*].

Azla : the widow of Arvalan, son of Kehama [Southey, *Curse of Kehama*].

Azo : the Marquis d'Este, who married Parisina, although she had been betrothed to his own son, Hugo [Byron, *Parisina*].

Bab, Lady : a lady's-maid that apes the airs of her mistress and is addressed as ' Lady Bab ' in the kitchen [Townley, *High Life Below Stairs*].

Baba : the chief eunuch at the Court of Sultana Gulbeyas [Byron, *Don Juan*].

———— **Ali :** the narrator of the story of the ' *Forty Thieves* ' [*Arabian Nights*].

———— **Cassim :** the brother of Ali Baba, who forgot the password ' sesame ' and so got shut into the cave [*Arabian Nights*].

———— **Hajji :** the hero of a romance the scene of which is laid in Persia [James Morier, *Adventures of Hajji Baba of Ispahan*].

———— **Mustapha :** the cobbler who pieced together Cassim's body after it had been cut up by the forty thieves [*Arabian Nights*].

Babe Christabel : *see* Christabel, Babe.

Babley, Richard : generally called Mr. Dick, a kindly lunatic, whose madness showed chiefly in relation to the head of King Charles I [Dickens, *David Copperfield*].

Bachelor, The : an old gentleman who sheltered Nell and her grandfather at a village where they halted in their wanderings [Dickens, *Old Curiosity Shop*].

Backbite, Sir Benjamin : a cynical scandal-monger, the nephew of Crabtree [Sheridan, *School for Scandal*].

Bacon, Frier : a conjuror and one of the leading characters [Greene, *Frier Bacon and Frier Bungay*].

Badger, Mr. and Mrs. Bayham : a doctor, the third husband of Mrs. Badger, and the man to whom Richard Carstone is apprenticed [Dickens, *Bleak House*].

———— **Squire :** a character in the drama [Fielding, *Don Quixote in England*].

———— **Will :** a favourite servant of Sir Hugh Robsart [Scott, *Kenilworth*].

Badman, Mr. : the chief character of the work [Bunyan, *Life and Death of Mr. Badman*].

Badoura : the daughter of Gaiour, King of China, the loveliest woman that ever lived [*Arabian Nights*].

Badroulboudour : the beautiful daughter of the Sultan of China, who married Aladdin [*Arabian Nights*].

Bagarag, Shibli : a whimsical youth who goes through most remarkable adventures and finally shaves Shagpat [George Meredith, *Shaving of Shagpat*].

Bagot, William : leading a Bohemian life in Paris with two friends and known as ' Little Billee '. He is the greatest artist of his age. The hero of the story who ultimately marries the heroine [Du Maurier, *Trilby*].

Bagshot : belonged to a gang of burglars who broke into Lady Bountiful's house [Farquhar, *Beaux' Stratagem*].

Bagman, The One-eyed : a jovial, elderly man whom Mr. Pickwick meets at Eatanswill and Bristol. He tells the '*Bagman's Story*' [Dickens, *Pickwick Papers*].

Bagstock, Major Joe : a retired military officer and friend of Miss Tox ; wooden-featured and blue-faced [Dickens, *Dombey & Son*].

Bahadar : Master of the Horse to the King of the Magi [*Arabian Nights*].

Bahman, Prince : eldest son of Sultan Khrosson-schah of Persia [*Arabian Nights*].

Bailey, Junior : a sharp boy in the service of Mrs. Todgers, at her boarding-house [Dickens, *Martin Chuzzlewit*].

Bailie, Giles : a gipsy, the father of Gabrael Faa [Scott, *Guy Mannering*].

Baillie [or Bailly], Harry : the host of the *Tabard Inn*, who is the first to propose the telling of tales by the way [Chaucer, *Canterbury Tales : Prologue*].

Bajazet : surnamed 'The Thunderbolt', Sultan of Turkey [Rowe, *Tamerlane*].

Bakbarah the Toothless : brother of the barber of Bagdad, known as 'The Silent Man' [*Arabian Nights*].

Balaam, Sir : 'a citizen of sober fame, a plain good man'. It is not known for whom the poet intended this [Pope, *Moral Essays*, Epistle iii.].

Balafré, Le : *see* Lesly, Ludovic.

Balak : this character was meant for Dr. Burnet, author of the *History of the Reformation* [Dryden and Tate, *Absalom and Achitophel*, pt. ii.].

Balan : brother of Balin ; a very valiant knight [Mallory, *History of Prince Arthur*].

Balance, Justice : the father of Sylvia [Farquhar, *Recruiting Officer*].

Balaustion : the subject of the poem ; a Greek girl of Rhodes. Her history is continued in '*Aristophanes' Apology*' [R. Browning, *Balaustion's Adventure*].

Balder : the hero of a long and rather stilted poem [Dobell, *Balder*].

—— the hero of a fine poem in three parts [Matthew Arnold, *Balder Dead*].

Balderstone, Caleb : the devoted servant of the Master of Ravenswood [Scott, *Bride of Lammermoor*].

Baldrick : ancestor of Eveline Berenger, who thinks she sees his ghost frowning upon her [Scott, *Betrothed*].

Baldringham, The Lady Ermengarde of : great-aunt of Eveline Berenger [Scott, *Betrothed*].

Baldwin : tutor of Rollo and Otto, Dukes of Norma(cy; afterwards put to death by Rollo [Beaumont, *Bloody Brother*].

—— **Count :** an obstinate old man whose wilfulness and indiscretion cause infinite woe to himself and all who belong to him [Southern, *Fatal Marriage*].

—— **Count :** one of the leaders of the First Crusade [Scott, *Count Robert of Paris*].

—— **de Oyley :** preceptor to the Knights Templars and esquire to Sir Bois Guilbert [Scott, *Ivanhoe*].

Balfour of Burley, John : a leader in the Covenanters' army [Scott, *Old Mortality*].

Balin : a very valiant knight, and brother of Balan [Mallory, *History of Prince Arthur*].

Baliol, Mrs. : a lady of position, who, upon her death, left two series of tales as a legacy to Mr. Croftangry [Scott, *Highland Widow*].

Ballendino, Don Antonio : intended for a portrait of Anthony Munday, the dramatist [Ben Jonson, *Case is Altered*].

Balmawhapple : a stupid, obstinate Scottish laird [Scott, *Waverley*].

Balthasar : a merchant [Shakespeare, *Comedy of Errors*].

—— Don Pedro's servant [Shakespeare, *Much Ado About Nothing*].

—— the name assumed by Portia when she pleads the cause of Shylock in the Law Courts [Shakespeare, *Merchant of Venice*].

Balthazar : the name of Romeo's servant [Shakespeare, *Romeo and Juliet*].

—— the father of Volante, Zamora and Juliana [Tobin, *Honeymoon*].

Balwhidder, Mr. Micah : the prejudiced, but kindly Presbyterian minister of the parish of Dalmailing. The writer of the Annals [Galt, *Annals of the Parish*].

Baly : an Indian king, who upheld justice and redressed wrongs [Southey, *Curse of Kehama*].

Bamber, Jack : a little old man whom Mr. Pickwick meets at the *Magpie and Stump* [Dickens, *Pickwick Papers*].

Bampfylde, Bertha : always called Bardie and known as the Maid of Sker. Cast away in infancy and rescued by David Llewellyn.

—— *Captain Drake :* son of Sir Philip Bampfylde, wrongly accused of the murder of his brother's children.

—— *Sir Philip :* the grandfather of ' Bardie '.

—— *Squire Philip :* father of Bardie and Harry Savage [Blackmore, *Maid of Sker*].

Ban, King : King of Benwick, brother of Bors, King of Gaul, and father of Sir Launcelot [Mallory, *History of Prince Arthur*].

Banastar, Humfrey : the adopted son of Henry, Duke of Buckingham, whom he betrayed to his death [attrib. Sackville, *Mirrour for Magistraytes*].

Banks : a farmer who is the terror of the Witch of Edmonton, Mother Sawyer [Rowley, Dekker and Ford, *Witch of Edmonton*].

—— **Nanse :** the schoolmistress of Dalmailing [Galt, *Annals of the Parish*].

Banquo : a Scottish thane, foully murdered by order of Macbeth ; his ghost afterwards appears at a banquet [Shakespeare, *Macbeth*].

Bantam, Angelo Cyrus, Esq., M.C. : a friend of Mr. Dowler and master of the ceremonies at a ball at Bath, attended by Mr. Pickwick [Dickens, *Pickwick Papers*].

Baptista : father of Katherine and Bianca [Shakespeare, *Taming of the Shrew*].

Baptisti Damiotti : a Paduan quack, the owner of a magic mirror [Scott, *Aunt Margaret's Mirror*].

Barabas : the hero of the play, but really little better than a monster [Marlowe, *Jew of Malta*].

—— servant of Captain Ralph de Lascours [Stirling, *Orphan of the Frozen Sea*].

Baradas, Count : succeeds Richelieu as chief minister to Louis XIII, but his triumph is shortlived, and he is arrested [Lytton, *Richelieu*].

Barbara : the housemaid at Mrs. Garland's, who marries Kit Nubbles [Dickens, *Old Curiosity Shop*].

Barbary, Roan : the favourite horse of King Richard II [Shakespeare, *King Richard II*].

Barbason : the name of a demon [Shakespeare, *Merry Wives of Windsor* and *King Henry V*].

Bardell, Mrs. Martha : she brings an action against Mr. Pickwick for breach of promise of marriage.

—— *Tommy :* the son of Mrs. Bardell [Dickens, *Pickwick Papers*].

Bardo de' Bardi : a wealthy Florentine scholar, the father of Romola [George Eliot, *Romola*].

Bardolph : an underbred, swaggering soldier, who ends on the scaffold [Shakespeare, *Merry Wives of Windsor* and *Henry IV*].

Barkis, Mr. : the carrier who becomes the husband of Clara Pegotty [Dickens, *David Copperfield*].

Barlasch : an old soldier of Napoleon's Guard [Merriman, *Barlasch of the Guard*].

Barlass, Kate : the woman who, to save the life of King James I of Scotland, thrust her arm through the staple of a door [D. G. Rossetti, *King's Tragedy*].

Barley, Bill : the father of Clara.

───── *Clara :* a gentle, pretty girl married to Herbert Pocket [Dickens, *Great Expectations*].

Barleycorn, Sir John : the personification of Ale and all liquors made from barley [Ballad, *Sir John Barleycorn*, also an ancient tract, *The Arraigning and Indicting of Sir John Barleycorn, Knt.*].

Barmicide : a rich man who gave to Schacabac, who came to him in distress for food, a make-pretence feast, where there was really nothing on the table, but who, upon his guest taking the jest in good part, relented and fed him [*Arabian Nights*].

Barnaby, Widow : a vulgar woman always in search of a second husband [Mrs. Trollope, *Widow Barnaby* ; also a sequel, *Widow Barnaby Married*].

───── Rudge : *see* Rudge, Barnaby.

Barnacle : the guardian of Precilla Tomboy [Bickerstaff, *The Romp*].

───── Ferdinand : private secretary to Lord Decimus Barnacle.

───── *Lord Decimus Tite :* a peer in great authority at the Circumlocution Office.

───── *Mr. Tite :* 'a man of family, a man of place,' who coaches the statesman at the head of the Circumlocution Office [Dickens, *Little Dorrit*].

Barney : a low-class Jew who served in the public-house frequented by Fagin [Dickens, *Oliver Twist*].

Barnstable, Lieutenant : a sailor in love with Kate Plowden ; he narrowly escapes hanging, by order of his own father [Fitzball, *The Pilot*].

Barnwell, George : an apprentice who falls in love with a girl who encourages him in evil ways. He robs his master and uncle, and ends by being condemned to death [Lillo, *George Barnwell*].

Barrabas : *see* Barabas.

Barraclough : a preaching Methodist tailor, the leader of those who wreck Robert Moore's mills [Charlotte Brontë, *Shirley*].

───── Rev. Amos : a Primitive Methodist minister, in love with Jessie Roantree [Kipling, *Life's Handicap*.

Barsisa, Santon : in *The Guardian*, the basis of M. G. Lewis' novel *The Monk*.

Barston : a Jesuit who corresponds with the Countess of Derby and assumes the name of Fenwicke [Scott, *Peveril of the Peak*].

Bartoldo : a rich old miser [Milman, *Fazio*].

Bartolus : a lawyer, and the husband of Amaranta [J. Fletcher, *Spanish Curate*].

Barton, Amos : a struggling, well-meaning but dull clergyman with small means and many children [George Eliot, *Scenes of Clerical Life : The Sad Fortunes of the Rev. Amos Barton*].

—— Sir Andrew : a Scottish admiral who, obtaining letters-of-marque, harried the Portuguese on the high seas [*Sir Andrew Barton*: a ballad].

—— Mary : a Lancashire factory-hand, the heroine of the story, whose lover is wrongfully accused of murder [Mrs. Gaskell, *Mary Barton*].

Basil : the Blacksmith of Grand Pré, to whose son Evangeline is betrothed [Longfellow, *Evangeline*].

—— Count : the hero of the drama [Joanna Baillie, *Count Basil*].

Basilisco : a foolish and boastful knight [*possibly* Kyd, *Soliman and Perseda*].

Basilius : the King of Arcadia [Sidney, *Arcadia*].

Bassanio : the friend for whom Antonio's life is nearly forfeited, and the husband of Portia [Shakespeare, *Merchant of Venice*].

Basset : a swindler and forger [Cibber, *Provoked Husband*].

Bassianus : the lover of Lavinia [Shakespeare, *Titus Andronicus*].

Bassino : Aurelia's 'perjured husband' [Mrs. Centlivre, *Perjured Husband*].

Bassiolo : a foolish and vain gentleman usher [Chapman, *Bassiolo*].

Bates : one of Henry V's sentinels on the eve of Agincourt, with whom the king talks [Shakespeare, *King Henry V*].

—— Charley : one of Fagin's most expert pupils [Dickens, *Oliver Twist*].

—— Frank : a sensible man who tries to check his friend Whittle's folly [Garrick, *Irish Widow*].

—— Miss : a good-natured, harmless fool; aunt of Jane Fairfax [Jane Austen, *Emma*].

Bath, Major : a poor, proud and honourable gentleman who seeks to hide his poverty [Fielding, *Amelia*].

—— Wife of : one of the 'Pilgrims' and one of the story-tellers, choosing 'Midas' as her subject [Chaucer, *Canterbury Tales : The Wife of Bath*].

Battle, Mrs. Sarah : 'Old Sarah Battle ... who next to her devotions loved a good game of whist' [Lamb, *Essays of Elia : Mrs. Battle's Opinions on Whist*].

Bawdin, Sir Charles : the hero of a ballad [Chatterton, *The Bristow Tragedy : or, The Death of Sir Charles Bawdin*].

Bayard : the charger of Fitz-James [Scott, *Lady of the Lake*].

Bayes : intended as a caricature of Dryden [Duke of Buckingham, *Rehearsal*].

Bayham, Fred : a kindly, unbusiness like Bohemian ; a friend of Pendennis [Thackeray, *Pendennis*].

Bazzard, Mr. : clerk to Mr. Grewgious [Dickens, *Edwin Drood*].

Beadle, Harriet : known as 'Tattycoram', a foundling, servant to Minnie Meagles [Dickens, *Little Dorrit*].

Beagle, Sir Harry : a commonplace country gentleman whose chief interest is horses, and for one of these he barters Harriet [Colman the Elder, *Jealous Wife*].

Beamish, Beau : the autocratic leader of society at a fashionable resort, whither came Duchess Susan, who was the unwitting cause of a tragedy [George Meredith, *Tale of Chloe*].

Bean, Alice : the daughter of a Highland robber who nurses Waverley.

—— *Lean, Donald :* a Highland robber-chieftain known by the name of Will Ruthven ; the father of Alice [Scott, *Waverley*].

Beatrice : niece of Leonato ; witty and high-spirited, she falls in love with and marries Benedick [Shakespeare, *Much Ado About Nothing*].

—— the chief character in the story. A beautiful woman of dangerous character [Nathaniel Hawthorne, *Rappacini's Daughter*].

—— **Joanna :** an unscrupulous girl who incites De Flores to murder a lover to whom she objects [Middleton, *Changeling*].

Beatrix : maid to Theodosia and Jacintha [Dryden, *An Evening's Love ; or, Mock Astrologer*].

—— *see* Castlewood, Beatrix.

Beauchamp, Nevil : a young naval officer who throws himself ardently into politics on the side of the advanced Radicals. He marries Jenny Denham after being in love with two other women. Is drowned rescuing a boy [George Meredith, *Beauchamp's Career*].

Beaufort : the lover of Maria Wilding [Murphy, *The Citizen*].

—— **Cardinal :** great-uncle of Henry VI, and Bishop of Winchester [Shakespeare, *Henry VI*, pt. ii.].

—— **Robert :** a deceitful humbug [Lytton, *Night and Morning*].

Beaugard, Captain : chief character in both plays [Otway, *The Soldier's Fortune* and *Atheist*].

────── **Old :** the extravagant father of Captain Beaugard [Otway, *Atheist*].

Beaujeu, Mons. le Chevalier de : the keeper of a gambling-house to which Nigel was taken [Scott, *Fortunes of Nigel*].

────── **Mons. le Comte de :** an officer in the Pretender's army [Scott, *Waverley*].

Beaumains : the nickname of Gareth, son of King Lot [Mallory, *History of Prince Arthur*].

Beaumanoir, Sir Lucas : Grand-master of the Knights Templars [Scott, *Ivanhoe*].

Beaupré : brother of Samira and son of Vertaigne [Beaumont and Fletcher, *Little French Lawyer*].

Beck, Gilead P. : an American who, whilst devoted to coining money himself, has an admiration for learning [Besant and Rice, *Golden Butterfly*].

────── **Madame :** the proprietress of a girls' boarding-school in Brussels [Charlotte Brontë, *Villette*].

Beckwith, Alfred : the man whom Julius Slinkton attempts to murder [Dickens, *Hunted Down*].

Bede, Adam : a village carpenter, in love with Dinah Morris [George Eliot, *Adam Bede*].

────── **Seth :** the brother of Adam Bede [George Eliot, *Adam Bede*].

Beder : son of Gulnare, King of Persia. He had the power of living under water as comfortably as on land [*Arabian Nights*].

Bedivere, Sir : ' first made and latest left of all the knights ' of the Round Table [Alfred Tennyson, *Passing of Arthur*].

Bedreddin Hassan : the son of Noureddin Ali, Grand Vizier of Basora, and nephew to the Vizier of Egypt. A man of resplendent beauty [*Arabian Nights*].

Bedwin, Mrs. : the kind, motherly housekeeper of Mr. Brownlow [Dickens, *Oliver Twist*].

Beefington, Milor : an English nobleman exiled through the tyranny of King John [Canning, *Rovers*].

Beelzebub : ' Than whom, Satan except, none higher sat ' [Milton, *Paradise Lost*].

Beevor, Sir Maurice : the would-be assassin of Arthur and Percy, that he might succeed to their estates. His evil designs came to naught [Lytton, *Sea-Captain*].

Beg, Toshach : acts as second to MacGillie Chattanach at the combat [Scott, *Fair Maid of Perth*].

Beggar, The Blind : the original 'blind beggar' is said to have been Henry, son of Simon de Montfort, who assumed blindness to escape detection after the battle of Evesham [Chettle and Day, *Blind Beggar of Bethnal Green*].

Behram : the captain of the ship which was to take Prince Assad to his death [*Arabian Nights*].

Beichan, Young : supposed to have been Gilbert Becket, the father of St. Thomas à Becket [*Young Beichan :* a ballad].

Belarius : a soldier in the army of Cymbeline who kidnapped the king's two sons, whom he afterwards restored to their father [Shakespeare, *Cymbeline*].

Belch, Sir Toby : a witty but dissipated old man; the uncle of Olivia [Shakespeare, *Twelfth Night*].

Belcour : a foundling adopted by a wealthy Jamaica merchant, whose grandson he proved to be [Cumberland, *West Indies*].

Beleses : a Chaldean prophet who told Arbaces that he would become King of Nineveh and Assyria [Byron, *Sardanapalus*].

Belfield, Andrew : an utter scamp who was on the point of committing bigamy with Sophia Dove.

―――― **Robert :** the brother of Andrew who becomes the husband of Sophia Dove [Cumberland, *Brothers*].

―――― a character said to have been dawn from that of a Mr. Percival Stockdale [Fanny Burney, *Cecilia*].

Belfond : a good-tempered man but dissolute [Thomas Shadwell, *Squire of Alsatia*].

Belford : one of the characters in this comedy [Colman and Garrick, *Clandestine Marriage*].

―――― the friend of Lovelace [Richardson, *Clarissa Harlowe*].

―――― **Major :** the affianced husband of Mdlle. Florival and the friend of Colonel Tamper [Colman the Elder, *The Deuce is in Him*].

Belgarde : a poor captain who, being cautioned not to appear at dinner in shabby clothes, dons his only other suit—one of full armour [Massinger, *Unnatural Combat*].

Belge : the mother of seventeen sons [Spenser, *Faëry Queene*].

Belial : a fallen angel whose 'tongue dropped manna, and could make the worse appear the better reason' [Milton, *Paradise Lost*].

Belianis, Don, of Greece : the hero of an old romance [*History of Don Belianis of Greece*].

Belinda : a kind-hearted, slatternly maid of-all-work in a lodging-house [H. J. Byron, *Our Boys*].

―――― a smart but very affected lady in love with Bell-mour [Congreve, *Old Bachelor*].

―――― one of the two heroines [Maria Edgeworth, *Belinda*].

―――― one of the more important female characters in the comedy [Etherege, *Man of Mode*].

―――― the daughter of Mr. Blandford, who loves Beverley the brother of Clarissa [Murphy, *All in the Wrong*].

―――― the heroine [Pope, *Rape of the Lock*].

―――― a rich woman [Charles Shadwell, *Fair Quaker of Deal*].

―――― a pretty heiress who marries Heartfree [Vanbrugh, *Provoked Wife*].

Bell, Adam : a noted outlaw, like Robin Hood, Clym of the Clough, etc. [Percy, *Reliques*].

―――― **Bessy, and May Gray :** the daughters of two gentle-men living near Perth who, with their lover, died of the plague [*Bessy Bell and May Gray : a* ballad].

―――― **Laura :** the lovable and patient girl whose con-stancy at last fixes the fickle fancy of Arthur Pen-dennis, whose wife she becomes [Thackeray, *Pen-dennis*].

―――― **Mr. Knight (M.R.C.S.) :** a member of the Mudfog Association who exhibits a wax model of a man's stomach [Dickens, *Mudfog Association*].

―――― **Peter :** the subject of the poem [Wordsworth, *Peter Bell, a Tale in Verse*].

Bellair : a French officer held prisoner at Lichfield [Far-quhar, *Beaux' Stratagem*].

―――― this character is said to have been the author's portrait of himself [Etherege, *Man of Mode*].

―――― **Miss Biddy :** in love with Captain Loveit, who, though she flirts with Flash and Fribble, absolutely declines to marry Stephen Loveit [Garrick, *Miss in Her Teens*].

Bellamira : the subject of a tragi-comedy in two parts [Killigrew, *Bellamire, Her Dream ; or, The Love of Shadows*].

―――― the heroine of the comedy [Sedley, *Bellamira ; or, The Mistress*].

Bellamy : Wildblood's friend ; a lively young 'blood' [Dryden, *An Evening's Love ; or, The Mock Astrologer*].

―――― a terribly sensible young man, who marries Jacintha with her fortune of £30,000 [Hoadly, *Sus-picious Husband*].

―――― **Lord :** a character in the comedy [Thomas Shad-well, *Bury-Fair*].

Bellario : the name of a page [Beaumont and Fletcher, *Philaster*].

Bellarmine : the despicable though fashionable lover of Leonora [Fielding, *Joseph Andrews*].

Bellaston, Lady : an immodest woman upon whose charity Tom Jones lives [Fielding, *Tom Jones*].

Bellefontaine, Benedict : the father of Evangeline [Longfellow, *Evangeline*].

Bellenden, Edith : in love with Morton, a leader of the Covenanters, but betrothed to Lord Evandale.

——— *Lady Margaret :* an enthusiastic royalist, the grandmother of Edith.

——— *Major :* the brother of Lady Margaret [Scott, *Old Mortality*].

Belleur : a blunt man, in love with Rosalura [J. Fletcher, *Wild Goose Chase*].

Bellicent : the daughter of Gorlois and Ygerne, and halfsister to King Arthur [Mallory, *History of Prince Arthur*].

Bellingham : a man about town [Dion Boucicault, *After Dark*].

Bellisant : sister of King Pepin and married to Alexander, Emperor of Constantinople [*Valentine and Orson*].

Bellmont, George : the hero, in love with Clarissa, to whom his father is opposed. Ultimately the lover triumphs.

——— *Sir William :* the father of George, a tyrannical and obstinate old man [Murphy, *All in the Wrong*].

Belloni, Sandra : the daughter of an exiled Italian and an English woman. Discovered by the Poles, singing in a wood, and received into their family. In love with Wilfred Pole, who discards her and then vainly tries to win her back [George Meredith, *Sandra Belloni*].

Belmont, Charles : a dissipated young man, the son of Sir Robert, who marries Fidelia.

——— *Sir Robert :* a friend of Sir Charles Raymond.

——— *Rosetta :* the witty daughter of Sir Robert, who marries Colonel Raymond [Edward Moore, *The Foundling*].

Bellmour : the friend of Jane Shore [Rowe, *Jane Shore*].

Belmour, Edward : a lively young man of the world [Congreve, *Old Bachelor*].

——— *Mrs. :* a widow with ' a feeling heart' [Murphy. *Way to Keep Him*].

Belphoebe : intended for Queen Elizabeth, and adorned with every virtue [Spenser, *Faëry Queene*].

Belshazzar : the hero of a drama by Milman, and of a Hebrew melody by Byron called *The Vision of Belshazzar.*

Beltham, Squire : a very rich and fierce-tempered county magnate, whose daughter Richmond Roy has secretly married. The old type of squire, strong, competent, racy of the soil [George Meredith, *Adventures of Harry Richmond*].

Selvawney, Miss : a member of Mr. Vincent Crummle's Company at the Portsmouth Theatre [Dickens, *Nicholas Nickleby*].

Belvidera : the heroine, whose sorrows so affect her mind that she becomes insane [Otway, *Venice Preserved*].

Belville : Peggy's lover [Garrick, *The Country Girl*].

Ben-Hur : a young Jew; the leading character in the book, the scene of which is laid in the time of Christ [Wallace, *Ben-Hur*].

Ben Jochanan : intended for the Rev. Samuel Johnson [Dryden and Tate, *Absalom and Achitophel*, pt. ii.].

Benaiah : intended for General Sackville [Dryden and Tate, *Absalom and Achitophel*, pt. ii.].

Benaskar : a merchant of Delhi [Ridley, *Tales of the Genii*].

Benevolus : intended for a portrait of John Courtney Throckmorton [Cowper, *The Task*].

Benedick : a witty and dashing young nobleman, the complement of Beatrice, whom he marries [Shakespeare, *Much Ado About Nothing*].

Benbow : a good-natured drunkard, whose follies caused him to end his days in the workhouse [Crabbe, *The Borough*].

Benbowie, Laird of : faithful friend and constant visitor of the Chief of Glenroy, but stupid, coarse, and uncouth [Susan Ferrier, *Destiny*].

Benjie, Little : Benjamin Colthred, a spy in the employ of Cristal Nixon [Scott, *Redgauntlet*].

Bennet, Brother : a monk at the Convent of St. Mary [Scott, *Monastery*].

——— **Elizabeth :** the most captivating of all this authoress's heroines. After sundry tribulations she marries Darcy.

——— *Jane :* the favourite sister of Elizabeth.

——— *Lydia :* a frivolous girl, the sister of the heroine. She elopes with Mr. Wickham from the garrison town near her home.

——— *Mrs. :* the foolish mother of the heroine.

——— *Mr. :* a witty and cynical recluse, bored to death by the follies of his wife and younger daughters [Jane Austen, *Pride and Prejudice*].

——— **Mrs. :** an intriguing woman of doubtful character [Fielding, *Amelia*].

Benson : the butler at Raynham Abbey, the seat of Sir Austin Feverel. Has a great mistrust for women, and is beaten by Richard Feverel for spying on him and Lucy Desborough [George Meredith, *Ordeal of Richard Feverel*].

Benton, Miss : Master Humphrey's housekeeper, to whom Tony Weller proposes marriage, but is rejected [Dickens *Master Humphrey's Clock*].

Benvolio : a quarrelsome member of the Montague faction. A friend of Romeo's [Shakespeare, *Romeo and Juliet*].

Beowulf : a Norse Viking and hero of the earliest known English poem [*Beowulf*].

Beppo : the husband of Laura, captured by Turks, and returning to Venice to find his wife at a ball with some one else [Byron, *Beppo*].

Berenger, Eveline : betrothed to Sir Hugo de Lacy, who relinquishes his claims in favour of Sir Damian de Lacy, his nephew.

—— *Sir Raymond :* an old Norman knight, the father of Eveline [Scott, *Betrothed*].

Berinthia : a young widow in love with Townly ; she flirts with Loveless so as to excite Townly's jealousy [Sheridan, *Trip to Scarborough*, adapted from Vanbrugh's *Relapse*].

Berkely, Lady Augusta : disguises herself as a minstrel, and finally marries Sir John de Walton [Scott, *Castle Dangerous*].

Berkley, Mr. : a kindly old English bachelor of eccentric habits [Longfellow, *Hyperion*].

Berkeley, Old Woman of : the subject of a ballad [Southey, *Old Woman of Berkeley*].

Berkrolles, Master Roger : the schoolmaster of Newton Nottage [Blackmore, *Maid of Sker*].

Bernardo : intended to represent Joseph Haslewood [T. F. Dibdin, *Bibliomania ; or, Book-Madness*].

—— an officer ; a friend of Hamlet's, to whom the Ghost appeared during his watch [Shakespeare, *Hamlet*].

—— del Carpio : a Spanish knight of the ninth century [Felicia D. Hemans, *Bernardo del Carpio* : a ballad].

Berry, Mrs. : the old nurse of Richard Feverel, and later on the tried friend of Lucy Feverel [George Meredith, *Ordeal of Richard Feverel*].

Bertha : a blind girl, the daughter of Caleb Plummer [Dickens, *Cricket on the Hearth*].

—— the reputed daughter of the Burgomaster of Bruges, but really Gertrude, the daughter of the Duke of Brabant [J. Fletcher, *Beggar's Bush*].

Bertha: alias Agatha. She eventually marries Hereward, one of the Emperor's guards [Scott, *Count Robert of Paris*].

Bertoldo: a knight of Malta and brother of the king of the two Sicilies. He loves Camiola, but jilts her for Aurelia [Massinger, *Maid of Honour*].

Bertram: a conspirator against the Republic of Venice who betrayed the plot [Byron, *Marino Faliero*].

—— **Edmund:** the most attractive of this writer's clergymen, and married to the heroine, Fanny Price.

—— *Julia:* married to Mr. Yates.

—— *Lady:* an indolent, self-indulgent woman. The aunt of Fanny Price, the heroine.

—— *Maria:* married to Mr. Rushworth; she finally elopes with Henry Crawford.

—— *Sir Thomas:* a rather punctilious but strictly honourable and really kindly man—the staunch friend of Fanny Price.

—— *Tom:* the scape-grace, eldest son of Sir Thomas Bertram [Jane Austen, *Mansfield Park*].

—— **Count:** an outlaw and leader of a robber-band, who is wrecked on the coast of Sicily. After committing various crimes he commits suicide [Maturin, *Bertram*].

—— **Count of Rousillon:** the man to whom Helena is married as a reward for restoring the King to health. He leaves her, but Helena wins his love in the end through a ruse [Shakespeare, *All's Well that Ends Well*].

—— **Frederick:** the son of Sir Stephen, who marries against his father's wishes but is finally taken back into favour.

—— *Sir Stephen:* a just but close-fisted man who disinherits his son for marrying a girl of no position. She proves to be rich, so he relents [Cumberland, *The Jew*].

—— **Henry:** the son of the Laird of Ellangowan, who marries Julia Mannering.

—— *Lucy:* sister of Henry Bertram, and, in the end, wife of Charles Hazlewood [Scott, *Guy Mannering*]. There are many other members of the family.

Bertulphe: the son of a serf who through industry wins wealth and power and is appointed Provost of Bruges [Knowles, *Provost of Bruges*].

Berwine: the maid of Lady Ermengarde [Scott, *The Betrothed*].

Bess: the daughter of the Blind Beggar [Chettle and Day *Blind Beggar of Bethnal Green*].

Besselia: the girl beloved by Captain Crowe [Smollett, *Sir Launcelot Greaves*].

Bessie Bell and **May Gray:** *see* Bell, Bessie.

Bessus: a cowardly, swaggering army captain [J. Fletcher, *King and No King*].

Bet or **Betsy:** a thief employed by Fagin, and an acquaintance of Nancy [Dickens, *Oliver Twist*].

Bettris: the country girl in love with George-a-Greene [Greene, *George-a-Greene*].

Bevan, Mr.: an American doctor who lends Martin Chuzzlewit and Mark Tapley money to help them back to England from America [Dickens, *Martin Chuzzlewit*].

Beverley: the rather questionable hero. Naturally of good instincts he allows himself to be led astray by Stukely and at last dies a miserable death.

—— *Charlotte:* sister of 'the Gamester' and ruined by him, but married by Lewson in spite of her poverty.

—— *Mrs.:* 'the Gamester's' faithful but unhappy wife [Edward Moore, *The Gamester*].

Beverley: a very jealous but constant lover, who marries Belinda Blandford.

—— *Clarissa:* betrothed to the son of Sir William Bellmont [Murphy, *All in the Wrong*].

—— *Ensign:* see Absolute, Captain.

Bevil: a witty society man [Charles Shadwell, *Epsom Wells*].

—— a very finished and courteous gentleman [Steele, *Conscious Lovers*].

—— **Francis, Harry** and **George:** three brothers all, unknowingly, suitors for the hand of the same lady. The youngest brother—a soldier—wins [O'Brien, *Cross Purposes*].

Bevis of Southampton, Sir: deserted on a desert as a baby, he was brought up as a shepherd, then exiled and sold to an Armenian who presented him to the king, whose daughter he married and eventually regained his lands and titles in England [Drayton, *Polyolbion*].

—— Lord Marmion's charger [Scott, *Marmion*].

Bianca: a beautiful character in the play [Massinger, Rowley and Fletcher, *Fair Maid of the Inn*].

—— married to Leontio, and a very beautiful woman, whose virtue is attempted by a bad woman [Middleton, *Women Beware Women*].

—— bears evidence against her husband, accusing him of murder, and then, upon his being condemned to death, goes mad and dies [Milman, *Fazio*].

—— the woman whom Iago persuades to steal Desdemona's handkerchief [Shakespeare, *Othello*].

Bianca : the younger sister of 'the Shrew,' who marries Lucentio as soon as Petrucchio has married Katherine [Shakespeare, *Taming of the Shrew*].

—— Capella : *see* Capella, Bianca.

Bibbet, Master : private secretary to General Harrison, a parliamentary commissioner [Scott, *Woodstock*].

Bickerton, Mrs. : of the *Seven Stars Inn*, York, the hostelry where Jeanie Deans stays on her way to London [Scott, *Heart of Midlothian*].

Biddy : the girl who married Joe Gargery after falling in love with Pip [Dickens, *Great Expectations*].

Bidmore, Hon. Augustus : pupil of Mr. Cargill.

—— *Lord :* patron of Mr. Cargill.

—— *Miss Augusta :* beloved by Mr. Cargill [Scott, *St. Ronan's Well*].

Biederman, Arnold : uncle of Anne and father of Rudiger, Ernest, Sigismund and Ulrich [Scott, *Anne of Geierstein*].

Biglow, Hosea : the pretended author of a lot of satirical political poems on the side of the anti-slavery movement [Lowell, *Biglow Papers*].

Biler,' The : *see* Toodle, Robin.

Billee, Little : *see* Bagot, William.

—— Little : one of three Bristol sailors who went to sea. Being on the point of starvation the others resolved to eat Little Billee [Thackeray, *Little Billee*].

Bimbister, Margery : the wife of Ranzelman [Scott, *Pirate*].

Bindloose, John : a banker at Marchthorn who also serves as sheriff's clerk [Scott, *St. Ronan's Well*].

Bingley, Mr. : a neighbour of the Bennet family, who ultimately marries Jane Bennet.

Bingleys, The Miss : the stuck-up, impertinent sisters of Mr. Bingley, the lover of Jane Bennet [Jane Austen, *Pride and Prejudice*].

Binks, Sir Bingo and Lady : visitors at the Spa : a fox-hunting baronet and his wife, who had been Miss Rachel Bonnyrigg [Scott, *St. Ronan's Well*].

Binnie, James : an old Anglo-Indian and a friend of Colonel Newcome's [Thackeray, *The Newcomes*].

Binnorie, The Twa Sisters o' : one sister, from motives of jealousy, drowns the other, etc., etc. [*Twa Sisters o' Binnorie*: a ballad].

Biondello : servant to Lucentio [Shakespeare, *Taming of the Shrew*].

—— Dr. : this is the name of a Christmas tale by Thackeray.

Birch, Harvey : one of the chief characters [Cooper, *The Spy* .

Birdlime : a man of evil character [Webster, *Westward Ho !*]

Bireno, Duke : destined by the King of Lombardy to wed Sophia, he plots to deceive him. In the end Bireno is slain by Paladore, the man who Sophia really loved [Jephson, *Law of Lombardy*].

Biron : a favourite of Henry IV of France, and the hero of two plays [Chapman, *Biron's Conspiracy* and *Biron's Tragedy*].

———— a witty, jesting attendant on King Ferdinand of Navarre, in love with Rosaline [Shakespeare, *Love's Labour's Lost*].

———— the eldest son of Count Baldwin; he marries Isabella, a nun, and is therefore disinherited by his father [Southern, *Fatal Marriage*].

———— **Harriet :** the girl with whom Sir Charles Grandison was in love [Richardson, *Sir Charles Grandison*].

Birtha : the only child of Astragon for whom she gathered 'simples' in spring, summer and autumn. She falls in love with Gondibert who plights his troth to her [Davenant, *Gondibert*].

Bitherston, Master : one of the boarders at Mrs. Pipchin's School [Dickens, *Dombey and Son*].

Bittlebrains, Lord and Lady : friends of Sir William Ashton, Lord-keeper of Scotland [Scott, *Bride of Lammermoor*].

Bitzer : a pupil of Mr. M'Cloakumchild's who becomes a light-porter at Bounderby's Bank, and is instrumental in the capture of Tom Gradgrind [Dickens, *Hard Times*].

Bizarre : a vivacious lady, the friend of Oriana, and apt to play the coquette [Farquhar, *The Inconstant*].

Black, Bell : niece of Mrs. St. Clair, who afterwards marries Major Waddell.

———— *Miss :* sister to Mrs. St. Clair.

———— *Miss Mary :* the invalid sister of Mrs. St. Clair [Susan E. Ferrier, *The Inheritance*].

Black-eyed Susan : *see* Susan, Black-eyed.

Blackacre, Widow : a perverse and quarrelsome woman [Wycherly, *Plain Dealer*].

Blackless, Tomalin : a guardsman in the army of Richard I [Scott, *Talisman*].

Blackpool, Stephen : a 'hand' in Bounderby's mill; the man on whom Tom Gradgrind cast suspicion when he robbed the bank [Dickens, *Hard Times*].

Bladamour : the friend of Paridel [Spenser, *Faëry Queene*].

Blair, Adam : a Scottish minister who strayed from the paths of virtue, but repented [Lockhart, *Adam Blair : a Story of Scottish Life*].

Blair, Father Clement : a Carthusian monk, the Confessor of Catherine Glover [Scott, *Fair Maid of Perth*].

Blaize, Mrs. Mary : the subject of a comic elegy [Goldsmith, *Mrs. Mary Blaize: an elegy on the Glory of her Sex*].

Blanchardine and Eglantine : a romance of the Middle Ages printed by William Caxton.

Blanche : the niece of King John of England [Shakespeare, *King John*].

———— **Lady :** vows, with Lady Anne, to remain unmarried, then promptly falls in love with Thomas Blount [Knowles, *Old Maids*].

Blanchefleur : the heroine of a mediaeval prose romance.

Blancove, Edward : ruins Dahlia Fleming, but afterwards repents and tries to marry her. In this he is unsuccessful [George Meredith, *Rhoda Fleming*].

Blandamour, Sir : an insolent knight who attacked Britomart but was undone by her enchanted spear [Spenser, *Faëry Queene*].

Blandeville, Lady Emily : a friend and neighbour of the Waverley family who marries Colonel Talbot [Scott, *Waverley*].

Blandford : the father of Belinda, whom he promised to George Bellmont ; but Belinda declined to marry any one but Beverley.

———— *Belinda :* she married Beverley against her father's wishes [Murphy, *All in the Wrong*].

Blandiman : serving-man to Bellisant [*Valentine and Orson.*]

Blandina : wife of Turpin, an uncouth, inhospitable man [Spenser, *Faëry Queene*].

Blandish, Mr. and Miss Letitia : both parasites and time-servers who bow down before Miss Alscrip, ' the heiress ' [Burgoyne, *The Heiress*].

Blaney : a wealthy man who brings himself to ruin by a life of dissipation [Crabbe, *The Borough*].

Blatant Beast, The : supposed to typify slander or public opinion [Spenser, *Faëry Queene*].

Blathers : one of the detectives engaged in investigating the burglary at Chertsey [Dickens, *Oliver Twist*].

Blattergrowl, The Rev. Mr. : minister of Trotcosey, near Monkbarns [Scott, *Antiquary*].

Bletson, Master Joshua : a parliamentary Commissioner sent by Cromwell to the Lees [Scott, *Woodstock*].

Bleys : supposed to teach Merlin, but his pupil knew more than he did himself [Alfred Tennyson, *Idylls of the King*].

Blifil : a deceitful friend of Tom's [Fielding, *Tom Jones*].

Blimber, Cornelia : a very learned young lady, the daughter of Paul Dombey's schoolmaster, who married Mr. Feeder, the usher in her father's school.

———— *Doctor and Mrs. :* the proprietors of the school to which Paul Dombey was sent at Brighton [Dickens, *Dombey and Son*].

Blinkinsop : a smuggler who plays a rather important part in the story [Scott, *Redgauntlet*].

Blister : an apothecary who courts Lucy [Fielding, *The Virgin Unmasked*].

Block, Martin : a minor character connected with the Estates of Burgundy when they refuse supplies to Charles the Bold [Scott, *Anne of Geierstein*].

Blondel de Nesle : the minstrel of Richard Coeur de Lion, who discovered his master's place of concealment [Scott, *Talisman*].

Blood, Colonel Thomas : the Duke of Buckingham's emissary [Scott, *Peveril of the Peak*].

Bloomfield, Louisa : in love with the young barrister, Charles Danvers, but betrothed to an old nobleman, Lord Totterly [Selby, *The Unfinished Gentleman*].

Blotton, Mr. (of Aldgate) : the member of the Pickwick Club who dares to call Mr. Pickwick a 'humbug' [Dickens, *Pickwick Papers*].

Blougram, Bishop : a low-minded bishop who had little sympathy with idealists [R. Browning, *Bishop Blougram's Apology*].

Blount, John : elder son of Master and Mistress Blount. A vain snob who made love to a lady's maid under the impression that she was a countess.

———— *Master and Mistress :* an honest and wealthy old London jeweller and his wife.

———— *Thomas :* younger son of the jeweller. A handsome man of fine character, who enters the army and marries Lady Blanche who had resolved to be an 'old maid' [J. S. Knowles, *Old Maids*].

———— **Nicholas :** master of the horse to the Earl of Sussex [Scott, *Kenilworth*].

———— **Sir Frederick :** a fop who could not, or did not, pronounce his 'r's' [Lytton, *Money*].

Blower, Mrs. Margaret : the widow of a shipowner, who takes for her second husband Dr. Quackleben [Scott, *St. Ronan's Well*].

Blowselinda : a shepherdess in love with Lobbin Clout [Gay, *Shepherd's Week*].

Blowzelinda : a country girl who feeds the pigs, milks the cows and performs a lot of lowly work [Gay, *Shepherd's Week*].

Blue-beard : Chevalier Raoul, a tyrant with a bluebeard, who disposes of one wife after another in a mysterious way until the brothers of his eighth victim slay him. A French story said to have been based on fact.

Bluett, The Hon. Rodney : nephew of Colonel Lougher, afterwards married to Bardie [Blackmore, *Maid of Sker*].

Bluff, Cap. Noll : the champion of fighting for fighting's sake [Congreve, *The Old Bachelor*].

Blumine : a 'young, hazel-eyed, beautiful, high-born maiden' with whom Teufelsdröckh falls in love [Carlyle, *Sartor Resartus*].

Blunt, Colonel : a royalist officer who, having declared he would bow to no woman, falls hopelessly in love with Arbella, an heiress [Howard, *The Committee*].

────── **Major General :** a brave and patriotic old cavalry officer [Thomas Shadwell, *The Volunteers*].

Blushington, Edward : an intensely shy young man, come into a considerable fortune. Afterwards the accepted suitor of Dinah Friendly [Moncrieff, *Bashful Man*].

Boabdelin, Mahomet : the last King of Granada [Dryden, *Conquest of Granada*].

Boadicea : wife of Praesutagus, King of the Iceni. She raised an army and burnt the Roman colonies in London, Colchester, etc. [J. Fletcher, *Boadicea*].

Boanerges : a parson who is a violent denouncer of all those who belong to other sects than his own, yet, out of the pulpit friendly enough [Mrs. Oliphant, *Salem Chapel*].

Boar of Ardennes, The Wild : Guillaume Comte de la Marck [Scott, *Quentin Durward*].

Bob the Grinder : *see* Toodle, Robin.

Bobadil, Captain : one of this author's best creations. A blustering, conceited coward with a panacea for the tranquilization of Europe [Ben Jonson, *Every Man in His Humour*].

Bobster, Miss Cecilia : the girl whom Newman Noggs mistakes for Miss Madeline Bray.

────── **Mr. :** a fierce old man, the father of Cecilia [Dickens, *Nicholas Nickleby*].

Boeuf, Front de, Reginald : 'very big and very fierce', a follower of John of England [Scott, *Ivanhoe*].

Boffin, Mrs. Henrietta : the daughter of a cat's-meat man, greatly beloved and admired by her husband.

────── **Nicodemus :** called by his friends, Noddy. Husband of Henrietta, the 'golden dustman'—a man of great simplicity and perfect honesty, who came into a large fortune and who shared it with the donors' son [Dickens, *Our Mutual Friend*].

Bohemond, Prince of Antioch : a crusader [Scott, *Count Robert of Paris*].

Bohort, Sir, or King : King of Gaul and brother of King Ban of Brittany. Also known as Bors, and Bort [Mallory, *History of Prince Arthur*].

Bois Guilbert, Brian de : a Knight Templar who insulted Rebecca and was slain by Ivanhoe [Scott, *Ivanhoe*].

Bokhara : the King of Bokhara tells his own story to his Vizier [Matthew Arnold, *Sick King of Bokhara*].

Bold, John : surgeon and reformer, in love with Eleanor Harding. The originator of the proceedings against the Wardenship of Hiram's Hospital.

——— *Mary :* his sister. A woman of sterling but unsentimental character [Anthony Trollope, *The Warden*].

Boldwig, Captain : a small, consequential and imperious man, on to whose grounds Mr. Pickwick and his party trespass whilst shooting, and in whose wheelbarrow Mr. Pickwick is found asleep [Dickens, *Pickwick Papers*].

Boldwood, Farmer : the man who shot Troy, Bathsheba's husband [Hardy, *Far from the Madding Crowd*].

Boleyn, Anne : second wife of Henry VIII, the subject of a dramatic poem [Milman, *Anne Boleyn*].

Bombardinian : general to King Chrononhotonthologos's army. He fights the king and is killed [Carey, *Chrononhonthologos*].

Bombastes Furioso : a general in the army of Artaxaminous, King of Utopia, who is jilted by Distaffina for a gift of half-a-crown. A burlesque in ridicule of the heroic style of Modern Operas [Rhodes, *Bombastes Furioso*].

Bomby, Hope-on-High : a Puritan, appearing in a morrisdance and denouncing worldly pleasures at the same time [J. Fletcher, *Women Pleased*].

Boniface : landlord of the inn at Lichfield [Farquhar, *Beaux' Stratagem*].

——— Father : the ex-abbot of Kennaquhair, who plays the part of Blinkhoodie, gardener at Kinross, and also as the gardener at Dundreman [Scott, *The Abbot*].

——— Abbot : becomes Superior of St. Mary's Convent, in succession to Ingelram [Scott, *Monastery*].

Bonnie Lesley : *see* Lesley, Bonnie.

Bonny : a waif, living with his jackass in a hollow of the South Downs, and who renders valuable service to the Lorraines [Blackmore, *Alice Lorraine*].

Booby, Lady : intended as a caricature of Pamela, in Richardson's novel [Fielding, *Joseph Andrews*].

Booth, Captain : said to be the author's portrait of himself. He is drawn as a vicious and mean man [Fielding, *Amelia*].

Borachia : a drunken woman of low character [Massinger, *A Very Woman*].

Borachio : a villian, who plots most of the mischief. He is a retainer of Don John, and betrothed to Margaret, Hero's maid [Shakespeare, *Much Ado About Nothing*].

—————— **Joseph :** landlord of the *Eagle*, in Salamanca, [Jephson, *Two Strings to Your Bow*].

Boroughcliff, Captain : a vulgar, boasting Yankee, the butt of Long Tom Coffin [Fitzball, *The Pilot*].

Borre, Sir : a Knight of the Round Table. The son of Arthur and Lyonors [Mallory, *History of Prince Arthur*].

Bors, Sir : *see* Bohort.

Bort, Sir : *see* Bohort.

Bossnowl, Lady Clarinda : beloved by, and ultimately married to, Captain Fitzchrome [Peacock, *Crotchet Castle*].

Bostana : one of the sisters whose task it was to administer the bastinado to Prince Assad, daily, during his captivity, and who, out of pity, secretly set him free [*Arabian Nights*].

Boswal : the hero of a Scottish romance dating from the sixteenth century [*Boswal and Lillian*].

Bothwell : Mary of Scotland's paramour : the hero of a Tale in verse by W. E. Aytoun, a Novel by James Grant, and a Drama by A. C. Swinburne.

Bottom, Nick : a weaver and the leading spirit amongst the yokels, who rehearse 'Pyramus and Thisbe previous to acting it before Theseus and Hippolyta [Shakespeare, *Midsummer Night's Dream*].

Boultby, the Rev. Dr. : Vicar of Whinbury and friend of Mr. Helstone [Charlotte Brontë, *Shirley*].

Bouncer, Mr. : friend of Verdant Green, who resorts to various ruses to aid his memory in examinations, and who owns two dogs of note, Huz and Buz [Cuthbert Bede (Edward Bradley), *Verdant Green*].

Bounderby, Josiah : the 'Bully of Humility'. A provincial banker, who makes a fortune and marries Louisa Gradgrind [Dickens, *Hard Times*].

Bountiful, Lady : an easy-tempered, generous, old country-gentlewoman [Farquhar, *Beaux' Stratagem*].

Bourgh, Lady Catherine de : the vulgar patroness of Mr. Collins [Jane Austen, *Pride and Prejudice*].

Bowley, Sir Joseph : an M.P. and, according to himself, 'the poor man's friend' [Dickens, *The Chimes*].

Bowling, Tom : the hero of a famous song [Charles Dibdin, *Tom Bowling*].

—— **Lieutenant Tom :** one of the old type of seamen ; rough, noisy, brave, and at heart tender as a woman [Smollett, *Roderick Random*].

Bows : a hunchbacked violinist, and friend of the Costigans [Thackeray, *Pendennis*].

Bowyer, Master : usher of the black rod to Queen Elizabeth [Scott, *Kenilworth*].

Bowzybeus : the singer of some of the best songs in the pastoral [Gay, *Shepherd's Week*].

Box and Cox : the names of the chief characters in a 'dramatic romance of real life' [J. M. Morton, *Box and Cox*].

Boxer : John Peerybingle's dog [Dickens, *Cricket on the Hearth*].

Boyet : one of the lords in attendance on the Princes of France [Shakespeare, *Love's Labour's Lost*].

Boythorne, Lawrence : a friend of Mr. Jarndyce, who had a huge voice but tender heart [Dickens, *Bleak House*].

Brabantio : the father of Desdemona ; a proud Venetian noble [Shakespeare, *Othello*].

Braccio : an employé of the republic of Florence who tried to discover actions to the discredit of General Luria, but failed [R. Browning, *Luria*].

Bracidas : the brother of Amidas and son of Milesio, who married Lucy [Spenser, *Faëry Queene*].

Brackley : the hero of a Scottish ballad, wherein the wife 'Peggy' eggs him on to fight against long odds and rejoices at his death [*Baron of Brackley*].

Bracy, Sir Maurice de : an unsuccessful suitor for the hand of Rowena [Scott, *Ivanhoe*].

Bradwardine, Baron Como Cosmyne : an adherent of Prince Charlie, and the father of Rose.

—— *Rose :* the heroine, who marries Waverley [Scott, *Waverley*].

Brady, Martha : a widow at twenty-three she had a suitor of sixty-three, whom she rejects in favour of his nephew [Garrick, *Irish Widow*].

Brag, Jack : a man of low birth and vulgar manners who strives to force his way into good society by the aid of bounce and servility [Hook, *Jack Brag*].

Bragela : the daughter of Sorglan and wife of Cuthullin who acted as regent during the minority of King Cormac [Ossian, *Fingal*].

Braggadochio : supposed to personify an unruly tongue [Spenser, *Faëry Queene*].

Brainworm : a man of many *aliases* and of shifty character [Ben Jonson, *Every Man in His Humour*].

Brakel, Adrian : a gypsy, at one time the master of Fenella, the pretended deaf-and-dumb girl [Scott, *Peveril of the Peak*].

Bramble, Matthew : a gouty, dyspeptic man, but kindly and generous.

—— *Miss Tabitha :* the sister of Matthew, who marries Captain Lismahago. She is prim and vain and altogether ridiculous [Smollett, *Humphrey Clinker*].

—— Frederick : nephew and adopted son of Sir Robert. Of generous and impulsive temper. He marries Emily Worthington.

—— *Sir Robert :* rich and generous [Colman, the Younger, *Poor Gentleman*].

Bran : the dog of Lamberg, the lover of Gelchossa [Ossian, *Fingal*].

—— the dog of Fingal, King of Morven [Ossian, *Fingal*].

Brampton, Lady : one of the characters in the play [Steele, *The Funeral*].

Brand, Alice : she makes the sign of the cross thrice on the brow of Urgan, and having restored him thus to human shape, discovers in him her own brother Ethert [Scott, *Lady of the Lake*].

—— Sir Denys : a country magnate who affects to be very humble, and whilst mounting his groom on a race-horse, rides a sorry nag himself [Crabbe, *The Borough*].

Brandan, St. : the saint who met Judas floating on an iceberg, Judas being respited from the flames of Hell for one brief day as a recompense for his goodness to a leper at Joppa [Matthew Arnold, *St. Brandan*].

Brandley, Mrs. : the lady who is to introduce Estella into society [Dickens, *Great Expectations*].

Brandon, Colonel : lover and afterwards husband of Marianne Dashwood [Jane Austen, *Sense and Sensibility*].

Brandt : the man who acted as leader to the Indians who destroyed Wyoming [Campbell, *Gertrude of Wyoming*].

Brangtons, The : a family of vulgar, malicious and jealous girls [Fanny Burney, *Evelina*].

Branville, Sir Anthony : a solemn, ponderous lover, who in thirteen years courts eight different women. A character acted by Garrick [Mrs. Sheridan, *The Discovery*].

Brass : the confederate of Dick Amlet [Vanbrugh, *The Confederacy*].

—— a deerhound belonging to Sheila [Black, *A Princess of Thule*].

Brass, Sally : the sister of Sampson, even cleverer, meaner, more repulsive than himself.

—— *Sampson :* a low-class attorney of Bevis Marks [Dickens, *Old Curiosity Shop*].

Bratts, Ned : he and his wife were both hanged for crimes which both confessed [R. Browning, *Dramatic Idylls*].

Bratti Ferravecchi : a goldsmith [George Eliot, *Romola*].

Bravassa, Miss : one of Mr. Crummles' company at the Portsmouth Theatre [Dickens, *Nicholas Nickleby*].

Bray, Madeline : a beautiful girl, who marries Nicholas Nickleby [Dickens, *Nicholas Nickleby*].

Bray, Vicar of : hero of a popular song. He is supposed to have been one Simon Aleyn. Bray is a village in Berkshire, and the song is supposed to have been written by an army officer in the reign of George I.

Braymore, Lady Caroline : daughter of Lord Fitz-Balaam ; she marries the Hon. Tom Shuffleton [Colman the Younger, *John Bull*].

Brazen, Captain : a recruiting officer in rivalry with Captain Plume [Farquhar, *Recruiting Officer*].

Brecan : a mythical king of Wales, supposed to be the father of twenty-four daughters [Drayton, *Polyolbion*].

Brechan, Prince : the father of St. Cadock the Martyr, and St. Canock the Confessor [Drayton, *Polyolbion*].

Breitmann, Hans : the hero of a lot of humorous ballads in Pennsylvanian Dutch dialect [Leland, *Hans Breitmann's Party*, etc.].

Brengwain : the go-between between Isolde and Sir Tristram [*Arthurian Cycle*].

—— wife of Gwenwyn, Prince of Powys-land [Scott, *The Betrothed*].

Brentford, The Two Kings : two characters in a farce, by some supposed to be intended for Charles II and James Duke of York, afterwards James I [Duke of Buckingham, *The Rehearsal*].

Breton, Captain : the lover of Clara [Mrs. Centlivre, *The Wonder*].

Briana : the lady who at her castle gate levied a toll of ' the locks of every lady and the beard of every knight that passed ' [Spenser, *Faëry Quesne*].

Brick, Mr. Jefferson : the war correspondent of the *New York Rowdy Journal* [Dickens, *Martin Chuzzlewit*].

Bridgemore, Lucinda : an ill-tempered girl engaged to Lord Abberville, but her temper so alarmed him that he forsook her.

—— *Mr. and Mrs. :* a vulgar and dishonest merchant, and his wife, who with as much vulgarity is more pretentious and therefore more offensive [Cumberland, *Fashionable Lover*].

Bridgenorth, Alice : the daughter of Ralph and the heroine of the story. She marries Julian Peveril.

—— *Major Ralph :* a Roundhead, the neighbour and friend of Julian Peveril, a Cavalier [Scott, *Peveril of the Peak*].

Bridget, Miss: the mother of Tom Jones [Fielding, *Tom Jones*].

—— **Mother :** the aunt of Catherine Seyton, and the Abbess of St. Catherine [Scott, *The Abbot*].

Bridgeward, Peter : the warder of the bridge at Kennaquhair, and also of that near St. Mary's Convent [Scott, *Abbot* and *Monastery*].

Brierly, Bob : a Ticket-of-Leave man [Tom Taylor, *Ticket-of-Leave Man*].

Brigadore : Sir Guyon's charger [Spenser, *The Faëry Queene*].

Briggs : surnamed ' Stoney ', because his brains were petrified by too much learning [Dickens, *Dombey and Son*].

—— **Matilda :** the companion of Miss Crawley and Mrs. Rawdon Crawley [Thackeray, *Vanity Fair*].

Brigida, Monna : a relative of Romola's [George Eliot, *Romola*].

Brilliant, Sir Philip : a fop, but at the same time a good and brave soldier. He falls in love with Lady Anne and marries her [Knowles, *Old Maids*].

Brisac, Charles : a son of the Justice and a learned man.

—— **Eustace :** a courtier ; the brother of Charles.

—— **Justice :** the brother of Miramont [J. Fletcher, *The Elder Brother*].

Brisk, Fastidious : ' a neat, spruce, affecting courtier, one that wears clothes well and in fashion ' [Ben Jonson, *Every Man Out of His Humour*].

—— a suitor for the hand of Lady Froth. A good-natured chatterbox who loved to be thought a wit [Congreve, *Double Dealer*].

Briskie : the ' loyal subject ', a captain in the Muscovite army, who assumed the name of Putskie for purposes of concealment [J. Fletcher, *The Loyal Subject*].

Britain, Benjamin : called ' Little Britain ', landlord of the *Nutmeg Grater Inn* and married to Clemency Newcome [Dickens, *Battle of Life*].

Britomart, or Britomartis : the personification of Chastity. The daughter of King Ryence of Wales [Spenser, *Faëry Queene*].

Briton, Colonel : a Scot, who, seeing Donna Isabella leap from a window, that she might escape from a distasteful marriage, took her to a friend's house, and in the end married her himself [Mrs. Centlivre, *The Wonder*].

Brittle, Barnaby : a character acted by Charles Macklin at Covent Garden.

———— *Mrs. :* his wife. A character acted by Mrs. Bracegirdle and Mrs. Oldfield [Betterton, *The Amorous Widow*].

Brittles : Mrs. Maylie's servant [Dickens, *Oliver Twist*].

Brocklehurst, Rev. Mr. : the clergyman at Lowood School [Charlotte Brontë, *Jane Eyre*].

Bronzely : a contemptible man whose ambition it was to be thought 'a general seducer' [Mrs. Inchbald, *Wives as they Were and Maids as they Are*].

Bronzomarte : the charger belonging to Sir Launcelot Greaves [Smollett, *Adventures of Sir Launcelot Greaves*].

Brook, Master : the name assumed by Ford [Shakespeare, *Merry Wives of Windsor*].

Brooke, Celia : the sister of Dorothea Casaubon. She marries Sir James Chettam [George Eliot, *Middlemarch*].

———— **Dorothea :** first married to Mr. Casaubon, a dry-as-dust scholar, and afterwards to Will Ladislaw the artist [George Eliot, *Middlemarch*].

Brooker : the man who kidnapped Ralph Nickleby's son, and placed him, under the name of 'Smike,' at Dotheboy's Hall [Dickens, *Nicholas Nickleby*].

Browdie, John : a bluff and noisy Yorkshireman [Dickens, *Nicholas Nickleby*].

Brown : the artist of the party, who gets himself arrested because he insists on sketching and the natives think he is a spy taking plans of their fortifications [Richard Doyle, *Adventures of Brown, Jones and Robinson*].

———— **Alice :** daughter of below, known as Alice Marwood. As a girl transported for burglary ; afterwards seduced by Carker.

———— *Mrs. :* the mother of Alice Marwood, by a former connection ; a horrid, ugly old woman [Dickens, *Dombey and Sons*].

———— **Jonathan :** landlord of the *Black Bear*, Darlington, the inn where Frank Osbaldistone and Rob Roy meet [Scott, *Rob Roy*].

———— **Mrs. :** an English 'type' ; a combination of native shrewdness and ignorance [Sketchley, *Mrs. Brown*].

———— **Tom :** a typical English schoolboy, fonder of sports than books ; honest, thoughtless, and good-natured [Tom Hughes, *Tom Brown's Schooldays*].

———— **Tom :** the above grown up, and at the University [Tom Hughes, *Tom Brown at Oxford*].

———— **Sally :** the heroine of a humorous poem [Thomas Hood, *Faithless Sally Brown*].

Brown Vanbust, Captain : alias Dawson, Dudley, and Harry Bertram. Son of the Laird of Ellangowan [Scott, *Guy Mannering*].

Browne, General : the guest of Lord Woodville who saw the vision in the 'tapestried chamber' [Scott, *Tapestried Chamber*].

Brownlow, Mr. : Oliver's friend and rescuer [Dickens, *Oliver Twist*].

Bruce, The : Robert I of Scotland is the hero of this Epic [Barbour, *The Bruce*].

Bruin : he is one of those opposed to Hudibras. The original was a butcher of the name of Talgol who served at Naseby [Butler, *Hudibras*].

—— a rough, uncultured man who treats his wife like a boor [Foote, *Mayor of Garratt*].

Brulgruddery, Dennis : landlord of the *Red Cow*, Muckslush Heath, 'an Irish gentleman bred and born'.

—— **Mrs. :** the illtempered wife of Dennis [Colman the Younger, *John Bull*].

Bruncheval : a knight who entered the lists against Sir Satyrane [Spenser, *The Faëry Queene*].

Brush : the impudent valet of Lord Ogleby [Colman and Garrick, *Clandestine Marriage*].

Brute : a mythical king of England, whose mother died at his birth, and who accidentally shot his father [Geoffrey of Monmouth, *Chronicles* ; Drayton, *Polyolbion* ; and Spenser, *Faëry Queene*].

—— **Lady :** driven to revenge against her brutal husband, she indulges in a flirtation with a former lover, Constant by name.

—— **Sir John :** a coarse, surly man, and a drunkard, whose chief delight is to try and provoke his wife [Vanbrugh, *The Provoked Wife*].

Brutus : a patriot who is prevailed upon by Cassius, 'a lean and hungry man', to head the conspiracy against Caesar [Shakespeare, *Julius Caesar*].

Bryan and Pereene : the characters in a ballad which is founded on an incident which occurred on the West Indian Island of St. Christopher.

Brydone, Elspeth : widow of Simon Glendinning [Scott, *Monastery*].

Bucket : the detective who discovered the murderer of Mr. Tulkinghorn [Dickens, *Bleak House*].

Bucklaw : *see* Hayston.

Budger, Mrs. : a rich little old widow, with whom Mr. Tupman dances at the Charity Ball at Rochester [Dickens, *Pickwick Papers*].

Buffone, Carlo : a jester, by some supposed to be intended for Marston, by others for Dekker [Ben Jonson, *Every Man Out of His Humour*].

Bulbo, Prince : one of the heroes of a ' fireside pantomime ' [Thackeray, *Rose and the Ring*].

Bull's-Eye : Bill Sikes's dog [Dickens, *Oliver Twist*].

Bullamy : porter of the ' Anglo-Bengalee Disinterested Loan and Life Insurance Company ' [Dickens, *Martin Chuzzlewit*].

Bullcalf, Peter : he was pricked for a recruit, but induced Bardolph to help him to get off serving [Shakespeare, *Henry IV*, pt. ii.].

Bullsegg, Mr. : Laird of Killancureit, and a friend of the Baron of Bradwardine [Scott, *Waverley*].

Bulmer, Mrs. Anne : the mother of Valentine, and the bigamous wife of the Earl of Etherington.

——— *Valentine :* titular Earl of Etherington, and married to Clara Mowbray [Scott, *St. Ronan's Well*].

Bumble, Mr. : the beadle at the workhouse where Oliver was born [Dickens, *Oliver Twist*].

Bumper, Sir Harry : the friend of Charles Surface [Sheridan, *School for Scandal*].

Bumpo, Natty : the real name of Hawkeye, as the Indians called the Deerslayer, who is also known as *The Pathfinder*, *The Last of the Mohicans*, and the *Pioneer* [Cooper, *The Deerslayer*].

Bunce, Mr. : the leading Bedesman of Hiram's Hospital, and devoted friend and supporter of Mr. Harding [Anthony Trollope, *The Warden*].

Bunch, Barnaby : a mender of old clothes [Webster, *The Weakest goeth to the Wall*].

——— **Mother :** a derisive name applied by Tucca to Mistress Miniver, an all wife [Dekker, *Satiro-Mastix;* used as a fancy author's name for jest-books, 1604 and 1760, and in *Mother Bunch's Fairy Tales*].

Buncle, John : married and survived seven wives; ' a prodigious hand at matrimony, divinity, a song, and a peck ' [Amory, *Life of John Buncle, Esq.*].

Bundle : the father of Wilhelmina and the friend of Tom Tug.

——— **Mrs. :** the nagging wife of Bundle, of whom he stands in great awe [C. Dibdin, *The Waterman*].

Bungay : a bookseller, and the publisher of the *Pall Mall Gazette*, which Captain Shannon edits [Thackeray, *Pendennis*].

Bungey, Friar : is credited with having ' raised mists and vapours ' at the battle of Barnet, which befriended the cause of Edward IV [Lytton, *Last of the Barons.*]

Bungey, Friar : a conjuror and one of the heroes [Greene, *Frier Bacon and Frier Bungay*].

Bunsby, Cap. Jack : owner of the 'Cautious Clara', and according to Captain Cuttle, a very mine of wisdom [Dickens, *Dombey and Son*].

Bunthorne : a would-be aesthetic youth who affects artistic airs, graces, and clothes : really commonplace in the extreme [Gilbert, *Patience*].

Bunting : the hero, who was so named because of his dress [R. Browning, *Pied Piper of Hamelin*].

Buonaventura, Father : really Charles Edward the Pretender [Scott, *Redgauntlet*].

Bur, John : the devoted servant of Job Thornberry, the brazier of Penzance [Colman the Younger, *John Bull*].

Burbon : the betrothed of Fordelis [*France*] who has been enticed away from him by Grantorto [*rebellion*]. Burbon recovers her in the end [Spenser, *Faëry Queene*].

Burchell, Mr. : really Sir William Thornhill, the true friend of the Primrose family. He marries Sophia [Goldsmith, *Vicar of Wakefield*].

Burd Helen : the heroine of a popular old Scottish ballad.

Burleigh, Lord : a Parliamentary leader [Scott, *Legend of Montrose*].

Burley, John : 'never sober, never solvent, but always genial and witty'—a poor ne'er-do-well [Lytton, *My Novel*].

Burlong : a giant, whose legs were cut off by Sir Tryamour [*Romance of Sir Tryamour*].

Burning Pestle, Knight of the : the hero of a comedy written to ridicule the old romances of chivalry [Beaumont, *Knight of the Burning Pestle*].

Burns, Helen : intended for the authoress's little sister, Maria Brontë [Charlotte Brontë, *Jane Eyre*].

Burris : the favourite of the Great-Duke of Muscovia [J. Fletcher, *Loyal Subject*].

Burton, James : an honest blacksmith of Chelsea.

———— **Samuel** : 'more fiendish than the snake, more savage than the shark'—a typical convict [Charles Kingsley, *Hillyars and Burtons*].

Busirane : an enchanter who bound Amoret to a brazen pillar, she being rescued by Britomart [Spenser, *Faëry Queene*].

Busiris : the hero of the tragedy [Young, *Busiris, King of Egypt*].

Bussy d'Ambois : the hero of the tragedy [Chapman, *Bussy d'Ambois*].

Butler, Reuben : a Presbyterian minister who marries Jennie Deans.

—— *Stephen :* grandfather of Reuben, and generally known as 'Bible Butler' [Scott, *Heart of Midlothian*]

Buttercup, John : a milkman [Brough, *A Phenomenon in a Smock Frock*].

Buzfuz, Serjeant : the advocate employed by Mrs. Bardell in her suit against Mr. Pickwick [Dickens, *Pickwick Papers.*]

Buzzard, Mr. Justice : an ignorant old magistrate, always open to a bribe [Fielding, *Amelia*].

Byron, Miss Harriet : an accomplished beauty, as good as she is beautiful, who marries the hero [Richardson, *Sir Charles Grandison*].

Cacafogo : a wealthy usurer who thinks that everything may be had for money [J. Fletcher, *Rule a Wife and have a Wife*].

Cacurgus : the fool or jester of Misogonus [Rychardes, *Misogonus*].

" **Caddy,**" *see* Jellyby, Caroline.

Cadenus : Dean Swift [Swift, *Cadenus and Vanessa*].

Cadwal : the name by which Cymbeline's son, Arviragus was known during his life in the wood [Shakespeare, *Cymbeline*].

Cadwallader, The Rev. Mr. : the provokingly good-tempered Rector of Middlemarch who 'even spoke well of his Bishop'.

—— *Mrs. :* the wife of the Rector of Middlemarch [George Eliot, *Middlemarch*].

—— intended for a Mr. Aprice, one of the author's friends, whom he ridiculed [S. Foote, *The Author*].

—— a misanthrope [Smollett, *Peregrine Pickle*].

Cadwallon : Prince Gwenwyn's favourite bard, who, under the name of Renault Vidal, entered the service of Sir Hugo de Lacy [Scott, *Betrothed*].

—— the son of Cynetha, the blind man [Southey, *Madoc*].

Caelestina : the bride of Sir Walter Terill [Dekker, *Satiro-mastix*].

Caesar, Don : an old man who courts a girl of sixteen in order to force his own daughter, Olivia, to marry [Mrs. Cowley, *A Bold Stroke for a Husband*].

Cain : the hero of the drama [Byron, *Cain : a Mystery*].

—— is also the subject of a poem [S. T. Coleridge, *Wanderings of Cain*].

Caius, Dr. : a French doctor [Shakespeare, *Merry Wives of Windsor*].

Caius Marius : the subject of a play [Otway, *History and Fall of aius Marius*].

Calantha : beloved by Ithocles, who is murdered before their marriage can take place. She dies of a broken heart [Ford, *Broken Heart*].

Calanthe : the affianced wife of Pythias the Syracusan [John Banim, *Damon and Pythias*].

Calderon : the hero of an historical romance [Lytton, *Calderon the Courtier*].

Caleb : intended for Lord Grey of Wark [Dryden, *Absalom and Achitophel*].

Caled : in command of the Arabs at the siege of Damascus [John Hughes, *Siege of Damascus*].

Calepine, Sir : rescued a child from the embrace of a bear and handed it to Matilde, the wife of Sir Bruin, to rear [Spenser, *Faëry Queene*].

Calianax : the father of Aspatia [Beaumont and Fletcher, *Maid's Tragedy*].

Caliban : a mis-shapen, brutish creature whom Prospero makes his servant [Shakespeare, *Tempest*].

Caliburn : the same as *Excalibur q.v.*

Calidore, Sir : the personification of courtesy and hero of the sixth book [Spenser, *Faëry Queene*].

Calis, The Princess : sister of Astorax, King of Paphos, in love with Polydore and beloved by Siphax [J. Fletcher, *Mad Lover*].

Calista : daughter of Sciolto, who though betrothed to Altamont had a guilty intrigue with Lothario. Lothario fell in a duel and Calista stabbed herself [Rowe, *Fair Penitent*].

———— the faithful wife of Cleander [Fletcher and Massinger, *Lover's Progress*].

———— one of the chief characters in the play [Massinger, *The Guardian*].

———— attendant on the Queen [Scott, *Talisman*].

Calistus : in love with Melibea [Anon., *Calistus : a tragical Comedy*]

Callipolis : a very beautiful woman [Peele, *Battle of Alcazar*].

Calmar : son of the Lord of Lara, in Connaught. Brave and impetuous he presses Cathullin to push forward, and his haste leads to defeat [Ossian, *Fingal*].

Calthon : one of the sons of Rathmor, the chief of Clutha [Ossian, *Calthon and Colmal*].

Calverley : a gamester, who, cruel to wife and children, is ruined by his vicious life [at one time attrib. Shakespeare, *Yorkshire Tragedy*].

Calvo, Baldassarre : a leading character in the novel [George Eliot, *Romola*].

Calypso : the heroine of a musical opera [John Hughes, *Calypso and Telemachus*].

Camaralzaman : a prince who fell in love with **Badoura** the moment he beheld her [*Arabian Nights*].

Camballo : second son of Cambuscan [Chaucer, *Canterbury Tales : The Squire's Tale*].

Cambina : the daughter of Agape [Spenser, *Faëry Queene*].

Cambuscan : a king of Tartary [Chaucer, *Canterbury Tales : The Squire's Tale*].

Cambyses, King : the hero of an allegorical play [Preston, *Lamentable Tragedy of King Cambyses*].

Cameron, General : the 'friend and patron' of Henry Douglas [Susan E. Ferrier, *Marriage*].

Camilla : the lady with whom Philautus falls in love [Lyly, *Euphues*].

—— 'a light, airy, poor and imprudent, but gentle' girl [Fanny Burney, *Camilla*].

Camillo : commanded by King Leontes to poison Polixenes, but instead, aided in his escape [Shakespeare, *Winter's Tale*].

—— husband of Vittoria Corombona [Webster, *White Devil*].

—— one of the characters in the play [Dryden, *Assignation*].

Camiola : in love with Bertoldo, with whom the Duchess of Sienna was also in love. Camiola finding herself jilted, exposed Bertoldo's duplicity and then retired into a convent [Massinger, *Maid of Honour*].

Campbell, Captain : known as 'Green Colin Campbell', or Barcaldine [Scott, *Highland Widow*].

—— **General :** 'Black Colin Campbell' [Scott, *Redgauntlet*].

—— **Sir Duncan :** of the Duke of Argyll's army, and sent as ambassador to the Earl of Montrose [Scott, *Legend of Montrose*].

—— **Murdoch :** the name assumed by the Duke of Argyll when he visited Dalgetty and M'Eagh [Scott, *Legend of Montrose*].

—— **Lady Mary and Lady Caroline :** daughters of the Duke of Argyll [Scott, *Heart of Midlothian*].

Camph, Lady : an eccentric aristocrat who makes merciless fun of General Ople and tries to cure him of his egoism. She finally marries him [George Meredith, *Case of General Ople and Lady Camph*].

Canace : a paragon among women : the heroine of the *Squire's Tale* [Chaucer, *Canterbury Tales*].

Candour, Mr : a backbiter and scandal-monger [Sheridan, *School for Scandal*].

Canton : Lord Ogleby's valet [Colman and Garrick, *Clandestine Marriage*].

Cantrips, Jessie : the daughter of Nanty Ewart's friend.

—————— *Mrs. :* the friend of Nanty Ewart [Scott, *Redgauntlet*].

Cantwell, Dr. : a meek and saintly hypocrite who behaves dishonourably to the wife of his closest friend [Bickerstaff, *Hypocrite*].

Capecchi, Cavalieri : the wicked brother of Lauretta [Shorthouse, *John Inglesant*].

Capella, Bianca : the wife of Cosmo de Medici [Lady Lytton, *Bianca Capella*].

Caponsacche, Giuseppe : the noble young priest who befriended Pompilia and was accused of criminal relations with her [R. Browning, *Ring and the Book*].

Capulet : father of Juliet and head of the family at enmity with the Montagues.

—————— *Lady :* mother of Juliet and wife of above [Shakespeare, *Romeo and Juliet*].

Carabas : ' servile, and pompous, and indefatigable, and loquacious', said to be intended for Lord Lyndhurst [Beaconsfield, *Vivian Grey*].

Caractacus : the subject of the drama [Mason, *Caractacus*].

Caradoc : a Knight of the Round Table, wedded to the one perfectly faithful wife among all the Queen's ladies [*Arthurian Cycle*].

Carathis : the mother of Vathek carried by an afrit to the abyss of Eblis on account of her wicked life [Beckford, *Vathek*].

Careless : ' A fellow that's wise enough to be but half in love, and makes his whole life a studied idleness ' [Cibber, *Double Gallant*].

—————— one of Charles Surface's boon companions [Sheridan, *School for Scandal*].

—————— *Colonel :* a suitor for the hand of Ruth Thoroughgood [Knight. *The Honest Thieves*; altered from the same character in a play by Howard, *The Committee*].

—————— *Ned :* the lover of Lady Pliant [Congreve, *Double Dealer*].

Cargill, The Rev. Josiah : tutor of Augustus Bidmore and suitor for the hand of Augusta Bidmore [Scott, *St. Ronan's Well*].

Carino : the father of Zenocia [Beaumont and Fletcher, *Custom of the Country*].

Carker, Harriet : a gentle and beautiful girl, the sister of John and James Carker ; she marries Mr. Morfin.

—————— *James ;* Mr. Dombey's business manager, who elopes with Mrs. Dombey. He is killed on a railway line.

Carker, John : the elder brother of James, who having robbed the firm and been forgiven makes restitution by years of faithful service [Dickens, *Dombey and Son*].

Carleton, Captain : an officer in the guards [Scott, *Peveril of the Peak*].

Carlos : the son of Don Antonio, and a bookworm, who developes into a man of fine character through the influence of his love for Angelina [Cibber, *Love Makes a Man*].

———— an unmitigated villain, a murderer and a thief, whose villainies find him out at last [Stirling, *Orphan of the Frozen Sea*].

———— **Don :** in love with Leonora, but he stands aside for his friend, Don Alonzo, who in return, in a fit of jealousy, causes him to be put to death [Young, *The Revenge*].

———— **Don :** the faithless husband of Donna Victoria, who in the end saves him from utter ruin [Mrs. Cowley, *A Bold Stroke for a Husband*].

Caro : the personification of the 'natural man', 'a hag of loathsome shape' [Phineas Fletcher, *Purple Island*].

Caroline : the subject of the poem, the second part of which is addressed to the Evening Star [Campbell, *Caroline*].

———— **Gann :** *see* Gann, Caroline.

Carstone, Richard : a ward in chancery—a nice fellow, but a rolling stone, who marries his cousin, Ada Clare [Dickens, *Bleak House*].

Carril : son of Kinfena, the bard of Cuthullin [Ossian, *Fingal*].

Carton, Sydney : the friend and 'double' of Charles Darnay, for whom he gave his life upon the guillotine [Dickens, *Tale of Two Cities*].

Carvel, Hans : the hero of a seventeenth century story [Prior, *Adventures of Hans Carvel*].

Casabianca : a young hero who gave his life in unswerving obedience to the call of duty [Felicia D. Hemans, *Casabianca*].

Casaubon, The Rev. Edward : an elderly pedant who marries Dorothea Brooke and makes her miserable by his indifference [George Eliot, *Middlemarch*].

Casca : one of the conspirators against Julius Caesar [Shakespeare, *Julius Caesar*].

Caschcasch : a hideous monstrosity who was called upon to determine which was the more beautiful, Prince Camaralzaman **or** Princess Badoura [*Arabian Nights*].

Casimere : a Polish emigrant [Canning, *The Rovers ; or The Double Arrangement*].

Caspar : the Baron of Arnheim's Master of the Horse [Scott, *Anne of Geierstein*].

Casby, Christopher : the landlord of *Bleeding Heart Yard*, who grinds down his tenants cruelly [Dickens, *Little Dorrit*].

Cass, Godfrey : the father of Eppie, and married to Nancy Lammeter [George Eliot, *Silas Marner*].

Cassandra : a prophetess, the daughter of Priam [Shakespeare, *Troilus and Cressida*].

Cassel, Count : an empty-headed nincompoop, suitor for the hand of Amelia Wildenhaim [Mrs. Inchbald, *Lover's Vows*].

Cassitane : the General of Candy [Beaumont and Fletcher, *Laws of Candy*].

Cassim : the brother of Ali Baba. He forgot the magic words, ' Open Sesame ', and so got shut into the robber's cave, where they found him and cut him to pieces with their sabres [*Arabian Nights*].

Cassio, Michael : Othello's lieutenant, ' amiably and nobly disposed, but easily seduced ' [Shakespeare, *Othello*].

Cassius : the discontented spirit that egged the noble Brutus on to plot against Julius Caesar [Shakespeare, *Julius Caesar*].

Castalio : twin-brother to Polydore, and, like him, in love with Monimia. Polydore's treachery results in the death of all three [Otway, *The Orphan*].

Castara : Lucy Herbert, who became the wife of the author of a collection of poems published under that title [Habington, *Castara*].

Castlewood, Beatrix : the vain beauty who nearly wrecks Henry Esmond's life and makes a failure of her own.

—— *Colonel Francis Esmond, Lord :* the father of Beatrix and first husband of Lady Rachel. A drunkard who neglects his wife, gambles away his substance, and is killed in a dual.

—— *Lady Rachel :* the mother of Beatrix, ' very sweet and pure ', who marries Henry Esmond as her second husband and goes out to Virginia with him [Thackeray, *Esmond*].

Catharick, Anne : the heroine [Collins, *Woman in White*].

Catherine : the history of Catherine Hayes, who was burned at Tyburn for the murder of her husband, formed the basis of this tale, which was written as a protest against the false sympathy sometimes lavished upon the vicious [Thackeray, *Catherine : A Story*].

Catherine, The Countess : she falls in love with a serf called Huon, and marries him, and he afterwards so distinguishes himself as to be created a prince [Knowles, *Love*].

Catherow, Phyllis : cousin of Mable Lovejoy and betrothed to Mabel's brother, Gregory [Blackmore, *Alice Lorraine*].

Cathlin of Clutha : the daughter of Cathmol [Ossian, *Cathlin of Clutha*].

Cathulla : King of Inistore, and brother of Comala [Ossian, *Carrick-Thura*].

Catius : intended for Charles Dartineuf [Pope, *Moral Essays*, Epistle i].

Cato : the hero of the tragedy, the prologue of which was written by Pope, the epilogue by Garth [Addison, *Cato*].

Caudle, Mrs. Margaret : the wife who lectures her long-suffering but erring husband, nightly, after they have gone to bed [Jerrold, *Mrs. Caudle's Curtain Lectures*].

Cauline, Sir : the knight whose duty it was to serve the king of Ireland with wine. He won the heart of the king's daughter, Christabelle [Percy, *Reliques : Sir Cauline*].

Caustic, Colonel : a fine gentleman of ' the good old times who constantly mourned the degeneracy of the present [Mackenzie, in *The Lounger*].

Cavall : ' King Arthur's hound of deepest mouth ' [Alfred Tennyson, *Idylls of the King : Enid*].

Cave, Mary : beloved by Matthewson Helston, and Hiram Yorke. She married Helstone [Charlotte Brontë, *Shirley*].

Cawdor, Thane of : a Scottish gentleman executed by order of Duncan, and to whose dignities Macbeth succeeds [Shakespeare, *Macbeth*].

Caxon, Jacob and Jenny : a humorous old barber, and his daughter, a milliner [Scott, *Antiquary*].

Caxton, Mr. : a scholar and a gentleman of retiring habits and unpractical mind.

—————— *Pisistratus :* his son and the hero of the story [Lytton, *Caxtons*].

Cayenne, Mr. : a Virginian loyalist who resigns wealth and ease for the sake of principles, and leaving Virginia settles at Dalmailing [Galt, *Annals of the Parish*].

Cecil : the hero of a novel which deals with life in London clubs [Mrs. Gore, *Cecil ; or, The Adventures of a Coxcomb*].

Cecilia : an heiress beloved by a Mr. Delville [Fanny Burney, *Cecilia*].

Cecilia Vaughan : *see* Vaughan, Cecilia.

Cecropia : probably intended for Catherine de Medici [Sidney, *Arcadia*].

Cedric : thane of Rotherwood, surnamed 'the Saxon', who disinherits his only son for following Richard I to the Holy Land [Scott, *Ivanhoe*].

Celadon : a witty but inconstant man who marries Florimel [Dryden, *Secret Love; or, The Maiden Queen*].

—— the lover of Amelia : they were both struck dead by lightning [James Thomson, *The Seasons*].

Celandine : a shepherd, in love with Marina, a shepherdess [Browne, *Britannia's Pastorals*].

Celia : an honest, affectionate girl courted by Antigonus and his son Demetrius [Beaumont and Fletcher, *Humorous Lieutenant*].

—— married to Corvino [Ben Jonson, *Volpone*].

—— daughter of the usurping Duke Frederick and the devoted friend and cousin of Rosalind [Shakespeare, *As You Like It*].

—— a girl of sixteen, the heroine [Whitehead, *School for Lovers*].

—— Brooke : *see* Brooke, Celia.

—— Dame : the mother of Faith, Hope, and Charity [Spenser, *Faëry Queene*].

Celinda : a victim to the vices of Count Fathom [Smollett, *Count Fathom*].

Cellide : courted by a father and son, Valentine and Francisco. The son, Francisco, is the successful suitor [J. Fletcher, *Monsieur Thomas*].

Cenci, Beatrice : she slew her father in horror at his misdeeds and was hanged [Shelley, *The Cenci*].

Cennini : a jeweller [George Eliot, *Romola*].

Cerdon : one of the leaders of the rabble : intended for Hewson, a preaching cobbler, a colonel in the Rump army [Butler, *Hudibras*].

Cerimon : a noble Ephesian who restored Thaisa to life [Shakespeare, *Pericles, Prince of Tyre*].

Chabot, Philippe de : Admiral of France, wrongfully accused of dishonesty. Though his innocence is established he dies from distress at the disgrace [Chapman and Shirley, *Tragedy of Philippe de Chabot*].

Chadband, The Rev. Mr. : a canting, hypocritical ranter [Dickens, *Bleak House*].

Chadwick. Mr. : the Bishop of Barchester's steward, who farmed the property connected with Hiram's Hospital [A. Trollope, *The Warden*].

Chaffington, Mr. Percy, M.P. : a stock-broker [J M. Morton, *If I had a Thousand a Year*].

Chainmail : the man who marries Susannah Touchandgo : he is a neighbour of Squire Crotchet's, who endeavours to live in a mediaeval fashion, and in his own opinion succeeds admirably in attaining the object of his ambition [Peacock, *Crotchet Castle*].

Chalkstone, Lord : a character rendered famous by the author's own acting of it [Garrick, *Lethe*].

Chamberlain, Matthew : a tapster and the successor of Roger Raine [Scott, *Peveril of the Peak*].

Chamont : the brother of Monimia and betrothed to Serina [Otway, *The Orphan*].

Champernel : the husband of Lamira, an old and lame man [Beaumont and Fletcher, *Little French Lawyer*].

Champneys, Miss : sister of Sir Geoffry, willing to marry Mr. Middlewick, the butterman, for his money.

———— *Sir Geoffry :* an old country gentleman, a staunch believer in ' blue blood '.

———— *Talbot :* his son, brainless but good-natured, who insists on marrying Mary Melrose, a penniless girl [H. J. Byron, *Our Boys*].

Chapman, Captain Stephen : son of Sir Remnant Chapman and suitor for the hand of Alice Lorraine. A man of low tastes and meagre intelligence.

———— *Sir Remnant :* a fox-hunting squire, the friend and neighbour of Sir Roland Lorraine [Blackmore, *Alice Lorraine*].

Chanson, Laura : so contrives that Paul Ferroll marries her instead of the girl he really loves—Elinor Ladylift. When he discovers the truth he murders Laura [Mrs. Archer Clive, *Paul Ferroll*].

Charalois : son of the Marshal of Burgundy, who, upon his father's corpse being seized by his creditors, redeemed it by being imprisoned himself in its place [Massinger, *Fatal Dowry*].

Charino : the father of Angelina, a hasty-tempered, obstinate old man [Cibber, *Love Makes a Man*].

Charles : a bookworm, who falls in love at first sight with Angelina [J. Fletcher, *Elder Brother*].

———— **Emmanuel :** the son of Victor Amadeus, King of Sardinia [R. Browning, *King Victor and King Charles*].

Charley : *see* Necket, Charlotte.

Charlotte : the betrothed of Wilmot, who remains faithful to his memory after he is thought to have perished at sea [Lillo, *Fatal Curiosity*].

———— daughter of Sir Gilbert Wrangle, in love with Frankly [Cibber, *The Refusal ; or, The Ladies Philosophy*].

Charlotte : the rough, low, servant of Sowerberry [Dickens, *Oliver Twist*].

—— the daughter of General Baynes ; she married Philip Firmin, the hero [Thackeray, *Adventures of Philip*].

—— a girl who apes deaf and dumbness to escape a distasteful marriage [Fielding, *Mock Doctor*].

—— the daughter of Sir John Lambert, in love with Darnley, whom she is fond of teazing [Bickerstaff, *Hypocrite*].

—— the Countess Wintersen's servant [B. Thomson, *Stranger*].

—— **Lady :** a servant who assumes the 'airs and graces' of her mistress [Townley, *High Life Below Stairs*].

Charmian : one of Cleopatra's attendants [Shakespeare, *Antony and Cleopatra*].

Charyllis : the name given by the poet to Anne Spenser in his pastoral [Spenser, *Colin Clout's Come Home Again*].

Chat, Dame : one of the characters in the comedy [attrib. Still, *Gammer Gurton's Needle*].

Chaunus : the personification of Arrogance [Phineas Fletcher, *Purple Island*].

Cheatly : a degraded inhabitant of the debtor's haunt, known as 'Alsatia,' who fleeces rich young men [Thomas Shadwell, *Squire of Alsatia*].

Chederazade : the mother of Hemjunah and wife of Zebenezer, Sultan of Cassimir [Ridley, *Tales of the Genii*].

Cheerly, Mrs. : a young widow, rich and beautiful, who after sundry misfortunes becomes the wife of Frank Hearall [Cherry, *Soldier's Daughter*].

Cheeryble Brothers, The (Charles and Edwin) : twin brothers, who rose to wealth by sheer industry and integrity, and were ever ready to stretch forth a helping hand to those in need.

—— *Frank :* nephew to the 'Brothers'. He became the husband of Kate Nickleby [Dickens, *Nicholas Nickleby*].

Cherry : daughter of Boniface, landlord of the *Lichfield Inn* [Farquhar, *Beaux' Stratagem*].

Cherub, The : *see* Wilfer, Reginald.

Cherubim, Don : a bachelor who finds himself in all sorts of difficult and unexpected situations [Lesage, *Bachelor of Salamanca*].

Chester, Edward : the son of Sir John Chester and the lover of Emma Haredale.

—— *Mr.* (later, *Sir John*) *:* a cold-hearted worldly fop, who falls in a dual with Geoffrey Haredale [Dickens, *Barnaby Rudge*].

Chesterfield, Charles : a young man of literary genius ; the hero [Mrs. Trollope, *Charles Chesterfield*].

Chesterton, Paul : nephew of Mr. Percy Chaffington, M.P. [J. M. Morton, *If I had a Thousand a Year*].

Chettam, Sir James : an easy-going, amiable baronet who marries Celia Brooke, Dorothea's sister [George Eliot, *Middlemarch*].

Chererel, Sir Christopher, and Lady : two of the leading characters in the story [George Eliot, *Scenes from Clerical Life : Mr. Gilfil's Love-Story*].

Cheveril, Hans : impulsive and generous, a ward of Mordent's. He falls in love with Joanna, a ' deserted daughter ', and marries her [Holcroft, *The Deserted Daughter*, later changed to *The Steward*].

Cheyne, Harvey : a spoilt and disagreeable American boy, who finds his salvation in an unintended cruise on the *Grand Banks* [Kipling, *Captain Courageous*].

Chick, Louisa : sister of Mr. Dombey, an unsympathetic, irritable woman, who counsels Mrs. Dombey, on her death bed, to ' make an effort '.

———— *Mr.* : Mr. Dombey's brother-in-law and the rather hen-pecked husband of Louisa Chick [Dickens, *Dombey and Son*].

Chicken, The Game : *see* Game Chicken, The.

Chickenstalker, Mr : a friendly ' body ' who keeps a general shop [Dickens, *The Chimes*].

Chickweed, Conkey : also known by the name of ' Nosey ' A thief who for a long time avoided detection by helping the police to chase innocent men [Dickens, *Oliver Twist*].

Chiffinch, Kate : the mistress of Thomas.

———— *Master Thomas* : employed by Charles II for private purposes ; he tries to carry off Alice Bridgenorth for the King [Scott, *Peveril of the Peak*].

Chignon : a French valet [Burgoyne, *The Heiress*].

Chilax : lieutenant to General Memnon [J. Fletcher, *Mad Lover*].

Child of Elle, The : he loved Emmeline, from whom he was divided by a family feud. In the end love was triumphant [Percy, *Reliques : Child of Elle*].

———— of Nature, The : the child is Amantis, the daughter of Alberto, who was unjustly exiled. Amantis falls in love with and marries her guardian, Almanza [Mrs. Inchbald, *Child of Nature*].

Childe, Harold : *see* Harold Childe.

———— Rowland : *see* Rowland Childe.

———— Waters : *see* Waters Childe.

Chillingly, Kenelm : the hero of the best of all this author's stories, it being free from much of his peculiarities of style and distinguished by simplicity of thought and diction [Lytton, *Kenelm Chillingly*].

Chillingworth, Roger : the betrayed and revengeful husband of Hester Prynne [Nathaniel Hawthorne, *Scarlet Letter*].

Chillip, Mr. : the doctor who attended Mrs. Copperfield at the birth of her son [Dickens, *David Copperfield*].

Chindasuintho : the King of Spain, father of Theodofred, and grandfather of Roderick [Southey, *Roderick*].

Chingachcook : an Indian chief called by the French *Le Gros Serpent*. He is prominent in four of the author's books [Cooper, *Last of the Mohicans ; Pathfinder ; Deerslayer ; Pioneer*].

Chinn, John : ' the slender little hookey-nosed boy ' who advocates vaccination [Kipling, *Tomb of his Ancestors*].

Chintz, Mary : maid to Miss Bloomfield and engaged to Jem Miller [Selby, *Unfinished Gentleman*].

Chitling, Tom : one of Fagin's apprentices, a ' half-witted dupe ', who makes an ' unsuccessful thief ' [Dickens, *Oliver Twist*].

Chivery, John, Senior : a non-resident turnkey of the Marshalsea.

———— *John, Junior :* one of Little Dorrit's lovers ; a very sentimental youth, who is very mournful when he learns that Little Dorrit is to be married to another [Dickens, *Little Dorrit*].

Chloe : the pretentious wife of a very honest but commonplace man [Ben Jonson, *The Poetaster*].

———— a shepherdess of unstable character [J. Fletcher, *Faithful Shepherdess*].

———— the self-given *nom-de-plume* of a wounded lady who lives at a resort of fashion. Her tragic end is told with a fine touch [George Meredith, *Tale of Chloe.*]

———— intended for Lady Suffolk, the Misstress of George II [Pope, *Moral Essays*, Epistle ii.].

———— a shepherdess [Sidney, *Arcadia*].

Choke : an American ; ' one of the most remarkable men in the century ' [Dickens, *Martin Chuzzlewit*].

Cholmondeley : the friend of Sir Geoffrey Peveril [Scott, *Peveril of the Peak*].

Cholmondeley : the Squire of Lord Guildford Dudley [Ainsworth, *Tower of London*].

Choppard, Pierre : a member of a gang of thieves, known as ' The Ugly Mug ' [Sterling, *Courier of Lyons*].

Chowne, Parson Stoyle : a bully and scamp, of whom the whole country-side stand in awe, who kidnaps the two grandchildren of Sir Philip Bampfylde [Blackmore, *Maid of Sker*].

Christabel : the heroine of an old romance [*Sir Eglamour of Artois*].

———— the heroine of a beautiful fragment [S. T. Coleridge, *Christabel*].

———— **Babe :** the subject of this elegy was one of the author's own children [Massey, *Babe Christabel*].

Christabelle : the daughter of a king of Ireland who loved Sir Cauline, and so the king banished the knight, who re-appeared at a tournament but was there slain, and Christabelle died of grief [Percy, *Reliques : Sir Cauline*].

Christian : the leading character in the allegory [Bunyan, *Pilgrim's Progress*].

———— captain of the patrol in the town where Mathis, whose daughter he marries, is Burgomaster [Ware, *Polish Jew*].

———— **Ann Charlotte de la Tremouille :** ' Auntie Nan', a sweet old lady that brings up Philip.

———— *Iron :* the great Deemster, grandfather of Philip.

———— *Peter :* younger son of Iron Christian, and a man of vicious habits.

———— *Philip :* the Deemster, son of Thomas and Mona Christian, betrayer of Catherine Cregeen and Peter Quilliam.

———— *Ross :* son of Peter Christian; a dissipated, evil liver.

———— *Thomas Wilson :* a man who ruins his career by marrying beneath him [Hall Caine, *The Manxman*].

———— **II :** the King of Norway, Sweden, and Denmark, who was successfully attacked by Gustavus Vasa [Brooke, *Gustavus Vasa*].

———— **Colonel William :** brother of Edward, who was arrested and shot.

———— *Edward :* a conspirator, who assumed the names of Richard Ganlesse and Simon Canter.

———— *Zarah (Fenella) :* the daughter of Edward [Scott, *Peveril of the Peak*].

———— **Fletcher :** mate of *The Bounty* and leader of the mutineers [Byron, *The Island*].

Christiana : Christian's wife, who, with Greatheart as guide, sets out, with her children, for the Celestial City [Bunyan, *Pilgrim's Progress*, pt. ii.].

Christie, John : a ship-chandler.

———— *Nelly :* wife of John, very pretty, and carried off by Lord Dalgarno [Scott, *Fortunes of Nigel*].

Christie of the Clint Hill : one of Julian Avenel's retainers [Scott, *Monastery*].

Christine : an attendant of the Countess Marie [Stirling, *Prisoner of State*].

—— the heroine of a metrical tale founded on the story of *The Meeting of the Bounty* [Milford, *Christine*].

Christopher : a head-waiter, who gives an amusing account of the trials of his class [Dickens, *Somebody's Luggage*].

Chrononhotonthologos : a pompous character in a burlesque [Carey, *Chrononhotonthologos*].

Chucks : a boatswain on Captain Savage's ship [Captain Marryat, *Peter Simple*].

Chuffey, Mr. : Anthony Chuzzlewit's old servant [Dickens, *Martin Chuzzlewit*].

Chump, Mrs. : a very common Irish woman to whom the Poles are compelled to be polite, as Mr. Pole has charge of her large fortune, with which he is speculating [George Meredith, *Sandra Belloni*].

Churchill, Ethel : the heroine of an historical novel [Letitia E. Landon, *Ethel Churchill*].

—— *Frank :* the rather shallow-hearted admirer of Jane Fairfax [Jane Austen, *Emma*].

—— *Mr. :* ' Nature had made him a poet, but destiny made him a schoolmaster ' [Longfellow, *Kavanagh*].

Chuzzlewit, Anthony : an avaricious old man, the father of Jonas.

—— *Goerge :* an elderly bachelor who apes youth.

—— *Jonas :* the son of Anthony ; a mean and brutal villain, who tries to poison his own father and murders Montague Tigg, makes his wife, Mercy Pecksniff, miserable, and then commits suicide to escape hanging.

—— *Martin, Junior :* the hero, who having been ' schooled ' by many misfortunes develops a fine character and marries Mary Graham.

—— *Martin, Senior :* the grandfather of the hero, whose kindly nature has been embittered by the wickedness of his family [Dickens, *Martin Chuzzlewit*].

Cid, The : the national champion of the Spaniards against the Moors. He occupies the same sort of position in Spanish romance as King Arthur occupies in English [Southey, *Chronicles of the Cid*].

Circuit, Serjeant : one of the characters in a farce [Foote, *Lame Lover*].

Cisley : the generic name for a dairymaid in English literature. [For example Tusser, *Five Hundred Points of Good Husbandry*].

Clara : the name given to the heroine in the English version of Molière's comedy [Otway, *Cheats of Scapin*].

Clara, the daughter of Don Guzman of Seville. She flies to a convent to escape the attentions of Don Ferdinand, whom she really loves. In the end she marries him [Sheridan, *The Duenna*].

—— **Donna :** betrothed to Octavio, who, having slain Don Felix in a duel, was obliged to hide. She seeks for and finds him, and they marry [Jephson, *Two Strings to Your Bow*].

Clare, Ada : a ward in Chancery and cousin of Richard Carstone, whom she marries [Dickens, *Bleak House*].

Claribel : [Alfred Tennyson, *Claribel : a Melody*].

—— **Sir :** surnamed ' The Lewd,' one of the six knights who contended for the hand of the false Florimel [Spenser, *Faëry Queene*].

Claridiana : marries the Knight of the Sun [*Mirror of Knighthood*].

—— the enchanted queen in a Spanish play by Mendoza, translated into English [Fanshawe, *Love for Love's Sake*].

Claridoro : a character in Mendoza's play, translated from the Spanish into English. He is the rival of Felisbravo [Fanshawe, *Love for Love's Sake*].

Clarinda : the heroine of the play, in love with Colonel Manly [Mrs. Centlivre, *Bean's Duel*].

—— niece of Sir Solomon Sadlife [Cibber, *Double Gallant*].

—— a good-natured and sprightly lady with whom Charles Frankly is in love [Hoadly, *Suspicious Husband*].

—— a niece of the hero ; she is in love with Longvil [Thomas Shadwell, *The Virtuoso*].

—— the confidential servant of Queen Radigund [Spenser, *Faëry Queene*].

Clarissa : the sister of Beverley and engaged to George Bellmont [Murphy, *All in the Wrong*].

—— a lackadaisical city lady, the wife of Gripe, a tight-fisted, mean old scrivener [Vanbrugh, *Confederacy*].

—— **Harlow :** *see* Harlow, Clarissa.

Claude : the hero of the poem [Clough, *Amours de Voyage*].

—— **Melnotte :** *see* Melnotte.

Claudia : the daughter of Count Zamora ; a Spanish girl, for whom Hillary Lorraine entertains a passing passion [Blackmore, *Alice Lorraine*].

Claudine : the old nurse of the deaf and dumb count, Julio, who recognizes him under his fictitious name of Theodore [Holcroft, *Deaf and Dumb*].

Claudio : the brother of Isabella, and suitor for the hand of Juliet [Shakespeare, *Measure for Measure*].

Claudio, Lord : the betrothed of Hero and friend of Don Pedro of Aragon [Shakespeare, *Much Ado About Nothing*].

Claudius : employed by Appius in his efforts to obtain possession of Virginia [Knowles, *Virginius*].

──── the usurping King of Denmark who, having poisoned his brother, married the widow. His villainy is exposed by Hamlet [Shakespeare, *Hamlet*].

Claverhouse : the Marquis of Argyll, a kinsman of Ravenswood [Scott, *Bride of Lammermoor*].

Clavering, Harry : jilted by the girl he loves, he becomes engaged to another, and then his first love becoming widowed she turns to him again [Anthony Trollope, *The Claverings*].

Claypole, Noah : a miserable hypocrite, sneak, and spy [Dickens, *Oliver Twist*].

Cleanthe : the sister of Siphax of Paphos [Beaumont and Fletcher, *Mad Lover*].

──── the girl whom the hero, Ion, loves [Talfourd, *Ion*].

Cleanthes : the son of Leonides and husband of Hippolita [Massinger, Middleton, and Rowley, *The Old Law*].

──── friend of Cleomenes and Captain of the Guard [Dryden, *Cleomenes*].

Cleaver, Fanny : a doll's dressmaker, known as ' Jenny Wren,' with whom Lizzie Hexham lodges.

──── *Mr. :* her good-natured but drunken father, called ' Mr. Dolls ' [Dickens, *Our Mutual Friend*].

Clegg, Holdfast : a staunch Puritan, and a millwright [Scott, *Peveril of the Peak*].

Cleishbotham, Jedediah : a schoolmaster and parish clerk ; the imaginary editor of *Tales of My Landlord* [Scott, *Tales of My Landlord*].

Clelia : a frivolous, vain and resourceless girl [Crabbe, *The Borough*].

Clemanthe : the heroine of the tragedy [Talfourd, *Ion*].

Clement, Justice : a good sensible man, with a sense of humour [Ben Jonson, *Every Man in His Humour*].

Clementina, The Lady : entertains a hopeless love for Sir Charles Grandison [Richardson, *History of Sir Charles Grandison*].

Clenham, Arthur : the reputed but really only the adopted son of Mrs. Clenham. He marries Little Dorrit.

──── *Mrs. :* a hard woman who suppresses a will by which Little Dorrit would have inherited a fortune [Dickens, *Little Dorrit*].

Cleon : the personification of Glory [Spenser, *Faëry Queene*].

──── the governor of Tarsus who, with his wife, is burnt to death by the citizens, who suppose him to be the murderer of Marina [Shakespeare, *Pericles, Prince of Tyre*].

'Cleopatra': *see* Skewton, The Hon. Mrs.

Cleopatra: Queen of Egypt [Shakespeare, *Antony and Cleopatra*].

Cleremont: the friend of Dinant [Beaumont and Fletcher, *Little French Lawyer*].

Cleriker: head of the firm in which Herbert Pocket and Pip were partners [Dickens, *Great Expectations*].

Clerimond: sister of the giant Ferragus, niece of the Green Knight and married to Valentine [*Valentine and Orson*].

Clerimont: Clarinda's lover and confidential friend of Atall and Careless [Cibber, *Double Gallant*].

—— a friend of Sir Dauphine [Ben Jonson, *The Epicene; or, The Silent Woman*].

Clessammor: son of Thaddu and brother of Morna. He was married to Moina but she was carried off by Reuda, a Briton, so he never saw her again [Ossian, *Carthon*].

Cleveland, Duchess of: one of the mistresses of Charles II [Scott, *Peveril of the Peak*].

—— **Capt. Clement:** son of Norna and in love with Minna Troil [Scott, *Pirate*].

Clever: Hero Sutton's man-servant, who assumed the guise of a Quaker to support his mistress in that character [Knowles, *Woman's Wit*].

Clifford, Mr.: the lover of Emily Gayville, afterwards her husband [Burgoyne, *The Heiress*].

—— **Paul:** a highwayman whose character is redeemed by love [Lytton, *Paul Clifford*].

—— **Rosamond:** 'Fair Rosamond'; the mistress of Henry II [Scott, *Talisman* and *Woodstock*].

—— **Sir Thomas:** the accepted lover of the 'hunchback's' daughter, Julia Walter [Knowles, *Hunchback*].

Clifton, Harry: a typical young English sailor, loving adventure and 'hair-breadth escapes' [Barrymore, *El Hyder, Chief of the Ghaut Mountains*].

Clincher, Bean: [Farquhar, *Constant Couple*].

Clinker, Humphry: the servant of Brambles, a methodistical but good sort of man [Smollett, *Humphry Clinker*].

Clippurse, Lawyer: the lawyer who draws up Sir Everard Waverley's will [Scott, *Waverley*].

Clodio: the younger son of Don Antonio; a vain snob engaged to Angelina, who jilts him in favour of his brother, a bookworm [Cibber, *Love Makes a Man*].

—— **Count:** a villain who torments Zenocia with his attentions [J. Fletcher, *Custom of the Country*].

Clodpate, Justice : a rough, coarse country-bumpkin who hates London. He is not devoid of public spirit [Charles Shadwell, *Epsom Wells*].

Clodpole : a countryman who experiences many disasters in a journey to London [Strutt, *Bumpkin's Disaster*].

Cloe : a coarse and wanton shepherdess, in love with Thenot who rejects her [J. Fletcher, *Faithful Shepherdess*].

Clon : the dumb porter at Cocheforêt [Weyman, *Under the Red Robe*].

Clora : the friend of Frances and sister of Fabritio [Beaumont and Fletcher. *The Captain*].

Clorinda : the shepherdess for whose sake Thenot turns a deaf ear to Cloe [J. Fletcher, *Faithful Shepherdess*].

Cloris : beloved by Prince Prettyman [Duke of Buckingham, *The Rehearsal*].

Cloten : the 'booby' rejected by Imogen [Shakespeare, *Cymbeline*].

Cloudesley, William of : a north-country freebooter and archer [Percy, *Reliques : Adam Bell, etc.*].

Clout, Colin : the name by which Spenser alludes to himself [Spenser, *Faëry Queene*].

—— **Colin :** the shepherd whom Marian loved, but who himself loved Cicely [Gay, *Pastoral*, ii.].

—— **Lobbin :** he loved Blowzelinda [Gay, *Pastoral*, i.].

Clumsy, Sir Tunbelly : the father of Miss Hoyden ; a mean-tempered Justice of the Peace [Sheridan, *The Relapse ; Trip to Scarborough*].

Clunch : husband to Old Madge ; he takes three strayed travellers to his house [Peele, *Old Wives' Tales*].

Cluppins, Mrs. Betsey : Mrs. Bardell's chief witness in her suit against Mr. Pickwick [Dickens, *Pickwick Papers*].

Cluricaune : an Irish Elf of evil propensities [*Irish Fairy Myths*].

Clutterbuck, Capt. Cuthbert : the supposed editor of some of Sir W. Scott's novels.

Clym of the Clough : a noted outlaw ; the companion of Adam Bell and William of Cloudesley [Percy, *Reliques : Adam Bell, etc.*].

Clymedes : a character in a sort of morality play [*History of Sir Clyomon and Clamydes*].

Clyomon, Sir : a character in what is a mixture of history and a moral play. Sir Clyomon is in love with Neronis, and Alexander the Great is introduced, and also an enchanter named Bryan Sansfoy, who keeps a dragon [*History of Sir Clyomon and Clamydes*].

Clytus : an officer in the army of Philip of Macedon [Lee, *Alexander the Great*].

Coatel : daughter of Aculthua and wife of Lincoya [Southey, *Madoc*].

Cob, Oliver : a friend and admirer of Captain Bobadil [Ben Jonson, *Every Man in His Humour*].

Cobb, Tom : a member of the Quadrilateral Club [Dickens, *Barnaby Rudge*].

———— the 'boots' in the *Holly Tree Inn* [Dickens, *Holly Tree Inn*].

Cocke : the prentice boy [attrib. to Still, *Gammer Gurton's Needle*].

Cockle, Sir John : the miller of Mansfield, and keeper of Sherwood Forest, who unwittingly arrests Henry VIII, mistaking him for a poacher [*The King and the Miller of Mansfield*].

Cockney, Nicholas : Prescilla Tomboy's guardian, a grocer in the city.

———— *Walter :* the grocer's son, who makes love to Prescilla [*The Romp*, altered from Bickerstaff's *Love in the City*].

Cockwood, Lady : under an assumption of religious devotion she conceals a compromising intrigue [Etherage, *She Would if She Could*].

Codlin, Tom : a travelling 'Punch and Judy' showman [Dickens, *Old Curiosity Shop*].

Coelebs : the hero of a novel [Hannah More, *Coelebs in Search of a Wife*].

Coelia : *see* Celia.

Coffin, Tom : a fine specimen of a sailor, 'heroic in action, and of a noble spirit' [Cooper, *The Pilot*].

Colax : Flattery personified [Phineas Fletcher, *Purple Island*].

Coldbrand : a Danish giant slain by the Earl of Warwick [Drayton, *Polyolbion*].

Coldstream, Sir Charles : a very *blasé* hero, who sees nothing to admire in the world [Charles Matthews, *Used Up*].

Cole, Mrs. : this is intended for Mother Douglas, a woman of bad character who lived by Covent Garden [Foote, *The Minor*].

Colein : the dragon which Sir Bevis of Southampton slew [Drayton, *Polyolbion*].

Colin Clout : *see* Clout, Colin.

———— and Lucy : [Tickell, *Colin and Lucy* : a ballad].

———— and Phoebe : [John Byron, *A Pastoral Poem*].

———— and Rosalinda : characters in the pastoral [Spenser, *Shepherd's Calendar*].

Colkitto : a Highland chief in Montrose's army. Also known as 'Vich Alister More' and 'Alister M'Donnell' [Scott, *Legend of Montrose*].

Colcan, May : the heroine of an old Scottish ballad.

Collins, Mr. : an intolerably vulgar and conceited toady who, rejected by Lizzie Bennet, marries Charlotte Lucas [Jane Austen, *Pride and Prejudice*].

Collet, Mary : one of the Little Gidding family [Shorthouse, *John Inglesant*].

Collingwood : a man with such a desire to improve his property that he planted acorns wherever he found a vacant space on his estate [Thackeray, *Vanity Fair*].

Colombe of Ravenstein : a duchess who refuses a prince that she may marry an advocate [R. Browning, *Colombe's Birthday*].

Colonna : a Neapolitan noble, much given to plain-speaking [Shiel, *Evadne ; or, The Statue*].

Colvin, May : the heroine of an old Scottish ballad.

Comal : was the son of Albion and the lover of Galbina. He slew his beloved in mistake, rushed to battle in despair, and was slain [Ossian, *Fingal*, ii.].

Comala : the daughter of Sarno, King of Inistore. She fell in love with Fingal, but he fell in battle before the marriage could take place [Ossian, *Fingal*].

Common, Dol : a friend of Subtle, the alchemist [Ben Jonson, *The Alchemist*].

Comnenus, Isaac : the hero of a story which is founded on history [Sir Henry Taylor, *Isaac Comnenus*].

Comparini, Pietro and Violante : the elderly couple who had reared Pompilia as their own child, the man really believing her to be so, and who, tempted by his social position, induced the girl to marry Guido Franceschini [R. Browning, *The Ring and the Book*].

Compeyson : a forger who jilted Miss Havisham, and was drowned at Greenwich [Dickens, *Great Expectations*].

Comus : the god of revelry, and the son of Circe, who lured the unwary to drink of his goblet [Milton, *Comus, a Masque*].

Conachar : the Highland apprentice of Simon Glover, who escaped death in the battle of the Clans which took place at Perth [Scott, *Fair Maid of Perth*].

Coningsby : this character is supposed to be a portrait of Lord Lytton. He is the hero of the tale [Beaconsfield, *Coningsby*].

—— Arthur : the hero of the only novel by this author [Sterling, *Arthur Coningsby*].

Conkey Chickweed : *see* Chickweed, Conkey.

Conlath : one of the sons of Morni. He was betrothed to Cuthona, Rumas' daughter, but she was kidnapped by Toscar of Ireland. Conlath and Toscar fought, and both fell [Ossian, *Conlath and Cuthona*].

Connal : the son of Colgar and friend of Cuthullin [Ossian, *Fingal*].

Conquest, Mrs. : a character in the comedy [Cibber, *Love's Last Stake*].

Conrad : the hero of the poem [Byron, *Corsair*].

———— a monk of Marpurg, and a Commissioner of the Pope for the suppression of heresy [Charles Kingsley, *Saint's Tragedy*].

Conrade : the Marquis of Montserrat, murdered in his tent by the Templar [*Talisman*].

———— a follower of Don John [Shakespeare, *Much Ado About Nothing*].

Constance : the heroine [Brome, *The Northern Lass*].

———— daughter of Nonesuch, and in love with Loveby [Dryden, *Wild Gallant*].

———— the daughter of Sir W. Fondlove. She marries her childhood's companion, Wildrake [Knowles, *Love Chase*].

———— daughter of the Provost and married to a knight of Flanders [Knowles, *Provost of Bruges*].

———— the mother of Prince Arthur and widow of Geoffrey Plantagenet [Shakespeare, *King John*].

———— the subject of a narrative poem [William Sotheby, *Constance de Castile*].

———— **of Beverley :** a Benedictine nun who fell in love with Marmion, and who, for breaking her vows, was walled up in the convent [Scott, *Marmion*].

Constant, Ned : a lover of Lady Brute, who renewed his attentions after her marriage [Vanbrugh, *Provoked Wife*].

———— **Sir Bashful :** unexpectedly wealthy through the death of his elder brother ; he marries an excellent woman but treats her with indifference, though loving her, because he thinks it ' the thing ' [Murphy, *Way to Keep Him*].

———— **Susan :** an old ballad quoted by Sir Toby Belch in *Twelfth Night*.

Constantia : the sister of Petruccio, Governor of Bologna [J. Fletcher, *The Chances*].

———— a girl befriended by Lady McSycophant, and in love with her son [Macklin, *Man of the World*].

Constanza : she follows her father into exile, disguised as a gipsy under the name of Pretiosa [Middleton, *Spanish Gipsy*].

Contest, Lady : young, lively and beautiful ; the second wife of Sir Adam.

———— **Sir Adam :** an elderly man married, for his second wife, to a young girl. After the marriage his first wife reappears, saved from a shipwreck [Mrs. Inchbald, *Wedding Day*].

Cophetua : a mythical African King, who fell in love with and married a beggar-maid [Percy, *Reliques*].

Copley, Sir Thomas : one of the Earl of Leicester's train at Woodstock [Scott, *Kenilworth*].

Copper, Captain : the real name of Michael Perez, a penniless adventurer who gets 'hoist with his own petard' [J. Fletcher, *Rule a Wife and Have a Wife*].

Copperfield, David : a posthumous child, who is made miserable by his stepfather. After a chequered existence he ends by marrying Agnes Wickfield.

―――― *Dora : see* Spenlow.

―――― *Mrs. Clara :* the mother of David, who for her second husband marries Mr. Murdstone, who tries to teach her 'firmness' but breaks her heart instead [Chas. Dickens, *David Copperfield*].

Cora : the wife of Alonzo and friend of Rollo [Sheridan, *Pizarro*].

―――― intended for Dr. Titus Oates [Dryden, *Absalom and Achitophel*].

Corbaccio : the confederate of Volpone. This character is supposed to have been acted by Ben Jonson himself [Ben Jonson, *Volpone ; or, the Fox*].

Cordelia : youngest of Lear's three daughters, and married to the King of France. As angelic as her sisters are fiendish [Shakespeare, *King Lear*].

Corflambo : the personification of sensual passion [Spenser, *Faëry Queene*].

Corinna : the daughter of Gripe and the wife of Dick Amlet [Vanbrugh, *Confederacy*].

Corinthian, Tom : companion of Jerry Hawthorn (Tom and Jerry) and sharing with him the rôle of hero [Pierce Egan, *Life in London*].

Coriolanus, Caius Marcius : the haughty and passionate but noble hero. He falls a victim to his great qualities almost as much as to his foibles [Shakespeare, *Coriolanus*].

Cormac II : King of Ireland, who succeeded his father Artho on the throne [Ossian, *Fingal ; Dar-Thula* and *Temora*].

Cormalo : a chief who lived near Lake Lano and stole the daughter of King Annir, for which deed he paid with his life [Ossian, *War of Inis-Thona*].

Cornelius : a friend of Dr. Faustus, who persuades him to sell his soul [Marlowe, *Dr. Faustus*].

Cornet : an attendant on Lady Fanciful [Vanbrugh, *Provoked Wife*].

Corney, Mrs. : matron of the workhouse w^here Oliver Twist first saw the light. She married Mr. Bumble [Dickens, *Oliver Twist*].

Cornflower, Henry : one of 'nature's gentlemen' though with a rough exterior.

—— **Mrs.** : his wife, abducted by Sir Chas. Courtly [C. I. M. Dibdin, *Farmer's Wife*].

Cornwall : the gloomy husband of Regan [Shakespeare, *King Lear*].

Coromboria, Vittoria : a very fiend in human shape [Webster, *The White Devil ; or, Vittoria Corombona*].

Corporal Nym : *see* Nym, Corporal.

—— **Trim** : *see* Trim, Corporal.

Corrouge : the sword of Sir Ortuel.

Corsand : a magistrate who presides at the examination of Dick Hatteraick [Scott, *Guy Mannering*].

Corsican Brothers : *see* Franchi.

Corvino : a Venetian merchant, the dupe of Mosca [Ben Jonson, *Volpone ; or, The Fox*].

Corydon : he wooed Pastorella, but had to stand aside for Sir Calidore, who, to make him some amends, gave him flocks and herds [Spenser, *Faëry Queene*].

Costard : the clown [Shakespeare, *Love's Labour's Lost*].

Costigan, Captain : a dram-drinking old scamp, the father of Miss Fotheringay.

—— **Emily** : an actress, with whom Arthur Pendennis falls in love. Her stage name is Fotheringay [Thackeray, *Pendennis*].

Cote Male-taile, Sir : the nickname of Sir Brewnor le Noyre [Mallory, *History of Prince Arthur*].

Cotta : intended for the Duke of Newcastle [Pope, *Moral Essays*, Epistle ii.].

Courtall : a libertine, who tries his wiles upon Lady Frances Touchwood, but ineffectively [Mrs. Cowley, *Belle's Stratagem*].

Courtland, Lord : the father of Lady Juliana, who, without consulting his daughter, promises her hand to an aged nobleman [Susan E. Ferrier, *Marriage*].

Courtley, Will : one of the characters in the *Tatler*.

Courtly, Charles : the son of Sir Harcourt, a fashionable young man, who cuts his father out in the affections of Grace Harkaway.

—— **Sir Harcourt** : an elderly man of fashion, who is suitor for the hand of an heiress named Grace Harkaway, but is rejected in favour of his own son [Dion Boucicault, *London Assurance*].

—— **Sir Charles** : the abductor of Mrs. Cornflower [C. I. M. Dibdin, *Farmer's Wife*].

Courtly, Sir James : a gamester ; witty, light-hearted, and
unprincipled [Mrs. Centlivre, *Basset-Table*].

—— Nice, Sir : *see* Nice, Sir Courtley.

Coventry, Peeping Tom of : the one person who ' peeped '
at Lady Godiva as she rode through Coventry clothed
only in her own hair [Alfred Tennyson, *Godiva*].

Coverdale, Miles : in this character the author to a large
extent painted his own portrait [Nathaniel Hawthorne,
Blithedale Romance].

Coverley, Sir Roger de : loyal to Church and King, and a
good landlord, he forms an ideal ' squire ' [Addison, in
Spectator].

Cox : *see* Box.

Crab : the guardian of Buck's fortune [Foote, *Englishman
Returned from Paris*].

Crabshaw, Timothy : the servant of Sir Launcelot's Squire
[Smollett, *Adventures of Sir Launcelot Greaves*].

Crabtree : the gardener at Fairport [Scott, *Antiquary*].

—— the uncle of Sir Benjamin Backbite [Sheridan,
School for Scandal].

—— an old deaf cynic ; a friend of Peregrine's [Smollett,
Peregrine Pickle].

Crackit, Toby : one of the burglars who took part in the
attempt upon Mrs. Maylie's house at Chertsey [Dickens,
Oliver Twist].

Cradlemont : King of Wales, who is vanquished by Arthur
[Alfred Tennyson, *Coming of Arthur*].

Cradock, Sir : the husband of the only lady at King
Arthur's Court who could wear the mantle of chastity
[Percy, *Reliques : Boy and the Mantle*].

Craigdallie, Adam : a baillie at Perth [Scott, *Fair Maid of
Perth*].

Craigengelt : one of Bucklaw's companions [Scott, *Bride
of Lammermoor*].

Cranbourne, Sir Jasper : the friend of Sir Geoffrey Peveril
[Scott, *Peveril of the Peak*].

Crane, Ichabod : a Yankee schoolmaster of cadaverous
appearance [Irving, *Sketch Book : Legend of Sleepy
Hollow*].

Cranstoun, Henry : lover of Margaret of Branksome, the
daughter of his hereditary foe. He wins her by im-
personating William of Daloraine in a trial by combat,
in which he comes off victorious [Scott, *Lay of the
Last Minstrel*].

Cratchit, Bob : Scrooge's underpaid and overworked clerk,
who in spite of poverty is happy.

—— *Tim :* Bob's little lame son [Dickens, *Christmas
Carol*].

Crawford, Henry : rejected by Fanny Price, he eventually elopes with her cousin, Mrs. Rushworth.

———— *Mary :* the frivolous sister of Henry [Jane Austen, *Mansfield Park*].

Crawley, Captain Rawdon : a dragoon and a 'blood about town'. A man with few brains and many faults, he yet loved his wife (Becky Sharp) truly, and when he discovered her real character his heart broke.

———— *Lady :* Sir Pitt's second wife, the daughter of a provincial ironmonger of little character.

———— *Miss :* the sister of the first Sir Pitt Crawley, who disinherited Rawdon when he married a governess.

———— *Mr. Pitt :* the brother of Rawdon ; an aggressive 'evangelical' who behaved with the utmost propriety [Thackeray, *Vanity Fair*].

———— *Sir Pitt :* a mean and vulgar, ignorant man, whose daughters Becky Sharp was expected to teach.

Creakle, Mr : the schoolmaster to whom David Copperfield was sent by his stepfather [Dickens, *David Copperfield*].

Credulous, Justice and Mrs. Bridget : the parents of Lauretta. A foolish but good-natured old couple [Sheridan, *St. Patrick's Day*].

Cregeen, Caesar : the father of Katherine, a self-righteous old scoundrel.

———— *Katherine :* the heroine, who first marries Peter Quilliam and afterwards Philip Christian [Hall Caine, *The Manxman*].

Crellin, Mona : an ignorant girl of low birth, who becomes the wife of Thomas Wilson Christian [Hall Caine, *The Manxman*].

Cresseid : the heroine of a poem founded on the Trojan legend and published in the late fifteenth century [Henrysoun, *Testiment of Fair Cresseid*].

Cressida : a giddy girl who falls in love with Troilus and afterwards deserts him [Shakespeare, *Troilus and Cressida*].

Cresswell, Madame : a woman of very bad character, whose funeral sermon was written by the Duke of Buckingham [Scott, *Peveril of the Peak*].

Crete, Hound of : a blood-hound [Shakespeare, *Midsummer Night's Dream*].

Crèvecour, Count Philip de : he carried Charles the Bold's defiance to Louis XI of France [Scott, *Quentin Durward*].

Crewler, Mrs. : a confirmed invalid, the wife of the Rev. Horace Crewler and mother-in-law of Traddles.

Crewler, Sophy : ' the dearest girl in the world ', afterwards Tommy Traddles' wife [Dickens, *David Copperfield*].

Cricca : servant to Pandolfo [Tomkis, *Albumazar*].

Crimora and Connal : Crimora accidentally shot her sweetheart, Connal, in trying to defend him. They both died and were buried in one grave [Ossian, *Carric-Thura*].

Crimsworth, Edward : the brother of William Crimsworth, to whom he is most cruel [Charlotte Brontë, *The Professor*].

Crispinella : sister to Beatrice, and a great contrast to her ; she is bright, lively, and witty [Marston, *Dutch Courtezan*].

Crispinus : the hero ; a thoroughly bad poet, intended for Marston, with whom Jonson had quarrelled [Ben Jonson, *Crispinus*].

Crites : supposed to have been intended by the author as a portrait of himself [Ben Jonson, *Cynthia's Revels*].

Croaker : a cynic who believes all life is vanity, but has a good heart. He is Miss Richland's guardian.

—— *Leontine :* his son, who falls in love with Olivia Woodville.

—— *Mrs. :* a light-hearted, cheerful woman—the very opposite to her husband [Goldsmith, *Good-natured Man*].

Croasse, La : intended for John Wilson Croker [Brougham, *Albert Lunel*].

Crocodile, Lady Kitty : Duchess of Kingston, who was tried for bigamy [Foote, *Trip to Calais*].

Croisnel, Renée de : a French girl, with whom Nevil Beauchamp falls in love at Venice. She is forced to marry an elderly French nobleman and is afterwards unhappy [George Meredith, *Beauchamp's Career*].

Croft, Admiral : a fine old gentleman and one of the heroes of Trafalgar [Jane Austen, *Persuasion*].

Croftangry, Mr. Crystal : a gentleman who has seen better days : said to be intended for the author's father [Scott, *Fair Maid of Perth*].

Crop, George : an honest farmer who cannot agree with his wife Dorothy [Hoare, *No Song, no Supper*].

Cropland, Sir Charles : an extravagant and heartless man of fashion [Colman the Younger, *Poor Gentleman*].

Crosbie, Mrs. : wife of the provost and a cousin of Redgauntlet.

—— *William :* the provost of Dumfries ; a friend of Mr. Fairford [Scott, *Redgauntlet*].

Crosbie, Mr.: a cowardly, shallow character, whose follies and wrong-doings lead however, to repentance [Anthony Trollope, *Small House at Allington*].

Crotchet, Squire: a retired man of business who settles in the country—an unscrupulous self-seeker [Peacock, *Crotchet Castle*].

Crothar: the 'lord of Atha' in Connaught [Ossian, *Temora*].

Crowdero: one of the leaders of the mob at the bear-baiting [Butler, *Hudibras*].

Crowe, Captain: the companion of Sir Launcelot in his efforts to reform the world. His real avocation was that of a captain of a merchant vessel [Smollett, *Adventures of Sir Launcelot Greaves*].

Croye, Countess Hameline of: aunt of Countess Isabella. She marries William de la Marck.

—— *Isabelle, Countess of:* a ward of the Duke of Burgundy, who marries Quentin Durward [Scott, *Quentin Durward*].

Croysado, The Great: intended for General Lord Fairfax [Butler, *Hudibras*].

Crummles, Miss Ninetta: 'the infant phenomenon'.

—— *Mr. Vincent:* the manager of the Portsmouth theatre where Miss Belvawney acts.

—— *Mrs. Vincent:* his wife, a kindly woman [Dickens, *Nicholas Nickleby*].

Cruncher, Jerry, Senior: an odd-job man at Tellson's Bank and a 'resurrection man'.

—— *Jerry, Junior:* his son and assistant at night, though not fully aware of the nature of the business [Dickens, *Tale of Two Cities*].

Crupp, Mrs.: the person with whom David lodged in Buckingham Street [Dickens, *David Copperfield*].

Crushton, The Hon. Mr.: a friend of Captain Dowler's [Dickens, *Pickwick Papers*].

Crusoe, Robinson: the shipwrecked sailor who lives in solitude for years. His story is based on the adventures of Alexander Salkirk [Defoe, *Robinson Crusoe*].

Cuddie Headrigg: *see* Headrigg, Cuddie.

Cuddy: a shepherd who admires Buxoma and sings her praises to the belittlement of Blouzelinda [Gay, *Pastoral* i.].

—— a herdsman [Spenser, *Shepherd's Calendar*].

Culling, Rosamund: the housekeeper of Lord Rompey, whom he marries. She entertains a great affection for Nevil Beauchamp [George Meredith, *Beauchamp's Career*].

Cully, Sir Nicholas: a very foolish knight [Etherege, *Comical Revenge; or, Love in a Tub*].

Cumnor, Lady Harriet: Molly Gibson's friend [Mrs. Gaskell, *Wives and Daughters*].

Cunobeline: son of Tasciovanus, and father of Caractacus, King of the Silures. Coins still exist bearing his name [Drayton, *Polyolbion*].

Curio: a gentleman in the train of the Duke of Illyria [Shakespeare, *Twelfth Night*].

Curryfin, Lord: an amiable young man, who has a mania for trying dangerous experiments [Peacock, *Gryll Grange*].

Curtio: Petruchio's servant [Shakespeare, *Taming of the Shrew*].

Custance, Dame Christian: a gay widow for whose hand Ralph Roister Doister is an unsuccessful suitor [Udall, *Ralph Roister Doister*].

—— daughter of the Emperor of Rome and betrothed to the Sultan of Syria. She survives many terrible adventures [Chaucer, *Canterbury Tales: The Man of Law's Tale*].

Cute, Alderman: 'resolved to put down everything', suicide, babies and poverty [Dickens, *The Chimes*].

Cuthona: daughter of Rumar, betrothed to Conlath [Ossian, *Conlath and Cuthona*]; *see also* Conlath.

Cuthullin: son of Semo, regent of Ireland [Ossian, *Fingal* and *Death of Cuthullin*].

Cutter: a merry man 'about town', and the leading character in the comedy [Cowley, *Cutter of Coleman Street*].

Cuttle, Cap. Edward: a retired mariner of extraordinary sweetness of character [Dickens, *Dombey and Son*].

Cymbeline: a mythical King of Britain whom Shakespeare has taken as the subject of this play. Imogen, the heroine, is his daughter [Shakespeare, *Cymbeline*].

Cymochles: the husband of the enchantress, Acrasia. He is slain by Arthur [Spenser, *Faëry Queene*].

Cynetha: son of Cadwallon, King of Wales, whose eyes were destroyed by his uncle Owen. He went with Madoc to North America [Southey, *Madoc*].

Cynthia: daughter of Lord and Lady Pliant, in love with Mellefont [Congreve, *Double Dealer*].

—— this has been the name of innumerable subjects of poems, amongst them one by Richard Barnfield, Sir W. Raleigh, Michael Drayton, and Ben Jonson.

Cythna: a character in the poem [Shelley, *Revolt of Islam*].

Dacier, Percy : a rising politician who falls in love with Diana Warwick. He tells her a State secret, which she gives away to a paper. Learning it from her lips, he breaks from her and at once engages himself to another woman [George Meredith, *Diana of the Crossways*].

Dagon : sixth in order in the hierarchy of hell [Milton, *Paradise Lost*].

Dagonet, Sir : the fool of King Arthur's Court [Alfred Tennyson, *Idylls of the King : Last Tournament*].

Dainty, Lady : a fashionable lady attached to ' dogs, doctors and monkeys ' [Cibber, *Double Gallant*].

Daisy, Solomon : parish clerk and bellringer of Chigwell [Dickens, *Barnaby Rudge*].

Dale, Lily : a character in the story, who is jilted by her lover [Anthony Trollope, *Small House at Allington*].

—— **Parson :** a clergyman of a sweet and kindly nature [Lytton, *My Novel*].

—— **Lætetia :** a romantic girl, whose father rents a cottage on Sir Willoughby Patterne's estate. She gradually has her eyes opened to the true character of Sir Willoughby and only engages herself to him under protest [George Meredith, *The Egoist*].

Dalgarno, Lord Malcolm of : son of the Earl of Huntinglen, a very profligate young nobleman [Scott, *Fortunes of Nigel*].

Dalgetty, Rittmaster Dugald : the Laird of Drumthwacket : a wearisome pedant but excellent soldier of fortune [Scott, *Legend of Montrose*].

Dalton, Reginald : the hero of the novel, who marries Helen Hesketh [Lockhart, *Reginald Dalton*].

Damas, Colonel : one of the characters in the play [Lytton, *Lady of Lyons*].

Damian : the lover of May, old January's wife [Chaucer, *Canterbury Tales : The Merchant's Tale*].

—— a young squire, who aspires to become a templar [Scott, *Ivanhoe*].

Damiotti, Dr. Baptisti : a Paduan quack who possesses a magic mirror [Scott, *Aunt Margaret's Mirror*].

Damocles : King of Arcadia [Greene, *Arcadia*].

Damon and Musidora : two lovers who misunderstood one another, but at last were happy [James Thomson, *Seasons*].

—— and Pythias : ' the most excellent comedie of two of the most faithfullest freendes ', of which the author was Richard Edwards.

—— and Pythias : a tragedy [Banim and Sheil, *Damon and Pythias*].

Damosel, The Blessed : the subject of a poem [Rossetti, *Blessed Damosel*].

Damply, Mrs. : a widow [Garrick, *Male Coquette*].

D'Amville : the murderer of his brother, Montferrers [Tourneur, *Atheist's Tragedy*].

Dandie Dinmont : *see* Dinmont, Dandie.

Dane, William : the villain who falsely accused Silas Marner and took his wife, Sarah, from him [George Eliot, *Silas Marner*].

Dangle : said to be intended for Thomas Vaughan, a playwright of mediocre abilities [Sheridan, *The Critic*].

Danhasch : one of the genii [*Arabian Nights*].

Daniel : the son of Widow Lackitt, very stupid but very wealthy [Southern, *Oroonoko*].

Danisburgh, Lord : the friend of Diana Warwick and prime minister. Out of their friendship springs a baseless scandal, which results in Mr. Warwick bringing an unsuccessful action for divorce against his wife [George Meredith, *Diana of the Crossways*].

Dapper : a foolish clerk who goes to Subtle for aid in his betting transactions [Ben Jonson, *Alchemist*].

Dapperwit : a foolish, vain and fast man [Wycherley, *Love in a Wood*].

Darby and Joan : a loving old couple, the subject of a ballad [attributed to Matthew Prior, *Happy Old Couple*].

Darch, Car and Nancy : the Queen of Spades, and Queen of Diamonds [Hardy, *Tess of the D'Urbervilles*].

Darcy : this aristocratic hero is at first the embodiment of snobbish pride and prejudice, but ends by marrying Elizabeth Bennet out of pure admiration for her good qualities [Jane Austen, *Pride and Prejudice*].

Dardu-Lena : the daughter of Foldath, General of the Firbolg or Belgae in the south of Ireland [Ossian, *Temora*].

Daredevil : a boastful coward who, when in danger, casts his principles aside and begins to pray. He is the hero of the comedy [Otway, *Atheist*].

Dargonet : slain by Hugo the Little in a combat between four against four [Davenant, *Gondibert*].

Darius, King : the leading character in a religious interlude, ' a prettie new enterlude both pithie and pleasant ' [*King Darius*].

Darlemont : the guardian of a deaf and dumb nephew—Julio of Harancour—and false to his trust [Holcroft, *Deaf and Dumb*].

Darnley : the lover of Charlotte Lambert [Bickerstaff, *Hypocrite*].

Darnay, Charles : Marquis St. Evrémonde, the lover of Lucie Manette, and the man for whom Sydney Carton gave his life on the guillotine [Dickens, *Tale of Two Cities*].

Darnel, Aurelia : a character in the novel [Smollett, *Adventures of Sir Launcelot Greaves*].

Dartle, Rosa : Mrs. Steerforth's companion, and in love with her son [Dickens, *David Copperfield*].

Dashall, The Hon. Tom : the cousin and companion of Rob Tallyho, Esq. [Pierce Egan, *Real Life in London*].

Dashwood : a satirical character in the comedy [Murphy, *Know Your Own Mind*].

———— *Elinor :* the heroine of the story—the embodiment of 'sense', who marries Edward Ferrars.

———— *Marianne :* the 'sensibility' of the story, who after much tribulation marries Colonel Brandon.

———— *Mr. John :* the stepbrother of the heroine and her sisters, who is always afraid his income may be encroached upon by them [Jane Austen, *Sense and Sensibility*].

Daura : daughter of Armin and affianced bride of Armar. He is drowned at sea and Daura dies of grief [Ossian, *Songs of Selma*].

Davenant, Charles : married to Marianne Dormer, his father's first wife.

———— *Lady :* 'a faultless wife' and very beautiful.

———— *Lord :* first married to Marianne Dormer, and then, whilst she still lived, to Louisa Travers [Cumberland, *The Mysterious Husband*].

David : intended for Charles II [Dryden, *Absalom and Achitophel*].

———— *King :* brother of Madoc and King of North Wales, he married Emma Plantagenet, and killed several of his brothers [Southey, *Madoc*].

———— Copperfield : *see* Copperfield, David.

Davilow, Mrs. : Gwendolen Harleth's mother [George Eliot, *Daniel Deronda*].

Daw, Sir David : a wealthy Monmouthshire baronet who pays court to Emily Tempest [Cumberland, *Wheel of Fortune*]

—·—·— Sir John : a coxcomb [Ben Jonson, *Epicene; or, Silent Woman*].

—·—·— Friar Tobias : the hero of a popular song, taking the side of the friars against the followers of Wiclif [*Friar Tobias Daw*].

Dawkins, John : one of Fagin's pupils, usually known as the 'Artful Dodger', a young but very accomplished thief [Dickens, *Oliver Twist*].

W.W.F.   G

Dawson, Bully: a London sharper alluded to in the *Spectator*, No. ii.

────── **Jemmy:** the subject of a ballad, which tells of Kitty's love for young Captain Dawson in the army of the young Chevalier [Shenstone, *Jemmy Dawson*].

────── **Phoebe:** 'the pride of Lammas Fair' [Crabbe, *Parish Register*].

Day, Abel: a foolish creature who aspires to the hand of the heiress, Arabella [Knight, *Honest Thieves*].

────── **Mr.:** the henpecked chairman of the Committee [Howard, *The Committee*].

Dazzle: an adventurer living on his wits, who cleverly contrives to become a guest of Squire Harkaway, at Oak Hall [Dion Boucicault, *London Assurance*].

De Courcy: an Irishman in love with an Italian woman and her daughter [Maturin, *Women*].

De Craye, Horace: the easy-going, unscrupulous friend of Sir Willoughby Patterne [George Meredith, *The Egoist*].

De Gard: a noble and much travelled gentleman, who goes in chase of Mirabel [J. Fletcher, *Wild-Goose Chase*].

De L'Epée, Abbé: the man who took pity on Julio Harancour, when he was deserted, and brought him up [Holcroft, *Deaf and Dumb*].

De Valmont, Count: the father of Florian and uncle of Geraldine [Dimond, *Foundling of the Forest*].

Dean, Mrs.: the housekeeper who tells the beginning of the story [Emily Brontë, *Wuthering Heights*].

Deane, Lucy: the rival and cousin of Maggie Tulliver [George Eliot, *Mill on the Floss*].

Deans, Davie: an Edinburgh cow-feeder, the father of Effie and Jeanie.

────── *Effie:* imprisoned and condemned to death for child-murder. Through the efforts of her sister the sentence is revoked and she dies in a convent.

────── *Jeanie:* the heroine. To save her sister she walks from Edinburgh to London and obtains an audience of the Queen [Scott, *Heart of Midlothian*].

Debarry, Sir Maximus: the Squire.

────── *Augustus:* brother of Sir Maximus.

────── *Philip:* the Squire's son [George Eliot, *Felix Holt*].

Debbitch, Deborah: the governess at the Peverils [Scott, *Peveril of the Peak*].

Deborah, Miss: *see* Jenkins, Miss Deborah.

Dedlock, Lady Honoria: a beautiful woman, but miserable with the secret of being the mother of an illegitimate child.

Dedlock, Sir Leicester : a proud, conservative man who believes in ' family ', and especially in his own [Dickens, *Bleak House*].

Deerslayer : the nickname of Natty Bumpo, *q.v.*

Defarge, Madame Thérèse : a terrible woman who sits and knits all day, but secretly aids towards the reign of terror.

——— *Mons. Ernest :* her husband, the keeper of a wine-shop, a meeting-place of the revolutionists [Dickens, *Tale of Two Cities*].

Degore, Sir : the hero of an old English romance.

Delaval, Maria : daughter of Colonel Delaval and betrothed to Mr. Versatile [Holcroft, *He's Much to Blame*].

Delmour, Lieut.-Col. Frederick : nephew of Lord Rossville and younger brother of the heir apparent to the earl-dom. Proud and accomplished, but unprincipled [Susan E. Ferrier, *Inheritance*].

Delville : one of the heroine's guardians [Fanny Burney, *Cecilia*].

Demetrius : the son of King Antigonus and in love with Celia [Beaumont and Fletcher, *Humorous Lieute-nant*].

——— intended for John Marston [Ben Jonson, *Poetaster*].

——— the young Athenian, who marries Helena [Shake-speare, *Midsummer Night's Dream*].

Dempster, Janet : the heroine of one of the scenes from *Clerical Life.* She is wretched in her home and nearly succumbs to the allurements of drink, but is rescued by a clergyman [George Eliot, *Janet's Repent-ance*].

Denham, Jenny : the ward of Dr. Shrapnel, who marries Nevil Beauchamp. A fine type of girl [George Mere-dith, *Beauchamp's Career*].

Dennis, Ned : the hangman who took an active part in the ' No Popery ' riots and was hung [Dickens, *Barnaby Rudge*].

Dennison, Jenny : Edith Bellenden's maid, who marries Cuddie Headrigg [Scott, *Old Mortality*].

Depazzi : an idiotically foolish man, who plays a part in the comedy [Shirley, *Humorous Courtier*].

Dermat O'Dyna : noted for his beauty and courage. He eloped with the Princess Grainia, and together they had many adventures [*Old Celtic Romance*].

Deronda, Daniel the hero. Discovering that he is of Jewish birth he resolves to restore his race to its lost position among the nations [George Eliot, *Daniel Deronda*].

Desborough, Colonel : a Parliamentary Commissioner [Scott, *Woodstock*].

Desborough, Lucy: married secretly to Richard Feverel. After the marriage, Sir Austin Feverel keeps them apart, to allow of the working of his system. This leads to unhappy results, and Lucy dies [George Meredith, *Ordeal of Richard Feverel*].

Deschappelles, Pauline: the daughter of a Lyons merchant; Beauseant, Glavis, and Claude Melnotte were all suitors for her hand. After ' serving ' for two years Melnotte won her [Lytton, *Lady of Lyons*].

Desdemona: the victim of a foul conspiracy which ended in her being slain by Othello, who doted on her [Shakespeare, *Othello*].

Despair, Giant: he dwelt in Doubting Castle and took Christian and Hopeful captive for sleeping in his grounds. But Christian with his key, called ' Promise ', set himself and his companion free [Bunyan, *Pilgrim's Progress*].

Devereux: the hero [Lytton, *Devereux*].

Dewy, Dick: the hero [Hardy, *Under the Greenwood Tree*].

Diamond: a son of Agape, slain by Cambalo [Spenser, *Faëry Queene*].

Diana: daughter of the woman with whom Helena stayed, and with whom Bertram, Helena's husband, fell in ove, she being blameless [Shakespeare, *All's Well that Ends Well*].

—— **de Lascours:** the daughter of Ralph and Louise, and affianced to Horace de Brienne, whom, however, her sister Martha marries [Stirling, *Orphan of the Frozen Sea*].

—— **of the Crossways:** *see* Warwick, Diana.

—— **Warwick:** *see* Warwick, Diana.

—— **Vernon:** *see* Vernon, Diana.

Diarmaid: =Dermat O'Dyna, *q.v.*

Dibutades: a potter whose daughter traced her lover's shadow on the wall. He applied the same method in his pottery and thereby produced sculpture in relief [Ouida, *Ariadne*].

Dick, Little: a pauper child with whom Oliver was boarded out at a branch workhouse [Dickens, *Oliver Twist*].

" Dick," Mr.: *see* Babley, Richard.

Didapper: a wealthy fop, very foolish, who has designs upon Fanny [Fielding, *Joseph Andrews*].

Diddler, Jeremy: a clever swindler who wheedles money out of people, partly by his wit [Kenney, *Raising the Wind*].

Didier, Henri: the loyal lover of Julie Lesurgues [Stirling, *Courier of Lyons*].

Dido : the Queen of Carthage, who fell in love with Æneas ; has been the subject of innumerable plays and poems ; amongst them are Nash and Marlowe, *Dido Queen of Carthage* ; D'Urfey, *Dido and Æneas* ; Purcell, *Dido and Æneas*, etc., etc.

Diego : a sexton who regrets the healthiness of the parish wherein his lot is cast [Beaumont and Fletcher, *Spanish Curate*].

———— **Don :** an elderly man who tries to train a country girl as his future wife. Just as he thinks her properly prepared she elopes with a younger man [Bickerstaff, *Padlock*].

Diggery : a stage-struck servant who infects his fellow-servants with his own complaint [Jackman, *All the World's a Stage*].

Diggon, Davie : a shepherd who professes to have travelled, and to have been shocked by the luxury of his kind, in foreign lands [Spenser, *Shephearde's Calendar*].

Diggory : was ' taken from the barn to make a show at the side-table ' [Goldsmith, *She Stoops to Conquer*].

Dimmesdale, Arthur : a Puritan clergyman, reverenced as a saint, but secretly conscious of having sinned with Hester Prynne [Nathaniel Hawthorne, *Scarlet Letter*].

Dimsdale, Sir Harry : a muffin-seller [Foote, *Mayor of Garratt*].

Dinah : the coloured cook at Mr. St. Clair's [Harriet Beecher Stowe, *Uncle Tom's Cabin*].

———— **Aunt :** the aunt who left Tristram £1,000 [Sterne, *Tristram Shandy*].

———— **Morris :** *see* Morris, Dinah.

Dinant : a sometime lover of Mrs. Champernel [Beaumont and Fletcher, *Little French Lawyer*].

Dinmont, Dandie and Ailie : an old farmer and his wife. Dandie (Andrew) was known as the ' Fighting Dinmont of Liddesdale '. He owned a famous breed of dogs [Scott, *Guy Mannering*].

Diogenes : a dog given to Florence Dombey by Toots in memory of Paul, who had been fond of it [Dickens, *Dombey and Son*].

Dion, Lord : the father of Euphrasia [J. Fletcher, *Philaster ; or, Love Lies A-bleeding*].

Dionysia : the wife of Cleon, governor of Tarsus, to whom Marina is entrusted during her motherless infancy. She is burnt to death [Shakespeare, *Pericles, Prince of Tyre*].

Dionysius : the tyrant of Syracuse, slain by Euphrasia [Murphy, *Grecian Daughter*].

Dipsas : a venomous serpent [Milton, *Paradise Lost*].

Dirk Hatteraick : *see* Hatteraick, Dirk.

Dirkovitch, Col. : a Russian soldier and spy travelling in India [Kipling, *Life's Handicap*].

Distaffina : betrothed to Bombastes, but she was tempted to desert him for Artaxaminous for half-a-crown [Rhodes, *Bombastes Furioso*].

Diver, Colonel : the editor of the *New York Rowdy Journal* [Dickens, *Martin Chuzzlewit*].

———— **Jenny :** she pretends to love Macheath, but helps to betray him into the hands of the constables [Gay, *Beggar's Opera*].

Dixon, Reuben : the village schoolmaster [Crabbe, *The Borough*].

Dizzy : a character in the play [Garrick, *Male Coquette*].

Dobbin, William, Colonel : the awkward and shy but large-hearted man of delicate feelings who loves Amelia and serves her faithfully for many years without recompense, though she marries him at last [Thackeray, *Vanity Fair*].

Dobbins, Humphrey : the servant of Sir Robert Bramble [Colman the Younger, *Poor Gentleman*].

Doctor Dove : *see* Dove, Doctor.

———— **Slop :** *see* Slop, Doctor.

———— **Squintum :** *see* Squintum, Doctor.

———— **Syntax :** *see* Syntax, Doctor.

Dodger, The Artful : *see* Dawkins, John.

Dodgson : a low-class lawyer [Tom Taylor, *Contested Election*].

Dods, Meg : landlady of the *Mowbery Arms* at St. Ronan's Well [Scott, *St. Ronan's Well*].

Dodson : the maiden name of Maggie Tulliver's three aunts — Aunt Pullet, Aunt Glegg, and Aunt Moss [George Eliot, *Mill on the Floss*].

———— a farmer who on his wedding day was summoned by Death. Upon his protesting Death said he should not be summoned until he had received three warnings— which were lameness, deafness and blindness. The last did not come till farmer Dodson was eighty [Mrs. Thrale, *Three Warnings*].

———— **and Fogg :** the lawyers who, acting for Mrs. Bardell, sue Mr. Pickwick for breach of promise [Dickens, *Pickwick Papers*].

Doeg : intended for Elkanah Settle, because he ' fell upon ' Dryden with his pen, but was only a ' driver of asses ' [Dryden, *Absalom and Achitophel*].

Dogberry : a city watchman who strives to teach his fellows how to do their duty, by avoiding it [Shakespeare, *Much Ado About Nothing*].

Doggrell : a poet [Mrs. Cowley, *The Guardian*, omitted in the later version of the play called *Cutter of Coleman Street*].

Doiley, Abraham : was a charity boy who amassed a large fortune and, uneducated himself, was determined that his son should not labour under the same misfortune.

———— *Elizabeth :* his daughter, who marries Captain Granger [Mrs. Cowley, *Who's the Dupe ?*].

Dolabella : though a friend of Mark Antony he loved Cleopatra [Dryden, *All for Love*].

Dollallolla, Queen : mother of Huncamunca, and wife of King Arthur, in the burlesque [Fielding, altered by O'Hara, *Tom Thumb*].

Dolly Varden : *see* Varden, Dolly.

Dolon : ' a man of subtle wit and wicked mind ', the father of Guizor [Spenser, *Faëry Queene*].

Dombey, Edith : Mr. Dombey's second wife ; the widow of Col. Granger and daughter of Mrs. Skewton. She elopes with Mr. Carker but leaves him at once.

———— *Fanny :* Mr. Dombey's first wife, the mother of Florence and Paul.

———— *Florence :* the despised and neglected daughter of Mr. Paul Dombey, and the loving companion of little Paul. She marries Walter Gay.

———— *Little Paul :* Mr. Dombey's son and heir, a delicate, pretty child with a ' wan and wistful face,' and thoughtful beyond his years. His health fails under the strain of school discipline and he dies.

———— *Mr. Paul :* proud, egoistic and pompous, and indifferent to the feelings of others, he neglects his wives and daughter, but dotes on his son, who dies [Dickens, *Dombey and Son*].

Dominic, Friar : the leading character in the play which was designed to lay bare the vices of the priesthood [Dryden, *Spanish Friar*].

Dominie Sampson : *see* Sampson, Dominie.

Dominique : an old gossip ; the footman at the Franvals [Holcroft, *Deaf and Dumb*].

Donald : Mr. Mordent's steward [Holcroft, *Deserted Daughter* ; changed to *The Steward*].

Donegild : mother of Alla, King of Northumberland, and the person who tried to get rid of Custance and her boy [Chaucer, *Canterbury Tales : Man of Law's Tale*].

Donica : a Finnish girl, who at the sound of a ' death-spectre ' fell lifeless into her lover's arms [Southey, *Donica*].

Donne, The Rev. Mr. : Curate of Whinbury, under Dr. Doultby, a vulgar upstart [Charlotte Brontë, *Shirley*].

Donnerhugel, Rudolph : one of the Swiss envoys to Charles the Bold [Scott, *Anne of Geierstein*].

Donovan : a thoughtful youth who passes through a phase of unbelief [Edna Lyall, *Donovan*].

Donnithorne, Arthur : the man who ruined Hetty Sorrel, and who rode up with her reprieve just as she was ascending the scaffold [George Eliot, *Adam Bede*].

Dony : a dwarf belonging to Florimel [Spenser, *Faëry Queene*].

Donzel del Phebo : the hero of a Spanish romance, who was 'most excellently fair', and whose lady-love was Rosiclear [*Mirrour of Knighthood*].

Doolan, Morgan : a journalist [Thackeray, *Pendennis*].

Doone, Lorna : the one girl in a family of outlaws dwelling on Exmoor. Her brothers terrorized the entire neighbourhood [Blackmore, *Lorna Doone*].

Doorm : an earl whom Geraint slew for his impertinence to Enid [Alfred Tennyson, *Idylls of the King : Geraint and Enid*].

Dora : the subject of an idyll [Alfred Tennyson, *Dora*].

Dorastus and Faunia : the hero and heroine of the romance upon which the *Winter's Tale* was founded [Greene, *Pandosto and the Triumph of Time*].

Dorax : the name taken by Alonzo when he deserted Sebastian of Portugal to join the Emperor of Barbary [Dryden, *Don Sebastian*].

Doricourt : betrothed to Letitia Hardy. A fashionable man about town, but also a man of honour [Mrs. Cowley, *Belle's Stratagem*].

—— the name of a character in the drama [Congreve, *Way of the World*].

Dorigen : a noble lady who, from pity, married Arviragus [Chaucer, *Canterbury Tales : The Franklin's Tale*].

Dorimant : a libertine : intended for the Earl of Rochester [Etherege, *Man of Mode ; or, Sir Fopling Flutter*].

Dorinda : daughter of Lady Bountiful and loving Aimwell [Farquhar, *Beaux' Stratagem*].

D'Ormeo : the Prime Minister of both King Victor and King Charles [R. Browning, *King Victor and King Charles*].

Dormer, Captain : engaged to Louisa Travers, she, being told by mischief-makers that he was false to her, married Lord Davenant instead.

—— *Marianne :* his sister, and married to Lord Davenant under a false name [Rich. Cumberland *Mysterious Husband*].

Dormer, Caroline : the orphan of a London merchant who loses her fortune through the dishonesty of her manager [Colman the Younger, *Heir at Law*].

Dornton, Harry : of a fine nature, spoilt through want of restraint. When on the brink of utter ruin he is saved by his marriage with Sophia Freelove.

———— *Mr. :* a wealthy banker, who sees his son on the road to ruin but has not the heart to restrain him [Holcroft, *Road to Ruin*].

Doron : a character which some have supposed to be intended for Shakespeare [Greene, *Menaphon*].

Dorothea : 'the peerless Queen of Scots' [Greene, *James the Fourth*].

———— a woman who gives evidence of the most devoted heroism [Massinger, *Virgin Martyr*].

Dorothy, Old : the housekeeper of Simon Glover [Scott, *Fair Maid of Perth*].

Dorriforth : a Roman Catholic priest, the guardian of Miss Milner, who is in love with him. Ultimately he is released from his vows and marries her [Mrs. Inchbald, *A Simple Story*].

Dorrillon, Miss Maria : daughter of Sir William, very beautiful and accomplished, but frivolous. Married to a man she loves, she reforms.

———— *Sir William :* a wealthy Anglo-Indian, with an only daughter [Mrs. Inchbald, *Wives as They Were and Maids as They Are*].

Dorrit, Amy : known as 'Little Dorrit', she spent her childhood in the Marshalsea when her father was a prisoner. She married Arthur Clennam.

———— *Edward :* known as 'Tip', the brother of Amy; an idler and a spendthrift.

———— *Fanny :* elder sister of Amy and a ballet dancer, who afterwards marries Mr. Sparkler.

———— *Frederick :* the uncle of Amy, who left off washing when dragged down by his brother's ruin, and consoled himself by playing a clarionet.

———— *Mr. Wm. :* a weak, shy man who is known as the 'Father of the Marchalsea'. He dies a rich man, having become heir to a large estate [Dickens, *Little Dorrit*].

———— John : the hero, and title of an old ballad.

———— John : the name of a character in the comedy.

Dory : Sir George Thunder's servant: faithful, but noisy [O'Reefe, *Wild Oats*].

D'Osborn, Count : the governor of Giant's Mount Fortress where the 'State Prisoner', Ernest de Fridberg, was incarcerated [Stirling, *State Prisoner*].

Dot : *see* Perrybingle, Mrs. Mary.

Douban : the doctor who healed the Greek king of leprosy [*Arabian Nights*].

Dougal Cratur, The : an untamed but faithful follower of Rob Roy [Scott, *Rob Roy*].

Douglas, Adelaide Julia Geraldine : one of the twin daughters of Henry and Lady Juliana Douglas.

―――― *Archibald, Major :* elder son of the Laird of Glenfern and brother of Henry Douglas.

―――― *Edward :* son of Henry and Lady Juliana Douglas, who marries Lady Emily Lindore.

―――― *Mary :* one of the twin daughters of Henry and Lady Juliana Douglas, and the heroine of the tale.

―――― *Miss Grizzy :* one of the three maiden aunts of Henry Douglas, and only distinguishable ' by her simple good nature' and general muddle-headedness.

―――― *Miss Jacky :* reckoned a ' very sensible woman' and greatly esteemed for her oratorical powers, but obstinate, illiberal, and interfering. An aunt of Henry Douglas.

―――― *Miss Nicky :* one of Henry Douglas's three maiden aunts, who, being the youngest, was fain to content herself with a subordinate rôle in the household.

―――― *Mrs. :* wife of Major Archibald Douglas, and afterwards the guardian of Mary Douglas, the heroine [Susan E. Ferrier, *Marriage*].

―――― *Clara :* beautiful in mind and body, and in love with Alfred Evelyn, whom she eventually marries [Lytton, *Money*].

―――― *Ellen :* the Lady of the Bleeding Heart [Scott, *Lady of the Lake*].

―――― *Jim :* an Englishman of great courage, who took part in the defence of Delhi [Flora A. Steele, *On the Face of the Waters*].

Dousterswivel : an astrologist and wielder of the divining rod [Scott, *Antiquary*].

Dove, Doctor : the hero of the novel, who has a horse called *Nobbs* [Southey, *Doctor Dove*].

―――― *Lady :* a termagant, who over-stepped the limits of Sir Benjamin's patience at last.

―――― *Sir Benjamin :* a little, feeble, henpecked knight.

―――― *Sophia :* daughter of Sir Benjamin, engaged to Robert Belfield though loving Andrew, whom she marries after all [Cumberland, *Brothers*].

Dowlas, Daniel : an old Gosport shopkeeper who unexpectedly succeeds to a peerage and large income. Just as he is about to enjoy his new honours the rightful heir appears.

——— *Dick :* his son, a wild ne'er-do-well, who falls in love with Cicely Homespun [Colman the Younger, *Heir at Law*].

Dowler, Captain and Mrs.: a noisy coward, whom Mr. Pickwick meets at the *White Horse Cellar*, and his wife [Dickens, *Pickwick Papers*].

Dowling, Captain : a great drunkard who dies tipsy [Crabbe, *The Borough*].

Downer, Billy : a porter, shoeblack and philosopher; the character from which the play takes its name [Selby, *Unfinished Gentleman*].

Downright : a straightforward, honest, country squire [Ben Jonson, *Every Man in His Humour*].

Dred : a runaway negro-slave living in the Dismal Swamp [Harriet Beecher Stowe, *Dred*; later edition called *Nina Gordon*].

Dowsabel : the daughter of Sir Cassemen [Drayton, *Dowsabel*].

Doxy, Betty : the girl whom Captain Macheath advises to 'stick to good wholesome beer' [Gay, *Beggar's Opera*].

Drawcansir : a boasting bully who spares 'neither friend nor foe' [Duke of Buckingham, *Rehearsal*].

Dreary, Wat : 'an irregular dog, with an underhand way of disposing of his goods' [Gay, *Beggar's Opera*].

Drood, Edwin : left an orphan very young, with his future bride selected for him by his father. The story was never finished [Dickens, *Mystery of Edwin Drood*].

Dromio of Ephesus and of Syracuse : twin brothers who are attendants upon twins, an arrangement which causes many complications [Shakespeare, *Comedy of Errors*].

Drugger, Abel : a tobacconist, a very innocent person, who puts himself in the hands of Subtle the alchemist [Ben Jonson, *Tobacconist*].

Drugget : a wealthy haberdasher, one of whose daughters has married a baronet.

——— *Mrs.:* a wise and loving wife who humours her husband's foibles [Murphy, *Three Weeks After Marriage*].

Drum, the Laird o' : an old Scottish ballad celebrating the loves of Alexander Irvine and Margaret Coutts.

Drummle, Bentley : a disagreeable, ill-tempered man, a pupil of Mr. Pocket's, who married Miss Havisham's adopted daughter Estella [Dickens, *Great Expectations*].

Drybob : a ridiculous sort of creature who tries to pass for a wit [Thomas Shadwell, *Humorist*].

Dryfesdale, Jasper : an old steward at Lochleven Castle who tries to poison Mary Stuart and her retinue [Scott, *The Abbot*].

Dubosc : a thief who robs the Lyons Mail [Stirling, *Courier of Lyons*].

Dubourg, Clement : a clerk in Osbaldistone's office.

———— *Mons. :* the father of Clement, a Bordeaux Merchant, and agent in that city for Mr. Osbaldistone [Scott, *Rob Roy*].

Dubrie, St. : Archbishop of the City of Legions, who set the crown upon King Arthur's head [Alfred Tennyson, *Idylls of the King : Coming of Arthur*].

Duchomar : in love with Morna, who loved Cathba; him he slew, then sued for Morna's hand again, but she stabbed him to the heart [Ossian, *Fingal*].

Dudley, Captain : a very poor though accomplished and noble-minded English officer.

———— *Charles :* his son, in love with Charlotte Rusport.

———— *Louisa :* beloved by and, in the end, married to Belcour, a wealthy West Indian [Cumberland, *West Indian*].

Dudu : one of the ladies in the harem [Byron, *Don Juan*].

Duessa : represents Falsehood, and is intended for Mary Queen of Scots [Spenser, *Faëry Queene*].

Dufoy : a French servant who supplies the motive to the comedy; his boastfulness and railings against women induce some of them to fasten him into a tub [Etherege, *Comical Revenge ; or, Love in a Tub*].

Dumachus : the impenitent thief [Longfellow, *Golden Legend*].

Dumaine : a French nobleman in the train of King Henry of Navarre [Shakespeare, *Love's Labour's Lost*].

Dumbello, Lady : an aristocratic but mindless doll [Anthony Trollope, *Small House at Allington*].

Dumbiedikes, Old Laird of : a taciturn and obstinate old man.

———— *Young Laird of :* a bashful young man in love with Jeanie Deans, who marries Reuben Butler [Scott, *Heart of Midlothian*].

Duncan : the 'meek' king of Scotland, who was murdered by Macbeth [Shakespeare, *Macbeth*].

Dunder, Lady : wife of Sir David ; a comfortable, homely person, fond of cooking.

———— *Sir David :* the father of Harriet and Kitty ; a whimsical old gentleman [Colman the Younger *Ways and Means*].

Dundreary, Lord : a very indolent, very gentlemanly noodle [Tom Taylor, *Our American Cousin*].

Dunrommath : the lord of Uthal, who carried off Oithona, the affianced bride of Gaul, and was slain by him in revenge [Ossian, *Oithona*].

Dunstane, Emma : an invalid ; the sympathetic friend of Diana Warwick [George Meredith, *Diana of the Crossways*].

Dunthalmo : the lord of Teutha, who slew Rathmor whilst he was banqueting [Ossian, *Calthon* and *Colmal*].

Dupely, Sir Charles : a man, who, priding himself on his power of reading character, proposed to Lady Bab Lardoon, a woman of fashion, thinking she was a simple country girl [Burgoyne, *Maid of the Oaks*].

Dupré : the servant of Mons. Darlemont [Holcroft, *Deaf and Dumb*].

Durance, Colney : a cynical, middle-aged, but loyal friend of the Radnors [George Meredith, *One of our Conquerors*].

Durandarte and Belerma : the characters in a ballad which first appeared in *The Monk* [Lewis, *Durandarte and Belerma*].

Durazzo : a lively old man, full of fun. The guardian of Caldoro [Massinger, *The Guardian*].

Durbeyfield, Tess : she is seduced and then executed for the murder of her seducer [Hardy, *Tess of the D'Urbervilles*].

Durden, Dame : the heroine of a popular glee.

—— **Dame :** the pet name for Esther Summerson [Dickens, *Bleak House*].

Duretete, Captain : a young man of a ponderous humour, who is shy with ladies, but not so with maids [Farquhar, *Inconstant*].

Durward, Quentin : a young Scott who by much courage and address made his way at the Court of France [Scott, *Quentin Durward*].

Dusronnal : one of Cuthullin's two chargers, the other being Sulin-Sifadda [Ossian, *Fingal*].

Duval, Dennis : the title of an unfinished novel by W. M. Thackeray.

Eames, Johnny : an amiable but weak character [Anthony Trollope, *Small House at Allington*].

Earine : a shepherdess with whom Eglamour was in love [Ben Jonson, *Sad Shepherd*].

Earnscliff, Patrick : the young laird [Scott, *Black Dwarf*].

Easy, Lady : his wife, who loving him dearly reforms his character.

Easy, Sir Charles : resolved ' to follow no pleasure that rises above the degree of amusement' so lazy was he [Cibber, *Careless Husband*].

—— Midshipman : the most popular of this author's heroes [Marryat, *Midshipman Easy*].

Ector de Maris, Sir : the brother of Sir Launcelot [Mallory, *History of Prince Arthur*].

Edgar : the son of Gloucester and his legal heir, though disinherited in favour of an illegitimate brother [Shakespeare, *King Lear*].

—— the master of Ravenswood, who fell in love with Lucy Ashton, who was forced by her father to marry the Laird of Bucklaw [Scott, *Bride of Lammermoor*].

Edging, Mistress : an indiscreet and mischief-making waiting-woman [Cibber, *Careless Husband*].

Edie Ochiltree : *see* Ochiltree, Edie.

Edith : the daughter of Baldwin, tutor to the Dukes of Normandy [Beaumont, *Bloody Brother*].

—— Lady : the mother of Athelstane the ' Unready ', thane of Coningsburgh [Scott, *Ivanhoe*].

—— the ' maid of Lorn ', who after many vicissitudes married Lord Ronald [Scott, *Lord of the Isles*].

—— Plantagenet, The Lady : married the Earl of Huntingdon. She was a kinswoman of Richard I and waiting-woman to Queen Berengaria [Scott, *Talisman*].

Edmonton, Witch of : *see* Sawyer, Mother.

Edmund : a natural son of the Earl of Gloucester, in whose favour Edgar was disinherited, and with whom both Goneril and Regan were in love [Shakespeare, *King Lear*].

Edmunds, John : condemned to death for crime, but his sentence commuted to fourteen years' transportation. The hero of ' *The Convict's Return* ' [Dickens, *Pickwick Papers*].

Edom O'Gordon : a Scottish ballad founded on a true event.

Edson, Mr a man who takes lodgings with Mrs. Lirriper for himself and wife, and then deserts his wife [Dickens, *Mrs. Lirriper's Lodgings* ; also *Mrs. Lirriper's Legacy*].

Edward, Sir : commits a murder, and having reason to believe his secret known to his secretary, swears him to secrecy [Colman the Younger, *Iron Chest*].

Edward : an old Scottish ballad generally attributed to Lady Wardlow.

Edwardes, Mr Murray : a friend of Hugh Flaxman's, who first finds work for Robert Elsmere in his new sphere, and after Robert's death carries out Robert's plans in the East End of London [Mrs. Humphrey Ward, *Robert Elsmere*].

Edwin : despised by his beloved, Edith, on account of his misshapen body, the fairies come to his rescue, and he finally triumphs over his rival, Sir Topaz [Parnell, *Edwin of the Green : a Fairy Tale*]

—— the hero in a play in which are also represented the characters of St. Dunstan and Leolf [Sir Henry Taylor, *Edwin the Fair*].

—— a lovely, studious youth who dwelt in the ' North countrie ' [Beattie, *The Minstrel*].

—— and Elgitha : the hero and heroine of an unsuccessful tragedy [Fanny Burney, *Edwin and Elgitha*].

—— and Emma : the hero and heroine of a ballad [Mallet, *Edwin and Emma*].

—— and Angelina : the hero and heroine of the ballad [Goldsmith, *The Hermit*].

—— of Deira : the subject of a long narrative poem [Alexander Smith, *Edwin of Deira*].

Edyrn : son of Nudd, who tried to win Enid for his wife, and when he failed in this, did his best to ruin her father [Alfred Tennyson, *Idylls of the King : Geraint and Enid*].

Eger, Sir : one of three heroes of an old English romance in verse [*Sir Eger, Sir Grahame and Sir Graysteel*].

Egerton, Audley : the rival of Henry L'Estrange for the hand of Nora Avenel [Lytton, *My Novel*].

Egeus : the father of Hermia [Shakespeare, *Midsummer Night's Dream*].

Egilona : the wife of Roderick the last of the Goths. She afterwards married Abdal-Aziz, the Moorish Governor of Spain [Southey, *Roderick*].

Egla : a Moorish woman, servant of Amaranta [J. Fletcher, *Spanish Curate*].

Eglamour : the person who helps the Duke of Milan's daughter, Silvia, to escape [Shakespeare, *Two Gentlemen of Verona*].

—— Sir, of Artois : the hero of an old English Romance of which no French original has been discovered [*Arthurian Cycle*].

—— Sir : the hero of a humorous ballad [Rowlands, printed in *The Melancholic Knight*].

Eglantine, Madame : the prioress who spoke French ' after the scole of Stratford-atte-Bow ', and who tells the *Prioress' Tale* [Chaucer, *Canterbury Tales*].

—— a daughter of King Pepin and married to her cousin Valentine [*Valentine and Orson*].

Eglett, Lady Charlotte : the kindly sister of Lord Ormont Strong-minded and full of character and commonsense [George Meredith, *Lord Ormont and His Aminta*].

Elaine : ' the lily maid of Astolat ', who loved Sir Launcelot [Alfred Tennyson, *Idylls of the King : Launcelot and Elaine*].

Elbow : a blundering, foolish constable [Shakespeare, *Measure for Measure*].

Eleazar : a dreadful man, insolent and blood-thirsty [Marlowe, *Lust's Dominion*].

Elene : the subject of an ancient poem [attrib. Cynewulf, *Elene ; or, The Finding of the Cross*].

Elfrida : the heroine of a tragedy based on the Greek model [Mason, *Elfrida*].

Elidure : surnamed ' the pius ', one of the sons of Morvidus [Drayton, *Polyolbion*].

Elissa : the half-sister of Medina and Perissa [Spenser, *Faëry Queene*].

Elizabeth : daughter of the King of Hungary, the heroine [Charles Kingsley, *Saints' Tragedy*].

Ella : the King of Northumberland, who married Custance [Chaucer, *Canterbury Tales : The Man of Law's Tale*].

Ellen : *see* Orson and Ellen.

—————— **Burd :** she followed her betrayer as his page, and gave birth to a son in a stable [Percy, *Reliques : Child Waters*].

Elliot, Anne : the heroine of the story ; a refined and womanly conception [Jane Austen, *Persuasion*].

—————— **Hobbie :** a farmer at Heugh-foot, and betrothed to Grace Armstrong [Scott, *Black Dwarf*].

Elmore, Margaret : the daughter of Matthew, who has to renounce her lover on account of her father's crime [Lovell, *Love's Sacrifice*].

Eloisa : the heroine of a poem founded on the pathetic story of Peter Abelard the priest and Heloisa, the niece of Fulbert [Pope, *Epistle from Eloisa to Abelard*].

Elphin : a Welsh prince, who is the victim of numerous misfortunes, but surmounts them at last [Peacock, *The Misfortunes of Elphin*].

Elpinus : the personification of Hope [Phineas Fletcher, *Purple Island*].

Elshender the Recluse : known as ' the Canny Elshi,' or ' The Wise Wight of Mucklestane Moor ' [Scott, *Black Dwarf*].

Elsie : the daughter of a Bavarian farmer, who offered to give her life to save that of Prince Henry of Hoheneck [Longfellow, *Golden Legend*].

Elsmere, Mrs : the generous, sympathetic, eccentric Irish mother of Robert.

—————— *Robert :* a man of many enthusiasms and of intellectual strength, who begins life as a keen Church of

England rector, but resigns his office for conscience sake [Mrs. Humphrey Ward, *Robert Elsmere*].

Elspat Lady : the heroine of an old ballad which tells how Lady Elspat obtains the release of her lover, who is wrongfully imprisoned by her mother.

Elspeth, Auld : the servant of Dandie Dinmont [Scott, *Guy Mannering*].

———— **Old :** of Craigburnfoot, the mother of Saunders Mucklebacket, and at one time in the service of the Countess of Glenallan [Scott, *Antiquary*].

Elspie : in love with Philip [Clough, *Bothie of Tober-na-Vuolich*].

Elsworthy : the clerk of St. Roques, and uncle of Rosa.

———— **Rosa :** a pretty, vain, empty-headed girl, who is betrayed by Tom Wodehouse [Mrs. Oliphant, *Chronicles of Carlingford: Perpetual Curate*].

Elton Mr. : a vulgar clergyman, who marries a still more vulgar wife [Jane Austen, *Emma*].

Elvira : the heroine of a play which is probably founded on an old Spanish drama [Earl of Bristol, *Elvira; or, The Worst not Always True*].

———— young and married to an old man; she has an intrigue with Lorenzo, who turns out to be her own brother [Dryden, *Spanish Fryar*].

———— married to Clodio, the son of Don Antonio [Cibber, *Love Makes a Man*].

———— gives up all for the love of Pizarro, whom she tries to influence for good, but in vain [Sheridan, *Pizarro*].

Emilia : heroine of the same story as that of Palamon and Arcite, which is introduced into the play [Beaumont and Fletcher, *Two Noble Kinsmen*].

———— beloved by Palamon and Arcite [Chaucer, *Canterbury Tales: The Knight's Tale*].

———— a beautiful woman beloved by both Palamon and Arcite [Dryden, *Palamon and Arcite*].

———— in attendance on Hermione [Shakespeare, *Winter's Tale*].

———— wife of Iago and persuaded by him to secure the handkerchief given by Othello to Desdemona. Upon Desdemona's death Emilia reveals the whole plot and is killed by Iago [Shakespeare, *Othello*].

———— beloved by Peregrine [Smollett, *Peregrine Pickle*].

Emily : betrothed to Colonel Tamper, whose duty summoned him to Havannah. On his return, to test Emily's affection, he assumes lameness, from which deceit many comic situations ensue [Colman the Elder, *The Deuce is in Him*].

———— the heroine [Mrs. Radcliffe, *Mysteries of Udolpho*].

Emily, Little : the niece of Daniel Peggotty ; she is betrayed and deserted by Steerforth [Dickens, *David Copperfield*].

Emma : *see* Henry and Emma.

———— **Plantagenet :** ' the Saxon ', wife of David, King of North Wales [Southey, *Madoc*].

Emmeline : a girl who for long labours under the stigma of illegitimacy ; this is removed and she enters upon a large inheritance [Mrs. Charlotte Smith, *Emmeline ; or, The Orphan of the Castle*].

Empedocles : a dramatic poem founded on the character of the historical philosopher, lawgiver and physician [Matthew Arnold, *Empedocles on Etna*].

Empson : flageolet-player to Charles II [Scott, *Peveril of the Peak*].

Enanthe : the mistress of Prince Demetrius. She assumes the name of Celia [Beaumont and Fletcher, *Humorous Lieutenant*].

Endell, Martha : a poor girl through whom Little Emily is restored to her family [Dickens, *David Copperfield*].

Enderby, Mrs. : mother of Mrs. Rowland and Philip Enderby.

———— *Philip :* the lover of Margaret Abbotson [Harriet Martineau, *Deerbrook*].

Endless : a scamp of a lawyer [Hoare, *No Song, no Supper*].

Endymion : a youth who fell in love with Diana, the Moon [John Keats, *Endymion*]. Many authors have chosen Endymion as their subject, and Lord Beaconsfield published a novel by that name.

Eneas, the Wandering Prince of Troy : an old English ballad founded on the story told by Virgil [Percy, *Reliques : Queen Dido ; or, The Wandering Prince of Troy*].

Enfield, Mrs. : the mistress of a house of ill-fame [Holcroft, *Deserted Daughter*].

Engelred : the squire of Sir Reginald Front de Boeuf [Scott, *Ivanhoe*].

Enguerraud : a crusader, and the brother of the Marquis of Montserrat [Scott, *Talisman*].

Enid : the daughter of Yniol, and hardly-used wife of Geraint. A type of spotless purity [Alfred Tennyson, *Idylls of the King : Geraint and Enid*].

Enoch Arden : *see* Arden, Enoch.

Epicene : the ' silent woman ' who, after her marriage, suddenly turns into a termagant and then proves to be a boy [Ben Jonson, *Epicene*].

Epinogris, Sir : son of the King of Northumberland [Malory, *History of Prince Arthur*].

Eppie : the little child adopted by Silas Marner, the weaver. She grows up and marries Aaron [George Eliot, *Silas Marner*].

———— the name of one of Josiah Cargill's servants, and also that of one at the *Mowbray Arms* [Scott, *St. Ronan's Well*].

Ereck : a Knight of the Round Table wedded to Enite [*Arthurian Cycle*].

Ereenia : a beneficent 'spirit' or 'glendoveer' [Southey, *Curse of Kehama*].

Erictho : a witch [Marston, *The Wonder of Women ; or, Sophonisba*].

Erillyab : the deposed Queen of the Hoamen, an Indian tribe dwelling on the Missouri [Southey, *Madoc*].

Ernest de Fridberg : the prisoner in the fortress of Giant's Mount, whose escape is contrived by his daughter Ulrica [Stirling, *Prisoner of State*].

Eromena : the heroine of a prose version of Chamberlayne's poem entitled Pharronida [*Eromena ; or, The Noble Stranger*].

Erota : a beautiful princess, beloved by Philander, Prince of Cyprus [Beaumont and Fletcher, *Laws of Candy*].

Erragon : the King of Lora [Ossian, *Battle of Lora*].

Error : a female monster who dwelt in 'Wandering Wood', who was slain by the Red Cross Knight [Spenser, *Faëry Queene*].

Errua : a legendary hero, whose superior wit enables him to pass triumphantly through many adventures [*Basque Legends*].

Escalus : a noble at the Court of the Duke of Vienna [Shakespeare, *Measure for Measure*].

———— Prince of Verona [Shakespeare, *Romeo and Juliet*].

Escanes : a Tyrian noble at the Court of Pericles [Shakespeare, *Pericles, Prince of Tyre*].

Escot, Mr. : 'the deteriorationist'; an eccentric member of the house-party at Squire Headlong's [Peacock, *Headlong Hall*].

Esher, Sir Ralph : the hero of the novel [Leigh Hunt, *Sir Ralph Esher*].

Eskdale, Lord : supposed to be intended for Lord Lonsdale [Beaconsfield, *Coningsby*].

Esmond, Henry : a cavalier in the reign of Queen Anne, who is deprived of his rightul inheritance, and afterwards voluntarily relinquishes it and emigrates to Virginia with his wife, Lady Castlewood [Thackeray, *Esmond*].

Espriella : the reputed author of some imaginary letters supposed to have been written by a Spaniard [Southey, *Letters from England*].

Etella : the adopted daughter of Miss Havisham, and the heroine of the story [Dickens, *Great Expectations*].

Estemere : King of England, the hero of an ancient legend [Percy, *Reliques : King Estemere*].

Esther : housekeeper to Muhldenau and in love with Hans, a fellow servant [Knowles, *Maid of Mariendorpt*].

Estifania : a low-class woman who palms herself off as an heiress [J. Fletcher, *Rule a Wife and Have a Wife*].

Estmere : *see* Estemere.

Estrildis : daughter of the Emperor of Germany and captured in war by Locrin, King of Britain [Drayton, *Polyolbion*].

Ethelinda : the heroine of the novel [Mrs. Charlotte Smith, *Ethelinda*].

Ettarre : beloved by Pelleas she rejects him for Gawain [Alfred Tennyson, *Idylls of the King : Pelleas and Ettarre*].

Euarchus : this is supposed to be a portrait of the poet's father [Sidney, *Arcadia*].

Eubulus : one of the characters in the play [Morton and Buckhurst, *Gorboduc*].

Eudocia : daughter of the Governor of Damascus [John Hughes, *Siege of Damascus*].

Eudon, Count : a partisan of the Moor, whose chief, however, ordered his head to be struck off [Southey, *Roderick*].

Eudoxia : wife of the Emperor Valentinian [Beaumont and Fletcher, *Valentinian*].

Eugene Aram : *see* Aram, Eugene.

Eugenia : the wife of Count Valmont and the mother of Florian, the 'foundling' [Dimond, *Foundling of the Forest*].

Eugenie : the witty but penniless nephew of Morose [Ben Jonson, *Epicene ; or, Silent Woman*].

Eugenius : supposed to be a portrait of John Hall Stevenson, a friend of the author [Sterne, *Life and Opinions of Tristram Shandy*].

Eumenes : Governor of Damascus, the father of Eudocia [John Hughes, *Siege of Damascus*].

Eumnestes : the personification of Memory [Spenser, *Faëry Queene*]

Euphrasia : daughter of Lord Dian, in love with Philaster [Beaumont and Fletcher, *Philaster ; or, Love Lies Bleeding*].

―――― represents the authoress [Clara Reeve, *Progress of Romance*].

―――― the daughter of Evander, the King of Syracuse. She rescued her aged father from starvation by feeding him from her own breast [Murphy, *Grecian Daughter*].

Euphues : a young Athenian, who after a life of pleasure in Italy returns home convinced of the vanity of life [Lily, *Euphues*].

Eurytion : a man who never slept either by night or day, but wandered about amongst his herds with his two-headed dog, Orthros [Spenser, *Faëry Queene*].

Eustace : an attendant on Sir Reginald Front de Boeuf [Scott, *Ivanhoe*].

—— **Charles :** secretly married and concealing his wife in a friend's room. This leads to misconstruction [Poole, *Scapegoat*].

—— **Father :** the Abbot of St. Mary's [*Monastery*].

—— **Jack :** a young man who obtains access to the girl he loves by assuming the guise of a music master [Bickerstaff, *Love in a Village*].

—— **Lady :** an opulent and aristocratic Becky Sharp [Anthony Trollope, *Eustace Diamonds*].

Eva : the daughter of a slave-owner and beloved by her father's slaves [Harriet Beecher Stowe, *Uncle Tom's Cabin*].

—— the daughter of Torquil of the Oak [Scott, *Fair Maid of Perth*].

Evadne : the wife of Amintor, who married her by order of the King although he was betrothed to Aspasia [Beaumont and Fletcher, *Maid's Tragedy*].

—— the sister of Colonna, betrothed to Vicentio, whom, after many trials, she marries [Shiel, *Evadne ; or The Statue*].

Evandale, Lord : in the Duke of Monmouth's army. One of Edith Bellenden's -suitors [Scott, *Old Mortality*].

Evander : the King of Syracuse, who was superseded by Dionysius the Younger [Murphy, *Grecian Daughter*].

Evangeline : the daughter of Benedict Bellefontaine and betrothed to Gabriel Lajeunesse. The story is founded on the expatriation of the French colonists from Nova Scotia [Longfellow, *Evangeline*].

Evangelist : the personification of a successful preacher [Bunyan, *Pilgrim's Progress*].

Evans, Sir Hugh : a Welsh parson and schoolmaster [Shakespeare, *Merry Wives of Windsor*].

—— **William :** a giant in the service of Charles I, as porter [Scott, *Peveril of the Peak*].

Evanthe : wife of Valerio. The Duke of Naples attempts her virtue but without avail [J. Fletcher, *Wife for a Month*].

Evelina : the heroine, who marries Lord Orville [Fanny Burney, *Evelina*].

Evelyn, Alfred : loves Clara Douglas, who returns his affection, but, on the score of poverty they are unable to marry. An immense fortune becomes his and alters the complexion of affairs [Lytton, *Money*].

────── **Hope :** *see* Hope, Evelyn.

────── **Sir George :** a man of fortune and noble character, who marries Maria Dorrillon [Mrs. Inchbald, *Wives as They Were and Maids as They Are*].

Evir-Allen : the daughter of Branno and sought by many. She was the mother of Oscar, Fingal's grandson [Ossian, *Fingal*].

Evrémonde, Marquis d' : the uncle of Charles Darnay [Dickens, *Tale of Two Cities*].

Ewain, Sir : the son of King Vrience and Morgan le Fay [Mallory, *History of Prince Arthur*].

Ewart, Nanty : captain of the smuggler's boat [Scott, *Redgauntlet*].

Excalibur : King Arthur's mystic sword [Alfred Tennyson, *Idylls of the King : Coming of Arthur*].

Eyre, Jane : a governess who wrestles bravely against heavy odds and at last marries Mr. Rochester, a very 'strenuous' hero [Charlotte Brontë, *Jane Eyre*].

Ezechias : a play founded upon the Second Book of Kings [Udall, *Ezechias*].

Ezzelin, Sir : the knight who, at Lord Otho's table recognizes Conrad the Corsair, in Lara. A duel is the result, and Ezzelin is never more seen [Byron, *Lara*].

Faa, Gabriel : a huntsman, and the nephew of Meg Merrilies [Scott, *Guy Mannering*].

Fabian : one of Olivia's servants [Shakespeare, *Twelfth Night*].

Fabritio : a soldier ; the friend of Captain Jacomo [Beaumont and Fletcher, *The Captain*].

Face : Lovewit's manservant, who tampers with alchemy and fortune-telling during his master's absence from home [Ben Jonson, *Alchemist*].

Faddle, William : a penniless ne'er-do-well [Edward Moore, *Foundling*].

Fadladeen : chamberlain to Aurungzebe's harem—very bombastic [Thomas Moore, *Lalla Rookh*].

Fadladinida : wife of King Chrononhotonthologos [Carey, *Chrononhotonthologos*].

Fag : Captain Absolute's steward, who 'scruples not to tell a lie at his master's command, but it pains his conscience to be found out' [Sheridan, *Rivals*].

Faggot, Nicholas : Matthew Foxley the Magistrate's clerk [Scott, *Redgauntlet*]

Faggus, Tom : a highwayman, and the cousin of John Ridd [Blackmore, *Lorna Doone*].

Fagin : an old Jew who trains thieves and lives upon their spoils [Dickens, *Oliver Twist*].

Fainall, Mr. and Mrs. : a couple who lead a cat and dog life together, each trying to over-reach the other [Congreve, *Way of the World*].

Fainasolis : daughter of the King of Shetland, who fled to Fingal for protection against Sora. Sora shot her with an arrow [Ossian, *Fingal, iii.*].

Fair Maguelone : *see* Magalona, The Fair.

—————— **Maid of Perth :** *see* Glover, Catherine.

—————— **Maid of the Exchange :** [Thomas Heywood, *The Fair Maid of the Exchange, with the Merry Humours and Pleasant Passages of The Cripple of Fenchurch, Furnished with a Variety of Delectable Mirth*].

—————— **Margaret and Sweet William :** an old ballad.

—————— **Penitent, The :** *see* Calista.

Fairbrother, Mr. : counsel for Effie Deans at her trial [Scott, *Heart of Midlothian*].

Fairfax, Jane : a young governess, clever but very poor, who marries Mr. Frank Churchill [Jane Austen, *Emma*].

Fairfield : the father of Patty, 'the maid of the mill '.

—————— **Patty :** the miller's daughter, the heroine, after whom the play is named.

—————— **Ralph :** an ignorant booby, jealous of his sister's superior mind, and in love with Fanny, a gipsy [Bickerstaff, *Maid of the Mill*].

—————— **Leonard :** beginning life as a literary hack, he developes into an eminent author [Lytton, *My Novel*].

Fairford, Mr. Saunders : a lawyer ; the father of Allan.

—————— **Allan :** the friend of Darcy Latimer, whose sister he marries [Scott, *Redgauntlet*].

Fairleigh, Frank : the hero of a novel, and the name under which its author wrote when editor of the *London Magazine* [Smedley, *Frank Fairleigh*].

Fairservice, Andrew : the self-seeking and humorous gardener at Osbaldistone Hall [Scott, *Rob Roy*].

Faithful : Christian's travelling companion on his way to the Celestial City [Bunyan, *Pilgrim's Progress*].

—————— **Jacob :** the hero of a nautical story [Marryat, *Jacob Faithful*].

Faithless Sally Brown : *see* Brown, Sally.

—————— **Nelly Gray :** *see* Gray, Nelly.

Falconer, Major : the brother of Lady Bothwell [Scott, *Aunt Margaret's Mirror*].

—————— **Mr. :** a friend of the old baron of Bradwardine [Scott, *Waverley*].

Falconer, Mr.: a serious, eccentric, good-hearted young man [Peacock, *Gryll Grange*].

—— **Mrs.:** a rugged Scottish Calvinist [Macdonald, *Robert Falconer*].

Faliero, Marino: the hero of the drama; a Venetian doge [Byron, *Marino Faliero*].

Falkland: the most interesting character in the book. A good man goaded on to commit a murder, the memory of which ruins his whole subsequent life [Godwin, *Caleb Williams*].

—— the hero of this author's first novel, which he afterwards withdrew from publication [Lytton, *Falkland*].

Falsetto, Signor: the 'fine weather friend' of Fazio [Milman, *Fazio*].

Falstaff, Sir John: the boon companion of Prince Hall, witty, unprincipled, and a coward [Shakespeare, *Merry Wives of Windsor* and *Henry IV*; also the hero of *Original Letters of Sir John Falstaff and His friends*, by James White: and of the *Comical Gallant; or, The Amours of Sir John Falstaff*, by John Dennis].

Fanciful, Lady: a vain beauty who flirts with Heartfree until her affectations alienate him from her [Vanbrugh, *Provoked Wife*].

Fan-Fan: the maker of sweet stuffs who makes love to Christine, maid to the Countess Marie [Stirling, *Prisoner of State*].

Fancy, Sir Patient: the hero of the comedy [Aphra Behn, *Sir Patient Fancy*].

Fang: a sheriff's officer [Shakespeare, *Henry IV*, pt. ii.].

—— **Mr.:** the magistrate who was upon the point of wrongfully convicting Oliver when Mr. Brownlow intervened on his behalf [Dickens, *Oliver Twist*].

Fanny: the heroine [Fielding, *Joseph Andrews*].

—— **Miss:** daughter of a wealthy merchant; she secretly marries Lovewell [Colman and Garrick, *Clandestine Marriage*].

Fardarougha: a miser in whom the tenderer instincts are still alive [Carleton, *Fardarougha the Miser; or, The Convicts of Lisnamona*].

Farebrother, the Rev Camden: an unpopular rector [George Eliot, *Middlemarch*].

Farina: the hero of the book bearing that name [George Meredith, *Farina*].

Farintosh, Beau: a society fop [Robertson, *School*].

—— **Marquis of:** aspired to the hand of Ethel Newcome [Thackeray, *The Newcomes*].

Farrell, Aminta: known as 'Browny'. She marries Lord Ormont, who is many years her senior, and who neglects her, with the result that she elopes with Weyburn [George Meredith, *Lord Ormont and His Aminta*].

Fashion, Sir Brilliant : a man who does everything he is called upon to do with a fashionable air [Murphy, *Way to Keep Him*].

—— **Sir Novelty :** the hero of this comedy, who in Vanbrugh's *Relapse* (its sequel) appears as Lord Foppington [Cibber, *Love's Last Shift*].

—— **Tom** (' Young ') : a younger brother of Sir Novelty Fashion (Lord Foppington), whom he supplants as the lover of Miss Hoyden the heiress [Vanbrugh, *The Relapse*; Sheridan, *Trip to Scarborough*].

Fastolfe, Sir John : lieutenant-general of the Duke of Bedford, not to be confounded with Sir John Falstaff the 'fat knight' [Shakespeare, *Henry VI*, pt. i.].

Fastrada : the daughter of Count Rodolph and one of Charlemagne's nine wives [Longfellow, *Golden Legend*].

Fat Boy : his real name was Joe. He divided his time between sleeping and eating, but contrived to see more than he was meant to see [Dickens, *Pickwick Papers*].

Fata Morgana : a sort of fairy who dwelt at the bottom of a lake ; the reputed sister of King Arthur [*Arthurian Cycle*].

Fathom, Ferdinand, Count : an utter villain, whom the author depicted as 'a beacon for the benefit of the inexperienced and unwary' [Smollett, *Adventures of Ferdinand, Count Fathom*].

Fatima : the mother of Prince Camaralzaman [*Arabian Nights*].

—— a holy Chinese woman who lived in seclusion and healed the sick. A magician won her secrets from her, murdered her, and then dressing up to represent her, got access to Aladdin, who, divining his trick, slew him [*Arabian Nights*].

—— the last of all Bluebeard's wives, who was saved by the timely arrival of her brothers at Bluebeard's castle [Perrault, *Contes de Fées*].

Faulconbridge, Philip : a natural son of Richard I, of generous temper, but hating all 'foreigners' [Shakespeare, *King John*].

Faulkland : the morbid, worrying lover of Julia Melville [Sheridan, *Rivals*].

Fauntleroy, Lord : a little child, born in America, who, coming to England, charms away the melancholy and fierceness of his grandfather, to whose title he is heir [Frances H. Burnett, *Little Lord Fauntleroy*].

Faustus : a famous magician who sold his soul to the devil on condition that during twenty-four years he might enjoy himself unconditionally [Marlowe, *Tragicall History of Doctor Faustus*].

Fawnia : the heroine [Greene, *Pandosto; or, Triumph of Time*].

Fax, Mr. : 'the champion of calm reason, the indefatigable explorer of the cold clear springs of knowledge' [Peacock, *Melincourt*].

Fazio : a Florentine, condemned to death for aiding at the death of Bartoldo, a miser, whose money he stole [Milman, *Fazio*].

Featherstone, Peter : an old man, a miser, whose chief delight consisted in tormenting his would-be heirs [George Eliot, *Middlemarch*].

Featherstonhaugh : the subject of a ballad, which was palmed off, by its author, upon Sir W. Scott as mediæval [Surtees, *Death of Featherstonhaugh*].

Fedalma : the heroine, daughter of a gipsy chief and beloved by a Spanish noble [George Eliot, *Spanish Gypsy*].

Feeble, Francis : one of Sir John Falstaff's recruits, a miserable, half-starved woman's tailor [Shakespeare, *Henry IV*, pt. ii.].

Feeder, Mr. : Dr. Blimber's usher, who marries Miss Blimber and takes over the school [Dickens, *Dombey and Son*].

Feenix Cousin : an old 'buck', and the nephew of Mrs. Skewton [Dickens, *Dombey and Son*].

Feignwell, Colonel : the suitor for Anne Lovely's hand, who at last obtained the consent of all her four guardians [Mrs. Centlivre, *Bold Stroke for a Wife*].

Felician, Father : the priest and schoolmaster of Grand Pré [Longfellow, *Evangeline*].

Felix : the monk who for a hundred years listened to the song of a milk-white bird [Longfellow, *Golden Legend*].

—— **Don :** a Portuguese nobleman who loved Violante [Mrs. Centlivre, *The Wonder*].

—— **Holt :** see Holt, Felix.

Fell, Alice : the motive of a ballad [Wordsworth, *Alice Fell; or, Poverty*].

Feltham, Black : a highwayman [Scott, *Fortunes of Nigel*].

Fenella : a girl who, that she may be a more effectual spy, pretends to be deaf and dumb. She is the daughter of Edward Christian [Scott, *Peveril of the Peak*].

Fenellan, Dartrey : the chivalrous friend of the Radnors, who marries Nesta Victoria.

Fenellan, Simeon : a wit. The friend of Victor Radnor and brother of Dartrey Fenellan [George Meredith, *One of Our Conquerors*].

Fenton : suitor of ' sweet Anne Page ' [Shakespeare, *Merry Wives of Windsor*].

Feramorz : the name assumed by the Cashmere prince when he disguises himself as a minstrel [Thomas Moore, *Lalla Rookh*].

Ferda : son of Damman and friend of Cathullin, general of the Irish army under Cormac I [Ossian, *Fingal*, ii.].

Ferdinand : a Spaniard in love with Leonora [Jephson, *Two Strings to Your Bow*].

———— the son of Alonso, King of Naples, who is in love with Miranda [Shakespeare, *Tempest*].

———— King of Navarre [Shakespeare, *Love's Labour's Lost*].

———— Count of Calabria, brother of the Duchess [Webster, *Duchess of Malfi*].

———— Don : in love with Clara, the daughter of Don Guzman [Sheridan, *Duenna*].

Fern, Will : a kindly, honest man who tried to live a good life in the face of heavy odds [Dickens, *Chimes*].

Fernando : a Venetian Captain in the service of Annophel [Beaumont and Fletcher, *Laws of Candy*].

———— married to Isoline, and on the night of their marriage slain in the massacre of the Sicilian Vespers [Knowles, *John of Procida*].

———— a man who is persuaded that he has experienced death, burial, and the torments of purgatory [Southerne, *Fatal Marriage*].

Fernandyne : the original character from which that of Jacques was drawn [Shakespeare, *As You Like It*].

Ferragus : the giant who protected Bellisant after her separation from Alexander, Emperor of Constantinople [*Valentine and Orson*].

Ferrar, Nicholas : founder of a religious society in Little Gidding [Shorthouse, *John Inglesant*].

Farrardo Gonzaga : a villain who tried to raise up strife between Leonardo, Duke of Mantua, and his wife Mariana [Knowles, *The Wife*].

Ferrars, Edward : lover, and afterwards husband, of Elinor Dashwood.

———— *Robert :* an empty-headed coxcomb, the brother of Edward Ferrars [Jane Austen, *Sense and Sensibility*].

Ferraugh, Sir : he who carried off the lady of snow and wax, the false Florimel, from Braggadoccio [Spenser, *Faëry Quëene*].

Ferret : a backbiter and slanderer [Cherry, *Soldier's Daughter*].

—— Lovel's most efficient, quick-witted servant [Ben Jonson, *New Inn*].

—— a morose, surly, silent man [Smollett, *Sir Launcelot Greaves*].

Ferrex : *see* Gorboduc.

Ferroll, Paul : in love with Elinor Ladylift. He is parted from her through the machinations of Laura Chanson, whom he marries. On discovering her duplicity he murders her [Mrs. Archer Clive, *Why Paul Ferroll Killed his Wife*].

Ferumbras, Sir : *see* Fierabras.

Feste : Olivia's Jester, gifted with a fine voice, a fertile wit, and a great love of money [Shakespeare, *Twelfth Night*].

Festus : meant for the presentment of a soul ' gifted ', ' beguiled ', ' stricken ', and ' purified ' [Bailey, *Festus*].

—— the friend of Paracelsus, before he started on his quest [R. Browning, *Paracelsus*].

Fetnab : the favourite of Haroun-al-Raschid [*Arabian Nights*].

Feverel, Richard : son of Sir Austin ; he casts his father's theories aside and marries Lucy Desborough. However, he again falls under their influence, and leaves his wife for a time, with bitter consequences.

—— *Sir Austin :* the father of Richard Feverel. He tries to bring him up on a ' system ' with disastrous results [George Meredith, *Ordeal of Richard Feverel*].

Fezon : daughter of the Duke of Aquitaine, she whom the Green Knight desired to marry ; but Orson overthrew the Green Knight and married Fezon himself [*Valentine and Orson*].

Fidele : the name under which Imogen set out on her journey to Milford Haven [Shakespeare, *Cymbeline*].

Fidelia : the heroine of a story published in Nos. 77, 78 and 79 of the Adventurer in 1753 [Hester Chapone, *Fidelia*].

—— her real name was Harriet Raymond ; she was motherless, and the woman to whose care he was committed sold her to one Villiard, and informed her father of her death. In the end the treachery was revealed and Harriet married to Sir Charles Belmont [Edward Moore, *Foundling*].

—— in love with Manly, whom she follows in the disguise of a boy [Wycherley, *Plain Lealer*].

Fidessa : the companion of Sansfoy, the ' faithless Saracen '. Fidessa was really Duessa, the daughter of Falsehood and Shame [Spenser, *Faëry Queene*].

Fido : the personification of Faith [Phineas Fletcher, *Purple Island*].

Fielding, Mary : engaged to Edward Plummer, whom, after many crosses in their love, she marries.

—— *Mrs. :* the mother of Mary, a peevish woman, much set upon her own dignity [Dickens, *Cricket on the Hearth*].

Fierabras, Sir : a Saracen who slew the giant who guarded the thirty-arched bridge of Mantible.

Fifine : the gipsy who attracts Don Juan [Browning, *Fifine at the Fair*].

Figaro : the lover of Susan, the Countess Almaviva's waiting woman [Holcroft, *Follies of a Day*].

Filch : a very skilful pickpocket, whom Mrs. Peachum declares will ' be a great man in history ' if he is not hung first [Gay, *Beggar's Opera*].

Filer : a ' lean and hungry ' man, devoted to statistics [Dickens, *Chimes*].

Fillan : the son of Fingal and Clatho, the most artistically drawn character in the poem [Ossian, *Temora*].

Fillpot, Toby : he ' among jolly topers bore off the bell ' [Fawkes, *Toby Fillpot*].

Filomena, Santa : intended for Florence Nightingale [Longfellow, *Santa Filomena*].

Finching, Mrs. Flora : a wealthy widow of middle age, too voluble, but good-hearted [Dickens, *Little Dorrit*].

Findlayson, C. E. : a plucky engineer [Kipling, *Bridge Builders*].

Fingal : the son of Comhal ; he was King of Morven, on the North-West Coast of Scotland. His soldiers were called *Feni*, and it is after them the *Fenians* were named [Ossian, *Fingal*].

Finney, Mr. : the attorney who acted for John Bold in his crusade against vested interests in Barchester [Anthony Trollope, *The Warden*].

Fion : a stupendous giant celebrated in Gaelic song.

Fionnuala : daughter of Lir, who was changed into a swan, which haunted the lakes and rivers of Ireland [Thomas Moore, *Irish Melodies : Song of Fionnuala*].

Fips : old Martin Chuzzlewit's agent, who engages Tom Pinch as librarian [Dickens, *Martin Chuzzlewit*].

Firouz Schah : son and heir of the King of Persia, who owned a magic horse which would carry him anywhere instantaneously [*Arabian Nights*].

Fisk : intended for Nicholas Fisk [Butler, *Hudibras*].

Fitzborn : supposed to be intended for Sir Robert Peel [Beaconsfield, *Vivian Grey*].

Fitz-both : Robert, Earl of Huntingdon, in love with Marian, the heroine [Peacock, *Maid Marian*].

Fitzdottrel : selfish, cunning, conceited, from a simple Norfolk squire he changes into an impostor [Ben Jonson, *Devil is an Ass*].

Fitz-Fulke, The Duchess of : a 'graceful, graceless grace' [Byron, *Don Juan*].

Fitzpatrick, Mrs. : one of the characters in the novel [Fielding, *Tom Jones*].

Fitzurse, Lord Waldemar : one of Prince John of Anjou's suite [Scott, *Ivanhoe*].

Fladdock, General : an American much devoted to titles. [Dickens, *Martin Chuzzlewit*].

Flagon, Moll : a low camp follower. The part being unfit for a woman to play Liston used to take it [Burgoyne, *Lord of the Manor*].

Fiamberge : the sword taken from Anthenor, the Saracen, by Maugis [*Romance of Maugis d'Aygremont et de Vivian son Frère*].

Flamborough, Solomon : a neighbour of the Primrose family—a farmer.

———— *The Misses* : Solomon's daughters—honest, homely girls [Goldsmith, *Vicar of Wakefield*].

Flammer, The Hon. Mr. Frisk : a young Cantab of small means and large requirements [Selby, *Unfinished Gentleman*].

Flammock, Rose : daughter of Wilkin. She waited on Lady Eveline.

———— *Wilkin* : a soldier at the Castle of Garde Douloureuse [Scott, *Betrothed*].

Flanders, Moll : of great beauty, but of blemished reputation [Defoe, *Fortunes of Moll Flanders*].

Flash, Captain : a coward, and a boaster [Garrick, *Miss in Her Teens*].

———— **Sir Petronel** : an adventurer who wishes to leave the city for the wilds of Virginia [Chapman, Marston and Jonson, *Eastward Ho !*].

Flaw : one of the Cozeners [Foote, *Cozeners*].

Flaxman, Hugh : a liberal-minded young aristocrat who ultimately marries Rose Leyburn [Mrs. Humphrey Warde, *Robert Elsmere*].

Fleance : the son of Banquo. He escaped to Wales and there married a Welsh princess, and from them were descended the royal House of Stuart [Shakespeare, *Macbeth*].

Fledgeby, Mr. : a foolish young dandy, nicknamed ' Fascination Fledgeby' by his friends [Dickens, *Our Mutual Friend*].

Fleecebumpkin : Mr. Ireby's bailiff [Scott, *Two Drovers*].

Fleeceem, Mrs. : intended for a Mrs. Rudd, who was a woman of evil reputation [Foote, *Cozeners*].

Fleetwood : the hero of the novel [Godwin, *Fleetwood ; or, New Man of Feeling*].

—— **Earl of :** a wealthy and pampered young nobleman, who, in a moment of impulse, engages himself to Carinthia Kirby. He marries her, then deserts her. When he afterwards tries to win her back he fails, and so becomes a monk [George Meredith, *Amazing Marriage*].

Fleming, Agnes : the mother of Oliver Twist [Dickens, *Oliver Twist*].

—— **Archdeacon :** the clergyman to whom Meg Murdochson confessed [Scott, *Heart of Midlothian*].

—— **Dahlia :** the pretty daughter of a Kentish farmer. She goes to London on a visit to her uncle, Anthony Hackbut, and gets led away by Edward Blancore. She is rescued by her sister.

—— *Farmer :* the stern but really tender-hearted father of Rhoda and Dahlia Fleming.

—— *Rhoda :* the sister of Dahlia. A simple, strong-hearted girl. She eventually marries Robert Armstrong [George Meredith, *Rhoda Fleming*].

—— **Lady Mary :** Maid of Honour to Mary Queen of Scots [Scott, *The Abbot*].

—— **Sir Malcolm :** at one time a suitor for the hand of Lady Margaret de Hautlieu [*Castle Dangerous*].

—— **Rose :** generally known as Rose Maylie, *q.v.*

—— **Paul :** in this narrative poem the hero, being disconsolate through the death of a friend, wanders from country to country for years, until he at last finds comfort in some words he sees graven on a tablet in a tiny chapel [Longfellow, *Hyperion*].

Flibbertigibbet : the fiend that ' squints the eye and makes the hare-lip ', etc., etc. [Shakespeare, *King Lear*].

—— the grandson of Gammer Sludge. He acts the part of imp in the entertainment at Kenilworth [Scott, *Kenilworth*].

Flimnap : the Premier of Lilliput [Swift, *Voyage to Lilliput*].

Flint, Lord : Minister of State to an Indian Sultan [Mrs. Inchbald, *Such Things Are*].

—— **Sir Clement :** an old bachelor, who, whilst professing disbelief in human nature, finds his own happiness in doing kindly acts [Burgoyne, *The Heiress*].

Flint, Solomon : a rich old miser, a 'fusty, shabby, money-loving, water-drinking, mirth-marring, amorous old hunk' [Foote, *Maid of Bath*].

Flintwinch, Affery : an old servant of Mrs. Clennam's who married Jeremiah Flintwinch.

———— *Jeremiah :* first Mrs. Clennam's servant, later her partner [Dickens, *Little Dorrit*].

Flip : a drunken commodore [Charles Shadwell, *Fair Quaker of Deal*].

Flippant, Lady : a widow on the look-out for a second husband [Wycherley, *Love in a Wood*].

Flippanta : a maidservant of Clarissa's, who aids and abets her in her follies [Vanbrugh, *Confederacy*].

———— **and Lissardo :** two servants—one a maid in love, the other a man, puffed up with vanity [Mrs. Centlivre, *The Wonder*].

Flite, Miss : a little half-crazed woman who haunts the Court of Chancery [Dickens, *Bleak House*].

Flockheart, Widow : the landlady of the rooms in the Canongate where the Baron of Bradwardine, Waverley and M'Ivor dine [Scott, *Waverley*].

Flora : Donna Violante's maid [Mrs. Centlivre, *The Wonder*].

———— niece of Farmer Freehold. Her beauty attracts Heartwell, and she marries him [Kemble, *Farm-House*].

Florac, The Comte de : an impecunious but light-hearted Frenchman [Thackeray, *The Newcomes*].

Floranthe, Donna : the lady to whom Octavian loses his heart [Colman the Younger, *Octavian*].

Florentius or Florent : a knight who promises to wed an old hag on condition that she tells him the answer to a riddle, on the solution of which his life depends [Gower, *Confessio Amantis*].

Floreski, Count : a Pole who loves and wins Lodoiska [Kemble, *Lodoiska*].

Florez : the son of Gerrard, the king of the beggars. He enters trade and become a wealthy merchant in Bruges, and marries Bertha, the supposed daughter of the Burgomaster [J. Fletcher, *Beggar's Bush*].

Florian : discovered and adopted by the Count de Valmont. Florian charms all who know him and marries Geraldine, De Valmont's ward [Dimond, *Foundling of the Forest*].

Floribel: the heroine of the tragedy [Beddoes, *Bride's Tragedy*].

Florimel : the personification of Grace and Chastity [Spenser, *Faëry Queene*].

Florinda : the heroine of the tragedy [Shiel, *Apostate*].

———— daughter of Count Julian. Violated by Roderick, Count Julian revenged the injury to his daughter by driving Roderick from the throne [Southey, *Roderick*].

Florio John : *see* Holofernes.

Florival, Mdlle. : the daughter of a French doctor. She fell in love with Major Belford [Colman the Elder, *Deuce is in Him*].

Florizel : the son of Polixenes, King of Bohemia, whc fell in love with Perdita, whom he married [Shakespeare *Winter's Tale*].

Flosky, Mr : a transcendentalist, said to have been intended for S. T. Coleridge [Peacock, *Nightmare Abbey*].

Flowerdale, Sir John : the father of the heroine, and a friend of Colonel Oldboy [Bickerstaff, *Lionel and Clarissa*].

Fluellen : a pedantic, hot-tempered Welsh captain, full of valour and very faithful [Shakespeare, *Henry V*].

Flur : the bride of Cassivelaun, with whom Caesar was in love [Alfred Tennyson, *Idylls of the King : Geraint and Enid*].

Flute : the bellows-mender who plays the part of Thisbe [Shakespeare, *Midsummer Night's Dream*].

Flutter : a silly, effeminate fop whom no one regarded [Mrs. Cowley, *Belle's Stratagem*].

—— **Sir Fopling :** this character is said to have been drawn from that of the son of a Herefordshire baronet [Etherege, *Man of Mode*].

Fly : a questionable character who had been a wandering gipsy, but afterwards earned a living as keeper of reckonings, etc., at the Inn [Ben Jonson, *New Inn*].

Fogg : *see* Dodson and Fogg.

Foible : the lady's-maid of Lady Wishfort, who married Mirabell's footman [Congreve, *Way of the World*].

Foigard, Father : an Irishman who belonged to a gang of thieves [Farquhar, *Beaux' Stratagem*].

Foker, Mr. Henry : a dashing young Cambridge undergraduate [Thackeray, *Pendennis*].

Folair, Mr. : one of Mr. Crummle's Company at the Portsmouth Theatre [Dickens, *Nicholas Nickleby*].

Foldath : general of the Belgae in the south of Ireland [Ossian, *Temora*].

Folio :=Thomas Rawlinson [Addison, *Tatler*, No. 158].

Folliott, The Rev. Dr. : a jovial old clergyman, of the muscular Christian type, and a hater of shams. A character said to have been drawn to propitiate the clergy, whom the author had ridiculed in previous works [Peacock, *Crotchet Castle*].

Follywit : a mischievous young spark who is for ever playing tricks upon his grandfather, Sir Bounteous Progress [Middleton, *A Mad World, My Masters*].

Fondlewife : a banker [Congreve, *Old Bachelor*].

Fondlove, Sir William : a sprightly old man of sixty who fancies himself to be still in his youth and who marries a widow of forty [Knowles, *Love-Chase*].

Foot-breadth : the sword of Thoralf Skolinson the Strong, of Norway.

Fopling Flutter, Sir : *see* Flutter, Sir Fopling.

Foppington, Lord : a character in Cibber, *The Careless Husband* and *Love's Last Shift* ; Vanbrugh, *The Relapse* (a sequel to them) ; Sheridan, *Trip to Scarborough*.

Ford, Master : the husband of one of the ladies with whom Falstaff is in love.

—— *Mrs. :* wife of above ; she turns the tables upon Falstaff and holds him up to ridicule [Shakespeare, *Merry Wives of Windsor*].

Foresight : a wealthy London citizen who practised astrology [Congreve, *Love for Love*].

Forester, Mr. : an admirable but despondent man with a strong trait of eccentricity in his nature. He introduces Sir Oran Hauton to Society [Peacock, *Melincourt*].

—— **Lady Jemima :** wife of Sir Philip, who discovers her husband's evil habits by means of ' the enchanted mirror.'

—— *Sir Philip :* a knight of low character. [Scott, *Aunt Margaret's Mirror*].

Forobosco : a Mountabank [J.Fletcher, *Fair Maid of the Inn*].

Fortinbras : the Prince of Norway [Shakespeare, *Hamlet*].

Fortunatus : the hero of an old Italian tale, on whom Fortune bestowed an inexhaustible purse. There are many versions of the story, and the character has come to represent good fortune, and is constantly referred to in all European literature.

Fortunio : the companion of Fidele [Munday, *Two Italian Gentlemen*].

Foscari, Francis : the Doge of Venice for thirty-five years [Byron, *Two Foscari*].

Foss, Corporal : an old soldier who, after he had left the army, continued in the service of Worthington, his old master [Colman the Younger, *Poor Gentleman*].

Fossile : supposed to have been intended for Dr. Woodward, a physician who devoted much time to antiquarian subjects [Pope, Gay and Arbuthnot, *Three Hours after Marriage*].

Foster, Anthony : the Earl of Leicester's agent at Cumnor Place [Scott, *Kenilworth*].

—— **Mr. :** ' the perfectibilian '—one of the cranks who met at Squire Headlong's [Peacock, *Headlong Hall*].

Fotheringay, Miss : *see* Costigan, Emily.

Fountain : one of Lady Heartwell's suitors [J. Fletcher, *Wit Without Money*].

Fourdelis : the personification of France [Spenser, *Faëry Queene*].

Fowler : a clever but unprincipled man, who is reformed by being gulled into thinking he is dead and suffering as a disembodied spirit for his vices [Shirley, *Witty Fair One*].

Foxchase, Sir Harry : a candidate for Parliament opposed by Colonel Promise and Lord Chase [Fielding, *Pasquin*].

Foxley, Squire Matthew : the magistrate who examined Darsie Latimer [Scott, *Redgauntlet*].

Fradubio : the wooer and winner of Duessa [Spenser, *Faëry Queene*].

Frail, Lady : really Lady Vane, a ' person of quality ', who had many adventures [Smollett, *Peregrine Pickle*].

—— **Mrs. :** a woman of bad repute, who married Tattle [Congreve, *Love for Love*].

Frampul, Lord : *see* Goodstock, The Host.

Frances : daughter of the Burgomaster of Bruges [J. Fletcher, *Beggar's Bush*].

Francesca : daughter of Menotti, the Governor of Corinth [Byron, *Siege of Corinth*].

—— the subject of a dramatic poem [Leigh Hunt, *Francesca da Rimini*].

Franceschini, Guido : the head of a noble but poor family of Arezzo who, for the sake of her money, married Pompilia, reputed daughter of Pietro and Violante, an elderly couple of obscure position. He treated her with cruelty and she fled. He pursued and killed her [R. Browning, *Ring and the Book*].

Francesco : the hero of an early novel [Greene, *Francesco's Fortunes*].

—— a character almost parallel to that of Iago in *Othello* [Massinger, *Duke of Milan*].

Franchi, Louis dei, and Fabian dei : the Corsican brothers. A translation from the French. The mysterious sympathy existing between these twins is the motive of the play [Dion Boucicault, *Corsican Brothers*].

Francis : the Confessor of Simon Glover [Scott, *Fair Maid of Perth*].

—— a monk quartered at Pamur [Scott, *Quentin Durward*].

—— a faithful and incorruptible servant [B. Thompson, *The Stranger*].

Francisco : the son of Valentine ; both loved the same girl, who chose the son [J. Fletcher, *Mons. Thomas*].

—— a musician [J. Fletcher, *The Chances*].

—— the younger brother of Valentine [J. Fletcher, *Wit Without Money*].

Frank : a girl who was desperately in love with the woman-hater, Captain Jacomo [Beaumont and Fletcher, *The Captain*].

—— **Mildmay :** *see* Mildmay, Frank.

Frankenstein : a man who tries to create a man from sundry chemicals and succeeds in creating a monster that he himself loathes [Mrs. Shelley, *Frankenstein*].

Frankford, Mr. : a man, whose wife having proved unfaithful, made her a liberal allowance and sent her from home. On her death-bed he forgave her.

—— *Mrs. :* the wife of the above [Heywood, *Woman Killed by Kindness*].

Franklin, Lady : a widow of great goodness of nature, who married Mr. Graves, a melancholy widower [Lytton, *Money*].

Frankly : one of the characters in a comedy [Cibber, *Refusal ; or, Ladies' Philosophy*].

—— **Charles :** in love with Clarinda, whom he wins [Hoadley, *Suspicious Husband*].

Franval, Madame : the mother of Marianne and opposed to her marriage with Captain St. Alme [Holcroft, *Deaf and Dumb*].

Frateretto : a fiend ; he is mentioned by Edgar [Shakespeare, *King Lear*].

Frederick : Celia's father, the usurping duke [Shakespeare, *As You Like It*].

—— the usurping King of Naples ; brother of Alphonso, the rightful king [J. Fletcher, *Wife for a Month*].

—— **Don :** a Portuguese merchant [Mrs. Centlivre, *The Wonder*].

Freehold : an old-fashioned gentleman-farmer who hates ' men of fashion '.

—— *Aura :* the daughter of the farmer, who marries Modely.

—— *Flora :* the niece of the farmer who marries Heartwell [Kemble, *Farm-House*].

Freelove, Lady : ' as mischievous as a monkey, and as cunning too ' [Colman the Elder, *Jealous Wife*].

—— **Sophia :** the daughter of Widow Warren, with whom Harry Dornton is in love [Holcroft, *Road to Ruin*].

Freeman : the friend of Manly and his lieutenant [Wycherley, *Plain Dealer*].

Freeman, Sir Charles : the friend of Aimwell, and a brother of Mrs. Sullen's [Farquhar, *Beaux' Stratagem*].

———— **Charles** : a friend of Lovel's [Townley, *High Life Below Stairs*].

Freeport, Sir Andrew : a shrewd yet perfectly honourable and upright London merchant [Addison and Steele, *Spectator*, Essays 174, 232, 549, etc.].

Friar Dominic : a comic character written in ridicule of the priesthood [Dryden, *Spanish Friar*].

———— **Laurence** : *see* Laurence, Friar.

———— **of Orders Grey** : the subject of a ballad compiled from fragments [Percy, *Reliques: a Friar of Orders Grey*.

———— **Tuck** : *see* Tuck, Friar.

Friars, The : two friars who detect each other in love intrigues [Dunbar, *The Friars of Berwick*].

Fribble : a despicable coxcomb troubled with weak nerves [Garrick, *Miss in Her Teens*].

———— a surly and conceited man ; a haberdasher by trade [Charles Shadwell, *Epsom Wells*].

Friday, Man : Robinson Crusoe's faithful coloured companion on the desert island [Defoe, *Robinson Crusoe*].

Friendly, Sir John : a simple country gentleman [Vanbrugh, *The Relapse*]. The same character under the name of Townley appears in Sheridan's adaptation of their play, *Trip to Scarborough*.

———— **Dinah** : the affianced wife of Edward Blushington, the 'Bashful Man' .

———— *Sir Thomas :* her father, a gouty old baronet [Moncrieff, *Bashful Man*].

Friscobaldo : ' a picture of a broken-hearted father with a sneer on his lips and a tear in his eye ' (Hazlitt) [Dekker, *Honest Whore*].

Fritchie, Barbara : an old old woman who at the risk of her own life defended the American flag [Whittier, *Barbara Fritchie*].

Fritz : an old gardener whose only love and sole source of conversation is flowers [Stirling, *Prisoner of State*].

Frolic, Sir Frederick : a man of good birth and good spirit, but aimless in life and given over to pleasure [Etherege, *Comical Revenge: or, Love in a Tub*].

Front de Boeuf, Reginald : *see* Boeuf, Front de.

Froth, Lady: a lady of literary proclivities and questionable morals.

———— *Lord :* her husband, most gallant and attentive in spite of his wife's shortcomings. He thought nothing was more ' unbecoming a man of quality than a laugh ' [Congreve, *Double Dealer*].

Froth, Master : a very foolish creature of no marked character [Shakespeare, *Measure for Measure*].

Frothal : son of Annir, overthrown by Fingal in single combat. Utha was his sister [Ossian, *Carric-Thura*].

Frugal, Luke : an ill-natured hypocrite ; the brother of Sir John [Massinger, *City Madam*].

Fudge, Foaming : said to be intended for a likeness of Lord Brougham [Beaconsfield, *Vivian Grey*].

—————— **Family :** a series of humorous and satirical poems in the form of letters from Phil Biddy, Bob Fudge and Phelim Connor to their friends at home [Thomas Moore, *Fudge Family in Paris*].

Fulgentio : a rising man at the Sicilian Court with a reputation for bribery [Massinger, *Maid of Honour*].

Fulmer : a shiftless, unsuccessful man.

—————— **Patty :** a swindler and scandal-monger, passing herself off as Fulmer's wife [Cumberland, *West Indian*].

Pungoso : a man distinguished for his ill-luck [Ben Jonson, *Every Man in His Humour*].

Fungus, Zachary : the principal character, played by the author himself [Foote, *The Commissary*].

Furor : the personification of Intemperate Anger [Spenser, *Faëry Queene*].

Fusbos : Minister of State to the King of Utopia, who kills Bombastes for having slain the King [Rhodes, *Bombastes Furioso*].

Gaberlunzie Man, The : the hero of a ballad ; a wandering beggar who carried a bag or gaberlunzie [ascribed to James V of Scotland, *Gaberlunzie Man*].

Gabor : he helped to rescue Count Stralenheim from the waters of the Oder instead of being his murderer, as was suspected [Byron, *Werner*].

Gabriel Lajeunnesse : *see* Lageunnesse.

Gadabout, Mrs. : one of the female characters in the play [Garrick, *Lying Valet*].

Gadsby, Captain : an officer of Hussars stationed in India [Kipling, *Story of the Gadsbys*].

Gaheris, Sir : nephew to King Arthur. Taken captive by Sir Turguine he was rescued by Sir Launcelot du Lac [Mallory, *History of Prince Arthur*].

Gaiour : the Emperor of China and father of Badoura [*Arabian Nights*].

Galahad, Sir : the purest of all King Arthur's Knights—the only one who had a full vision of the Holy Grail [Alfred Tennyson, *Idylls of the King : The Holy Grail*].

Galahalt : the son of Sir Brewnor ; a quite distinct character from Sir Galahad, though also a Knight of the Round Table [*Arthurian Cycle*].

Galantyse : the charger given to Grande Amoure by Melyzyus [Hawes, *Passe-tyme of Pleasure*].

Galapas : an enormous giant whom King Arthur slew [Mallory, *History of Prince Arthur*].

Galatea : a statue modelled by Pygmalion with which he fell in love and which became animated [Gilbert, *Pygmalion and Galatea*].

—— a lady in the suite of the princess [Beaumont and Fletcher, *Phylaster ; or, Love Lies Bleeding*].

Galathea and Phillida : two girls who dress up as men, meet one another and fail in love with one another [Lyly, *Galathea*].

Galatine : Sir Gawain's Sword [Mallory, *History of Prince Arthur*].

Galbraith, Major Duncan : an officer in the militia [Scott, *Rob Roy*].

Galoshio : a clown [J. Fletcher, *Nice Valour*].

Gamelyn : the youngest of the five sons of Sir Johan di Boundys, who was very cruelly treated by his eldest brother. He ends by becoming the king's chief ranger, and seeing his persecutor executed [Chaucer, *Canterbury Tales : The Coke's Tale of Gamelyn*].

Game Chicken, The : a low teacher of fencing, betting, etc., who gives Mr. Toots some lessons in those arts [Dickens, *Dombey and Son*].

Gammer Gurton : *see* Gurton, Gammer.

Gammon, Master : a servant of the Flemings, known as Mas' Gammon—' the slowest old man of his time'. A deliberate but trustworthy creature [George Meredith, *Rhoda Fleming*].

—— Oily : a low-class, hypocritical solicitor [Warren, *Ten Thousand a Year*].

Gamp, Sarah : a drunken sick nurse of the old type, who nurses Martin Chuzzlewit through a fever [Dickens, *Martin Chuzzlewit*].

Ganderetta : the heroine of a burlesque [Somerville, *Hobbinol*].

Ganem : the hero of a tale called ' *The Slave of Love* ' [*Arabian Nights*].

Gann, Caroline : the heroine, whom we meet again in another story from the same pen, i.e. *The Adventures of Philip* [Thackeray, *A Shabby Genteel Story*].

Garagantua : a giant who swallowed five pilgrims, staves and all, in a salad [*History of Garagantua*].

Gardiner, Mr. and Mrs. : the good and sensible aunt and uncle of the Bennets, who aid in the rescue of Lydia [Jane Austen, *Pride and Prejudice*].

Gareth : the son of Queen Bellicent. He bound himself by an oath to serve as a scullion in King Arthur's kitchen for a year and a day. He married Lynette [Alfred Tennyson, *Idylls of the King : Gareth and Lynette*].

Gargery, Joe : a blacksmith of fine nature, married to a termagant [Dickens, *Great Expectations*].

—— *Mrs. :* Joe's wife, and Pip's sister ; an ill-tempered virago [Dickens, *Great Expectations*].

Garland, Mr. : a little, fat, kindly man whose horse Kit Nubbles holds, and to whom Kit goes as servant after he leaves Little Nell.

—— *Mr. Abel :* his son, articled to Mr. Witherden, and afterwards his partner.

—— *Mrs. :* his wife, as placid and kindly as himself [Dickens, *Old Curiosity Shop*].

Garth, Caleb : a yeoman of singularly direct and truthful character.

—— *Mary :* the daughter of Caleb, who marries Fred Viney [George Eliot, *Middlemarch*].

Gartha : the sister of Prince Oswald, who does her best to stir up civil war [Davenant, *Gondibert*].

Gas, Charlatan : this character is supposed to be intended for Canning [Beaconsfield, *Vivian Grey*].

Gashford, Mr. : a detestable man, the secretary of Lord George Gordon. To satisfy his private spite he eggs the rioters on to burn Haredale's house. He ends by committing suicide [Dickens, *Barnaby Rudge*].

Gaster, Rev. Dr. : a self-satisfied and worldly cleric, whose main wish is for personal comfort. One of those visiting Squire Headlong [Peacock, *Headlong Hall*].

Gaspard : the faithful servant of Count de Valmont [Dimond, *Foundling of the Forest*].

Gaudiosa, Lady : high-minded and brave, she was the devoted wife of Pelayo [Southey, *Roderick*].

Gaul : the son of Morni and affianced to Oithona, who died before the wedding-day [Ossian, *Oithona*].

Gauntgrim : a wolf [Lytton, *Pilgr ms of the Rhine*].

Gauntlett, Emilia : the heroine [Smollett, *Peregrine Pickle*]; *see also* Emilia.

Gauvaine or Gawain : a bold but irreverent Knight of the Round Table [Alfred Tennyson, *Idylls of the King : Pelleas and Ettarre*]. This character is the subject of many other poems and romances.

Gawrey : a woman with wings which served her as clothing as well as means of progression [Paltock, *Peter Wilkins*].

Gawtrey, Stephen : a man of honest purpose but strong passions, who offends against law and society [Lytton, *Night and Morning*].

Gay, Lucien : supposed to be intended for Theodore Hook [Beaconsfield, *Coningsby*].

—— **Walter :** an honest youth in the employ of Dombey and Son, who suffers shipwreck, but survives, and marries Florence Dombey. Captain Cuttle is his great friend [Dickens, *Dombey and Son*].

Gayless : the penniless lover of Melissa [Garrick, *Lying Valet*].

Gayville, Lady Emily : sister of Lord Gayville, in love with Mr. Clifford.

—— **Lord :** betrothed to the heiress, Miss Alscrip, but loving Miss Alton, whom he ultimately marries [Burgoyne, *The Heiress*].

Gazette, Sir Gregory : an absurd man who, having no comprehension of politics, yet delights in political news [Foote, *The Knights*].

Gazingi, Miss : a member of Mr. Crummle's Company at the Portsmouth Theatre [Dickens, *Nicholas Nickleby*].

Geddes, Joshua : an elderly quaker who befriends Darsie Latimer when he is overtaken by the tide in the Solway Firth [Scott, *Redgauntlet*].

Geierstein, Anne of : daughter of Count Albert and Baroness of Arnheim, the ' Maiden of the Mist'.

—— **Count Albert :** brother of Count Arnold. He appears under various disguises, i.e. as president of the secret tribunal, as a monk, and as the black priest of St. Paul.

—— **Count Arnold :** his brother. [Scott, *Anne of Geierstein*].

Geith, George : a man full of moral courage and an unflagging devotion to duty [Mrs. Trafford (Riddell), *George Geith*].

Gelert : the favourite dog of Llewellyn that, by killing a wolf, saved his master's child.

Gellatley, Davie : a half-witted, at the same time shrewd, servant of the Baron of Bradwardine [Scott, *Waverley*].

General, Mrs. : a widow lady engaged by Mr. Dorrit to teach his daughters [Dickens, *Little Dorrit*].

Genevieve : the subject of a ballad [S. T. Coleridge, *Genevieve*].

George Barnwell : *see* Barnwell, George.

—— **Captain :** the keeper of a shooting gallery, ' a fine, bluff-looking man of a frank free bearing ', whose real name is Rouncewell [Dickens, *Bleak House*].

George-a-Greene : a boon companion of Robin Hood, a pinner of Wakefield [Greene, *History of George-a-Greene, the Pinner of Wakefield*].

Geraint, Sir : a Knight of the Round Table who proves but a sorry husband, at first, to Enid, his wife [Alfred Tennyson, *Idylls of the King : Geraint and Enid*].

Geraldin, Lord : son of the Earl of Glenallan. He marries Isabella Wardour [Scott, *Antiquary*].

Geraldine : the heroine of a 'romance of the age'. She is noble, but falling in love with a peasant poet bestows her hand on him [Elizabeth B. Browning, *Lady Geraldine's Courtship*].

——— a young man who finds, on returning from long travels, the girl he loves married to an old man, who treats him with great hospitality—a hospitality which he resolves not to abuse [Heywood, *The English Traveller*].

——— Fair : supposed to be Lady Elizabeth Fitzgerald, who married the Earl of Lincoln. Henry Howard, Earl of Surrey, addressed love sonnets to her.

——— The Lady : the 'serpent-woman' whom Christabel met in the forest [S. T. Coleridge, *Christabel*].

——— Lady : an orphan and the ward of her uncle, Count de Valmont. She marries Florian, 'the foundling', who turns out to be her uncle's son [Dimond, *Foundling of the Forest*].

Gerardine : the lover of Maria [Middleton, *Family of Love*].

Gerrard : the father of Florez, the merchant of Bruges, and himself king of the beggars. He assumes the name of Clause [J. Fletcher, *Beggar's Bush*].

——— a scented fop who assumes the rôle of a dancing-master so as to prosecute an intrigue with Hippolita under the eyes of her guardians [Wycherley, *Gentleman Dancing Master*].

Gertrude of Wyoming : the heroine, daughter of the patriarch Albert. The story relates to the destroying of the Pennsylvanian village of Wyoming by Indians [Campbell, *Gertrude of Wyoming*].

——— Queen of Denmark : the mother of Hamlet, married to his uncle [Shakespeare, *Hamlet*].

Gerundio : the hero of a Spanish romance [Isla, *Life of Friar Gerund*].

Geryoneo : a monster with three bodies, whom King Arthur slew [Spenser, *Faëry Queene*].

Giaffir : father of Zuleika. He shoots Zuleika's lover, Selim, and she dies of grief [Byron, *Bride of Abydos*].

Giant Despair : *see* Despair, Giant.

Giant Grim : *see* Grim, Giant.

—— **Slay-good :** *see* Slay-good, Giant.

Giaour, The : Leilah falls in love with him and flees from the harem of Hassan. Hassan pursues the lovers and is slain by the Giaour. On his death-bed the Giaour confesses his crime, and at his own request is buried without a name [Byron, *Giaour*].

Giauhare : was the daughter of the King of Samandal [*Arabian Nights*].

Gib : a cat [wrongly attrib. Bp. Still, *Gammer Gurton's Needle*].

Gibbet : a convict who 'left his country for his country's good' [Farquhar, *Beaux' Stratagem*].

Gibbie Galbraith, Sir : the hero of the tale [Macdonald, *Sir Gibbie*].

—— **Guse :** a half-witted boy in the service of Lady Bellenden [Scott, *Old Mortality*].

Gibby : the awkward blundering servant of Colonel Briton [Mrs. Centlivre, *The Wonder*].

Gibson, Dr. : the medical man of Hollingford.

—— **Molly :** Dr. Gibson's motherless daughter [Mrs. Gaskell, *Wives and Daughters*].

Giglio, Prince : one of the two heroes of a 'fireside pantomime' [Thackeray, *Rose and the Ring*].

Gilbert : hero of a ballad [Longfellow, *Sir Humphrey Gilbert*].

—— **Sir :** a Knight of the Round Table, whose sword and cerecloth had a wonderful healing power [Mallory, *History of Prince Arthur*].

—— **with the White Hand :** one of Robin Hood's companions mentioned in *Lyttell Geste of Robyn Hode*.

Gilderoy : a famous robber who flourished in the seventeenth century and is said to have exercised his talents upon Oliver Cromwell and Cardinal Richelieu. His feats are celebrated in a Scottish ballad.

Giles : a hard-working but rough farmer who loved Patty, 'the Maid of the Mill' [Bickerstaff, *Maid of the Mill*].

—— **Mr. :** Mrs. Maylie's butler and steward [Dickens, *Oliver Twist*].

—— the hero of the poem, which is arranged in four parts after the seasons of the year [Bloomfield, *Farmer's Boy*].

—— **Gideon :** a journeyman roper, discharged by his master, and afterwards imprisoned, under an unjust law, for hawking his own manufactures [Miller, *Gideon Giles, the Roper*].

Gilfil, The Rev. Maynard : the hero, who, only a crusty, commonplace, conscientious country parson, to outward seeming, 'had known all the deep secrets of devoted love, had struggled through its days and nights of anguish, and trembled under its unspeakable joys' [George Eliot, *Scenes of Clerical Life: Mr. Gilfil's Love-Story*].

Gilflory, Mrs. General : a widow, lively, good-natured and uncultured [Woolf, *Mighty Dollar*].

Gill, Harry : the farmer who forbade Goody Blake to carry home sticks from his land [Wordsworth, *Goody Blake and Harry Gill*].

Gills, Solomon : a ship's instrument maker, and the uncle of Walter Gay [Dickens, *Dombey and Son*].

Gilpin, John : a draper and 'train-band Captain' of 'famous London town' [Cowper, *John Gilpin*].

Gimcrack, Sir Nicholas : the hero of the comedy—a man full of scientific crotchets [Thomas Shadwell, *The Virtuoso*].

Ginevra : a young bride who in a game of hide-and-seek hid herself in an old chest, which closed with a spring. She was never found until years afterwards when the chest was sold; there lay her skeleton [Rogers, *Italy*].

—— the subject of this ballad is the same as that by Rogers [Bailey, *Ginevra*].

Ginx's Baby : a poor little gutter-child [Jenkins, *Ginx's Baby*].

Glasher, Mrs. Lydia : the woman whom Grandcourt had wronged, and who was the mother of his children [George Eliot, *Daniel Deronda*].

Glass, Mrs. : a tobacconist in London who befriended Jeanie Deans [Scott, *Heart of Midlothian*].

Glauce : Britomart's nurse [Spenser, *Faëry Queene*].

Glaucus : the chief male character in the novel [Lytton, *Last Days of Pompeii*].

Glee-Maiden : a girl called Louise, to whom the king's son makes love. After his death she throws herself over a precipice [Scott, *Fair Maid of Perth*].

Glegg, Mrs. : one of Maggie Tulliver's aunts [George Eliot, *Mill on the Floss*].

Glenallan, Lord : unsuccessful suitor for the hand of Mary Douglas [Susan E. Ferrier, *Marriage*].

Glenalvon : the heir to Lord Randolph, slain by Noval [Home, *Douglas*].

Glenarvon, Lord : = Lord Byron, in a novel where nearly all the characters are drawn from life [Lady C. Lamb, *Glenarvon*].

Glencairn, Miss Mally : Mrs. Pringle's correspondent [Galt, *Ayrshire Legatees*].

Glendinning, Sir Halbert : the Knight of Avenel, Lady Mary's husband [Scott, *The Abbot*].

Glendinnings, The : a family of modest pretentions raised to a position of eminence through pure merit [Scott, *Monastery*.]

Glendower, Owen : a highly accomplished Welsh chief, descended from King Llewellyn [Shakespeare, *Henry IV*, pt. i.].

Glenfern, The Laird of : father of Henry Douglas [Susan E. Ferrier, *Marriage*].

Glenroy, Chief of : a proud, prejudiced and irascible Highland chieftain wrapped up in a son and nephew to the exclusion of his daughter [Susan E. Ferrier, *Destiny*].

Glenthorn, Lord : the personification of *Ennui*, the natural result of over-indulgence [Maria Edgeworth, *Ennui*].

Glenvarloch, Lord : *see* Olifaunt, Nigel.

Glibun, Avery : the hero of the story [R. H. Newell (Orpheus C. Kerr), *Avery Glibun ; or, Between Two Fires*].

Gloriana : 'the greatest, glorious queen of Faëry-land,'. She sends her knights out on their various missions and represents Queen Elizabeth in the allegory [Spenser, *Faëry Queene*].

Glossin, Gilbert : an unrighteous lawyer [Scott, *Guy Mannering*].

Glover, Catherine : the heroine, who has many admirers but gives her hand to Henry Smith, the armourer.

—— *Simon :* father of Catherine [Scott, *Fair Maid of Perth*].

Glowry, Mr. : the father of Scythrop and owner of Nightmare Abbey [Peacock, *Nightmare Abbey*].

—— *Scythrop :* son of above, a misanthrope, in love with Marionetta O'Carroll and Celinda Toobad at the same time. Supposed to be intended for P. B. Shelley [Peacock, *Nightmare Abbey*].

Glumdalca : in a burlesque ; she is queen of the giants and in love with Tom Thumb [Fielding, *Tom Thumb the Great*].

Glumdalclitch : a girl of nine who is forty feet high. Gulliver was commited to her care during his visit to Brobdingnag [Swift, *Gulliver's Travels*].

Glycine : a character in the tale [S. T. Coleridge, *Zapolya*].

Gnotho : an old man who wants to avail himself of 'The Old Law' in order to exchange an old wife for a young one [Massinger, Middleton and Rowley, *Old Law*].

Gobble, Justice : an insolent magistrate [Smollet, *Sir Launcelot Greaves*].

Gobbo, Launcelot : the boy who forsakes Shylock's service for Bassanio's.

———— *Old :* Launcelot's father, an old, blind man [Shakespeare, *Merchant of Venice*].

Gobilvve, Godfrey : the assumed name of False Report—a hideous dwarf [Hawes, *Passe-tyme of Pleasure*].

Godfrey, Sir Edmondbury : a magistrate who actively denounced the plots of the papists and was, in revenge, slain by them [Scott, *Peveril of the Peak*].

———— **Miss :** the daughter and heiress of an Indian official [Foote, *The Liar*].

Godiva, Lady : wife of Leofric, Earl of Mercia. She undertook to ride naked through the town if her husband would remit a tax which weighed heavily on the people. She actually did as she had promised, first ordering that all doors and windows should be closed and none look out. All obeyed her except one, who was ever after known as 'Peeping Tom'.

Godmer : a British giant whom Canutus slew [Spenser, *Faëry Queene*].

Godolphin : the hero [Lytton, *Godolphin*].

Gold Hair : a story about a young girl of Pornic who was buried near the high altar in the church. Years afterwards, when the pavement was removed, thirty double louis were discovered to have been buried in her hair [R. Browning, *Gold Hair*].

Goldfinch, Charles : a common, low man who carries on a flirtation with Widow Warren and plots with her to destroy her husband's will [Holcroft, *Road to Ruin*].

Goldiebirds, Messrs. : the firm to whom Sir Arthur Wardour owes money [Scott, *Antiquary*].

Goliath : the second character in the poem [Drayton, *David and Goliath*].

Golightly, Mr. : the would-be borrower [J. M. Morton, *Lend Me Five Shillings*].

Goltho : loved Birtha, the daughter of Astragan, but Birtha loved Gondibert [Davenant, *Gondibert*].

Gomaz : a rich old banker married to a young wife, who amuses herself with one Lorenzo, who proves to be her own brother [Dryden, *Spanish Friar*].

Gondibert, Duke : in a faction fight limited to two representatives on either side, Gondibert slew Oswald, and his own wounds were healed by Astragon, to whose daughter, Birtha, he is affianced [Davenant, *Gondibert*].

Goneril : eldest daughter of King Lear and wife of the Duke of Albany [Shakespeare, *King Lear*].

Gonzalo : counsellor to the King of Naples [Shakespeare, *Tempest*].

—————— a Venetian nobleman [J. Fletcher, *Laws of Candy*].

Goodchild, Charlotte : a wealthy orphan with many suitors ; of these only one remains faithful upon hearing that her fortune is lost, and that is Sir Callaghan O'Brallaghan [Macklin, *Love à-la-Mode*].

Goodenough, Dr. : a physician [Thackeray, *Adventure of Philip*].

Goodfellow, Robin : a knavish sprite, the son of Oberon, King of the Fairies, often called ' Puck '.

Goodlucke, Gawin : one of the characters in the play [Udall, *Ralph Roister Doister*].

Goodstock, The Host : assumes the position of a gentleman, and pretends to be the landlord of the *Light Heart* Inn at Barnet [Ben Jonson, *New Inn*].

Goodwill : a tradesman who had amassed a fortune. He had one only child, his daughter Lucy.

—————— *Lucy :* a girl of sixteen, whose father tries to force her into a family marriage so as to keep his money in the family. She declines and marries Thomas, a footman [Fielding, *The Virgin Unmasked*].

Goody, Blake : *see* Gill, Harry.

Gorboduc : a mythical British king, father of Ferrex and Porrex. On this tradition our first historical play was based [Morton and Buckhurst. *The Tragedy of Gorboduc*].

Gorbrias : the father of King Arbaces [Beaumont and Fletcher, *King or No King*].

Gordon, Lord George : the leader of the ' no Popery ' riots at the close of the eighteenth century [Dickens, *Barnaby Rudge*].

Gorlois : lord of Tintagel, and husband of Igrayne ; he is the traditionary father of King Arthur [Alfred Tennyson, *Idylls of the King : Coming of Arthur*].

Gosling, Giles : landlord of the *Black Bear* at Cumnor [Scott, *Kenilworth*].

Goswin : a wealthy merchant of Bruges, a son of Gerrard, king of the beggars. Betrothed to Bertha, not knowing her to be the daughter of the Duke of Brabant [J. Fletcher, *Beggar's Bush*].

Gotham, The Men of : the heroes of an attempt to foil King John in a plan to pass through Gotham, whereby the villagers would have been put to great expense [*Merry Tales of the Men of Gotham*].

Gottlieb : a poor farmer with whom Prince Henry of Hoheneck lived when he became a leper. Elsie his daughter, it was, who offered her life for the Prince [Longfellow, *Golden Legend*].

Gourlay, Ailsie : one of the sibyls present at Alice Gray's death [Scott, *Bride of Lammermoor*].

Gow, Henry : otherwise Henry Smith, the armourer who married Catherine Glover [Scott, *Fair Maid of Perth*].

Gowan, Henry : an artist, who marries Miss Minnie Meagles

—— **Mrs. :** his mother, a stately old lady [Dickens, *Little Dorrit*].

Gowkthrapple, Maister : a Covenanting preacher and 'chosen vessel' [Scott, *Waverley*].

Gracchus, Caius : the hero of the tragedy [Knowles, *Caius Gracchus*].

Grace, Lady : sister of Lady Townly, and engaged to Manly, an unpretending, home-loving woman [Vanbrugh and Cibber, *Provoked Husband*].

Gradgrind, Mr. Thomas : a retired hardware merchant devoted to 'facts and calculations'.

—— **Mrs. :** his wife, a nervous, peevish invalid.

—— **Louisa :** his eldest daughter, married to Josiah Bounderby, and devoted to Tom.

—— **Tom :** his son, a sullen, self-indulgent young man, who ends by robbing a bank and trying to throw suspicion on another [Dickens, *Hard Times*].

Graeme, Adam : the hero of a Scottish story [Mrs. Oliphant, *Adam Graeme of Mossgray*].

—— **Magdalene :** the grandmother of Roland.

—— **Roland :** the heir of the Avenels, and page to Mary, Queen of Scots [Scott, *The Abbot*].

Graham, Mary : the companion of old Martin Chuzzlewit, and betrothed to the younger Martin [Dickens, *Martin Chuzzlewit*].

Grahame, Colonel John : afterwards Viscount Dundee, serving in the Duke of Monmouth's army.

—— **Cornet Richard :** his nephew [Scott, *Old Mortality*].

—— **Sir :** see Eger, Sir.

—— **The :** the hero of an heroic poem [Blacklock, *The Grahame*].

Grandamour : the hero of an allegorical romance [Hawes, *Passe-tyme of Pleasure*].

Grandcourt, Henleigh : the man who marries Gwendolen Harleth, the heroine [George Eliot, *Daniel Deronda*].

Grandison, Sir Charles : intended for an ideal English gentleman. The original of the character is supposed to have been Robert Nelson, author of '*The Whole Duty of Man*' [Richardson, *Sir Charles Grandison*].

Graneangowl, Rev. Mr. : Sir Duncan Campbell's chaplain at Ardenvohr Castle [Scott, *Legend of Montrose*].

Granger : one of the characters in the comedies [Southern, *Maid's Last Prayer*; and Cibber, *The Refusal*].

Granger, Edith : *see* Dombey, Edith.

—— **Captain :** loves Elizabeth Doiley, an old trades-man's daughter, whose father wishes her to marry a scholar [Mrs. Cowley, *Who's the Dupe ?*].

Grantam, Miss : the friend of Miss Godfrey, and herself engaged to Sir James Elliot [Foote, *The Liar*].

Grantly, Bishop : Bishop of Barchester, 'a bland and kind old man, opposed by every feeling to authoritative demonstration and episcopal ostentation'. The warm friend of Mr. Harding. Father of the Archdeacon [Anthony Trollope, *The Warden*].

—— **The Rev. Dr. Theophilus :** Archdeacon of Bar-chester, a stern and inflexible pillar of the church, possessed of 'all the dignity of an ancient Saint with the sleekness of a modern Bishop'.

—— **Mrs. :** who had been Susan Harding. The arch-deacon's wife, and the only person to whom he ever un bent [Anthony Trollope, *The Warden*].

Grantmesnil, Sir Hugh de : one of the challengers at the tournament [Scott, *Ivanhoe*].

Grantorto : the personification of Rebellion [Spenser, *Faëry Queene*].

Gratiano : a friend of Antonio and Bassanio [Shakespeare, *Merchant of Venice*].

—— the brother of Brabantio [Shakespeare, *Othello*].

Granville, Juliet : the heroine ; married to a man she despises, from whom she runs away, and who pursues her relentlessly until his death [Fanny Burney, *The Wanderer*].

Graveairs, Lady : a lady of doubtful character [Cibber, *Careless Husband*].

—— the hero [Cooper, *The Pilot*].

Gray, Auld Robin : a ballad [Lady Anne Barnard, *Auld Robin Gray*].

—— **Duncan :** wooed Maggie, but she turned him a deaf ear, so off he went ; then she fell sick and was like to die, so Duncan came back to her [Burns, *Duncan Gray*].

—— **Dr. Gideon :** the Middlemas Surgeon.

—— *Menie :* his daughter, who had a narrow escape from spending her life in the harem of Toppoo Saib. Rescued by Hyder Ali, she returned to her own country [Scott, *Surgeon's Daughter*].

—— **Lucy :** a little child ; the subject of a ballad [Words-worth, *Lucy Gray ; or, Solitude*].

—— **Mary :** *see* Bell, Bessie.

—— **Nelly :** the title of a humorous poem [Thomas Hood, *Faithless Nelly Gray*].

Gray, Old Alice : a tenant on the Ravenswood estate [Scott, *Bride of Lammermoor*].

—— **Robin :** was the name of a herdsman in the service of Lord Balcarras [Lady Anne Barnard, *Auld Robin Gray*].

—— **Rosamond :** the heroine of a 'miniature romance' replete with grace and fine feeling and quite unique of its kind [Lamb, *Rosamond Gray and Blind old Margaret*].

Gray-Steel, Sir : *see* Eger, Sir.

Greatheart, Mr. : Christiana's trusty guide when she and her children set out for the Celestial City [Bunyan, *Pilgrim's Progress*, pt. ii.].

Greaves, Sir Launcelot : a young English squire of high ideals and fine character, who sets forth to right the wrong and uphold the good ; an English Don Quixote [Smollett, *Adventures of Sir Launcelot Greaves*].

Greedy, Justice : a 'lean and hungry' man, who could be bribed to give any verdict for the sake of a good meal [Massinger, *New Way to pay Old Debts*].

Green, George à- : *see* George à-Green.

—— **Mr. and Mrs. Paddington :** a clerk of Somerset House, and his wife [J. M. Morton, *If I had a Thousand a Year*].

—— **Knight, The :** overthrown by Gareth at the entrance to Castle Perilous [Mallory, *History of Prince Arthur*].

—— **Verdant :** an Oxford undergraduate, the object of many practical jokes [Cuthbert Bede (Rev. E. Bradley) *Verdant Green*].

—— **Widow :** a wealthy widow of forty. She had first married for money, but the second time 'to please her vanity' [Knowles, *Love-Chase*].

Greenhorn, Mr. Gilbert : an attorney, Mr. Gabriel Grinderson's partner.

Gregory : a faggot-maker, who began his education in a charity school, and then improved it whilst acting as servant to an Oxford undergraduate. The play is an adaptation from Molière [Fielding, *Mock Doctor*].

Gregsbury, Mr. : the M.P. to whom Nicholas applies for a situation as secretary [Dickens, *Nicholas Nickleby*].

Gremio : one of Bianca's suitors [Shakespeare, *Taming of the Shrew*].

Grendel : half monster, half man, he haunted marshy places. Beowulf went forth at the head of a band of warriors and slew him [*Beowulf*].

Grenville, Sir Richard : he commanded the *Revenge* 'at Flores in the Azores '—one ship against fifty-three

[Alfred Tennyson, *The Revenge*]. The same hero is commemorated in Charles Kingsley's *Westward Ho!*

Gresham, Beatrice : one of the characters in the novel [Anthony Trollope, *Doctor Thorne*].

Grewgious, Hiram, Esquire : 'a particularly angular man ; Miss Rosa Bud's guardian [Dickens, *Edwin Drood*].

Grey, Agnes : the heroine of the novel [Anne Brontë, *Agnes Grey*].

———— **Elliot :** the central character in the play [Wallack. *Rosedale*].

———— **Henry :** the Provost of St. Anselm's ; a philosopher. The teacher and inspirer of Robert Elsmere [Mrs. Humphry Ward, *Robert Elsmere*].

———— **Lady Jane :** this unfortunate Queen has been made the subject of several tragedies, amongst others one by Nicholas Rowe, Ross Neil, and Alfred Tennyson.

———— **Mr. and Mrs. :** a provincial corn and timber merchant and his wife. Worldly people but dissenters, and given to picking holes in their neighbours [Harriet Martineau, *Deerbrook*].

———— **Valentine de :** in love with Hero Sutton, whom he marries [Knowles, *Women's Wit ; or, Love's Disguises*].

———— **Vivian :** this character is said to have been intended by the author for a portrait of himself [Beaconsfield, *Vivian Grey*].

Gride, Arthur : an old miser, who wished to marry Madeline Bray, who refused him [Dickens, *Nicholas Nickleby*].

Gridley, Mr : 'the man from Shropshire' ruined by a suit in Chancery [Dickens, *Bleak House*].

Griflet, Sir : knighted by King Arthur at Merlin's request [Mallory, *History of Prince Arthur*].

Grim, Giant : slain by Greatheart for stopping pilgrims on their way to the Celestial City [Bunyan, *Pilgrim's Progress*].

———— the hero of a curious old comedy, writer unknown [J.T., *Grim the Collier of Croydon*].

Grime : a usurer, the partner of Item [Holcroft, *Deserted Daughter*].

Grimes, Peter : a drunken thief and a murderer [Crabbe, *The Borough*].

Grimwig, Mr. : Mr. Brownlow's testy old friend, who was always offering to 'eat his head' [Dickens, *Oliver Twist*].

Grinder, Mr. : a showman [Dickens, *Old Curiosity Shop*].

Grinderson, Mr. Gabriel : an attorney, the partner of Mr. Greenhorn [Scott, *Antiquary*].

Grip : Barnaby Rudge' raven [Dickens *Barnaby Rudge*].

Gripe : one of the characters taken from Molière's play, *Les Fourberies de Scapin*. In the French play Gripe is called Géronte [Otway, *Cheats of Scapin*].

―――― a close-fisted scrivener, married to Clarissa. He entertained too strong a regard for his friend Moneytrap's wife [Vanbrugh, *Confederacy*].

―――― an old usurer [Wycherley, *Love in a Wood*].

―――― **Sir Francis :** the elderly guardian and admirer of Miranda, an heiress, but she prefers Sir George Airy, a younger man [Mrs. Centlivre, *Busy Body*].

Grippy, Leddy : the heroine [Galt, *Entail*].

Griselda, Patient : a type of wifely devotion and patient submission. The daughter of a charcoal-burner, she becomes the wife of a marquis [Chaucer, *Canterbury Tales : The Clerk's Tale*].

Griskinessa : wife of Artaxminous, King of Utopia [Rhodes, *Bombastes Furioso*].

Grizzle, Lord : the first peer of the realm at King Arthur's Court, and in love with the Princess Huncamunca [Fielding, *Tom Thumb*].

Groffin, Thomas : one of the jury in the case of Bardell *v.* Pickwick [Dickens, *Pickwick Papers*].

Groom, Squire : a gentleman-jockey who, having wasted his substance on horses and dogs, etc., strives to retrieve his financial position by marriage [Macklin, *Love à-la-Mode*].

Groveby, Sir Harry : the nephew of old Groveby of Gloomstock Hall, and engaged to Maria [Burgoyne, *Maid of the Oaks*].

Grovelgrub, Dr. : one of the characters in the novel [Peacock, *Melincourt*].

Grove, Jem : landlord of the *Valiant Soldier Inn* [Dickens, *Old Curiosity Shop*].

Grub, Emily : the handsome daughter of Jonathan, who marries Captain Bevil of the Guards.

―――― *Jonathan :* a wealthy stock-broker.

―――― *Mrs. :* his wife, who would fain forget sordid things and figure as a woman of fashion. [Wm. O'Brien, *Cross Purposes*].

―――― **Gabriel :** the hero of the story of ' the Goblins who stole a Sexton ' [Dickens, *Pickwick Papers*].

Grudden, Mrs. : a general *factotum* attached to the Portsmouth Theatre Company [Dickens, *Nicholas Nickleby*].

Grueby, John : the servant of Lord George Gordon [Dickens, *Barnaby Rudge*].

Grumio : one of Petrucchio's servants [Shakespeare, *Taming of the Shrew*].

Grundy, Mrs. : the person of whom Mrs. Ashfield, the farmer's wife, stood in awe, always wondering what she would say [J. M. Morton, *Speed the Plough*].

Gryll, Morgana : the charming niece of Squire Gryll. She marries Mr. Falconer [Peacock, *Gryll Grange*].

Gualberto, St. : the heir of Valdespesa, who was trained to believe in the avenging of blood, but one day, whilst lying in wait for Anselmo, the wickedness of the belief struck him, and throwing aside his dagger he entered a convent [Southey, *St. Gualberto*].

Gubbins, Margery : the girl who was loved by Moore of Moore Hall [Carey, *Dragon of Wantley*].

Guendolen : a fairy, of human parentage, with whom King Arthur fell in love. He deserting her she attempt d to destroy him by poison [Scott, *Bridal of Triermain*].

Guenever, cr, Guinever : daughter of King Leodegrance of Camelyard. She married King Arthur but was not true to him [Mallory, *History of Prince Arthur*].

Guenevra : the wife of the dwarf Nectabanus [Scott, *Talisman*].

Guest, Stephen : Maggie Tulliver's lover [George Eliot, *Mill on the Floss*].

Guiderius : the elder son of Cymbeline, kidnapped as an infant by Belarius [Shakespeare, *Cymbeline*].

Guildenstern : one of Hamlet's friends, who tries to turn his thoughts into a happier channel [Shakespeare, *Hamlet*].

Guinevere : King Arthur's Queen, who loves Sir Launcelot and breaks her faith with the King [Alfred Tennyson, *Idylls of the King : Guinevere*].

Guisla : the sister of Pelayo and in love with Numacian, a renegade [Southey, *Roderick*].

Guizor : the bridge-ward of Pollente's estate, bound to let no man pass without paying 'the passage-penny'. He was slain by Sir Artegel [Spenser, *Faëry Queene*].

Gulbeyaz : the Sultana, who causes Juan to be introduced into the harem dressed up as a woman [Byron, *Don Juan*].

Gulchenrous : son of Ali Hassan the 'most lovely youth in the world' [Beckford, *Vathek*].

Gulliver, Lemuel : first a surgeon, then a sea-captain, who visits Lilliput, Brobdingnag, Laputa and Houyhnhnms [Swift, *Gulliver's Travels*].

Gulnare : wife of the Sultan, who aids the Corsair in his escape from prison and follows him disguised as a page [Byron, *Corsair*].

Gumbo : the coloured servant who came with Harry Warrington to England [Thackeray, *Virginians*].

Gummidge, Mrs.: 'a lovelorn creeture'; the widow of Peggotty's partner [Dickens, *David Copperfield*].

Guppy, William: clerk in the firm of Kenge & Carboy [Dickens, *Bleak House*].

Gurney, Gilbert: the hero. The novel is mainly auto-biographical [Theodore Hook, *Gilbert Gurney*].

Gurth: a swineherd and a thrall of Cedric's [Scott, *Ivanhoe*].

—— the most devoted of King Harold's brothers [Lytton, *Harold*].

Gurton, Gammer: the heroine of an old comedy. Whilst mending her man Hodge's breeches she loses her needle, and upon its discovery the fun of the piece turns [wrongly attrib. Bishop Still, *Gammer Gurton's Needle*].

Guse, Gibbie: *see* Gibbie, Guse.

Guster: maid-of-all-work to the Snagsbys. Overworked and given to fits [Dickens, *Bleak House*].

Guthrie, John: an archer in Louis XI's Scottish Guard [Scott, *Quentin Durward*].

Guy Mannering: *see* Mannering, Guy.

—— Sir, Earl of Warwick: an English knight who performed many feats of valour and has been the hero of song and romance for many generations. Chaucer and Drayton mention him.

Guyon, Sir: personifies Temperance [Spenser, *Faëry Queene*].

Gwendolen Harleth: *see* Harleth, Gwendolen.

Gwenhidwy: a mermaid [Alfred Tennyson, *Idylls of the King: The Holy Grail*].

Gwynn, Miss: governess at the Westgate House Establishment for Young Ladies [Dickens, *Pickwick Papers*].

Gyneth: daughter of King Arthur, who married De Vaux upon awakening from a trance that had lasted 500 years [Scott, *Bridal of Triermain*].

Gyp: Blushington's college servant, who helped himself freely to Blushington's goods [Moncrieff, *Bashful Man*].

Hackburn, Simon of: Hobbie Elliot's friend [Scott, *Black Dwarf*].

Hackbut, Anthony: the brother-in-law of Farmer Fleming. Thought to be wealthy, he is in fact only the messenger of a bank. In a fit of madness he steals money [George Meredith, *Rhoda Fleming*].

Hackum, Captain: an inhabitant of Alsatia (a low Thames-side quarter of London), and a bully [Thomas Shadwell, *Squire of Alsatia*].

Hadgi, Abdallah el: the Soldan's envoy [Scott, *Talisman*].

Hadwin, Mrs.: Mr. Frank Wentworth's landlady [Mrs. Oliphant, *Chronicles of Carlingford: Perpetual Curate*].

Hafed : the leader of a band of patriots resolved to liberate their country, or die in the attempt [Thomas Moore, *Lalla Rookh*].

Haiatalnefous : daughter of King Armanos ; one of Prince Camaralzaman's two wives [*Arabian Nights*].

Haidee : 'the beauty of the Cyclades', the daughter of a Greek pirate. She loved Don Juan [Byron, *Don Juan*].

Hajji Baba : *see* Baba, Hajji.

Hakeem, or, **Hakem :** the chief of the Druses [R. Browning, *Return of the Druses*].

Hakim, Adonbec el : the Saladin, who, assuming the disguise of a physician, goes to his enemy, Coeur de Lion, to cure him [Scott, *Talisman*].

Halcro, Claud : the bard of Magnus Troil [Scott, *Pirate*].

Hales, The Rev. Struan : a fox-hunting parson, the uncle of Alice. He took for his motto, 'Ride on, ride on' [Blackmore, *Alice Lorraine*].

Halifax, John : a boy whose sole inheritance was a book with the inscription in it, 'John Halifax, gentleman', showing that his ancestry was good, and this inspired him to struggle up from sheer poverty to a position of affluence [Dinah Muloch, *John Halifax, Gentleman*].

Halkett, Cecilia : an heiress, between whom and Nevil Beauchamp there is great friendship. She eventually marries a very steady, ordinary Englishman [George Meredith, *Beauchamp's Career*].

Hall, Father : an intriguing priest [Shorthouse, *John Inglesant*].

—— **The Rev. Cyril :** Vicar of Nunnely, 'near-sighted, spectacled, . . . abstracted. To old ladies he was kind as a son. To men of every occupation and grade he was acceptable' [Charlotte Brontë, *Shirley*].

Haller, Mrs. : she deserted her husband, Count Waldbourg, for years, but by the instrumentality of friends, and the sight of their children, they were reconciled [B. Thompson, *The Stranger*].

Hamako : a madman [Scott, *Talisman*].

Hamartia : the personification of Sin [Phineas Fletcher, *Purple Island*].

Hamet : the son of a Chinese Mandarin [Murphy, *Orphan of China*].

—— a black slave of Sir Brian de Bois Guilbert [Scott, *Ivanhoe*].

Hamlet : essentially a man of thought, called upon by circumstances to be a man of action [Shakespeare *Hamlet*].

Hamley, Osborne : elder son of Squire Hamley, secretly married to a French girl.

—— *Roger :* second son of Squire Hamley, who marries Molly Gibson [Mrs. Gaskell, *Wives and Daughters*].

Hammerlein, Claus : one of the Liége insurgents, a smith [Scott, *Quentin Durward*].

Hamond : stabs the Duke of Normandy, and is himself stabbed by Rollo [J. Fletcher, *Bloody Brother*].

Handford, Julius : *see* Harmon, John.

Handy, Abel : a discontented pensioner of Hiram's Hospital [Anthony Trollope, *The Warden*].

—— **Lady Nelly :** wife of Sir Abel, raised from the position of a domestic servant. Extravagant and overbearing.

—— *Robert :* son of Sir Abel, by his first wife, married to Farmer Ashfield's daughter Susan.

—— *Sir Abel :* an inventor always behind the age in his inventions [J. M. Morton, *Speed the Plough*].

—— **Andy :** the hero of a novel [Lover, *Handy Andy*].

Hannah : the heroine [Mrs. Inchbald, *Nature and Art*].

Hannibal and Scipio : the subjects of a tragedy acted in 1635 [Nabbes, *Hannibal and Scipio*].

Hanno : a slave [Dr. J. Moore, *Zeluco*].

Hans : in love with Esther, and in the end marrying her [Knowles, *Maid of Mariendorpt*].

Happer : the miller who serves St. Mary's Convent.

—— *Mysie :* his daughter, who gets up as a page and in that guise serves Sir Piercie Shapton [Scott, *Monastery*].

Happuck : brother of the enchantress Ulin, and the intending assassin of the Sultan. His intentions being detected he is himself killed [Ridley, *Tales of the Genii*].

Happy Old Couple : *see* Darby and Joan.

Harapha : a descendant of Anak, who went to mock at Samson in prison, but whose courage failed him [Milton, *Samson Agonistes*].

Harcourt : a character in the play [Wycherley, *Country Wife*].

Hardcastle, Miss Kate : a pretty girl who assumes the rôle of chambermaid so as to ' conquer ' the shyness of young Marlow.

—— *Mr. :* Tony Lumpkin's step-father, and father of Kate, who ' stoops ' to win young Marlow.

—— *Mrs. :* his wife, the mother of Tony Lumpkin, a foolish, fond and vain old woman [Goldsmith, *She Stoops to Conquer*].

Harding, Eleanor : the heroine, who marries John Bold.

—— *The Rev. Septimus :* her father, sometime Minor

Canon of Barchester, afterwards Precentor of the
Cathedral, and Warden of Hirem's Hospital. The
hero, who upon conscientious grounds resigns a lucra-
tive post [Anthony Trollope, *The Warden*].

Hardy, Letitia : betrothed to Dorincourt, whose affection
she secures by a ' stratagem '.

―――― *Mr. :* father of Letitia, a rather foolish though
meritorious man [Mrs. Cowley, *Belle's Stratagem*].

Hardy-dardy : the jester in a curious old miracle play
[*Godly Queen Hester*].

Haredale, Emma : Geoffrey's niece and ward, her father
having been murdered. She loves Edward Chester.

―――― *Mr. Geoffrey :* a papist, and the uncle of Emma.
He killed Sir John Chester in a duel, and, escaping,
took refuge in a monastery.

―――― *Reuben :* the murdered father of Emma [Dickens,
Barnaby Rudge].

Hargrave : a man of fashion, and the hero of the story
[Mrs. Trollope, *Hargrave*].

Harkaway, Grace : an heiress [Dion Boucicault, *London
Assurance*].

Harleth, Gwendolen : the heroine ; she marries Grandcourt [George Eliot, *Daniel Deronda*].

Harley : a man of great sensibility and genuine goodness,
but too retiring to give his noble sentiments effect
[Mackenzie, *Man of Feeling*].

―――― *Adrian :* known as the ' Wise Youth '. A relation
of the Feverels, with whom he lives. Though existing
mainly for pleasure, he is cunning enough to do so under
a cloak of great respectability [George Meredith,
Ordeal of Richard Feverel].

Harlow, Miss : the heroine of a farce, aged forty-two
[Murphy, *Old Maid*].

Harlowe, Clarissa : has been described as ' the sweetest
martyr in fiction ' [Richardson, *Clarissa Harlowe*].

Harmachis : directly descended from the Pharaohs, and
a model of manly strength [Haggard, *Cleopatra*].

Harmon, John : he sometimes took the name of Handford,
sometimes Rokesmith. Heir to the Harmon estates, he
is attacked, thrown into the Thames, and supposed to
be dead. Eventually he regains his own [Dickens,
Our Mutual Friend].

Harmony, Mr. : a universal peace-maker [Mrs. Inchbald,
Every One has his Fault].

Harold : the central figure of this historical romance
[Lytton, *Harold*].

―――― the last Saxon King, is the hero of this drama
[Alfred Tennyson, *Harold*].

Harold, Childe : supposed to be autobiographical, but this Lord Byron denied. It is the picture of a man sated with the world, who roams from place to place seeking distraction [Byron, *Childe Harold's Pilgrimage*].

—— **the Dauntless :** son of Witikind the Dane, 'rocked on a buckler and fed from a blade' [Scott, *Harold the Dauntless*].

Haroun al Raschid : Sultan of the Saracen Empire and hero of many eastern tales [*Arabian Nights*].

Harpalus : the hero of an old pastoral; the lover of Phillada [in *Songs and Sonnets*].

—— probably intended for the Earl of Dorset [Spenser, *Colin Clout's Come Home Again*].

Harpier, or Harper : a familiar spirit referred to in the mediaeval demonology.

Harriet : daughter of Sir David and Lady Dunder. She loved Scruple, and to avoid marriage with Lord Snolts arranges an elopement [Colman the Younger, *Ways and Means*].

Harrington : the hero of the novel [Maria Edgeworth, *Harrington*].

—— **Evan :** the son of a country tailor, with all the instincts of a gentleman. After many remarkable episodes, he finally marries Rose Jocelyn, the rich daughter of a county family.

—— **Mrs. Melchisedec :** the mother of Evan Harrington. Her husband was a kind of gentleman-tailor, but she sternly sets herself to prevent Evan following in his father's steps [George Meredith, *Evan Harrington*].

Harris, Mr. : a showman, better known as 'Short' or 'Trotters' [Dickens, *Old Curiosity Shop*].

—— **Mrs. :** the often-quoted but purely imaginary friend of Sarah Gamp [Dickens, *Martin Chuzzlewit*].

Harrison, Dr. : a wise philanthropist [Fielding, *Amelia*].

Harrowby, Dame : wife of John.

—— *John :* a Kentish farmer, tactless but very kind-hearted.

—— *Mary :* daughter of John.

—— *Stephen :* his son, who suffers from warlike enthusiasm [Colman the Younger, *Poor Gentleman*].

Harry, Blind : the blind friend of Henry Smith, the armourer; a minstrel [Scott, *Fair Maid of Perth*].

—— **Sir :** the servant of a baronet, who tries to assume the airs and habits of his master [*High Life Below Stairs*].

Harthouse : tries to persuade Louisa, the wife of Bounderby, to elope with him, but fails [Dickens, *Hard Times*].

Hartley, Adam : apprenticed to Dr. Gray, and in love with Menie, his daughter. He goes to India and rises rapidly in his profession [Scott, *Surgeon's Daughter*].

———— **Mike :** an Antinomian weaver who attempts to shoot Robert Moore [Charlotte Brontë, *Shirley*].

Hartwell, Lady : a widow with many admirers [J. Fletcher, *Wit Without Money*].

Hassan : owner of the seraglio in which was Leila who loved the Giaour, who slays Hassan [Byron, *Giaour*].

———— **Abu :** hero of the tale, ' *The Sleeper Awakened* ', the son of a Bagdad Merchant [*Arabian Nights*].

———— **Al :** an Arabian Emir of Persia, and father of Hinda [Thomas Moore, *Lalla Rookh*].

———— **Al Habbal :** became fabulously rich through his wife finding a huge diamond in a fish that he caught [*Arabian Nights*].

Hastie, Robin : a smuggling inn-keeper [Scott, *Redgauntlet*].

Hastings : the friend of young Harlow, who elopes with Miss Neville [Goldsmith, *She Stoops to Conquer*].

Haswell : a benevolent physician who devoted himself to work in Indian prisons [Mrs. Inchbald, *Such Things Are*].

Hatchway, Lieutenant : a retired naval officer who lived with Commodore T-union [Smollett, *Peregrine Pickle*].

Hatteraick, Dirk : half smuggler, half pirate, and wholly a villain [Scott, *Guy Mannering*].

Haut-ton, Sir Oran : a tame monkey prepared by the hero for entrance into Parliament [Peacock, *Melincourt*].

Hautlieu, Lady Margaret de : disguised as Sister Ursula and betrothed to Sir Malcolm Fleming [*Castle Dangerous*].

Havelok the Dane : son of Birkabegn, King of Denmark, and reared by a fisherman, who rescued him from the sea. Through various adventures he succeeds to his father's throne [*Havelok the Dane*].

Havisham, Estella : Miss Havisham's adopted child, who married Bentley Drummle.

———— *Miss :* a very eccentric old maid, the daughter of a wealthy brewer [Dickens, *Great Expectations*].

Hawdon, Captain : father of the girl known as Esther Summerson.

———— *Esther :* known best as Esther Summerson, the daughter of Hawdon and Lady Dedlock. She is a ward in Chancery and marries Allan Woodcourt [Dickens, *Bleak House*].

Hawk, Sir Mulberry : an unprincipled knave and gambler who had a marked talent for ruining young men [Dickens, *Nicholas Nickleby*].

Hawkeye : the name given to Natty Bumpo, the Deer-slayer, by the Red Indians [Cooper, *Deerslayer*].

Hawthorn : a universal favourite who found his own happiness in doing good to others [Bickerstaff, *Love in a Village*].

——— **Jerry :** a rustic, the co-hero with Corinthian Tom [Pierce Egan, *Life in London*].

Hayston, Frank : the laird of Bucklaw, to whom Sir Wm. Ashton promised Lucy, and to whom he was married, only to be assassinated on his bridal night [Scott, *Bride of Lammermoor*].

Hazeldean, Squire : ' a bluff old English squire ' [Lytton, *My Novel*].

——— **Jock o' :** the hero of an old ballad modernized by Sir Walter Scott.

Hazelwood Charles : son of Sir Robert, who marries Lucy Bertram.

——— *Sir Robert :* an old baronet [Scott, *Guy Mannering*].

Headlong, Caprioletta : the Squire's sister, who acted as hostess to his guests.

——— *Squire Harry :* a Welsh squire who gathers round him, at his ancestral home, a large number of eccentric people [Peacock, *Headlong Hall*].

Headrigg, Cuddie : a ploughman who saves himself from an ignominious death by astuteness, when under examination [Scott, *Old Mortality*].

Headstone, Bradley : a schoolmaster who loves Lizzie Hexam, and dies in a hand-to-hand fight with Rider-hood [Dickens, *Our Mutual Friend*].

Heartall, Frank : falls in love with a widow, whom he marries.

——— *Governor :* a peppery but simple-minded old bache-lor, Frank's uncle [Cherry, *Soldier's Daughter*].

Heartfree, Jack : a railer against women ; nevertheless he falls in love [Vanbrugh, *Provoked Wife*].

Heartwell : falls in love with Flora Freehold, whom he marries [Kemble, *Farm-House*].

Heathcliff : an example of how ill-usage in youth may utterly warp an otherwise respectable character [Emily Brontë, *Wuthering Heights*].

Heathen Chinee, The : the hero of a humorous poem [Bret Harte, *Heathen Chinee*].

Heatherblutter, John : gamekeeper to the Baron of Brad-wardine [Scott, *Waverley*].

Heathfield, Alfred : a young medical student engaged to Marion Jeddler [Dickens, *Battle of Life*].

Hector de Mares : a brother of Sir Launcelot du Lac, and a Knight of the Round Table [*Arthurian Cycle*].

Hector of the Mist : an outlaw killed by Allan M'Aulay [Scott, *Legend of Montrose*].

Hedon : a self-indulgent, voluptuous courtier [Ben Jonson, *Cynthia's Revels*].

Heeltap, Crispin : a cobbler [Foote, *Mayor of Garratt*].

Heep, Mrs. : the mother of Uriah, and very like him.

—— *Uriah :* an oily, detestable hypocrite, who always pretends to be 'umble' [Dickens, *David Copperfield*].

Heidelberg, Mrs. : a vulgar, rich woman, the widow of a Dutch merchant, keeping house for her brother, Mr. Sterling [Colman and Garrick, *Clandestine Marriage*].

Helbeck, Alan : a Roman Catholic landowner, in love with Laura [Mrs. Humphry Ward, *Helbeck of Bannisdale*].

Helen : the heroine of the novel [Maria Edgeworth, *Helen*].

—— beloved by Modus [Knowles, *Hunchback*].

—— Burd : *see* Burd, Helen.

—— **Lady :** loved Sir Edward Mortimer, who, in avenging an insult, murdered her uncle. He confessed his crime to her and died [Colman the Younger, *Iron Chest*].

—— **of Kirconnell :** the heroine of a Scottish ballad, of which many versions have been printed.

—— **Queen of Corinth :** in love with Amphialus [Sidney, *Arcadia*].

Helena : an Athenian woman in love with Demetrius [Shakespeare, *Midsummer Night's Dream*].

—— the daughter of Gerard de Narbon. She loved Bertram, who scorned her love, and after marrying her at once left her to go to the wars. She won him to her in the end [Shakespeare, *All's Well that Ends Well*].

Helinore, Dame : wife of Malbecco ; she eloped with Sir Paridel [Spenser, *Faëry Queene*].

Hellebore : the president of a Medical College ; a part played by the author himself [Foote, *Devil Upon Two Sticks*].

Hellicanus : minister of Pericles, who left him to govern in his own absence from Tyre. The Crown was offered to Hellicanus, but he remained true to Pericles [Shakespeare, *Pericles, Prince of Tyre*].

Helstone, Caroline : a fatherless girl, brought up by her uncle, the Rector. She marries her cousin, Robert Moore [Charlotte Brontë, *Shirley*]

—— *the Rev. Matthewson :* Rector of Briarfield. A brave, conscientious, fiery old man, but unsympathetic, with a poor opinion of women in general, and a violent Tory. Generally called a 'clerical cossack' [Charlotte Brontë, *Shirley*].

Hempskirke : serving as captain in the army of the usurping Earl of Flanders [J. Fletcher, *Beggar's Bush*].

Henri, Mdlle. : first pupil, then wife of the 'Professor, [Charlotte Brontë, *The Professor*].

Henrique, Don : the reputed husband of Violante, and father of Ascanio [Beaumont and Fletcher, *Spanish Curate*].

Henry : a soldier who deserts on hearing that his affianced bride is about to marry another. Condemned to death he is reprieved through the efforts of his beloved [Thomas Dibdin, *The Deserter*].

—— nephew to Sir Philip Blandford, who had attempted the life of Henry's father for the sake of winning Henry's mother to wife [J. M. Morton, *Speed the Plough*].

—— **and Emma :** the characters in a poem modelled on the ballad of the *Nut Brown Maid* [Prior. *Henry and Emma*].

—— **Poor :** the leper prince, for whose sake Elsie offers to forfeit her life [Longfellow, *Golden Legend*].

Henslowe : Squire Wendover's low-minded agent [Mrs. Humphry Ward, *Robert Elsmere*].

Hepar : the personification of the Liver [Phineas Fletcher, *Purple Island*].

Heraud, Sir: a character in the romance [*Sir Guy of Warwick*].

Hercules : the hero of a play adapted from the Greek of Seneca [Jasper Heywood, *Hercules Furens*].

—— the subject of a moral poem [Shenstone, *Judgment of Hercules*].

—— **Oetaeus :** a play written in the Alexandrine measure and adapted from the Greek of Seneca [Studley, *Hercules Oetaeus*].

Hereward : one of the Varangian Guard of the Emperor of Greece [Scott, *Count Robert of Paris*].

—— **the Wake :** the 'last of the English,' who for long held out against William of Normandy [Charles Kingsley, *Hereward the Wake*].

Herman : the deaf and dumb jailer of the Giant's Mount dungeon [Stirling, *Prisoner of State*].

Hermegyld : a convert to Christianity through the teaching of Constance. She had the power of restoring sight to the blind [Chaucer, *Canterbury Tales : Man of Law's Tale*].

Hermegild : a friend of Oswald's and in love with Oswald's sister, Gartha [Davenant, *Gondibert*].

Hermesind : the daughter of Pelayo and Gaudiosa, betrothed to Alphonso [Southey, *Roderick*].

Hermia : daughter of Egeus and betrothed to Demetrius, though she marries Lysander [Shakespeare, *Midsummer Night's Dream*].

Hermion : wife of Damon, the Pythagorean [Banim and Shiel, *Damon and Pythias*].

Hermione : wife of Damon and Pythias [Banim and Shiel, *Damon and Pythias*].

—— daughter of Meneläos, King of Sparta. Loved by Orestes but loving Pyrrhus. She died by her own hand [Philips, *Distressed Mother*].

—— privately married to Lord Dalgarno [Scott, *Fortunes of Nigel*].

—— wrongly suspected of infidelity by her husband Leontes, she is parted from him for sixteen years, and then restored to him as a living statue [Shakespeare, *Winter's Tale*].

Hermit, The : *see* Edwin and Angelina.

—— **The :** the hero of a book written in imitation of Robinson Crusoe, of which the authorship is not known [*The Hermit; or, Unparalleled Adventures of Philip Quarll*].

Hermite, Tristan l', or, Tristan of the Hospital : Provost-marshal of France [Scott, *Quentin Durward* ; also, *Anne of Geierstein*].

Hermstrong : the hero of the tale, which is a sequel to one entitled *Man as He Is* [Bage, *Man as He Is Not*].

Hero : daughter of the Governor of Messina. A quiet, serious girl on the eve of her marriage to Claudio denounced as unfaithful to him. Her innocence is proved and the marriage proceeds [Shakespeare, *Much Ado About Nothing*].

—— **and Leander :** a long narrative poem in six sestiads [Marlowe and Chapman, *Hero and Leander*].

Herries, Lord : a friend and supporter of Mary, Queen of Scots [Scott, *The Abbot*].

Hesketh, Helen : the heroine [Lockhart, *Reginald Dalton*].

—— **Ralph :** landlord of the ale-house where the fight takes place between Robin Oig and Harry Wakefield [Scott, *Two Drovers*].

Hesperus, Sir : known as the Green Knight, *q.v.*

Hester : the subject of this poem was a Miss Savory, a quakeress [Lamb, *Hester*].

Hetty Sorrel : *see* Sorrel, Hetty.

Hew : *see* Hugh of Lincoln.

Hexham, Charley : son of Jesse, a pupil of Headstone's. Selfish and cold.

—— *Jesse :* a 'waterside character', whose chief occupation is the recovering of dead bodies from the Thames. Generally called ' Gaffer '.

—— *Lizzie :* daughter of Jesse. She rescues Eugene Wrayburn from a watery grave, and marries him [Dickens, *Our Mutual Friend*].

Heyling, George : a prisoner for debt in the Marshalsea, and hero of ' The Old Man's Tale about a Queer Client' [Dickens, *Pickwick Papers*].

Hiawatha : a Red Indian, the prophet and teacher of his tribe [Longfellow, *Hiawatha*].

Hickathrift, Thomas or Jack : a poor labourer who killed a huge giant with an axletree and cartwheel ; the hero of a popular old English story.

Hick Scorner : the hero derives his name from his inveterate habit of scoffing at religion. He is the chief character in an old Morality play [printed by Wynkyn de Worde, *Hick Scorner*].

Hieronimo : the leading character in the drama, which is very bombastic in style [Kyd, *Hieronimo*].

Higden, Mrs. Betty : an old woman who kept a ' minding-school' and a mangle, in a back street of Brentford, and loathed the idea of a workhouse more than death [Dickens, *Our Mutual Friend*].

Highland Mary : the original of this song was a servant in the family of a Mr. Hamilton [Burns, *Highland Mary*].

Hilda : an artist and a native of New England [Nathaniel Hawthorne, *Marble Faun*].

Hillary, Tom : afterwards Captain Hillary. He was apprenticed to the Town Clerk, Mr. Lawford [Scott, *Surgeon's Daughter*].

Hinchcliffe, Henry Salt : an engine room artificer full of resource and courage [Kipling, *Their Lawful Occasions*].

Hinchup, Dame : a peasant present at the execution of Meg Murdochson [Scott, *Heart of Midlothian*].

Holmes, Sherlock : a marvellous detective and unraveller of plots [Conan Doyle, *Adventures of Sherlock Holmes*].

Hinda : daughter of the Emir of Persia and beloved by Hafed [Thomas Moore, *Lalla Rookh*].

Hint, Betty : the prying servant of the Mac Sycophants [Macklin, *Man of the World*].

Hippolita : the bride of Theseus [J. Fletcher, *Two Noble Kinsmen*].

———— the leading female character in the comedy, with whom the dancing master carries on an intrigue [Wycherley, *Gentleman Dancing Master*].

Hippolyta : a wealthy woman who entertains a dishonourable passion for Arnoldo [J. Fletcher, *Custom of the Country*].

———— betrothed to Theseus, Duke of Athens [Shakespeare, *Midsummer Night's Dream*].

Hippolytus : the hero of a play adapted from the Greek of Seneca [Studley, *Hippolytus*].

Hiren : the heroine, but of doubtful character [Peele, *Turkish Mahomet and Hyren, the Fair Greek*].

Hobbididance : one of the five fiends that possessed 'poor Tom' [Shakespeare, *King Lear*].

Hobbinol : intended for Gabriel Harvey, a physician and old college friend of the author's [Spenser, *Shepheards' Calendar*].

Hocus, Humphry : the attorney who acted for John Bull against Lewis Baboon. Intended for the Duke of Marlborough [Arbuthnot, *History of John Bull*].

Hodeirah : the husband of Zeinab and father of Thalaba [Southey, *Thalaba*].

Hodge : Gammer Gurton's husband, whose garments she was mending when she lost her needle [attrib. wrongly to Bishop Still, *Gammer Gurton's Needle*].

Hoel : the son of King Hoel, kidnapped by Ocellopan, an Aztec, and confined in a cave [Southey, *Madoc*].

Hoffmann : the hero of a most gory tragedy [Chettle, *Hoffmann ; or, Revenge for a Father*].

Hohensteil-Schwangau, Prince : the hero of this poem tries to describe the events of his reign as they appear in his own eyes or measured by the generally accepted rules of conduct [R. Browning, *Prince Hohensteil-Schwangau*].

Holdenough, Nehemiah : a Presbyterian preacher [Scott, *Woodstock*].

Holdfast, Aminadab : a friend of Simon Pure [Mrs. Centlivre, *Bold Stroke for a Wife*].

Holgrave, Mr. : the daguerreotypist who persuades Hepzibah Pyncheon to let him live in one of the gables of the old house. His real name is Maule, and his family the hereditary foes of the Pyncheons [Nathaniel Hawthorne, *House of the Seven Gables*].

Hollingsworth : one of the characters in the story—the only one with any pretentions to being a man of action [Nathaniel Hawthorne, *Blithedale Romance*].

Holofernes : a schoolmaster. The name is said to be an anagram on J'h'nes Floreo or John Florio, the philologist and lexicographer [Shakespeare, *Love's Labour's Lost*].

Holt, Felix : the champion of the working men, and the hero [George Eliot, *Felix Holt, the Radical*].

Homespun, Cicely : Zekiel's sister, who marries Dick Dowlas.

—— *Zekiel :* turned out of his farm, he seeks his fortune in London, and wins a lot of money in a lottery [Colman the Younger, *Heir at Law*].

Honeycomb, Will : a great authority on the fashions, and, ' where women are not concerned, an honest and worthy man ' [Steele, *Spectator*, Essay 77, 359, 499, 511, 530, etc.].

Honeycombe, Mr. : a self-willed old gentleman that tries to force his daughter's wishes by locking her into her room.

—— *Mrs. :* a foolish half-tipsy old woman, his wife.

—— *Polly :* their daughter, with her head stuffed with romance [Colman the Elder, *Polly Honeycombe*].

Honeyman, Charles : a worldly, unprincipled clergyman [Thackeray, *The Newcomes*].

Honeythunder, Mr. Luke : the guardian of Neville and Helena Landless ; a large man with a big voice [Dickens, *Edwin Drood*].

Honeywood : the hero, who eventually marries Miss Richland, when he has learnt to ' reserve his pity for real distress, and his friendship for true merit '.

—— *Sir William :* his uncle, a high-minded gentleman [Goldsmith, *Good-natured Man*].

—— **Patty : the girl** whom Verdant Green loves [Cuthbert Bede (Rev. Edward Bradley), *Verdant Green*].

Honora : daughter of General Archas and sister of Viola [Beaumont and Fletcher, *Loyal Subject*].

Honoria : beloved by Theodore of Ravenna though she hated him [Dryden, *Theodore and Honoria*].

Honour, Mrs. : Sophia Western's waiting-woman [Fielding, *Tom Jones*].

Hood, Robin : a famous outlaw whose favourite haunt was Sherwood Forest, Nottinghamshire. He has for centuries been a favourite subject for English ballads and romances.

Hope, Edward : the Deerbrook doctor who upholds his political views at the expense of local persecution [Harriet Martineau, *Deerbrook*].

—— **Evelyn :** a young girl of sixteen on whom a middle-aged man fixes his affections [R. Browning, *Dramatic Lyrics : Evelyn Hope*].

Hopeful : Christian's companion after Faithful's death [Bunyan, *The Pilgrim's Progress*].

Hopkins, Jack : a medical student and friend of Bob Sawyer's [Dickens, *Pickwick Papers*].

Horace de Brienne : engaged to Diana de Lascours, but marries her sister Ogarita [Stirling, *Orphan of the Frozen Sea*].

Horatia : daughter of the ' Roman Father ', and slain by her brother Publius [Whitehead, *Roman Father*].

Horatio : the friend of Lord Allamont, who discovers

Lothario's treachery to him. Allamont fights Lothario and kills him [Rowe, *Fair Penitent*].

Horatio: Hamlet's one true and faithful friend and counsellor [Shakespeare, *Hamlet*].

—— the hero of the novel [Horace Smith, *Horatio; or, Memoirs of the Davenport Family*].

Horatius Cocles: the man who 'held the Bridge, in the brave days of old', against the hosts of Tarquin [Macaulay, *Lays of Ancient Rome: Horatius*].

Horn, King: the hero of a metrical romance, dating back, according to Bishop Percy, to the twelfth century.

Hortense, Mademoiselle: intended for a portrait of Mrs. Manning, the murderess [Dickens, *Bleak House*].

Hortensio: a very valiant and chivalrous man [Massinger, *Bashful Lover*].

—— suitor for Bianca [Shakespeare, *Taming of the Shrew*].

Houseman: a character in the novel [Lytton, *Eugene Aram*].

Hounslow: one of the gang of thieves who arranged to rob Lady Bountiful [Farquhar, *Beaux' Stratagem*].

Houssain, Prince: the owner of a magic carpet, that he had only to sit upon in order to be transported wherever he wished [*Arabian Nights*].

Howe, Miss: Clarissa's friend and adviser [Richardson, *Clarissa Harlowe*].

Howie, Jamie: Malcolm Bradwardine's baillie [Scott, *Waverley*].

Howlaglass, Master: a preacher, and the friend of Maul-statue [Scott, *Peveril of the Peak*].

Howleglas, Father: plays the part of the Abbot of Un-reason at the revels at Kennaquhair Abbey [Scott, *The Abbot*].

Hoyden, Miss: an ignorant, country romp [Vanbrugh, *The Relapse*], also in Sheridan's adaptation of same play, *Trip to Scarborough*].

Hrothgar: the King of Denmark delivered by Beowulf from the Monster, Grendel [*Beowulf*].

Hubble, Mr. and Mrs.: a wheelwright and his wife, very much his junior. Friends of Mrs. Joe Gargery [Dickens, *Great Expectations*].

Hubert: a brother of Prince Oswald, and wounded by Hurgonel [Davenant, *Gondibert*].

—— in love with Jaculin, the daughter of Gerrard, King of the Beggars [J. Fletcher, *Beggar's Bush*].

—— King John's chamberlain, and ordered by him to have Prince Arthur's eyes put out [Shakespeare, *King John*].

Hudibras : the hero of a satire directed against the Puritans [Butler, *Hudibras*].

———— **Sir :** a melancholy man in whom, it is thought, the author wished to portray the Puritans [Spenser, *Faëry Queene*].

Hudjadge : a Shah of Persia, to cure whose sleeplessness Moradbak told the *Oriental Tales* [Comte de Caylus, *Oriental Tales*].

Hudson, Sir Geoffrey : a dwarf, and page to Queen Henrietta Maria [Scott, *Peveril of the Peak*].

Hugh : servant at the *Maypole Inn*, Chigwell, and leader of the ' No Popery ' riots, for which he was executed [Dickens, *Barnaby Rudge*].

———— **of Lincoln :** it is asserted that the Jews of Lincoln kidnapped and crucified a little boy of eight, and then cast him into a pit. The story is constantly referred to in the literature of the Middle Ages [Chaucer, *Canterbury Tales : The Prioress's Tale ;* also Percy, *Reliques : The Jew's Daughter*].

Hugo : the natural son of the Marquis of Este [Byron, *Parisina*].

———— of diminutive height but very brave ; the brother of Arnold [Davenant, *Gondibert*].

Hughie Graham : the subject of a Scottish ballad, who was hanged for stealing a bishop's mare [*Border Minstrelsy*].

Humgudgeon, Grace-be-here : a corporal in Cromwell's army [Scott, *Woodstock*].

Humphrey Clinker : *see* Clinker, Humphrey.

———— **Master :** deformed old gentleman, very kindly, the founder of a club of which Mr. Pickwick becomes a member [Dickens, *Master Humphrey's Clock*].

Huncamunca : the daughter of King Arthur and Queen Dollallolla [Fielding, *Tom Thumb the Great*].

Hunsden, Mr. : a rough but kindly manufacturer [Charlotte Brontë, *Professor*].

Hunter, Mr. and Mrs. Leo : for ever hunting up society ' lions ' [Dickens, *Pickwick Papers*].

Huntingdon, David, Earl of : Prince royal of Scotland, who first appears as Sir Kenneth, and later as the Nubian slave, Zohauk [Scott, *Talisman*].

———— **Earl of :** a baron outlawed by King Henry II. He lives in the woods and is finally restored to his own. In spite of difficulties he married Maid Marian [Peacock, *Maid Marian*].

———— **Robert, Earl of :** generally called Robin Hood : *see* Hood, Robin.

Huon : a serf who falls in love with his pupil, Lady Catherine [Knowles, *Love*].

—— **of Bordeaux, Sir :** married Esclairmond and succeeded Oberon as King of Fairyland [*Old Romance*].

Hurgonel, Count : affianced to Orna, the sister of Gondibert [Davenant, *Gondibert*].

Hurlothrumbo : the hero of an absurd play which is a jumble of dialogues [Dr. S. Johnson, *Hurlothrumbo; or, The Supernatural*].

Hurry : the manservant at Oldworth Oaks [Burgoyne, *Maid of the Oaks*].

Hushai : intended for Hyde, Earl of Rochester [Dryden, *Absalom and Achitophel*].

Hurst, Mrs. : a married sister of Mr. Bingley's [Jane Austin, *Pride and Prejudice*].

Hutley, Jem : known as 'Dismal Jemmy', an actor and friend of Mr. Alfred Jingle [Dickens, *Pickwick Papers*].

Hyanisbe : a character supposed by some to be intended for Queen Elizabeth [Barclay, *Argenis*].

Hyde, Mr. : the second self of Dr. Jekyll [Stevenson, *Strange Case of Dr. Jekyll and Mr. Hyde*].

Hyder Ali Khan Behauder : the Nawaub of Mysore [Scott, *Surgeon's Daughter*].

Hypatia : the daughter of Theon ; very learned in mathematics and philosophy, which she taught in Alexandria. She was attacked by a band of fanatics and killed. She is the heroine of a novel [Charles Kingsley, *Hypatia*].

Hyperion : god of the son who, upon the fall of the Titans, had to make way for the new sun-god, Apollo [Keats, *Hyperion*].

—— the subject of a prose romance [Longfellow, *Hyperion*].

Hythloday, Raphael : Portuguese adventurer who discovered Utopia [Sir Thomas More, *Utopia*].

Iachimo : a treacherous Italian whose conduct brings much sorrow to Imogen [Shakespeare, *Cymbeline*].

Iago : the villain who poisons Othello's mind against Desdemona [Shakespeare, *Othello*].

Ianthe : one of the characters which the noted actress, Mrs. Betterton, used to take [Davenant, *Siege of Rhodes*].

—— one of the characters in a narrative poem [Shelley, *Queen Mab*].

Ibbotson, Hester : cousin to Mr. Grey. She marries Edward Hope, the doctor.

—— *Margaret :* her sister, who marries Philip Enderby [Harriet Martineau, *Deerbrook*].

Ida : a believer in the emancipation of women, for which purpose she founds a college [Alfred Tennyson, *The Princess*].

Idenstein : nephew of the governor of Prague and married to Adolpha [Knowles, *Maid of Mariendorpt*].

Igerna, or **Igrayne** : wife of Gorlois, Duke of Tintagil, and mother of King Arthur. Tennyson spells the name Ygerne [Alfred Tennyson, *Idylls of the King : Passing of Arthur*].

Ignaro : foster-father of Orgoglio ; he looked one way and walked another [Spenser, *Faëry Queene*].

Ilchester, Janet : the heiress of Squire Beltham, after he has disinherited Harry Richmond. A spoilt girl, who develops into a fine type of woman. She marries Harry Richmond [George Meredith, *Adventures of Harry Richmond*].

Imlac : traveller and poet, and the son of a wealthy merchant. Imlac was Rasselas's companion on his rambles [Dr. S. Johnson, *Rasselas*].

Imogen : falsely accused of infidelity to Posthumus, she, after much tribulation, establishes her innocence [Shakespeare, *Cymbeline*].

Imogine, The Fair : *see* Alonzo.

Imoinda : her father migrated to Angola, and she married Oronooko, a coloured man [Southern, *Oronooko* (a play) ; Mrs. Aphr-Behn, *Oronooko* (a novel)].

Inez, Donna : the mother of the hero [Byron, *Don Juan*].

—— **de Castro** : secretly married to Prince Pedro of Portugal, whose father, King Alfonso, compelled her to drink poison [Rose Neil, *Inez de Castro ; or, Bride of Portugal*].

' Infant Phenomenon ' : *see* Crummles, Miss Ninetta.

Ingelram, Abbot : at one time superior at St. Mary's Convent [Scott, *Monastery*].

Inglesant, John : Played an important and noble rôle in the courts of England and Italy during the English Civil War [Shorthouse, *John Inglesant*].

Inglewood, Squire : a magistrate [Scott, *Rob Roy*].

Inglis, Corporal : in the Duke of Monmouth's army [Scott, *Old Mortality*].

Ingram, Edward : the great friend of Sheila Mackenzie and Frank Lavender, through whom they came to know one another. He marries an American girl [Black, *Princess of Thule*].

Inkle, Mr. Thomas : marries an Indian girl named Yarico, whom he afterwards sells into slavery [Steele, *Spectator*, No. 11].

Interpreter, Mr.: intended to symbolize the Holy Spirit. He lives just beyond the Wicket Gate [Bunyan, *Pilgrim's Progress*].

Intrigo: a character upon which Mrs. Centlivre based hers of Marplot [Fane, *Love in the Dark*].

Iolande: the heroine [Sir Henry Taylor, *St. Clement's Eve*].

Iphigenia: the subject of a tragedy taken from the story of Iphigenia in Tauris, and acted in 1700 at Lincoln's Inn Fields [Dennis, *Iphigenia*].

—— a girl who has been brought up as a man, and whose notions of propriety are vague [Suckling, *Brennoralt*].

Ipomydon: the subject of an Early English Romance [*Life of Ipomydon*].

Iras: an attendant on the Queen of Egypt [Shakespeare, *Anthony and Cleopatra*; also Dryden, *All for Love*].

Irene: wife of the Emperor of Greece [Scott, *Talisman*].

—— daughter of the Greek renegade, Horush Barbarossa, and married to Selim [Brown, *Barbarossa*].

Irenus: the personification of Peaceableness [Phineas Fletcher, *Purple Island*].

Ironside, Sir: 'the Red Kight of the Red Lands', who kept the lady Lyonors or Lionês a prisoner in Castle Perilous [Mallory, *History of Prince Arthur*].

Ironsides, Captain: uncle of Belfield and friend of Sir Benjamin Dove [Cumberland, *Brothers*].

Irwin, Ellen: the subject of a legendary poem [Wordsworth, *Ellen Irwin; or, the Braes of Kirtle*].

—— **Lady Eleanor:** wife of Lord Norland.

—— **Mr.:** married to a daughter of Lord Norland, he robs him, but repents and returns the money [Mrs. Inchbald, *Every One has His Fault*].

Irwine, Mr.: a clergyman [George Eliot, *Adam Bede*].

Isaac Mendoza: *see* Mendoza, Isaac.

—— **of York:** a rich Jew persecuted by the followers of King John [Scott, *Ivanhoe*].

Isabell: the sister of Lady Hartwell [Beaumont and Fletcher, *Wit Without Money*].

Isabella: the heroine of a story taken from Boccaccio [Keats, *Isabella; or, The Pot of Basil*].

—— wife of Hieronimo [Kyd, *Spanish Tragedy*].

—— the mother of the Duke [Massinger, *Duke of Milan*].

—— the sister of Claudio, and in love with Angelo [Shakespeare, *Measure for Measure*].

—— a nun, who marries Biron and then marries Villeroy, believing Biron to be dead. She goes mad [Southern, *Fatal Marriage*].

—— assists Zanga in his plots against Don Alonzo [Young, *The Revenge*].

Isabella Donna : daughter of Don Pedro. To avoid a distasteful marriage she leaps from a window and marries her rescuer [Mrs. Centlivre, *The Wonder*].

—— **The Countess :** the wife of Roberto. After a life of crime, she is executed [Thomas Morton, *Wonder of Women ; or, Sophonisba*].

—— **The Lady :** a lovely girl who was, by her step-mother's orders, cut up and 'made into a meat-pie' [Percy, *Reliques : The Lady Isabella's Tragedy*].

Isabinda : the daughter of Sir Jealous Traffick. She, by a ruse, marries the man she loves instead of the one her father favours [Mrs. Centlivre, *Busy Body*].

Isenbras, Sir : a hero of mediaeval romance.

Iseult : Tristram's lady-love, though the wife of King Mark [Alfred Tennyson, *Idylls of the King : Last Tournament ;* also Matthew Arnold, *Tristram and Iseult*].

Ishbosheth : intended for Richard Cromwell, son of the Protector [Dryden, *Absalom and Achitophel*].

Ismael : the hero of an oriental tale published when the author was only fifteen [Lytton, *Ismael*].

Isolde, Isolt, Isond, Yseult, or Ysolt : *see* Iseult.

Isoline : daughter of the governor of Messina and wife of Fernando. Father and husband both died in the 'Sicilian Vespers', and Isoline died of a broken heart [Knowles, *John of Procida*].

Isumbras, Sir : the hero of an early English romance, in verse.

Item : a money-broker and a thorough villain [Holcroft, *Deserted Daughter*].

Ithocles : in love with Calantha, a Princess of Sparta [Ford, *Broken Heart*].

Ithuriel : one of the angels whose duty it was to watch over Adam and Eve at night [Milton, *Paradise Lost*].

Ivanhoe, Wilfred of : son of Cedric the Saxon ; disinherited for becoming a Crusader [Scott, *Ivanhoe*].

Ivan Ivanovitch : the subject of the poem, the scene of which is laid in Russia [R. Browning, *Dramatic Idylls : Ivan Ivanovitch*].

I'wain : the Knight of the Lion [*Arthurian Cycle*].

Jabos, Jack : postilion at the *Golden Arms*, the inn of which Mrs. M'Candlish was landlady [Scott, *Guy Mannering*].

Jachin : the parish clerk. He stole the Holy Communion money [Crabbe. *The Borough*].

Jacintha : reputed wife of Octavio [Beaumont and Fletcher, *Spanish Curate*].

Jacintha : an heiress and ward of Mr. Strickland, who elopes with Bellamy [Hoadley, *Suspicious Husband*].

Jack, Colonel : the hero [Defoe, *History of the Most Remarkable Life and Extraordinary Adventures of the truly Hon. Colonel Jacque, vulgarly called Colonel Jack*].

—— intended for John Calvin [Arbuthnot, *History of John Bull* ; also Swift, *Tale of a Tub*].

Jackman, Major Jemmy : one of Mrs. Lirriper's lodgers [Dickens, *Mrs. Lirriper's Lodgings*].

Jackson, Mr. : a clerk of Messrs. Dodson and Fogg [Dickens, *Pickwick Papers*].

Jacomo : a woman-hater, with whom Frederick's sister is in love [Beaumont and Fletcher, *The Captain*].

Jacqueline : the subject of a story told in verse [Rogers, *Jacqueline*].

Jacques : manservant to the Duke of Aranza ; the duke deputes him to personate himself [Tobin, *Honeymoon*].

Jaculin : daughter of the king of the beggars, and loved by Lord Hubert [J. Fletcher, *Beggar's Bush*].

Jacynth : the maid who slept whilst her mistress was being bewitched by a gipsy [R. Browning, *Flight of the Duchess*].

Jaffier : Belvidera's husband [Otway, *Venice Preserved*].

Jaggers, Mr. : an old Bailey advocate [Dickens, *Great Expectations*].

Jakin, Bob : the packman who is kind to Tom Tulliver [George Eliot, *Mill on the Floss*].

James, Truthful : the supposed author of the Heathen Chinee and other humorous poems [Bret Harte, *Heathen Chinee*].

Jamie, Don : the ill-treated younger brother of Don Henrique [Beaumont and Fletcher, *Spanish Curate*].

Jamieson, Bet : nurse at Dr. Gray's, the Middlemas surgeon [Scott, *Surgeon's Daughter*].

Janet : Miss Betsey Trotwood's housemaid [Dickens, *David Copperfield*].

—— **Dempster :** *see* Dempster, Janet.

Jane Eyre : *see* Eyre, Jane.

—— **Shore :** *see* Shore, Jane.

Janfaries, Katherine : the heroine of the ballad on which Scott based his ' *Young Lochinvar* '.

Jaquenetta : a country girl courted by Don Adriano de Armado [Shakespeare, *Love's Labour's Lost*].

Jaques : servant to Sulpitia, a woman of ill repute [J. Fletcher, *Custom of the Country*].

—— a miser [Ben Jonson, *Case is Altered*].

—— ' could suck melancholy out of a song, as a weasel sucks eggs ' [Shakespeare, *As You Like It*].

Jarley, Mrs.: owner of the wax-work show with which Little Nell and her grandfather travel [Dickens, *Old Curiosity Shop*].

Jarndyce, John: a philanthropist, whose suite in Chancery is intended as a satire on that Court [Dickens, *Bleak House*].

Jarvie, Baillie Nicol: a shrewd and very cautious Glasgow magistrate [Scott, *Rob Roy*].

Jarvis: a devoted servant who tries to shield Beverley from his passion for the gaming table [Edward Moore, *Gamester*].

Jasper: a highway robber, and a murderer, who becomes a maniac [Southey, *Jaspar:* a ballad].

Jasper, Sir: the father of Charlotte. The play is based on Molière's *Le Medecin Malgré Lui* [Fielding, *Mock Doctor*].

Javan: the chief character in a sort of allegorical play [Montgomery, *World Before the Flood*].

Jeames de la Pluche: a footman who unexpectedly inherits a large fortune [Thackeray, *Diary of Jeames de la Pluche, Esq.*].

Jeanie Morrison: *see* Morrison, Jeanie.

Jeanne of Alsace: a girl ruined by the highwayman Dubosc [Stirling, *Courier of Lyons*].

Jeddler, Doctor Anthony: a kind and generous man who esteemed himself a great philosopher.

———— *Grace and Marion:* his beautiful daughters, both in love with the same man [Dickens, *Battle of Life*].

Jekyll, Dr.: a noble-minded doctor whose second self was the villain Hyde [Stevenson, *Strange Case of Jekyll and Mr. Hyde*].

Jellicot, Old Goody: servant at the under-keeper's hut ᴀ Woodstock [Scott, *Woodstock*].

Jellyby, Caroline: generally called ‘Caddy’. Over worked and neglected but good. She marries Prince Turveydrop.

———— *Mrs.:* a pleasant-looking woman who is so devoted to philanthropy outside her own home that she has no time to attend to her domestic duties.

———— ‘*Peepy*’: her neglected son [Dickens, *Bleak House*].

Jenkin: the servant of the Pinner of Wakefield [Greene, *George-à-Green, the Pinner of Wakefield*].

Jenkins, Miss Deborah: a profound admirer of Dr. Johnson and a great stickler for form and ceremony.

———— *Miss Mattie:* the gentle little sister of Miss Deborah Jenkins, whom every one loved and honoured, and who was rescued from want by her brother Peter.

Jenkins, Mr. Peter : their brother, who runs away as a boy, and returns to make Mattie happy when he hears she is poor and alone [Mrs. Gaskell, *Cranford*].

—————— Winifred : Miss Tabitha Bramble's maid [Smollett, *Humphry Clinker*].

Jenkinson, Ephraim : a swindler who imposes upon the Vicar, and upon Moses Primrose [Goldsmith, *Vicar of Wakefield*].

—————— Mrs. Mountstuart : a rich, clever widow who rules the county in which Sir Willoughby Patterne lives [George Meredith, *The Egoist*].

Jenkison, Mr. : 'the statu-quoite', an amiable crank in the party at Squire Headlong's [Peacock, *Headlong Hall*].

Jennings, Mrs. : a vulgar but good-natured match-maker [Jane Austen, *Sense and Sensibility*].

Jenny Diver : *see* Diver, Jenny.

—————— Wren : *see* Cleaver, Fanny.

Jermyn, Matthew : a lawyer, the husband of Mrs. Transome and father of Harold [George Eliot, *Felix Holt*].

Jerningham, Master Thomas : in the service of the Duke of Buckingham [Scott, *Peveril of the Peak*].

Jerome, Don : father of Don Ferdinand and Louisa ; pig-headed but affectionate [Sheridan, *Duenna*].

Jeronimo, or Heironymo : the principal character in the play [Kyd, *Spanish Tragedy*].

Jerry : the owner of a troop of performing dogs [Dickens, *Old Curiosity Shop*].

Jervis, Mrs. : the squire's housekeeper [Richardson, *Pamela*].

Jess : the woman who patiently viewed the world from her cottage window for twenty years [Barrie, *Window in Thrums*].

Jessamy : a popinjay who proposes to Clarissa Flowerdale and is rejected by her [Bickerstaff, *Lionel and Clarissa*].

Jessica : the daughter of Shylock, who elopes with Lorenzo [Shakespeare, *Merchant of Venice*].

Jessie, the Flower o' Dunblane : the subject of a song [Tannahill, *Charming Young Jessie*, etc.].

Jew, The Wandering : varying stories relate to him. One is, that, as Jesus rested for a moment, bearing His cross, a cobbler, Ahasuerus by name, pushed him, crying, 'Get on, away with you,' and Jesus answered, 'Truly I go away quickly, but tarry thou till I come'. Ahasuerus has had to wander about, waiting, ever since.

Jewkes, Mrs. : an offensive character [Richardson, *Pamela*].

Jin Vin : Jenkin Vincent, an apprentice in love with Margaret Ramsay [Scott, *Fortunes of Nigel*].

Jingle, Alfred : a strolling actor, and a swindler, who sponges on Mr. Pickwick [Dickens, *Pickwick Papers*].

Jiniwin, Mrs. : the mother of Mrs. Quilp [Dickens, *Old Curiosity Shop*].

Jinkins, Mr.: a character in ' The Bagman's Story ' [Dickens, *Pickwick Papers*].

Jip : Dora's pet dog [Dickens, *David Copperfield*].

Jo : a poor crossing-sweeper known as ' Toughey ' [Dickens, *Bleak House*].

Joanna : Mr. Mordent's deserted daughter [Holcroft, *Deserted Daughter*].

Jobling, Tony : a law-writer known as ' Weevle' [Dickens, *Bleak House*].

———— **Dr. John :** medical officer to a Loan and Life Insurance Company [Dickens, *Martin Chuzzlewit*].

Jobson, Joseph : clerk to Squire Inglewood [Scott, *Rob Roy*].

Jobson, Neil : Zekel's meek wife, taught by blows to obey.

———— *Zekel :* a cobbler who ruled his wife with a rod of iron [Coffey, *Devil to Pay*].

Jocelyn, Lady : the mother of Rose Jocelyn. A woman full of strong common-sense and kindness.

———— *Rose :* a high-spirited girl of good position. She meets Evan Harrington in Portugal, and after many difficulties marries him [George Meredith, *Evan Harrington*].

Jock o' Hazeldean : *see* Hazeldean, Jock o'.

Joe, The Fat Boy : Fat Boy.

John Anderson : *see* Anderson, John.

———— **Don :** a rather foolish but honourable Spaniard [Beaumont and Fletcher, *The Chances*].

———— **Don :** an ill-conditioned man who tries to injure Hero in the eyes of Claudio, on the eve of their marriage [Shakespeare, *Much Ado About Nothing*].

———— **Friar :** a Franciscan Friar [Shakespeare, *Romeo and Juliet*].

———— **Little :** one of Robin Hood's companions often referred to in ballads, etc.

Johnnie of Braidislee : an outlaw and deerstealer, the hero of an old ballad [*Johnnie of Braidislee*].

Johnny : Betty Higden's baby, who died [Dickens, *Our Mutual Friend*].

Johnstone, Auld Willie : an old fisherman [Scott, *Guy Mannering*].

Joliffe, Joceline : under-keeper at Woodstock [Scott, *Woodstock*].

Joliquet, Bibo : the waiter at the *White Lion*, an inn kept by Jerome Lesurques [Stirling, *Courier of Lyons*].

Jollup, Sir Jacob : owner of Gerratt, a pompous and vulgar man [Foote, *Mayor of Garratt*].

Jonas : intended for the attorney-general, Sir William Jones [Dryden, *Absalom and Achitophel*].

Jonathan : a man whom Sir Benjamin Dove had raised from want and who served him as butler [Cumberland, *Brothers*].

Jones, Tom : generous and manly but dissipated [Fielding, *Tom Jones*].

Jorkins, Mr. : Mr. Spenlow's partner [Dickens, *David Copperfield*].

Josceline, Sir : a crusader [Scott, *Talisman*].

José, Don : husband of Donna Inez, and father of Don Juan [Byron, *Don Juan*].

Joseph : a very generous and benevolent Jew [Knowles, *Maid of Mariendorpt*].

—— the canting servant of Heathcliff [Emily Brontë, *Wuthering Heights*].

—— Andrews : *see* Andrews, Joseph.

Josephine : the mother of Werner [Byron, *Werner*].

Josian : wife of Sir Bevis of Southampton, who gave him his sword ' Morglay ', and ' Arundel ' his charger [Drayton, *Polyolbion*].

Joyeuse : the Emperor Charlemagne's sword.

Juan : a troubadour [George Eliot, *Spanish Gypsy*].

—— Don : a native of Seville, son of Don José and Donna Inez [Byron, *Don Juan*].

Juba : a friend of Cato's and loving Cato's daughter, to whom he was married [Addison, *Cato*].

Judith, Aunt : the sister of George Heriot [Scott, *Fortunes of Nigel*].

Juletta : Alinda's maid [J. Fletcher, *Pilgrim*].

Julia : the hunchback's ward, betrothed to Sir Thomas Clifford [Knowles, *Hunchback*].

—— the heroine of the novel [Mackenzie, *Julia de Roubigné*].

—— a lady loved by Protheus [Shakespeare, *Two Gentlemen of Verona*].

—— the patient object of Falkland's jealousy [Sheridan, *Rivals*].

—— Donna : a Sevillian of Moorish extraction, with whom Juan fell in love at the age of sixteen [Byron, *Don Juan*].

Julian : the subject of a tragedy [Mary R. Mitford, *Julian*].

—— and Maddalo : Julian is intended for Shelley himself, Maddalo for Lord Byron [Shelley, *Julian and Maddalo : a Conversation*].

Julian, Count : the hero of a very impressive tragedy. The author's first attempt in the field of drama [Landor, *Count Julian*].

―――― **Count :** the chief instrument in the fall of Roderick. It was he who invited the Moors to force him from the Spanish throne [Southey, *Roderick*].

Juliana : a saintly woman, the wife of Virolet [Beaumont and Fletcher, *Double Marriage*].

―――― married to the Duke of Aranza, who schools her from pride and arrogance to affectionate modesty [Tobin, *Honeymoon*].

―――― **Lady :** daughter to Lord Courtland, a frivolous and extravagant girl, who elopes with Henry Douglas, a penniless lifeguardsman [Susan E. Ferrier, *Marriage*].

Julie de Mortemar : an orphan under the guardianship of Richelieu. Louis XIII was one of many admirers, but she married Adrien de Mauprat [Lytton, *Richelieu*].

Juliet : beloved by Claudio [Shakespeare, *Measure for Measure*].

―――― the daughter of the Capulets, whose self-devotion was rendered of no avail because of Romeo's despair [Shakespeare, *Romeo and Juliet*].

Julio : in love with Lelia, a widow of no repute [Beaumont and Fletcher, *The Captain*].

―――― **of Harancour :** a deaf and dumb boy abandoned in the streets of Paris. He is rescued and brought up by De l'Epée, and afterwards recognized and restored to his rightful position as Count of Harancour [Holcroft, *Deaf and Dumb*].

Jupe, Cecilia : the daughter of the clown, adopted by Thomas Gradgrind [Dickens, *Hard Times*].

―――― **Signor :** a clown in a circus [Dickens, *Hard Times*].

Kailyal : the heroine—a daughter of Ladurlad [Southey, *Curse of Kehama*].

Kalasrade : the wife of Sedak [Ridley, *Tales of the Genii*].

Kaled : the name assumed by Gulnare when she disguised herself as Lara's page [Byron, *Lara*].

Kamal : an outlaw and border chief, who allows his son to enter the Empress of India's service [Kipling, *East and West*].

Karenina, Anna : the heroine [Tolstoi, *Anna Karenina*].

Katerfelto : a noted quack [Cowper, *The Task*].

Katherine : one of the Princess of France's attendants [Shakespeare, *Love's Labour's Lost*].

―――― the 'Shrew', elder daughter of Baptista of Padua [Shakespeare, *Taming of the Shrew*].

Kathleen : the heroine of a very popular Irish song [Mrs. Crawford, *Kathleen Mavourneen*].

Katinka: one of the three beautiful girls in the harem into which Don Juan penetrated in disguise [Byron, *Don Juan*].

Katusha: a girl sent to Siberia for a crime she did not commit [Tolstoi, *Resurrection*].

Kavanagh: a clergyman, who marries Cecilia Vaughan, the heroine [Longfellow, *Kavanagh*].

Kay, Sir: King Arthur's foster-brother, and seneschal at his court [Mallory, *History of Prince Arthur*].

Kearney, Kate: the subject of a pathetic Irish song [Lady Morgan, *Kate Kearney*].

Kecksey: a wretched old man who pretends he prefers a termagant and a flirt as wife [Garrick, *Irish Widow*].

Keeldar, Shirley: the heroine. 'To admire the great, reverence the good, and be joyous with the genial, was very much the bent of Shirley's soul.' She marries Louis Moore [Charlotte Brontë, *Shirley*].

Keene, Abel: a village schoolmaster who became a clerk. He commits suicide [Crabbe, *The Borough*].

Kehama: a mighty rajah who was cursed with 'immortal death' [Southey, *Curse of Kehama*].

Keiner, General: Governor of Prague [Knowles, *Maid of Mariendorpt*].

Kempferhausen: one of the speakers [Wilson, *Noctes Ambrosianae*].

Kenge, Mr.: known as 'Conversation Kenge' because he so loved to hear his own voice [Dickens, *Bleak House*].

Kennedy, Frank: an excise officer who is murdered by smugglers [Scott, *Guy Mannering*].

Kenneth, Sir: the 'Knight of the Leopard', really the Prince Royal of Scotland [Scott, *Talisman*].

Kenrick, Felix: a faithful servant: the foster-father of Caroline Dormer [Colman the Younger, *Heir at Law*].

Kent, Earl of: under the name of Caius he waits on Lear, and takes him to Dover Castle [Shakespeare, *King Lear*].

Kenwigs, Mr. and Mrs.: an ivory turner and his wife, who consider themselves very 'genteel'.

—— **The Misses:** pupils of Nicholas [Dickens, *Nicholas Nickleby*].

Kera Khan: a Tartar chief at war with Poland [Kemble, *Ladoiska*].

Kettle, Captain: an amusing, pugnacious man, the hero of several books [Hyne, *Adventures of Captain Kettle*].

Kettledrummle, Gabriel: a Covenanter preacher [Scott, *Old Mortality*].

Kevin, St.: fled to a rock at Glendalough to escape from the fascinations of Kathleen. She followed him thither and he cast her into the sea [Thomas Moore, *Irish Melodies : St. Kevin*].

Kew, Countess of : a domineering society lady [Thackeray, *The Newcomes*].

Key, Sir : *see* Kay, Sir.

Kezia : a 'bad-tempered, good-hearted housemaid' [George Eliot, *Mill on the Floss*].

Kickleburys, The : the heroes of a Christmas book [Thackeray, *Kickleburys on the Rhine*].

Kifri : the personification of Atheism and Blasphemy. He was an enchanter and a giant [Ridley, *Tales of the Genii : Enchanter's Tale*].

Kilmansegg, Miss : an heiress with a golden leg [Thomas Hood, *Miss Kilmansegg*].

Kim : the son of an English soldier, reared by a half-caste [Kipling, *Kim*].

King, Tom : 'a rowdy, joking dog' [Moncrieffe, *Mon. Tonson*].

Kinmont, Willie : a notorious freebooter, the hero of a ballad [*Border Minstrelsy*].

Kionis : a strange, hot-tempered gipsy girl, half in love with Harry Richmond [George Meredith, *Adventures of Harry Richmond*].

Kirby, Carinthia Jane : an English girl brought up in Austria. On her first entry into society she meets and accepts the Earl of Fleetwood and marries him, but is at once forsaken, and when he attempts a reconciliation she declines.

—— **Chillon John :** the brother of the Countess of Fleetwood. An athletic and handsome man who marries the beautiful Henrietta Fakenham [George Meredith, *Amazing Marriage*].

Kirkpatrick, Cynthia : Dr. Gibson's step-daughter.

—— *Mrs. :* becomes the second wife of Dr. Gibson [Mrs. Gaskell, *Wives and Daughters*].

Kirkrapine : a robber of churches, giving the proceeds of his thefts to Abessa [Spenser, *Faëry Queene*].

Kit : *see* Nubbles, Christopher.

Kite, Sergeant : a recruiting officer [Farquhar, *Recruiting Officer*].

Kitely : a rich London merchant, very jealous of his wife [Ben Jonson, *Every Man in His Humour*].

Kitty : a wild, harum-scarum girl who arranges to elope with Random [Colman the Younger, *Ways and Means*].

—— one of Mr. Lovel's servants, who ape the manners of their masters and mistresses [Townley, *High Life Below Stairs*].

Knag, Miss : Mme. Mantalini's forewoman, who first adores, then hates, Kate Nickleby [Dickens, *Nicholas Nickleby*].

Knight, The : the type of noble, courageous, yet humble chivalry [Chaucer, *Canterbury Tales : The Knight's Tale*].

Knightley, Mr. : the hero of the tale, who in the end marries Emma Woodhouse [Jane Austen, *Emma*].

Knockwinnock, Sybil : wife of Sir Richard of the Redhand, and mother of Malcolm Misbegot [Scott, *The Antiquary*].

Knowell, the Elder : a character supposed to have been acted by Shakespeare. He is an elderly man of sententious humour, very anxious about the moral well-being of his son [Ben Jonson, *Every Man in His Humour*].

Koëldwethout, Baron Von : hero of one of the tales told at the inn where Nicholas and Squeers were detained by an accident to the coach [Dickens, *Nicholas Nickleby*].

Krook, Mr. : the drunken proprietor of a rag and bone shop, said to have died of spontaneous combustion [Dickens, *Bleak House*].

Kubla Khan : the prince who built the ' pleasure-dome ' the poet saw in his dream [S. T. Coleridge, *Kubla Khan*].

La Creevy, Miss : a merry little woman, a miniatur painter [Dickens, *Nicholas Nickleby*].

La Roche : a Swiss Pastor travelling through France with his daughter [Mackenzie, *Story of La Roche*].

La Vallière, Louise, Duchesse de : betrothed to the Marquis de Bragalone, but in love with Louis XIV [Lytton, *Duchess de la Vallière*].

Labe Queen : Queen of the Island of Enchantments, who got transformed into a mare [*Arabian Nights*].

Lackitt, Widow : falls in love with Charlotte Weldon when that lady impersonates Mr. Weldon [Southern, *Oroonoko*].

Lacy, Sir Damian de : nephew of Sir Hugo.
———— *Sir Hugo de :* a crusader, and the constable of Chester.
———— *Sir Randal de :* cousin to Sir Hugo, who appears under various guises [Sir W. Scott, *Betrothed*].

Ladislaus : a humorous cynic [Massinger, *The Picture*].

Ladislaw, Will : an artist in love with Dorothea, whom he marries after Casaubon's death [George Eliot, *Middlemarch*].

W.W.F.   M

Ladurlad : the father of Kailyal [Southey, *Curse of Kehama*].
Lady of the Bleeding Heart : *see* Douglas, Ellen.
—— **of the Lake :** *see* Vivien; also Douglas, Ellen.
Ladylift, Elinor : the girl Paul Ferrol loved, though he was inveigled by Laura Chanson into marrying her instead [Mrs. Archer Clive, *Why Paul Ferrol Killed His Wife*].
Laertes : his wife having been spared by Gustavus Vasa, he henceforth is the trusty servant of the king's daughter, Christina [Brooke, *Gustavus Vasa*].
—— son of Polonius, and brother of Ophelia, it is he who uses a poisoned rapier in his duel with Hamlet [Shakespeare, *Hamlet*].
Laila : daughter of Okba, the sorcerer. She died to save Thalaba's life [Southey, *Thalaba*].
Lajeunesse, Gabriel : the lover of Evangeline, who was parted from her when the inhabitants of Grand Pré were driven from their homes. They met again when he was on his deathbed [Longfellow, *Evangeline*].
Lalla Rookh : the Princess to whom the stories contained in the poem were related on her journey from Delhi to Cashmere [Thomas Moore, *Lalla Rookh*].
Lambert, Charlotte : daughter of Sir John and Lady Lambert and beloved by Darnley.
—— *Lady :* wife of Sir John. She aids in exposing Dr. Cantwell's hypocrisy.
—— *Sir John :* the dupe of Dr. Cantwell, on whom he bestows £4,000 a year [Bickerstaff, *The Hypocrite*].
—— Hetty : daughter of Colonel Lambert. She eggs Henry Warrington on till he becomes a soldier. Afterwards she marries him [Thackeray, *Virginians*].
Lambro : the father of Haideé—a Greek pirate [Byron, *Don Juan*].
Lamderg : and Ullin both loved Gelchossa, so they fought and Lamderg won, but afterwards died of his wounds, and in three days Gelchossa died of a broken heart [Ossian, *Fingal*].
Lamia : a serpent-woman who married a Corinthian youth [Keats, *Lamia*].
Lamira : the daughter of the noble Vertaigne, and wedded to Champernel [J. Fletcher, *Little French Lawyer*].
Lammermoor, Bride of : parted from the man she loves, and wedded to another, she goes mad [Scott, *Bride of Lammermoor*; *see also* Ashton, Lucy].
Lammeter, Nancy : the girl that Godfrey Cass marries, and who urges him to claim his child Effie [George Eliot, *Silas Marner*
Lammikin, or Lamkin : a monster who used blood as the

chief constituent in the mortar with which he built his castle [*Scottish Ballad*].

Lammle, Mr. and Mrs. Alfred : adventurers and fortune-hunters. Each marries the other for money, only to find, too late, that neither has any [Dickens, *Our Mutual Friend*].

Lamoracke, Sir : a Knight of the Round Table, and son of Sir Pellinore [Mallory, *History of Prince Arthur*].

Lampedo : a country surgeon, very poor, the ' sketch and outline of a man ' [Tobin, *Honeymoon*].

Lance : a falconer and the servant of Valentine's father [J. Fletcher, *Wit Without Money*].

Lancelot of the Lake : a Scottish metrical romance [Percy, *Reliques : Sir Launcelot du Lake*].

—— **Sir** : chief Knight of the Round Table, who harbours a guilty love for Guinevere which has a disastrous influence on the Court. He repents and dies ' a holy man ' [Alfred Tennyson, *Idylls of the King : Lancelot and Elaine : Guinevere*].

Langham, Edward : an Oxford tutor whose intellectual gifts and many fine qualities of head and heart are all rendered neutral by an invincible shyness and morbid indecision of character [Mrs. Humphry Ward, *Robert Elsmere*].

Langley, Sir Frederick : a Jacobite conspirator and suitor for the hand of Miss Vere [Scott, *Black Dwarf*].

Languish, Miss Lydia : an insatiable novel-reader, who tries to act the characters she admires [Sheridan, *Rivals*].

Lapet, Mons. : an abject coward who wrote a book upon duelling [J. Fletcher, *Nice Valour ; or, Passionate Madman*].

Lapraick : the friend of Steenie in Wandering Willie's tale [Scott, *Redgauntlet*].

Lara : the name taken by the Corsair after Medora's death [Byron, *Lara*].

—— **the Count of** : in love with Preciosa [Longfellow, *Spanish Student*].

Lardoon, Lady Bab : a fashionable gambler, who renounces such weaknesses upon her marriage to Sir Charles Dupely [Burgoyne, *Maid of the Oaks*].

Larkins, Miss : an imposing young woman for whom David experiences a violent ' calf-love ' [Dickens, *David Copperfield*].

Larthmoor : King of Berrathon, a Scandinavian island [Ossian, *Berrathon*].

Larynx, Rev. Mr. : a cheery, jovial clergyman [Peacock, *Nightmare Abbey*].

Las-Casas : a fine old Spaniard who denounced the barbarities perpetrated by his compatriots [Sheridan, *Pizarro*].

Lascours, Martha de : cut adrift in a boat, in infancy, she was found and reared by an Indian tribe.

—— *Ralph de :* father of Martha and Captain of the *Urania* [Stirling, *Orphan of the Frozen Sea*].

Lathmon : a British prince who attacks Morven. Fingal defeats him but releases him unharmed [Ossian, *Lathmon*].

Latimer, Darsie : supposed to be the son of Mr. Ralph Latimer, really that of Sir Henry Redgauntlet.

—— *Mr. Ralph :* the reputed father of Darsie [Scott, *Redgauntlet*].

Laud, Will : a smuggler, beloved by Margaret Catchpole. He helps her to escape from Ipswich Gaol [Cobbold, *Margaret Catchpole*].

Launce : the servant of Protheus [Shakespeare, *Two Gentlemen of Verona*].

Launcelot, Sir : *see* Lancelot, Sir.

Launfal, Sir : a Knight of the Round Table, and the subject of the poem [Lowell, *Vision of Sir Launfal*].

Laura : beloved by both Arnold and Hugo. As both were slain in a faction fight, she married neither [Davenant, *Gondibert*].

—— a frivolous woman whose husband, being captured by Turks, embraces their faith [Byron, *Bappo*].

Laurana : daughter of the King of Thessaly, beloved by Parismus [Foord, *History of Parismus*].

Laurence, Friar : the friendly friar who gives Juliet the sleeping draught [Shakespeare, *Romeo and Juliet*].

Lauretta di Guardino : the wife of John Inglesant, who dies of the plague [Shorthouse, *John Inglesant*].

Laurie, Annie : the original of this song was the eldest of the three daughters of Sir Robert Laurie of Maxwelton [Douglas, *Annie Laurie*].

Lauringtons, The : this novel is meant as a satire on a certain class of people [Mrs. Trollope, *The Lauringtons*].

Lavaine, Sir : a knight of Arthur's Court, brother to Elaine [Alfred Tennyson, *Idylls of the King : Lancelot and Elaine*].

Lavender, Frank : an artist. A self-indulgent young man who at first, having won her, neglects his wife, but her nobility of character at last has its reward and he becomes wholly hers [Black, *Princess of Thule*].

Lavengro : the author is himself the hero of this story, much of it being strictly autobiographical [Borrow, *Lavengro, the Scholar, the Gipsy and the Priest*].

Lavington, Squire : the squire who denied that the ownership of property carried duties with it [Charles Kingsley *Yeast*].

Lavinia : sister of Lord Altamont and the wife of Horatio [Rowe, *Fair Penitent*].

—— daughter of the Roman general, Titus Andronicus. Her hands were cut off and her tongue cut out by Goths [Shakespeare, *Titus Andronicus*].

—— in love with Palemon [James Thomson, *Seasons : Autumn*].

Lazarillo : a poor needy, hungry courtier, greedy and voluptuous [Beaumont and Fletcher, *Woman-Hater*].

—— a servant who tries to wait on two masters and commits many blunders in the effort [Jephson, *Two Strings to Your Bow*].

—— a punctilious Spaniard [Middleton, *Blurt, Master Constable*].

Lazie, Sir Lawrence : a man who served ' the Schoolmaster, his Wife, the Squire's Cook, and the Farmer '. A popular old chap-book [*The Infamous History of Sir Lawrence Lazie*].

Le Beau : a courtier in the train of the usurping Duke, Frederick [Shakespeare, *As You Like It*].

Le Castre : the father of Mirabel, the ' wild-goose ' [J. Fletcher, *Wild-goose Chase*].

L'Eclair, Philippe : a boasting army orderly who courts Rosabelle, a serving-maid [Dimond, *Foundling of the Forest*].

Le Febre : a poor lieutenant [Sterne, *Tristram Shandy*].

L'Estrange, Harley : a ' shy, dreamy, and delicate ' young nobleman, who falls in love with Nora Avenel, a girl socially his inferior [Lytton, *My Novel*].

Lea : an angel who was sent to earth on a message fell in love with her as she saw her bathing. She rose as a spirit to heaven [Thomas Moore, *Loves of the Angels*].

Leander : a young man of Abydos who swam the Hellespont nightly to visit his love—Hero—is the theme of many poems and romances.

—— a young Spanish student who falls in love with Leonora, who was betrothed to Don Diego. Diego is old, Leander young, so the latter wins [Bickerstaff, *Padlock*].

Lear : a mythical King of Britain, who is driven mad by the cruelty and neglect of two of his daughters [Shakespeare, *King Lear*].

Learoyd, John : ' a slow-moving, heavy-footed Yorkshireman ' [Kipling, *Life's Handicap*].

Leatherhead : supposed to be a portrait of Inigo Jones, the architect [Ben Jonson, *Bartholomew Fair*].

Leatherstocking, Natty : the nickname of Natty Bumpo, a half-civilized man whom we meet in five stories by the same author [Cooper, *Deerslayer, Prairie, Last of the Mohicans, Pathfinder, Pioneer*].

Leblanc, René : notary of Grand Pré, whose goods were confiscated with those of the other settlers there [Longfellow, *Evangeline*].

Ledbrain, Mr. X. : vice-president of Section C. at the Mudfog meeting [Dickens, *Mudfog Association*].

Ledbrook, Miss : a member of Mr. Crummles' Company at the Portsmouth Theatre [Dickens, *Nicholas Nickleby*].

Ledbury : the hero of a novel [Albert Smith, *Adventures of Mr. Ledbury*].

Lee, Annabel : the subject of the poem [Poe, *Annabel Lee*].

—— *Alice :* the heroine ; daughter of Sir Henry. She marries Markham Everard.

—— *Colonel Albert :* son of Sir Henry and the friend of Charles II.

—— *Sir Henry :* an old royalist, and head ranger of Woodstock Forest, who gives shelter to Charles II [Scott, *Woodstock*].

—— **Simon :** the subject of a lyric [Wordsworth, *Simon Lee, the Old Huntsman*].

Leeford, Edward : *see* Monks.

Lefevre, Lieutenant : an officer who died of starvation [Sterne, *Tristram Shandy*].

Legend, Ben : a sailor, the younger son of Sir Sampson Legend.

—— *Sir Sampson :* a testy old gentleman who tries to substitute his younger for his elder son as his heir [Congreve, *Love for Love*].

Legree : the brutal overseer of a slave plantation [Harriet Beecher Stowe, *Uncle Tom's Cabin*].

Leicester, Countess of : *see* Robsart, Amy.

Leigh, Amyas : the hero of the story [Charles Kingsley, *Westward Ho !*].

—— **Aurora :** the heroine of a long narrative poem.

—— *Romney :* the cousin and lover of Aurora : a wealthy philanthropist. Not until he becomes blind does she marry him [Elizabeth B. Browning, *Aurora Leigh*].

Leila : the heroine. A young Turkish child, who at the siege of Ismail is rescued by Don Juan [Byron, *Don Juan*].

—— a beautiful slave who falls in love with the Giaour [Byron, *Giaour*].

Leila : the heroine of the novel [Lytton, *Leila ; or, Siege of Granada*].

Lenkenstein, Lena and Anna two high-born Austrian women, full of pride and fierce patriotism [George Meredith, *Vittoria*].

Lennox, Colonel Charles : the hero of the tale who marries the heroine, Mary Douglas [Susan E. Ferrier, *Marriage*].

Lenore : the name of the heroines of two poems by the same author [Poe, *The Raven* ; also *Lenore*].

Lenville : the tragedian of Mr. Crummles' Company at the Portsmouth Theatre [Dickens, *Nicholas Nickleby*].

Leoline and Sydanis : characters in an early seventeenth century heroic romance [Kynaston, *Leoline and Sydanis*].

Leoline : deputed to murder the orphan daughter of Pericles [Shakespeare, *Pericles, Prince of Tyre*].

Leon : the hero. He exercises great forbearance, kindness, and wisdom in subduing a wilful wife, and he gains the day [J. Fletcher, *Rule a Wife and Have a Wife*].

Leonard : a true scholar who earns his living by keeping a poor school [Crabbe, *The Borough*].

Leonardo : Duke of Mantua, married to Mariana, after surviving two terrible accidents, and the plots of enemies to part them [Knowles, *The Wife*].

Leonato : the Governor of Messina, and father of Hero [Shakespeare, *Much Ado About Nothing*].

Leonidas : a character in the play [Dryden, *Marriage à la Mode*].

——— the hero of a poem in twelve books, at one time very popular [Glover, *Leonidas*].

Leonora : a portionless girl who captivates the fancy of an old man who undertakes her education, intending to marry her, but Leander, a young man, arranges to elope with her. Diego, the old man, sanctions the match [Bickerstaff, *Padlock*].

——— sister of Alfonso II, Duke of Ferrara. Tasso, the poet, loved this princess from afar [Byron, *Lament of Tasso*].

——— wrongful Queen of Aragon, who loves Torrismond, son of the rightful king. This leads to the restoration of the lawful sovereign [Dryden, *Spanish Fryar*].

——— betrothed to Ferdinand, a young Spaniard [Jephson, *Two Strings to your Bow*].

——— the faithful wife of Don Alonzo, but as she had been at one time affianced to Don Carlos, charges of infidelity are brought against her. She takes her own life [Young, *The Revenge*].

Leonora : the heroine of the novel which bears her name [Maria Edgeworth, *Leonora*].

Leontes : falsely accuses his wife of infidelity and loses her for sixteen years in consequence [Shakespeare, *Winter's Tale*].

Leontius : a valiant and cheery old soldier [J. Fletcher, *Humorous Lieutenant*].

Leopold : a sea-captain in love with Hippolyta [J. Fletcher, *Custom of the Country*].

—— the Austrian Archduke who captured Richard I on his return from Palestine [Scott, *Talisman*].

Leporello : a character in the play which used to be taken by the actor J. Liston [Thomas Shadwell, *The Libertine*].

Lesley, Bonnie :=Miss Leslie Baillie, the daughter of a gentleman of Ayrshire is the person thus immortalized [Burns, *Bonnie Lesley*].

—— **Bonnie :** pet name of one of the female characters [Black, *Kilmeny*].

—— **Ludovic :** an old archer in Louis XI's Scotch Guard known as Le Balafré [Scott, *Quentin Durward*].

Lesurques, Jerome : an impoverished solicitor who tries to add to his income by secretly owning the *White Lion Inn.*

—— *Joseph :* his son, whose likeness to the highwayman Dubosc causes him to be accused of robbing the Lyons mail.

—— *Julie :* daughter of Joseph, in love with Didier [Stirling, *Courier of Lyons*].

Leucippe : wife of Menippus, a woman of ill fame [J. Fletcher, *Humorous Lieutenant*].

—— an Athenian soldier who loves Pygmalion's sister Myrine [Gilbert, *Pygmalion and Galatea*].

Lewis : the Landgrave of Thuringia, and husband of Elizabeth [Charles Kingsley, *Saint's Tragedy*].

—— **Don :** no scholar, but loving scholarship, he is devoted to his learned nephew Carlos [Cibber, *Love Makes a Man*].

Lewiston, Jacob : an impostor; cousin of the real father of Gertrude, who blackmails Mrs. St. Clair by threatening disclosure [Susan E. Ferrier, *Inheritance*].

Lewsome, Mr. : the man from whom Jonas Chuzzlewit obtains the drugs with which he poisons old Anthony [Dickens, *Martin Chuzzlewit*].

Lewson : in love with Charlotte Beverley, whom he marries in spite of her poverty [Edward Moore, *Gamester*].

Leyburn, Agnes : the practical one of the family ; sister to Mrs. Robert Elsmer~

Leyburn, Catherine : the beautiful and saintly, but narrow-minded woman who becomes Mrs. Robert Elsmere.

────── *Mrs. :* the mother of Mrs. Robert Elsmere.

────── *Rose :* the wayward but gifted and beautiful sister of Mrs. Robert Elsmere, who marries Hugh Flaxman [Mrs. Humphry Ward, *Robert Elsmere*].

Lieschen : Teufelsdroch's general domestic factotum [Carlyle, *Sartor Resartus*].

Lightwood, Mortimer : a solicitor, the friend of Eugene Wrayburn, and at one time the admirer of Bella Wilfer [Dickens, *Our Mutual Friend*].

Lilian : the heroine [Charles Kingsley, *Alton Locke*].

────── ' Airy, fairy Lilian,' a portrait [Alfred Tennyson, *Lilian*].

Lilinau : a woman who followed a phantom that waved to her from amongst the pines in her father's woods [Longfellow, *Evangeline*].

Lillia-Bianca : daughter of Nantolet, and courted by Pinac [J. Fletcher, *Wild-goose Chase*].

Lilly : she is the wife of Andrew, Charles Brisac's servant [J. Fletcher, *Elder Brother*].

Lillyvick, Mr. : a water-rate collector, who marries Miss Petowker, the actress [Dickens, *Nicholas Nickleby*].

Limberham : supposed to be intended for the Duke of Lauderdale [Dryden, *Limberham*].

Limmason, Lieut. : an officer of Hussars imprisoned in Siberia, whence he escapes, a wreck [Kipling, *Life's Handicap*].

Limp, Sir Luke : the leading character, which was acted by the author himself [Foote, *Lame Lover*].

Lincoya : ' the flower of all his nation ', a captive of the Aztecas [Southey, *Madoc*].

Lindabrides : one of the heroines of the romance [*Mirrour of Knighthood*].

Lindore, Lady Emily : daughter of the first Lord Lindore and cousin of Mary Douglas. She marries Edward Douglas, Mary's brother.

────── *Lord, the Elder :* afterwards Lord Courtland. Brother to Lady Juliana Douglas.

────── *Lord, the Younger :* cousin and lover of Adelaide Douglas, with whom she ultimately elopes [Susan E. Ferrier, *Marriage*].

Linet : daughter of Sir Persaunt. The same whom Tennyson calles Lynette [Mallory, *History of Prince Arthur*].

Linkinwater, Tim : the faithful clerk of Cheeryble Bros. [Dickens, *Nicholas Nickleby*].

Linne, The Heir of : subject of an old ballad [Percy, *Reliques : The Heir of Linne*].

Linnet, Kitty : an actress ; the heroine of the play [Foote, *Maid of Bath*].

Lionel and Clarissa : the hero and heroine of an opera [Bickerstaff, *Lionel and Clarissa*].

Lirriper, Mrs. Emma : the letter of lodgings at No. 81, Norfolk Street, Strand [Dickens, *Mrs. Lirriper's Lodgings*].

—— **Jemmy Jackman :** son of Mr. Edson, adopted by Mrs. Lirriper [Dickens, *Mrs. Lirriper's Legacy*].

Lisa, Monna : mother of Tessa [George Eliot, *Romola*].

Lismahago, Captain : the wounded warrior who marries Tabitha Bramble [Smollett, *Humphry Clinker*].

Lissardo : *see* Flippanta and Lissardo.

Listless, the Hon. Mr. : an aimless and stupid young man ; a friend of Scythrop's [Peacock, *Nightmare Abbey*].

Littimer : Steerforth's meretricious servant [Dickens *David Copperfield*].

Little Billee : *see* Billee, Little.

—— **Britain :** *see* Britain, Benjamin.

—— **Dorrit :** *see* Dorrit, Amy.

—— **John :** *see* John, Little.

—— **Nell :** *see* Trent, Nell.

Livia : a worldly, malicious woman, who betrays Bianca [Middleton, *Women Beware Women*].

Livingstone, Guy : the hero of a novel, fiery, wanting in self-restraint, but generous [Lawrence, *Guy Livingstone*].

Llaian : the mother of Prince Hoel ; she went with Madoc to America [Southey, *Madoc*].

Llewellyn : grandson of Owen, King of North Wales ; he was set aside in succession to the throne because of a disfigured face [Southey, *Madoc*].

—— **Bunny :** the orphan grand-daughter of David Llewellyn, who marries Watkin Thomas.

—— **David :** the wily old fisherman and marine, who tells the story [Blackmore, *Maid of Sker*].

Loadstone, Lady : a character in the play [Ben Jonson, *Magnetick Lady*].

Loathly Lady, The : as soon as she is married to the knight she changes into a beautiful woman [*Marriage of Sir Gawain*, old ballad].

Lobbs, Maria : very pretty, and beloved by Nathaniel Pipkin.

—— **Old :** Maria's father, a wealthy saddler [Dickens, *Pickwick Papers*].

Lochiel : one of the speakers in a lyrical dialogue [Campbell, *Lochiel's Warning*].

Lochinvar : the hero of a ballad, who carries off a bride under the very nose of the bridegroom, at the wedding festival [Scott, *Marmion*].

Locke, Alton : a poetical tailor, who turns Chartist [Charles Kingsley, *Alton Locke*].

Lockit : the gaoler who loaded his prisoners with chains in inverse ratio to the fees which they paid.

—————— *Lucy :* his daughter, who aided in Macheath's escape [Gay, *Beggar's Opera*].

Locksley : an outlawed archer generally known as Robin Hood [Scott, *Ivanhoe*].

Locrine : a mythical King of England who was made the subject of a drama [ascribed to Peele and Tilney, *Locrine*], 1595.

Lodowick : the name under which the Duke of Vienna concealed his identity when he wished to remain unknown [Shakespeare, *Measure for Measure*].

Lofty : a vulgar toady, who boasted of his acquaintances among the aristocracy [Goldsmith, *Good-natured Man*].

—————— **Sir Thomas :** a man of small abilities, who sets up to be a man of parts [Foote, *The Patron*].

Log, King : appointed by Jupiter to be king amongst the Frogs when they petitioned him for a ruler [*Aesop's Fables*].

Lolah : she was ' dark as India ', and was one of the three beauties of the harem into which Don Juan penetrated in disguise [Byron, *Don Juan*].

Long Tom : the hero of a popular story [*Merry Conceits of Long Tom, the Carrier*, etc., etc.].

—————— **Tom Coffin :** *see* Coffin, Tom.

Longaville : a young lord, in the train of Ferdinand of Navarre [Shakespeare, *Love's Labour's Lost*].

Lopes, Don : the father of Don Felix, and Donna Isabella [Mrs. Centlivre, *The Wonder*].

Lord Beichan : *see* Beichan, Young.

Loredano, James : one of the Venetian Council of Ten. An enemy of the Foscari [Byron, *Two Foscari*].

Lorel : a swineherd ; the lover of Earine [Ben Jonson, *Sad Shepherd*].

Lorenzo : Jessica's lover, with whom she elopes [Shakespeare, *Merchant of Venice*].

—————— an atheist and evil liver [Young, *Night Thoughts*].

Lorma : wife of Erragon, King of Sora, who fell in love with a Scottish soldier. The king challenged and killed him, and Lorma died of grief [Ossian, *Battle of Lora*].

Lorna Doone : *see* Doone, Lorna.

Lorraine, Mrs. Felix : a capable but conceited woman, supposed to be intended for Lady Caroline **Lamb** [Beaconsfield, *Vivian Grey*].

Lorraine, Alice : the heroine, who, declining Captain Stephen Chapman, marries Colonel Aylmer, a hero of Waterloo.

—— *Hilary :* the brother of Alice. A highly romantic, impetuous young man, who, trained as a lawyer, becomes a soldier instead, and falling in love with a Kentish farmer's daughter ultimately marries her.

—— *Lady Valeria :* a stern old lady, mother and ruler of the household of Sir Roland Lorraine.

—— *Sir Roland :* a solitary dreamer, but the pink of old fashioned courtesy [Richard D. Blackmore, *Alice Lorraine*].

Lorrequer, Harry : a boisterous, rollicking Irishman, the hero [Lever, *Harry Lorrequer*].

Lorrimite : a horrid witch who helped to persecute Kailyal [Southey, *Curse of Kehama*].

Lorry, Mr. Jarvis : confidential clerk at Tellson's bank and a friend of the Manette family [Dickens, *Tale of Two Cities*].

Losberne, Mr. : ' The doctor ', a good-humoured surgeon, a friend of the Maylies [Dickens, *Oliver Twist*].

Lot : King of Orkney and father of Gawain and Modred. [Alfred Tennyson, *Idylls of the King : Coming of Arthur*].

Lothair : the hero, a young noble of undecided views, who coquettes with the church of Rome [Beaconsfield, *Lothair*].

Lothario : a libertine who is supposed to have suggested the character of Lovelace to Richardson [Rowe, *Fair Penitent*].

Lougher, Colonel Henry : chief landowner in Newton-Nottage and friend to Bardie [Blackmore, *Maid of Sker*].

Louisa : is turned from home for declining to marry Mendoza, and remaining faithful to Antonio [Sheridan, *Duenna*].

—— daughter of bailiff Russet, for whose sake Henry deserts the colours [Charles Dibden (from the French), *The Deserter*].

Louise : the name of the glee-maiden [Scott, *Fair Maid of Perth*].

—— de Lascours : wife of Ralph and mother of Martha the ' orphan ' [Stirling, *Orphan of the Frozen Sea*].

Love, Sir Antony : the leading character in the comedy. A lady who assumes male attire, fights duels, is hail-fellow-well-met with men, etc., etc. [Southerne, *Sir Antony Love ; or, the Rambling Lady*].

Lovegold : a miserly old man of sixty who wants to marry his son's sweetheart [Fielding, *The Miser*], based on *L'Avare*, by Molière.

Lovegood : Valentine's uncle [J. Fletcher, *Wit Without Money*].

Lovejoy, Gregory : brother of Mabel Lovejoy and lover of Phyllis Catherow.

—— *Mabel :* the girl with whom Hilary Lorraine falls in love and ultimately marries.

—— *Martin :* a Kentish ' grower ' and father of Mabel and Gregory Lovejoy [Richard D. Blackmore, *Alice Lorraine*].

Lovel : a scholarly soldier [Ben Jonson, *New Inn*].

—— =John Lamb, father of the essayist [Lamb, *Old Benchers of the Inner Temple*].

—— the page of Lord Beaufort, for whom he stands aside, when he finds they both love Lady Frances Murphy, *The Citizen*].

—— the subject of a novel founded on a comedy by the same author called *The Wolves and the Lamb* [Thackeray, *Lovel the Widower*].

—— **Lord :** the hero of an old Scottish ballad, at one time very popular.

—— **Lord :** appears as a ghost [Clara Reeve, *Old English Baron*].

—— **Peregrine :** a rich man who suspects his servants of extravagant living [Townley, *High Life Below Stairs*].

Lovelace : an aristocratic suitor for the hand of Miss Drugget, the daughter of a rich tradesman [Murphy, *Three Weeks After Marriage*].

—— an evil liver whose showy qualities gave him all the more power to harm [Richardson, *Clarissa Harlowe*].

Loveless, The Elder : claimant for the hand of the scornful lady.

—— *The Younger :* a repentant sinner [Beaumont and Fletcher, *Scornful Lady*].

—— **Edward :** wedded to Amanda, he flirts with Berinthia. He learns the error of his ways [Sheridan, *A Trip to Scarborough*]. The same character is dealt with by Cibber, *Love's Last Shift*, and Sir J. Vanbrugh, *The Relapse.*

Lovell, Benjamin : a banker, addicted to the gaming table.

—— *Elsie :* the daughter of Benjamin, and loving Victor Orme [Reeve, *Parted*].

—— **Lord :** destined by Sir Giles Overreach for his daughter Margaret, but marrying Lady Allworth instead [Massinger, *New Way to Pay Old Debts*].

Lovely, Anne : the heroine [Mrs. Centlivre, *A Bold Stroke for a Wife*].

Lovemore : a pleasure-loving man who finds home dull, so neglects his wife and seeks his pleasures abroad.

Lovemore, Mrs.: exerts herself manfully to make home more attractive, and succeeds in winning her husband back [Murphy, *Way to Keep Him*].

Loverule, Lady: a termagant who led her husband a dreadful life until Zakel Jobson, a cobbler, taught her better.

———— **Sir John:** a good sort of fellow who had no authority at home [Coffey, *Devil to Pay*].

Lovewell: secretly married to Fanny Sterling [Colman and Garrick, *Clandestine Marriage*].

Lovinski, Baron: guardian of Princess Lodoiska. He betrays his trust by making love to her [Kemble, *Lodoiska*].

Loys de Dreux: a Breton noble who joins the Druses and is created prefect [R. Browning, *Return of the Druses*].

Lreux: King Arthur's Seneschal, a boastful coward [*Arthurian Cycle*].

Luath: the 'swift-footed hound' of Fingal [Ossian, *Fingal*].

Lucan, Sir: King Arthur's butler, and a Knight of the Round Table. Also called Sir Lucas [Mallory, *History of Prince Arthur*].

Lucasta: = Miss Lucy Sacheverell, the lady loved by Richard Lovelace. She, hearing that Lovelace had died of wounds at Dunkirk, married some one else.

Lucia: beloved by both of Cato's sons and marrying Porcius [Addison, *Cato*].

———— daughter of Thrifty and sister of Octavian [Otway, *The Cheats of Scapin*, from the French of Molière].

———— dresses up as a man and follows her lover about in order to win him. She gives the second title to the play [Southerne, *Sir Antony Love; or, The Rambling Lady*].

Luciana: sister-in-law of Antipholus of Syracuse [Shakespeare, *Comedy of Errors*].

Lucifer: the spirit of evil, quite inhuman in its conception [Bailey, *Festus*].

———— one of the characters introduced [Longfellow, *Golden Legend*].

Lucifera: the impersonation of Pride [Spenser, *Faëry Queene*].

Lucile: the heroine of a novel in verse [Lytton, *Lucile*].

Lucinda: in love with Jack Eustace and the friend of Rosetta [Bickerstaff, *Love in a Village*].

———— = Lucy Fortescue, wife of Lord George Lyttelton [James Thomson, *Seasons: Spring*].

Lucio: an unstable sort of man, with some redeeming characteristics [Shakespeare, *Measure for Measure*].

Lucippe : in the train of the Princess Calis, sister of Astorax [Beaumont and Fletcher, *Mad Lover*].

Lucrece : a character accepted as the type of conjugal fidelity in the middle ages is the subject of this poem [Shakespeare, *Rape of Lucrece*].

Lucretia : the heroine of a novel much condemned by the critics on its publication [Lytton, *Lucretia ; or, Children of the Night*].

—— supposed to have been intended for Madame Zichy [Beaconsfield, *Coningsby*].

Lucy : Polly's rival [Gay, *Beggar's Opera*].

—— the subject of a ballad [Laidlaw, *last verse*, Hogg, *Lucy's Flitting*].

—— the heroine [Mackenzie, *Man of the World*].

—— affianced bride of Amidas, and forsaken by him because poor. Braciday, his brother, marries her [Spenser, *Faëry Queene*].

—— **Lockit :** *see* Lockit, Lucy.

Ludovico : a deep-dyed villain, caught in his own wiles, and killed [Sheil, *Evadne ; or, The Statue*].

Ludwal : son of Roderick the Great of North Wales, who declined to pay tribute to England [Drayton, *Polyolbion*].

Lufra : ' the fleetest hound in all the North,' belonged to Douglas [Scott, *Lady of the Lake*].

Luke : a hypocrite who begins life poor, and ends by being very wealthy. The hero [Massinger, *City Madam*].

Lumbercourt, Lady Rodolpha : daughter of Lord Lumbercourt, who failing Egerton McSycophant, marries his brother Sandy [Macklin, *Man of the World*].

—— **Lord :** an impecunious voluptuary, who, for the sake of money, consents to give his daughter to Egerton McSycophant, who declines her [Macklin, *Man of the World*].

Lumbey, Dr. : the doctor who attended Mrs. Kenwigs [Dickens, *Nicholas Nickleby*].

Lumley, Captain : in Montrose's army [Scott, *Old Mortality*].

Lumpkin, Tony : an ignorant, conceited, and mischievous country squire, the son of Mrs. Hardcastle [Goldsmith, *She Stoops to Conquer*].

Lundie, Lizzie : a huntsman's daughter, noted for her beauty, who married Lewiston, and whose daughter was adopted by Mrs. St. Clair and passed off as her own [Susan E. Ferrier, *Inheritance*].

Lupin, Mrs : the landlady of the *Blue Dragon* [Dickens, *Martin Chuzzlewit*].

Lurewell, Mistress : a revengeful jilt [Farquhar, *Constant Couple*].

Luria : a Moor who serves the Florentines faithfully as commander of their forces against Pisa, and is rewarded by ingratitude [R. Browning, *Luria*].

Lusignan : the last of the line of the Christian kings of Jerusalem [Hill, *Zara*], from the French of Voltaire.

Lycidas : Edward King, Milton's friend, who was drowned crossing between England and Ireland [Milton, *Lycidas*].

Lycidus : the hero [Mrs. Aphra Behn, *Lycidus; or, Lover in Fashion*].

Lydgate, Mr. : the doctor who marries Rosamond Viney and has his life ruined by her [George Eliot, *Middlemarch*].

Lydia : ‘a miracle of virtue as well as beauty’, who ran from home and went into service to escape an objectionable marriage [Knowles, *Love-Chase*].

Lyle, Annot : daughter of Sir Duncan Campbell and the wife of the Earl of Menteith [Scott, *Legend of Montrose*].

———— **Mr. :** intended as a portrait of Lord Surrey [Beaconsfield, *Coningsby*].

Lyndon, Barry : an Irishman and a sharper, who tells his own story [Thackeray, *Barry Lyndon*].

Lyndsay, Edward : nephew of the Earl of Rosseville and his ward. The hero of the tale, who in the end marries Gertrude [Susan E. Ferrier, *Inheritance*].

Lynedale, Lord : a liberal and progressive peer [Charles Kingsley, *Alton Locke*].

Lynette : sister of Lady Lyonors of Castle Perilous, who marries Gareth [Alfred Tennyson, *Idylls of the King : Gareth and Lynette*].

Lyon, Esther : the daughter of Rufus Lyon [George Eliot, *Felix Holt*].

———— **Rufus :** a dissenting minister [George Eliot, *Felix Holt, the Radical*].

Lyonors : mother of Sir Borre, a knight of the Round Table [Mallory, *History of Prince Arthur*].

———— **Lady :** of Castle Perilous, held captive there, and delivered thence by Gareth [Alfred Tennyson, *Idylls of the King : Gareth and Lynette*].

Lysander : a young Athenian, who loves Hermia [Shakespeare, *Midsummer Night's Dream*].

Lysimachus : governor of Metaline and husband of Marina, the daughter of Pericles [Shakespeare, *Pericles, Prince of Tyre*].

Mab : Queen of the Fairies, constantly celebrated in English Literature.

Mab, Queen : one of the characters in a long, speculative poem [Shelley, *Queen Mab*].

MacAlpine, Jeanie : the landlady of the clachan, or inn, at Aberfoyle [Scott, *Rob Roy*].

MacAnaleister, Eachin : one of Rob Roy's followers [Scott, *Rob Roy*].

McAndrews : a Scottish engineer ; he loved his engines, and was, though irreverent in speech, really religious [Kipling, *McAndrew's Hymn*].

Macaulay, Allan : 'of the Red Hand', 'a seer' who loved Annot Lyle.

———— *Angus :* brother of Allan, Chief of his clan and a follower of Montrose [Scott, *Legend of Montrose*].

———— **Mary :** the humble but devoted friend of the Glenroy family [Susan E. Ferrier, *Destiny*].

Macbeth : prompted by ambition and egged on by his wife, he murders King Duncan.

———— *Lady :* her husband's evil genius, who, sympathizing with his ambition, supplies the courage and will which he lacks [Shakespeare, *Macbeth*].

Macbriar, Ephraim : a religious enthusiast and preacher [Scott, *Old Mortality*].

Macbride, Miss : an heiress and the heroine of a narrative poem [Saxe, *Miss Macbride*].

Maccabee, Father : the name and title taken by Roderick after his fall [Southey, *Roderick*].

Mac Choakumchild : an assistant in Mr. Gadgrind's school : choke-full of facts and the triumphant passer of many examinations [Dickens, *Hard Times*].

McDow, The Rev. Duncan : a coarse-minded, self-advertising parish minister [Susan E. Ferrier, *Destiny*].

Macduff : Thane of Fife, whose wife and children were slain by Macbeth, who was in revenge slain by Macduff [Shakespeare, *Macbeth*].

MacEagh, Ranald : one of the 'Children of the Mist' and an outlaw [Scott, *Legend of Montrose*].

Macey, Mr. : one of the characters in the novel [George Eliot, *Silas Marner*].

McFingall : a New England squire of Royalist sympathies in the American revolt [Trumball, *MacFingall*].

MacFlecknoe : = Thomas Shadwell, the poet [Dryden, *MacFecknoe*].

McFlimsey, Flora : the heroine of a satirical poem, by an American author [W. A. Butler, *Nothing to Wear*].

Macgregor : *see* Rob Roy.

———— **Hamish and Robert :** sons of Rob Roy, the outlaw.

———— *Helen :* wife of Rob Roy, the outlaw [Scott, *Rob Roy*].

Macheath, Captain : the leader of a band of highwaymen, who married Polly Peachum [Gay, *Beggar's Opera*].

Mac Ian, Eachin, or Hector : known as Conachar and apprenticed to Glover, whose daughter he loves [Scott, *Fair Maid of Perth*].

Mac Intyre, Captain Hector : nephew of the ' Antiquary ', Mr. Jonathan Oldbuck.

—— *Maria :* Hector's sister [Scott, *Antiquary*].

Mac Ivor, Fergus and Flora : the Chief of Glennaquoich, and his sister, the heroine of the tale. They befriend Prince Charlie [Scott, *Waverley*].

Mackage, Sandy : a canny old Scottish second-hand book-seller who befriends the hero [Charles Kingsley, *Alton Locke*].

Mackenzie, Mr. : the father of Sheila, an old Scottish laird, known as the King of Borva.

—— *Sheila :* the Princess of Thule, who marries Frank Lavender, an artist [Black, *Princess of Thule*].

—— *Rosa :* the pretty, empty-headed girl whom Clive Newcome marries as his first wife [Thackeray, *The Newcomes*].

Macklin, Sir : a priest who preached sermons that ran into their ' twenty-firstly ' and ' twenty-secondly ' [Gilbert, *Bab Ballads*].

Maclaughlan, Lady : an over-bearing but good-hearted woman, whose opinions ruled the country-side ; ' a scion of a noble house '.

—— *Sir Sampson :* a superannuated and invalid ' warrior ' with a ' distressing cough ' [Susan E. Ferrier, *Marriage*].

Macleod, Colin : one of Lord Abberville's servants, who looks after the household finances. Honest and economical [Cumberland, *Fashionable Lover*].

Mac Murrough : the bard of Fergus Mac Ivor, of Glennaquoich [Scott, *Waverley*].

Macoma : a beneficent spirit who shields the good from the machinations of evil genii [Ridley, *Tales of the Genii : Enchanter's Tale*].

Macrabin, Peter : one of the interlocutors [Wilson, *Noctes Ambrosianae*].

Macready, Pate : a pedlar. The friend and confidant of Andrew Fairservice, the cannie gardener at Osbaldistone Hall [Scott, *Rob Roy*].

Macri, Theresa : the maid of Athens [Byron, *Maid of Athens*].

Macrothumus : the personification of long-suffering [Phineas Fletcher, *Purple Island*].

Mac Sarcasm, Sir Archie : a proud Scotch knight possessed of a barbed tongue that spares no one's feelings [Macklin, *Love à la Mode*].

Mac Sillergrip : a Scotch pawnbroker, who starts in pursuit of his runaway apprentice.

—— *Mrs. :* his wife [Charles Matthews, *At Home in Multiple*].

Macstinger, Mrs. : Captain Cuttle's violent landlady, who marries Captain Busby [Dickens, *Dombey and Son*].

Mac Sycophant, Charles Egerton : son of Sir Pertinax. He declines to marry Rodolpha, preferring his mother's protégé Constantia.

—— *Sir Pertinax :* a Scottish baronet who destined his elder son for Rodolpha Lumbercourt [Macklin, *Man of the World*].

McTab, The Hon Miss Lucretia : a proud and poor Scottish maiden lady [Colman the Younger, *Poor Gentleman*].

Mac Tavish, Hamish Bean : the son of Elspat, who when he joins a Highland regiment drugs him, in order to detain him. Arrested for desertion he is tried and shot [Scott, *Highland Widow*].

Mac Turk, Captain Hector : one of the managing committee at the Spa Hotel, who throws oil on ruffled waters [Scott, *St. Ronan's Well*].

Madeline : the heroine [Lytton, *Eugene Aram*].

—— 'smiling, frowning, evermore' [Alfred Tennyson, *Madeline*].

Mademoiselle : Lady Fanciful's French maid [Vanbrugh, *Provoked Wife*].

Madge Wildfire : *see* Murdochson, Madge.

Madoc : youngest son of Owain Gwynedd, King of North Wales, known as 'The Perfect Prince' [Southey, *Madoc*].

—— **ap Iddon :** was King of Gwent, in South Wales [Stephens, *Literature of the Kymri*].

Mador, Sir : a Scottish knight, who brought charges of malpractices against Queen Guinevere for which Sir Launcelot challenged and vanquished him [*Arthurian Cycle*].

Magalona, The Fair : a daughter of the King of Naples, the heroine of an old romance, French in origin [*History of the Fair Magalone and Peter, son of the Count of Provence*].

Maggs, Molly : a young and impudent housemaid who is in love with Robin [Poole, *Scapegoat*].

Maggy : half-witted, the result of a fever, she was the grand-daughter of Mrs. Bangham [Dickens, *Little Dorrit*].

Magi, the, or Three Kings of Cologne : the 'wise men from the East'—Melchior, 'King of Light'; Balthazar, 'Lord of Treasures'; and Gaspar or Caspar, 'The White One'.

Magnano : one of those who assaulted Hudibras at a bear-baiting [Butler, *Hudibras*].

Magnetic, The Lady : the subject of a comedy [Ben Jonson, *Lady Magnetic*].

Magnus, Peter : 'a red-haired man with an inquisitive nose', who inquires of Mr. Pickwick as to the best way to propose to a lady [Dickens, *Pickwick Papers*].

Maguelone, Fair : see Magalona, The Fair.

Magwitch, Abel : sometimes known by the name of Provis ; a convict. He is the father of Miss Havisham's adopted child Estella [Dickens, *Great Expectations*].

Mahldenau, Meeta : daughter of the minister and betrothed to Rupert Roselheim [Knowles, *Maid of Mariendorpt*], based on a novel by Jane Porter, *Village of Mariendorpt*].

Mahoud : the spendthrift son of a Delhi jeweller and condemned to be burnt alive, but was changed into a toad [Ridley, *Tales of the Genii : Enchanter's Tale*].

Maid Marian : see Marian, Maid.

—— **of Athens :** see Macri, Theresa.

—— **of Mariendorpt :** see Mahldenau, Meeta.

—— **of Perth, Fair :** see Glover, Catherine.

—— **of the Mill :** see Fairfield, Patty.

Maiden of the Mist : see Geierstein, Anne of.

Maimoune : the fairy daughter of Damriat, 'King of a legion of geni', who changed herself into a flea [*Arabian Nights*].

Maimuna : a sorceress [Southey, *Thalaba*].

Malachi : the assistant of Turnbull [Scott, *Redgauntlet*].

Malagrowther, Sir Mungo : an ill-tempered old courtier, soured by misfortune [Scott, *Fortunes of Nigel*].

Malaprop, Mrs. : aunt of Lydia Languish. Notorious for her misuse of words [Sheridan, *Rivals*].

Malbecco : 'a cankered, crabbed carl', wealthy and stingy, and married to a young wife [Spenser, *Faëry Queene*].

Malcolm : eldest son of Duncan, who, upon the murder of his father, fled with his brother, Donalbain, to Ireland [Shakespeare, *Macbeth*].

—— **Captain :** the father of the hero of the story.

—— *Edith :* a gentle, beautiful and intellectual girl, the daughter of the Chief of Glenroy, and heroine of the story.

—— *Mungo :* Laird of Inch Orran, and cousin of

Glenroy, owner of an estate much coveted by the latter.

Malcolm, Norman : the only son and heir of the Chief of Glenroy, who died in boyhood.

———— *Reginald :* nephew to the Chief of Glenroy and long betrothed to his daughter, to whom he proved faithless, finally wedding Florinda Waldegrave.

———— *Ronald :* cousin of Glenroy, the hero of the story, who after an adventurous life, ends by marrying Edith, the Chief's daughter [Susan E. Ferrier, *Destiny*].

———— *Mrs. :* a poor but very pious widow whose children all prosper [Galt, *Annals of the Parish*].

Malecasta : the lady of Castle Joyous, and the personification of lust [Spenser, *Faëry Queene*].

Maleffort : Lady Briana's Seneschal, whom Sir Calidore slew [Spenser, *Feëry Queene*].

Maleger : the son of the Earth, who, whenever he touched her derived new strength, so that when Arthur wished to kill him he had to cast him into a lake [Spenser, *Faëry Queene*].

Malengrin : the personification of guile [Spenser, *Faëry Queene*].

Mal-Fet, The Chevalier : the name taken by Sir Launcelot during the term of his madness [Mallory, *History of Prince Arthur*].

Malfort, Mr. and Mrs. : a young man who ruins himself and his wife by unwise speculations. Their distresses are relieved by Frank Heartall and Mrs. Cheerly [Cherry, *Soldier's Daughter*].

Malfy, Duchess of : sister of the Duke of Calabria, she fell in love with her steward, at which her brothers were so outraged that they caused her to be strangled [Webster, *Duchess of Malfy*].

Malgo : a mythical King of Britain [Drayton, *Polyolbion*].

Malinal : when the Aztecas declared war against the white men Malinal took the white men's side, and defended the white women [Southey, *Madoc*].

Malone, the Rev. Peter Augustus : curate of Briarfield ; fonder of using his fists than his brains [Charlotte Brontë, *Shirley*].

Mal-Orchol : King of Fuärfed [Ossian, *Oina-Morul*].

Maltravers, Ernest : the hero of the story [Lytton, *Ernest Maltravers*].

Malvil : it was upon this character that Sheridan based his of Joseph Surface [Murphy, *Know Your Own Mind*].

Malvina : the daughter of Toscar and engaged to Oscar, Ossian's son [Ossian, *Temora*].

Malvoisin, Sir Albert : preceptor to the Knights Templars.

Malvoisin, Sir Philip : one of the challengers at the tournament [Scott, *Ivanhoe*].

Malvolio : Olivia's steward, on whom Sir Toby, Sir Andrew Aguecheek and Maria play a trick [Shakespeare, *Twelfth Night*].

Mamillius : Prince of Sicilla [Shakespeare, *Winter's Tale*].

Mammon, Sir Epicure : a wealthy fool, who gives the alchemist, Subtle, the money for his quackery [Ben Jonson, *Alchemist*].

—— the personification of earthly ambition [Spenser, *Faëry Queene*].

Man in Black : said to be intended for the Rev. Henry Goldsmith, the author's father [Goldsmith, *Citizen of the World*].

Mandane : wife of the Mandarin Zamti, and mother of Hamet [Murphy, *Orphan of China*].

Manette, Doctor Alexander : for eighteen years a prisoner in the Bastille, and released just on the eve of the revolution.

—— *Lucie :* his daughter, who devotes herself to him during his remaining years, and marries Charles Darnay [Dickens, *Tale of Two Cities*].

Manfred : sells himself to the Devil, who assigns him seven demons to do his bidding [Byron, *Manfred*].

Manly : a young man, the friend of Wittipol [Ben Jonson, *Devil is an Ass*].

—— replete with noble traits and the cousin and good genius of Sir Francis Wronghead [Vanbrugh and Cibber, *Provoked Husband*].

—— a morose sea-captain, who disbelieves in everybody and everything, including himself [Wycherley, *Plain-Dealer*].

—— Captain : betrothed to Arabella [Knight, *Honest Thieves*].

—— Colonel : a straightforward, honourable soldier [Mrs. Centlivre, *Beau's Duel*].

Mannering, Guy : the father of Julia, who marries the hero, Harry Bertram.

—— *Julia :* his daughter, rather hare-brained ' [Scott, *Guy Mannering*].

Mansfield, The Miller of : a good-natured countryman, who offered shelter to Henry VIII when he lost his way on a hunting expedition [*King and the Miller of Mansfield*].

Mantalini, Madame : a fashionable milliner and dressmaker near Cavendish Square.

—— *Mr. Alfred :* her husband, his share in the business

being confined to spending the money [Dickens, *Nicholas Nickleby*].

Marcelia : the wife of Sforza, who doted on her, but listened to evil tongues, flew into a jealous rage and slew her [Massinger, *Duke of Milan*].

Marcella : a lady attendant on the Queen, the only other female character in the play [Norton and Buckhurst, *Gorboduc*].

────── a young and impulsive girl with socialistic leanings [Mrs. Humphry Ward, *Marcella*].

Marcellin de Peyras : first elopes with the lady Ernestine and then falls in love with his cousin Margaret [Stirling, *Gold Mine ; or, Miller of Grenoble*].

Marcellus : intended for Edmund Malone [T. F. Dibdin, *Bibliomania*].

────── the officer to whom the ghost appeared when he was on guard on the ramparts [Shakespeare, *Hamlet*].

March, Ursula : the girl who marries John Halifax [Mrs. Craik, *John Halifax, Gentleman*].

Marchioness, The : the poor little drudge who nurses Dick Swiveller, and afterwards marries him [Dickens, *Old Curiosity Shop*].

Marcia : beloved by both Sempronius and Juba [Addison, *Cato*].

Marck, William de la : the 'Wild-Boar of the Ardennes' [Scott, *Quentin Durward*].

Mardonius : a captain [J. Fletcher, *King and No King*].

Margoul : only child of Sir Giles Overreach, who rejects Lord Lovel for simple Tom Allworth [Massinger, *New Way to Pay Old Debts*].

Margaret : wife of Vanduuke, the tipsy Burgomaster of Bruges [J. Fletcher, *Beggar's Bush*].

────── the heroine of an American novel, by some called 'the New England Classic' [Judd, *Margaret*].

────── **Ladye** : 'the flower of Teviot', daughter of Lord Walter Scott of Branksome Hall [Scott, *Lay of the Last Minstrel*].

Margaretta : ran away from home to avoid an unpalatable marriage, and earned her living by singing [Hoare, *No Song, No Supper*].

Margaritta, Donna : a wealthy, wilful girl, who is tamed by a wise and forbearing husband [J. Fletcher, *Rule a Wife and Have a Wife*].

Margery, Dame : the nurse of Eveline Berenger [Scott, *Betrothed*].

Margiana, Queen : married to Prince Assad [*Arabian Nights*].

Marguerite : the wife of St. Leon [Godwin, *Marguerite*].

Marhaus, Sir : a knight of the Round Table, who met Sir Tristram in single combat and was defeated by him [Mallory, *History of Prince Arthur*].

Maria : engaged to Groveby. Supposed to be the ward but really the daughter of Oldworth [Burgoyne, *Maid of the Oaks*].

—— the wife of Frederick, brother of the King of Naples. He is a wicked man, she a virtuous woman [J. Fletcher, *Wife for a Month*].

—— daughter of Thorowgood, who loved her father's apprentice, George Barnwell, but he was convicted of robbery and murder [Lillo, *George Barnwell*].

—— beloved by Longaville, a noble in the train of Ferdinand of Navarre [Shakespeare, *Love's Labour's Lost*].

—— the witty waiting-woman to Olivia, who plays a trick on Malvolio [Shakespeare, *Twelfth Night*].

—— the heroine, in love with Charles Surface [Sheridan, *School for Scandal*].

—— a mad girl who played Vesper hymns on a pipe [Sterne, *Sentimental Journey*].

Mariamne : the subject of two tragedies—one by Alexandre Hardy, 1601; and the other by Elijah Fenton, 1723.

Marian : a foundling adopted by Kate Macone, an Irish cook, who rears her tenderly [Mrs. S. C. Hall, *Marian ; or, Young Maid's Fortunes*].

—— loved Colin Clout, who scorned her for Cicely [Gay, *Pastorals*, ii.].

—— daughter of Robert, the wrecker, and promised to a young sailor named Edward [Knowles, *The Daughter*].

—— Margaret, Countess of Cumberland [Spenser, *Colin Clout's Come Home Again*].

—— Maid=Matilda, daughter of Robert Lord Fitzwater. Poisoned by a poached egg sent her by King John, because she rejected his advances [Drayton, *Polyolbion*].

—— Maid : the heroine of the book. The daughter of a baron, she marries another baron, who has been outlawed, and lives with him in Sherwood Forest [Peacock, *Maid Marian*].

Mariana : this was the girl whom Lovegold, the miser, desired to marry [Fielding, *Miser*].

—— the daughter of a Swiss ; she nurses Leonardo through a dreadful accident and falls in love with him. After many trials they are married [Knowles, *The Wife*].

—— sister of Ludovico Sforza, Duke of Milan [Massinger, *Duke of Milan*].

Mariana : the wife of Angelo [Shakespeare, *Measure for Measure*].

—————— **and Mariana in the South :** two poems for which Tennyson is said to have taken the idea from Mariana in *Measure for Measure* [Alfred Tennyson, *Mariana*, and *Mariana in the South*].

Marie, Countess : the mother of Ulrica, by her lover, Ernest de Fridberg, the 'prisoner' [Stirling, *Prisoner of State*].

—————— **Magdalene :** the subject of an interlude [Lewis Wager, *Life and Repentance of Marie Magdalene*].

Marigold, Dr. : the hero of a Christmas story. Marigold is a Cheap-Jack, whose little child dies in his arms whilst he is entertaining a crowd [Dickens, *Dr. Marigold's Prescription*].

Marina : she tried to drown herself for love of Celandine, who disregarded her love, but was rescued by a shepherd [Browne, *Britannia's Pastorals*].

—————— wife of Jacopo Foscari, son of the Doge of Venice [Byron, *Two Foscari*].

—————— the daughter of Pericles [Shakespeare, *Pericles, Prince of Tyre*].

Marinel : the son of Cymoent. He permitted no one to pass the cave wherein he dwelt without fighting with him ; but Britomart felled him to the ground. Marinel was loved by Florimel [Spenser, *Faëry Queene*].

Marino, Faliero : the forty-ninth Doge of Venice, who at the age of seventy-six was beheaded on the 'Giant's Staircase' [Byron, *Marino Faliero*].

Marion de Lorme : the conspiritors met in her house, so that she was enabled to keep Richelieu informed of all their plans [Lytton, *Richelieu*].

Mark, Sir : King of Cornwall, who wedded Ysolde the Fair, of Ireland, who loved Sir Tristram [Mallory, *History of Prince Arthur*].

Markleham, Mrs. : the mother of Mrs. Strong and known as 'the old soldier' [Dickens, *David Copperfield*].

Marks, Will : the hero of the tale which Mr. Pickwick submits to Master Humphrey as his qualification for admission to the Club [Dickens, *Master Humphrey's Clock*].

Marley, The Ghost of Jacob : Marley had been Scrooge's partner, and his ghost plays an important rôle in the story [Dickens, *Christmas Carol*].

Marlow, Sir Charles : an old friend of Squire Hardcastle.

—————— *Young :* his son, who is overcome by shyness whenever in the presence of women of any social standing. Kate Hardcastle 'stoops to conquer' him [Goldsmith, *She Stoops to Conquer*].

Marmion : a valiant English knight, who fell on Flodden Field [Scott, *Marmion*].

Marner, Silas : a poor lonely weaver deserted by his wife. He finds a tiny strayed child and takes it to his heart and rears it [George Eliot, *Silas Marner*].

Marplot : a good-natured, interfering young man, always meddling with other people's affairs [Mrs. Centlivre, *The Busy-Body*].

—— **Sir Martin :** the hero of a comedy founded on Molière's *L'Etourdi* [Duke of Newcastle, *Sir Martin Marplot*].

Marrall, Jack : a false, cringing employé of Sir Giles Overreach [Massinger, *New Way to Pay Old Debts*].

Mar-Text, Sir Oliver : a clergyman [Shakespeare, *As You Like It*].

Martha : sister to the 'Scornful Lady' [Beaumont and Fletcher, *Scornful Lady*].

—— *alias* **Ulrica :** mother of Bertha, who becomes Hereward's wife [Scott, *Count Robert of Paris*].

Martia : in love with Virolet ; she is one of the heroines of the play [J. Fletcher, *Double Marriage*].

Martin, Dame : Darsie Latimer's partner at the fisherman's merrymaking [Scott, *Redgauntlet*].

—— **Robert :** an honest young farmer, in love with Harriet Smith [Jane Austin, *Emma*].

Marton, Mr. : the old schoolmaster who gave shelter to Little Nell and her grandfather [Dickens, *Old Curiosity Shop*].

Marwood, Alice : *see* Brown, Alice.

—— **Mistress :** a despiser of all men, the result of having been jilted by one [Congreve, *Way of the World*].

Mary : the Mayor of Ipswich's pretty housemaid, who becomes Mrs. Sam Weller [Dickens, *Pickwick Papers*].

—— the niece of Valentine and Alice. She loves Mons. Thomas [J. Fletcher, *Mons. Thomas*].

—— **Ambree :** *see* Ambree, Mary.

—— **Ashburton :** *see* Ashburton, Mary.

—— **Graham :** *see* Graham, Mary.

—— **Morrison :** *see* Morrison, Mary.

—— the **Maid of the Inn :** a bright and happy girl, the pride of the village, who went mad on discovering her lover to be a murderer [Southey, *Mary, the Maid of the Inn*].

—— **Trevellyn :** *see* Trevellyn, Mary.

Maskwell : a cunning hypocrite, who feigns love and friendship for all sorts of people he despises [Congreve, *Double Dealer*].

Mason, Bertha : Rochester's lunatic wife, who set fire to his house [Charlotte Brontë, *Jane Eyre*].

———— **Lady :** a woman who forges a codicil to a will in favour of her own son. She is a woman whose character is a strange mixture of good and evil, weakness and strength [Anthony Trollope, *Orley Farm*].

Massey, Bartle : a schoolmaster with a great contempt for all women-kind [George Eliot, *Adam Bede*].

Mat-o'-the-Mint : a highwayman whose friend says he 'may raise good contributions on the public if he does not cut himself short by murder' [Gay, *Beggar's Opera*].

Matilda : daughter of Sophia and sister of Rollo and Otto [J. Fletcher, *Bloody Brother*].

———— daughter of Rokeby and in love with Redmond, her father's page [Scott, *Rokeby*].

Matthew, Master : a stupid, gullable, quarrelsome fellow [Ben Jonson, *Every Man in His Humour*].

Matthias : a miller in debt, who follows a wealthy Polish Jew one night and kills him, pays his debts and wins respect. On the eve of his daughter's wedding he dies in a fit, haunted by the sound of sledge-bells [Ware, *Polish Jew*].

Mattie : Bailie Nicol Jarvie's servant, whom he makes his wife [Scott, *Rob Roy*].

———— **Miss :** *see* Jenkins, Miss Mattie.

Maud : 'Faultily faultless, icily regular, splendidly null' [Alfred Tennyson, *Maud*].

Maude : wife of Peter Pratefast, who, failing other towels, 'wyped her dishes with her dogges tayll' [Hawes, *Passe-Tyme of Pleasure*].

Maugrabin, Hayraddin : a Bohemian gipsy, who assumes the disguise of Rouge Sanglier.

———— *Zamet :* his brother, hung near Plessis les Tours [Scott, *Quentin Durward*].

Maugraby : one of the greatest magicians who ever lived, and son of the founder of Dom-Daniel [*Arabian Nights*].

Maul : a giant who assaulted Greatheart with a club, but had his head cut off for his pains [Bunyan, *Pilgrim's Progress*].

Maule : *see* Holgrave, Mr.

Mauprat, Adrien de : 'the wildest gallant and bravest knight of France' [Lytton, *Richelieu*].

Mauxalinda : she loved Moore of Moore Hall, who slew the dragon of Wantley, but was by him forsaken [Carey, *Dragon of Wantley*].

Mawworm : an ignorant and vulgar man who thinks he has a vocation to preach [Bickerstaff, *Hypocrite*].

Maxime : a Roman officer who was converted to Christianity [Chaucer, *Canterbury Tales : Second Nun's Tale*].

Maximin : a Roman tyrant [Dryden, *Tyrannic Love; or, Royal Martyr*].

Maxwell : deputy chamberlain at Whitehall [Scott, *Fortunes of Nigel*].

—— **Mr. Pate :** called 'Pate in Peril', one of Redgauntlet's fellow conspirators [Scott, *Redgauntlet*].

—— **Right Hon. William :** a royalist officer in the king's army [Scott, *Old Mortality*].

May : the heroine of a poem 'full of passion, incident, and melody' [R.Browning, *Rhyme of the Duchess May*].

—— the girl who marries a Lombard baron of sixty [Chaucer, *Canterbury Tales : Merchant's Tale*].

—— **Baby :** the subject of a graceful little lyric [Bennett, *Baby May*].

—— **Queen :** *see* Alice.

Mayflower, Phoebe : Sir Henry Lee's servant at the lodge at Woodstock [Scott, *Woodstock*].

Maylie, Harry : the son of Mrs. Maylie, who marries Rose.

—— **Mrs. :** a lady living at Chertsey, who befriends Oliver.

—— **Rose :** Mrs. Maylie's adopted daughter, whose real name is Rose Fleming, and who proves to be the aunt of Oliver [Dickens, *Oliver Twist*].

—— **Mr. :** an affected, blasé man who dresses to perfection and is adored by foolish young ladies [Fanny Burney, *Cecilia*].

Meadows, Sir William : a kindly country gentleman, the friend of Jack Eustace.

—— **Young :** son of Sir William, who, to escape an undesired marriage, leaves home and goes as gardener to Mr. Woodcock, at whose house he falls in love with the very girl he had tried to escape from [Bickerstaff, *Love in a Village*].

Meagles, Minnie : called 'Pet'. Ultimately marries Henry Gowan.

—— **Mr. :** a well-to-do, kindly man who prides himself on being practical.

—— **Mrs. :** his wife, as kind and cheery as himself [Dickens, *Little Dorrit*].

Medina : the personification of the Golden Mean [Spenser, *Faëry Queene*].

Medley : some have supposed this to be a portrait of the author himself [Etherege, *Man of Mode*].

—— **Matthew :** 'handy man' to Sir Walter Waring, who marries the woodcutter's daughter, Dolly Fairlop [Dudley, *Woodman*].

Medora : the faithful and greatly beloved wife of the Corsair [Byron, *Corsair*].

Meeta : *see* Mahldenan, Meeta.

Meercraft : a dishonest speculator [Ben Jonson, *Devil is an Ass*].

Meg : the daughter of Toby Veck, married on New Year's Day to Richard [Dickens, *Chimes*].

Megissogwon : a magician, who wrought all kinds of evil to man, and whom Hiawatha was for ever opposing. He had one vunerable point on his person, and that was beneath a tuft of hair on his head. Into this Hiawatha sent an arrow [Longfellow, *Hiawatha*].

Meiklewham, Mr. Saunders : the legal authority on the board of management at the Spa Hotel [Scott, *St. Ronan's Well*].

Melantha : a lady of fashion, impertinent but attractive [Dryden, *Marriage à la Mode*].

Melantius : brother to Evadne. Brave and honest, but rough, and though trusting, relentless in punishing proved misdeeds [Beaumont and Fletcher, *Maid's Tragedy*].

Meldrum, Squire : the hero of a curious old Scottish poem [Sir David Lindsay, *The History of a Nobil and Wailzeand Squyre, William Meldrum*].

Melema, Tito : son of Baldassare Calvo. Of Greek parentage and very handsome, but unprincipled, false and pleasure-loving. The husband of Romola [George Eliot, *Romola*].

Meliades : =Henry, son of James I. It is an anagram of *Miles a De* (*o*) ' God's Soldier '. Upon his death an elegy on him appeared [Drummond, *Tears on the Death of Meliades*].

Meliadus del Espinoy and **Meliadus le Noir Oeil** were both Knights of the Round Table—the thirty-seventh and thirty-eighth in order [Robinson's *Ancient Order*].

Melibee : a shepherd, father of Pastorella, who married Sir Calidore. Melibee=Sir Francis Walsingham, and Calidore=Sir Philip Sidney, who married Walsingham's daughter, Frances [Spenser, *Faëry Queene*].

Melibeus : the husband of Prudence, a ' noble wyf', noted for her forgiving spirit [Chaucer, *Canterbury Tales : Chaucer's Tale of Melibeus*].

Melinda : in love with Worthy, whom she marries, after teazing him unmercifully for a year [Farquhar, *Recruiting Officer*].

Mell, Mr. : an assistant master at Mr. Creakle's school, persecuted by Steerforth [Dickens, *David Copperfield*].

Mellefont : nephew of Lady Touchwood, and deeply attached to Cynthia Pliant [Congreve, *Double Dealer*].

Mellida : *see* Antonio and Mellida.

Melmoth : the central figure of the novel, who makes a compact with the Devil that he may live 100 years [Maturin, *Melmoth the Wanderer*].

Melnotte, Claude : the hero of the play, who, though only a gardener's son, passes himself off as a prince and marries Pauline [Lytton, *Lady of Lyons*].

Melrose, Mary : the penniless cousin of Violet, who marries Talbot Champneys.

—— *Violet :* the rich bride of Charles Middlewick [H. J. Byron, *Our Boys*].

Melusina : a fairy who, as a punishment for ill-treating her father, was turned into a serpent every Saturday. Her husband had promised never to visit her that day, but he broke his word and she was compelled to leave him [*Jean d'Arras*].

Melvil, Sir John : betrothed to Miss Sterling, but preferring her sister Fanny, who is discovered to be already married [Colman and Garrick, *Clandestine Marriage*].

Melville, Julia : the ward of Sir Anthony Absolute. She fell in love with Faulkland [Sheridan, *Rivals*].

—— **Sir Robert :** a member of the embassy sent to Mary, Queen of Scots, from the privy council [Scott, *The Abbot*].

Melyhalt, The Lady : Sir Galiot invaded her territory, but nevertheless was chosen by her as her chevalier [*Arthurian Cycle*].

Memnon : a general in the army of Astorax, King of Paphos. He is the hero [Beaumont and Fletcher, *Mad Lover*].

Menander : intended for Thomas Warton [T. F. Dibdin, *Bibliomania*].

Mendoza, Isaac : a rich Portuguese Jew who is very wise in his own conceit, but always being duped [Sheridan, *Duenna*].

Mengs, John : the innkeeper at Kirchhoff [Scott, *Anne of Geierstein*].

Menippus : *see* Philonides and Menippus.

Menteith, Earl of : marries Annot Lyle, the heroine [Scott, *Legend of Montrose*].

Mephistopheles : is one of the characters which materially differs in conception from that drawn by Goethe. There is 'an awful melancholy', says Hallam, about that of the English poet [Malowe, *Faustus*].

Mercilla : a 'Maiden Queen of great power and majesty', who is menaced by a soldan. The Queen is Elizabeth, the soldan is Philip II of Spain [Spenser, *Faëry Queene*].

Mercutio : 'a gentleman that loves to hear himself talk' [Shakespeare, *Romeo and Juliet*].

Mercy : a young friend of Christiana, who goes with her to Zion [Bunyan, *Pilgrim's Progress*].

Merdle, Mr. : a banker who is ruined and commits suicide.

———— *Mrs. :* his wife, and the mother of Mr. Edmund Sparkler [Dickens, *Little Dorrit*].

Meredith, Mr. : one of Redgauntlet's co-conspirators [Scott, *Redgauntlet*].

Merida, The Marchioness : affianced bride of Count Valantia [Mrs. Inchbald, *Child of Nature*].

Meridies : or 'Noonday Sun', who helped to guard the entrances to Castle Perilous [Alfred Tennyson, *Idylls of the King : Gareth and Lynette*].

Merlin : the bard and wizard of King Arthur's Court, the son of Matilda, and an evil 'sprite'. Frequent allusions are found to him in old English literature [Mallory, *History of Prince Arthur*].

Merope : the subject of a classical tragedy [Matthew Arnold, *Merope* ; also George Jeffreys, *Merope*].

Merrilies, Meg : a gipsy, thief, smuggler, and a kidnapper of children [Scott, *Guy Mannering*].

Merrygreek, Matthew : Ralph Roister Doister's servant [Udall, *Ralph Roister Doister*].

Merrylegs : a performing dog at Sleary's Circus that belongs to Signor Jupe [Dickens, *Hard Times*].

Merton, Tommy : one of the leading characters in this once popular tale for boys [Day, *Sandford and Merton*].

Mertoun, Basil : known as Vaughan, at one time a pirate.

———— *Mordaunt :* the son of Basil. Married to Brenda Troil [Scott, *Pirate*].

———— **Henry, Earl of :** the lover of Mildred Tresham, who is killed by her brother to conceal her shame [R. Browning, *Blot on the Scutcheon*].

Mervyn, Mr. Arthar : the guardian of Julia Mannering [Scott, *Guy Mannering*].

Methos : Drunkenness personified. He is Gluttony's twin-brother [Phineas Fletcher, *Purple Island*].

Meyrick : the name of a family which occupies a considerable place in the novel [George Eliot, *Daniel Deronda*].

Micawber, Miss Emma : daughter of Mr. and Mrs. Micawber, who marries Mr. Ridger Begs, and goes to Australia.

———— *Mr. Wilkins :* an improvident, impecunious man, always 'waiting for something to turn up'.

Micawber, Mrs. : his wife, whose spirits are almost as elastic as his own.

—— *Wilkins :* their son, a chorister boy in Canterbury Cathedral [Dickens, *David Copperfield*].

Michal : is intended for Queen Catherine, the wife of Charles II [Dryden and Tate, *Absalom and Achitophel*, pt. ii.].

Michael : loved Maria Mosby, and is persuaded by her brother to let some ruffians enter Arden's house to murder him [Lillo, *Arden of Feversham*].

Michelot : a grasping, low-minded coward, who does all he can to penetrate the mystery of 'the Gold-mine' [Stirling, *Gold-Mine; or, Miller of Grenoble*].

Micklewham, Mr. : schoolmaster and sessions clerk at Garnock, to whom Dr. Pringle addresses his letters [Galt, *Ayrshire Legatees*].

Midas, Justice : it was his duty to decide between the rival merits of Pol and Pan. He gave the preference to Pan, whereupon Pol cast aside his disguise and revealed himself as Apollo and caused Midas henceforth to wear the ears of an ass [O'Hara, *Midas*]. Lily also wrote a play by this name.

Middlemas, Mr. Matthew : the assumed name of General Witherington.

—— *Richard :* his son; though as a foundling he has been apprenticed to Dr. Gray. He goes to India and is crushed to death by an elephant [Scott, *Surgeon's Daughter*].

Middleton, Clara : a charming girl who is engaged to Sir Willoughby Pattern, but discovers his true character in time and breaks off her engagement. In love with Vernon Whitford.

—— *Dr. :* the sententious and learned father of Clara Middleton [George Meredith, *The Egoist*].

—— **Sir John** : the squire of the neighbourhood where Mrs. Dashwood and her daughters settle [Jane Austen, *Sense and Sensibility*].

Middlewick, Charles : son of Mr. Perkyn Middlewick, who marries Violet Melrose, an heiress, against his father's wishes.

—— *Mr. Perkyn :* a retired butterman, a neighbour of Sir Geoffrey Champneys. Vulgar but good [H. J. Byron, *Our Boys*].

Midge : a miller's son and one of Robin Hood's companions [*Robin Hood and Allan-a-Dale*].

Miggs, Miss : the disagreeable and mischief-making servant of the Vardens [Dickens, *Barnaby Rudge*].

Mildmay, Frank : the hero, whose adventures are said to

be those of the author himself, though it is not supposed to be a portrait [Marryat, *Frank Mildmay*].

Mildred, Little : the junior subaltern with an income of £4,000 a year [Kipling, *Man Who Was*].

Milford, Jack : the companion of Harry Dornton on ' the road to ruin ' [Holcroft, *Road to Ruin*].

Millamant : in love with Mirabell, an accomplished, fine lady, who rejoices in her power of giving pain [Congreve, *Way of the World*].

Millbank : supposed to be intended for Thomas Hope, who wrote a romance called *Anastasius* [Beaconsfield, *Vivian Grey*].

Miller, Daisy : the subject of a novel [James, *Daisy Miller*].

———— **James** : brought up in the stable and on the turf, he became ' tiger ' to Mr. Flammer and engaged to Miss Bloomfield's maid, Mary Chintz [Selby *Unfinished Gentleman*].

Million, Mrs. : a lady possessed of fabulous wealth [Beaconsfield, *Vivian Grey*].

Mills, Miss : a lady of blighted affections ; the friend of Dora [Dickens, *David Copperfield*].

Millwood, Sarah : a woman of evil life, who spurs George Barnwell on to the commital of all sorts of crimes, and then bears evidence against him [Lillo, *George Barnwell*].

Milner, Miss : in love with Mr. Dorriforth, a young Roman Catholic priest [Mrs. Inchbald, *Simple Story*].

Milvey, Mrs. Margaretta : a pretty, bright, plucky little woman.

———— *The Rev. Frank* : a young curate with small means and a large family [Dickens, *Our Mutual Friend*].

Mincing : Millamant's maid [Congreve, *Way of the World*].

Minikin, Lady : hates her husband and coquettes with Colonel Tivy because it is the ' correct thing '.

———— *Lord* : a married man who flirts with other women because that too is ' the thing ' [Garrick, *Bon Ton*].

Minnehaha=laughing water, the wife of Hiawatha [Longfellow, *Hiawatha*].

Minns, Mr. : the subject of the first of the ' sketches ' [Dickens, *Sketches by Boz*].

Minotti : governor of Corinth, who, when that city was stormed by the Turks in 1715, himself fired a train of gunpowder, blowing up the Turkish camp. Minotti himself was killed [Byron, *Siege of Corinth*].

Mirabel : the subject of the play ; a woman-hater, he is pursued by Oriana and captured by her [J. Fletcher, *Wild-Goose Chase*].

Mirabel, Old : tries to trap his son, to whom he is devoted, into marriage, but in vain.

──── **Young :** an inconstant young man who, though he loves, wishes to retain his freedom [Farquhar, *Inconstant*].

Mirabell, Edward : in love with Millamant, whose very faults attracted him [Congreve, *Way of the World*].

Mirabella : ' a maiden fair clad in mourning weeds ', but very ' scornful and proud ' withal [Spenser, *Faëry Queene*].

Miramont : an ignorant old man himself, he nevertheless admired learning. He was uncle to Charles and Eustace [J. Fletcher, *Elder Brother*].

Miranda : the rich ward of Sir Francis Gripe [Mrs. Centlivre, *Busy Body*].

──── the daughter of Prospero, with Caliban for her only comrade save her father and Ariel [Shakespeare, *Tempest*].

──── **Léonce :** the son of a rich jeweller, he fell in love with Clara Mulhausen, an adventuress, and lived with her at Clairvaux, where he eventually committed suicide [R. Browning, *Red-Cotton Night-cap Country*].

Mirza : a holy man who, living at Bagdad, has a vision of the Bridge of Life [Addison, *Spectator : The Vision of Mirza*, No. 159].

Misbegot, Malcolm : the son of Sybil Knockwinnock and an ancestor of Sir Arthur Wardour [Scott, *Antiquary*].

Mishe-Mokwa : the mighty bear which Mudjekeewis slays [Longfellow, *Hiawatha*].

Mishe-Nahma : an enormous sturgeon from which Hiawatha showed the Indians how to make oil. It swallowed Hiawatha but he smote its heart with his fist, and thus killing it, Hiawatha escaped [Longfellow, *Hiawatha*].

Misnar : an Indian sultan transformed into a toad [Ridley, *Tales of the Genii*].

Mite, Sir Matthew : a dissolute, pig-headed, East Indian merchant [Foote, *The Nabob*].

Mivers, Chillingly : a cynical journalist [Lytton, *Kenelm Chillingly*].

Mivins, Mr. : known as ' the Zephyr ' and detained in the Fleet Prison at the same time as Mr. Pickwick [Dickens, *Pickwick Papers*].

Mizen, Mat : a harum-scarum, dare-devil English sailor [Barrymore, *El Hyder, Chief of the Ghaut Mountains*].

Moath : the father of Thalaba's bride, Oneiza [Southey, *Thalaba*].

Moddle Mr. Augustus : one of Mrs. Todger's boarders

who falls in love with Mercy Pecksniff, and is entrapped into an engagement with her sister Charity. He escapes to Van Dieman's Land [Dickens, *Martin Chuzzlewit*].

Modelove, Sir Philip : one of Anne Lovely's guardians, and a regular old fop [Centlivre, *Bold Stroke for a Wife*].

Modely : an unprincipled, worldly-minded man, constantly being smitten, but never really loving until he meets AuraFreehold,a farmer's daughter[Kemble,*FarmHouse*].

Modish, Lady Betty : flirts with Lord Foppington to annoy Lord Morelove, her genuine love, for whom she will not admit any regard until brought to reason by his flirtations with Lady Graveairs [Cibber, *Careless Husband*].

Modo : a murder-inciting fiend, and one of the five who possess 'poor Tom' [Shakespeare, *King Lear*].

Modred : the knight whom King Arthur slew with the last blow he ever gave with Excalibur [Alfred Tennyson, *Idylls of the King : Passing of Arthur*].

Modus : the frowsy, musty bookworm whom Helen loved [Knowles, *Hunchback*].

Moechus : the personification of Adultery [Phineas Fletcher, *Purple Island*].

Moeliades : *see* Meliades.

Mog, Molly : the subject of a ballad in praise of an innkeeper's daughter at Oakingham, Berkshire [Gay, *Molly Mog : or, Fair Maid of the Inn*].

Mogg, Peter : a barrister who seeks election to Parliament [Sterling, *Election*].

Mohareb : an evil spirit that dwelt in a cave under the ocean called Dom-Daniel [Southey, *Thalaba*].

Mohun, Lord : a fashionable rake, gambler and man-about-town [Thackeray, *Esmond*].

Moidart, John of : an officer in Montrose's army [Scott, *Legend of Montrose*].

Mokanna : a prophet-chief, who, to hide a face disfigured in battle, always wore a veil [T. Moore, *Lalla Rookh : The Veiled Prophet of Khorassan*].

Molly : at one time Abel Magwitch's mistress and the mother of Estella, afterwards housekeeper to Mr. Jaggers [Dickens, *Great Expectations*].

Molozane, Beryl : beloved by George Geith. A saintly and much loved woman who, after enduring many sorrows, died young [F. G. Trafford (Mrs. Riddell), *George Geith*].

Monaldeschi, Marquis : grand Equerry to Queen Christina, who caused him to be executed for insulting her with his love [R. Browning, *Christina and Monaldeschi*].

Moncada, Matthias de : a stern man who, ignoring all natural affections, causes his daughter to be arrested the day after she has given birth to a son.

—— *Zilia de :* his daughter. The wife of General Witherington [Scott, *Surgeon's Daughter*].

Moneytrap : wedded to Araminta, but allowing his affections to stray to his friend Gripe's wife, Clarissa [Vanbrugh, *Confederacy*].

Monflathers, Miss : the keeper of a girl's day and boarding school [Dickens, *Old Curiosity Shop*].

Monford : the man who arranges to elope with Charlotte Whimsey [Cobb, *First Floor*].

Monimia : secretly married to the son of her guardian [Otway, *The Orphan*].

Monk, The : the hero of a romantic tale written and published when the author was only nineteen [Lewis, *The Monk*].

Monkbarns, Laird of : *see* Oldbuck, Jonathan.

Monks : Edward Leeford, half-brother to Oliver Twist. A ne'er-do-weel who does his best to injure Oliver [Dickens, *Oliver Twist*].

Monmouth, Lord : a 'refined voluptuary', the grandfather of Coningsby [Beaconsfield, *Coningsby*].

Monnema : wife of Quiara, living in Paraguay at the time of an epidemic of smallpox ; they flee to the Mondai Woods, where Quiara is devoured by a jaguar [Southey, *Tale of Paraguay*].

Montague : head of the house that was hereditary enemy to the Capulets, and the father of Romeo [Shakespeare, *Romeo and Juliet*].

Montalban, Count : suitor to Volante, Belthazer's daughter ; he disguised himself as a priest so as to obtain access to her, but she detected the fraud at once [Tobin, *Honeymoon*].

Montanto : a boastful master of fence [Ben Jonson, *Every Man in His Humour*].

Montespan, Madame de : wife of the Marquis, and mistress of Louis XIV.

—— *The Marquis de :* a heartless, empty-headed fop [Lytton, *Duchess de la Vallière*].

Montorio : a villain who persuades his supposed nephews to murder their own father, and after the crime is accomplished discovers that the assassins are his own sons [Maturin, *Fatal Revenge*].

Montreville, Mme. Adela : the Begum Mootee Mahul, known as 'the Queen of Sheba' [Scott, *Surgeon's Daughter*].

Montrose: the subject of a ballad [Aytoun, *Execution of Montrose*].

Moody: a brawling boasting man of the old school [Dryden, *Sir Martin Mar-all*].

—— **Alithea:** John's sister. She jilts Sparkish and marries Harcourt.

—— *John:* brings up his ward, Peggy Thrift, in isolation, then at the age of fifty wishes to marry her. She rejects him in favour of Belville, a younger man [Garrick, *Country Girl*].

Moore, Hortense: sister of Robert and Louis Moore.

—— *Louis Gérard:* brother of Robert, and tutor to Henry Sympson, Shirley's cripple cousin. Louis Moore marries Shirley.

—— *Robert Gérard:* owner of Hollow's Mill, which is wrecked by the mill-hands upon his substituting modern frames for hand-looms. He marries Caroline Helstone [Charlotte Brontë, *Shirley*].

—— of Moore Hall: a legendary hero whom the author has pressed into his service. In the burlesque he loves Margery Gubbins, of Rothram Green [Carey, *Dragon of Wantley*].

Moorna: daughter of Monnema and Quiara, and born in the Mondai Woods [Southey, *Tale of Paraguay*].

Mopes, Mr. Tom: very dirty, and very nasty, and dressed in a blanket and skewer, he lived by himself on Tom Tiddler's Ground, a veritable ' hermit ' [Dickens, *Christmas Number : Tom Tiddler's Ground*].

Mopsa: Hobbinol's deserted lady-love [Somerville, *Hobbinol*].

Mora: affianced bride of Oscar, who vanishes mysteriously on the eve of his marriage. Allan, his brother, wins the bride, and then is found to have murdered Oscar [Byron, *Oscar of Alva*].

Morakanabad: Grand Vizier of the Caliph Vathek [Beckford, *Vathek*].

Mordecai, Beau: a rich Jewish suitor for the hand of the heiress, Charlotte Goodchild, who withdraws when he learns that her fortune is lost [Macklin, *Love à-la-Mode*].

—— a Jew who believed himself the bearer of an inspired mission to his race. The character is drawn from a man of the name of Cohn, who belonged to a club that used to meet in Red Lion Square, Holborn, some forty or fifty years ago, having for its object the redemption of Palestine for Israel [George Eliot, *Daniel Deronda*].

Mordent : the father of Joanna, who deserts her and leaves her to strangers, that he may marry Lady Anne.

—— *Joanna :* motherless, and left to the care of strangers, after surviving many dangers, is married to a young hero called Cheveril.

—— *Lady Anne :* a long-suffering, much neglected wife [Holcroft, *Deserted Daughter*].

Mordred : the treacherous knight slain by Arthur, and who gave Arthur his death wound [Mallory, *History of Prince Arthur*] ; see also *Modred.*

Mordure : son of the Emperor of Germany, who loved the mother of Sir Bevis of Southampton. Having slain her first husband she married Mordure [Drayton, *Polyolbion*].

—— the name of the magic sword which Merlin gave to Arthur [Spenser, *Faëry Queene*].

Morecraft : first a miser, afterwards a spendthrift [Beaumont and Fletcher, *Scornful Lady*].

Morelove, Lord : in love with Lady Betty Modish, who torments him by constant flirtation with Lord Foppington, for whom she has no real feeling, whilst she cares for Morelove all the time [Cibber, *Careless Husband*].

Morûn, Mr. : an elderly bachelor. Head clerk to Dombey & Son. He marries Harriet Carker [Dickens, *Dombey and Son*].

Morgadour, Sir : one of the Knights of the Round Table [*Arthurian Cycle*].

Morgan : Major Pendennis's valet, who entertains him with society gossip [Thackeray, *Pendennis*].

—— la Fée·: one of King Arthur's three fairy sisters [Mallory, *History of Prince Arthur*].

Morgan, Mrs. : the rector's loyal and sympathetic, but larger-natured wife.

—— *The Rev. William :* Rector of Carlingford, old-fashioned, narrow and prejudiced, but striving to be honest [Mrs. Oliphant, *Chronicles of Carlingford : Perpetual Curate*].

Morgane : a fairy, to whose care Passelyon and Bennucq were entrusted [*Perceforest*].

Morgause : the mother of Gowain, Agravain, Gaheris, Gareth and Mordred [Mallory, *History of Prince Arthur*].

Morgiana : the slave of Ali Baba, whom he gave to his son in marriage [*Arabian Nights*].

Morglay : the sword of Sir Bevis of Southampton ; a gift from his wife Josian [Drayton, *Polyolbion*].

Moria : ' the guardian of the nymphs '. . . . ' A lady made all of voice and air, talks anything of anything ' [Ben Jonson, *Cynthia's Revels*].

Morice, Gil : the son of Lady Barnard, slain by Lord Barnard in a fit of jealousy [Percy, *Reliques : Gil Morice*].

Morland, Catherine : an attractive girl, the heroine of the book. ' Artless, guileless, with affections strong but simple ' [Jane Austen, *Northanger Abbey*].

——— **Henry :** the heir of Baron Duberly, supposed to have been lost at sea [Colman the Younger, *Heir at Law*].

Morna : daughter of Cormac, King of Ireland. She loved Câthba, but Duchômar loved her and slew Câthba, and then asked Morna to be his bride, but she thrust his own sword through his heart [Ossian, *Fingal*].

Mornay : the seneschal at Earl Herbert's seat at Peronne [Scott, *Quentin Durward*].

Morose : a close-fisted old man, upon whose wealth his nephew, Sir Dauphine, has designs. He tricks the old man into a marriage with a ' silent woman ', who turns out to be a boy in disguise [Ben Jonson, *Epicoene*].

Morrell : a shepherd who has a partiality for high ground, and tries to induce Thomalin to follow him [Spenser, *Shepherd's Calendar*].

Morris, Dinah : a factory girl and a methodist preacher, who devotes herself to Hetty Sorrel when she is condemned to death for the murder of her child [George Eliot, *Adam Bede*].

——— **Mr. :** a timid man who travelled with Frank Osbaldistone [Scott, *Rob Roy*].

Morrison, Jeanie : the subject of a ballad [Motherwell, *Jeanie Morrison*].

——— **Mary :**

> A thought ungentle canna be.
> The thought of Mary Morrison.
>   [Burns, *Mary Morrison*].

Mortality, Old : *see* Old Mortality.

Mortcloke, Mr. : the undertaker at Mrs. Bertram's funeral [Scott, *Guy Mannering*].

Mortemar, Alberick of : the hermit of Engaddi, who assumes the name of Theodorick [Scott, *Talisman*].

Mortimer : a character in a play of which only a very small portion is now extant [Scott, *Fall of Mortimer*].

——— **Mr. :** ' he did a thousand noble acts without the credit of a single one ' [Cumberland, *Fashionable Lover*].

——— **Sir Edward :** he committed a murder on a drunken man who had heaped insults upon him. He was tried and acquitted, but eventually confessed his crime [Colman the Younger, *Iron Chest*].

Morton : a retainer of the Earl of Northumberland [Shakespeare, *King Henry IV*, pt. ii.].

—— Earl of : in the service of Mary, Queen of Scots [Scott, *Monastery* ; also *Abbot*].

—— Colonel Silas : the father of Henry.

—— *Henry :* an officer in the army of the Covenanters.

—— *Ralph :* the uncle of Henry [Scott, *Old Mortality*].

Mosby : the wretch who seduced the wife of Arden of Feversham, and then three times attempted Arden's life [Lillo, *Arden of Feversham*].

Mosca : a confederate of Volpone, a regular parasite, who eventually betrays his master [Ben Jonson, *Volpone ; or, The Fox*].

Moth : an antiquary fond of quoting Chaucer in scraps [Cartwright, *Ordinary*].

—— page to Don Adriano de Armado [Shakespeare, *Love's Labour's Lost*].

—— one of the fairies [Shakespeare, *Midsummer Night's Dream*].

Mother Bunch : *see* Bunch, Mother.

Motte, La : a character that is exceptionally well drawn [Mrs. Radcliffe, *Romance of the Forest*].

Mould, Mr. : an undertaker to whom the 'tap, tap' of a coffin, in the making, was quite exhilarating [Dickens, *Martin Chuzzlewit*].

Mouldy, Ralph : pricked for a recruit, Falstaff lets him off in spite of the remonstrances of Justice Shallow [Shakespeare, *Henry IV*, pt. ii.].

Mowbray, Clara : sister to John and betrothed to Frank Tyrrel. She, however, marries Valentine Bulmer in the end.

—— *Mr. John :* the Lord of the Manor of St. Ronan's [Scott, *St. Ronan's Well*].

—— *Frederick :* eldest son of Sir Miles, who marries Clara Middleton.

—— *Sir Miles :* a meddlesome opinionated old man who meant well but made mischief [Cumberland, *First Love*].

—— Harriet : a friendless orphan who is secretly married to Charles Eustace [Poole, *The Scapegoat*].

—— Helen : in love with Walsingham, but her reputation suffering through the evil offices of Lord Athunree, Walsingham casts her off. In the end all goes well [Knowles, *Woman's Wit*].

Mowcher, Miss : a fashionable ladies' hairdresser, dealer in cosmetics, etc., and a dwarf [Dickens, *David Copperfield*].

Mowis : the snow-bridegroom who won a lovely bride, but when the dawn broke melted away [Longfellow, an American-Indian legend told in *Evangeline*].

Mucklebackit, Saunders : an old fisherman [Scott, *Antiquary*].

Mucklewrath, Habakkuk : a fanatical preacher [Scott, *Old Mortality*].

Muckworm, Sir Penurious : uncle and guardian of Arbella, whom he destines for Squire Sapskull. Arbella succeeds in marrying Gaylove, the man she loves [Carey, *Honest Yorkshireman*].

Muddle : a carpenter in the employ of Captain Savage [Marryat, *Peter Simple*].

Mudjekeewis : the father of Hiawatha [Longfellow, *Hiawatha*].

Muff, Professor : remarkable for the urbanity of his manners and the manner in which he can adapt himself to circumstances [Dickens, *Mudfog Association*].

—— **Sir Henry :** an unsuccessful candidate for Parliament [Dudley, *Rival Candidates*].

Muggins, Dr. : a physician who suited 'his physic to his patient's taste' [Rhodes, *Bombastes Furioso*].

Muhldenau : the minister of Mariendorpt, who, whilst searching for a lost child, was seized and imprisoned in Prague.

—— *Meeta :* his daughter, who hearing of his misfortune, walks to Prague and petitions for his release, and thus discovers her lost sister [Knowles, *Maid of Mariendorpt*].

Mulhausen, Clara : beloved and secretly married by Leonce Miranda [R. Browning, *Red-Cotton Night-cap Country*].

Müller, Maud : the subject of a ballad [J. G. Whittier, *Maud Müller*].

Mullet, Professor : the 'most remarkable man' in North America [Dickens, *Martin Chuzzlewit*].

Mullion, Mordecai : supposed to be intended as the personification of the people of Glasgow [Wilson, *Noctes Ambrosianae*].

Multon, Sir Thomas de : a Crusader and Master of the Horse to Richard I [Scott, *Talisman*].

Mulvaney : an Irish private in the army. Full of humour, good-temper, and recklessness [Kipling, *Soldiers Three*].

Mumblazen, Master Michael : an old servitor of Sir Hugh Robsart who acts as his herald [Scott, *Kenilworth*].

Mumblecrust, Madge : a character which was reproduced in various comedies, etc. [Udall, *Ralph Roister Doister*].

Munchausen, Baron : the hero of many marvellous adventures [Raspe, *Baron Munchausen*].

Munera : the lovely daughter of Poliente. Talus cut off her golden hands and silver feet and cast her into a moat [Spenser, *Faëry Queene*].

Mungo : Don Diego's black slave [Bickerstaff, *Padlock*].

Murcraft : 'a projector' [Ben Jonson, *Devil's an Ass*].

Murdochson, Madge : known as Madge Wildfire. Ruined and discarded, and her baby killed by her mother, Madge went mad [Scott, *Heart of Midlothian*].

—— **Meg :** the mother of Madge Wildfire, a thieving gipsy [Scott, *Heart of Midlothian*].

Murdstone, Miss Jane : sister of Mr. Edward Murdstone as severe and gloomy as himself.

—— *Mr. Edward :* David's step-father, a terrible, gloomy man who breaks Mrs. Copperfield's heart [Dickens, *David Copperfield*].

Murray, The Bonnie Earl of : son-in-law of James Stuart, and known as the 'Good Regent'. He was assassinated in 1570. The subject of a ballad [*Bonnie Earl of Murray*].

Muscarol : the king of all flies, and the most beautiful [Spenser, *Muiopolmas ; or, Butterfly's Fate*].

Musgrave, Little, and Lady Barnard : an old ballad telling how these two sinned together and were discovered in their sin and killed by Lord Barnard [Percy, *Reliques : Little Musgrave and Lady Barnard*].

—— **Sir Richard :** the English champion who fought the Scottish champion, Sir William of Deloraine [Scott, *Lay of the Last Minstrel*].

Musidore : beloved by Damon [James Thomson, *Seasons : Summer*].

Musidorus : Prince Thessalia, who loved Pamela, and is the hero of the pastoral [Sidney, *Arcadia*].

Muslin : a parsite of Mrs. Lovemore's, who is attracted by William, a footman [Murphy, *Way to Keep Him*].

Mustafa : the father of Aladdin, a poor tailor [*Arabian Nights : Aladdin and the Wonderful Lamp*].

Mutch : one of Robin Hood's company of outlaws.

Muxworthy, Betty : humble friend and servant of the Ridds [Blackmore, *Lorna Doone*].

Muzzle, Mr. : a diminutive, ill-shapen footman in the service of George Nupkins, Esq. [Dickens, *Pickwick Papers*]

Myrine : sister of Pygmalion, and in love with Leucippe [Gilbert, *Pygmalion and Galatea*].

Myrrha : an Ionian slave beloved by the king, with whom she perished in the flames of a funeral pile lighted by her own hand [Byron, *Sardanapalus*].

Mysis : wife of Sileno, and mother of Daphne and Nysa [O'Hara, *Midas*].

Mystic, Moley : a caricature of the extreme forms of retrograde transcendental mysticism [Peacock, *Melincourt*].

Nab : a fairy who, seeing Orpheus in the infernal regions, offered him food in the shape of a flea's thigh, rainbow tart, etc. [King, *Orpheus and Eurydice*].

Nabob, The : the subject of a lyric [Susanna Blamire, *The Nabob*].

Nacien : a hermit who conducted Gelahad to the only seat left vacant at the Round Table, reserved for him who should find the Holy Grail [Mallory, *History of Prince Arthur*].

Nadab : intended for the profligate Lord Howard of Esrick [Dryden, *Absalom and Adritophel*].

Naddo : the unsympathetic critic of the poet's mission [R. Browning, *Sordello*].

Nadgeth : Tom Pinch's landlord, whose vocation was that of a detective [Dickens, *Martin Chuzzlewit*].

Naggleton, Mr. and Mrs. : types of an inharmonious pair, who could never agree upon trifles [*Punch*, 1864–5].

Nailor, John : generally known as Little John ; *see* John, Little.

Nama : a human being with whom the angel Zaraph was in love [Thomas Moore, *Loves of the Angels*].

Namby, Major : a much-married, retired officer who used to deliver all his domestic orders, in a shouting voice, from the garden path to those within [Collins, *Pray Employ Major Namby*].

Namouna : an enchantress [Thomas Moore, *Lalla Rookh : Light of the Harem*].

Nancy : Mrs. Pattypan's pretty servant, a flirt herself and ready to help with the ' love-affairs ' of others [Cobb, *First Floor*].

———— the heroine of one of the songs [Charles Dibden, *Sea Songs*].

———— a young woman who loves Bill Sykes, and whilst aiding in his robberies has some womanly instincts left. She tries to shield Oliver and is killed by her paramour [Dickens, *Oliver Twist*].

Narcissa : intended for Mrs. Oldfield, the actress [Pope, *Moral Essays*, Ep. i.].

———— intended for the author's step-daughter, Mrs. Temple [Young, *Night Thoughts*].

Nathaniel, Sir : the absurd curate in the play [Shakespeare, *Love's Labour's Lost*].

Nathos : one of the sons of Usnoth, who took over the command of the Irish army upon the death of Cuthullin [Ossian, *Dar-Thula*].

Natty Bumpo : *see* Bumpo, Natty.

Nealliny : a suttee : the widow of Kehama's son Arvalan [Southey, *Curse of Kehama*].

Neckett, Charlotte : called 'Charley', the daughter of a sheriff's officer [Dickens, *Bleak House*].

Neddy : a man confined in the Fleet Prison for debt [Dickens, *Pickwick Papers*].

Nekayah : the sister of Rasselas, who escapes with him from the 'happy valley', whither, after long wanderings, they return [Johnson, *Rasselas*].

Nell, Little : *see* Trent, Nell.

Nello : a barber [George Eliot, *Romola*].

Nemo : the name by which Captain Hawdon was known at Krooks, where he lodged [Dickens, *Bleak House*], *see also* Hawdon, Captain.

Nerestan : son of D'Outremer, King of Jerusalem, and brother of Zara [Hill, *Zara*]. This play is based on that by Voltaire.

Nereus : father of the water-nymphs [Milton, *Comus*].

Nerissa : Portia's confidential maid, who marries Antonio's friend Gratiano [Shakespeare, *Merchant of Venice*].

Neuha : a native of the island on which the mutineers of the '*Bounty*' landed. She married Torquil [Byron, *The Island*].

Neville, Marmaduke : the lover of Sybil Warner [Lytton, *Last of the Barons*].

———— **Miss :** the friend of Kate Hardcastle, and intended for the bride of Tony Lumpkin. She married Hastings, Marlow's friend [Goldsmith, *She Stoops to Conquer*].

———— **Major :** the assumed name of Lord Geraldin, son of Earl Geraldin.

———— *Mr. Geraldin :* uncle to Major Neville [Scott, *Antiquary*].

Newcome, Clemency : married Benjamin Britain, her fellow servant at Dr. Jeddler's, and became thereby landlady of the *Nutmeg-Grater*' [Dickens, *Battle of Life*].

———— **Clive :** the hero. He is an artist and marries his cousin Ethel as his second wife.

———— *Colonel :* a perfect English gentleman, who, becoming poor, enters the Charterhouse as a pensioner. The father of Clive.

———— *Ethel :* the Colonel's niece, who afterwards marries Clive.

———— *Sir Barnes :* a thoroughgoing snob, but a keen business man [Thackeray, *The Newcomes*].

Newcome : the ritualistic Vicar of Mottringham : a friend of Robert Elsmere's [Mrs. Humphry Ward, *Robert Elsmere*].

Newfangle, Nichol : the hero of an old 'moral' play [Fulwell, *Like Will to Like, quod the Devil to the Collier*].

Newman, Oliver : the hero of a tale told in verse [Southey, *Oliver Newman : New England Tale*].

Nice, Sir Courtly : the hero of the comedy [Crowne, *Sir Courtly Nice*].

Nicholas : a poor scholar in love with Alison, his landlord's wife [Chaucer, *Canterbury Tales : The Miller's Tale*].

—————— **Brother :** a monk at St. Mary's convent [Scott, *Monastery*].

Nickleby, Godfrey : the father of Ralph and Nicholas, the elder.

—————— *Kate :* sister to Nicholas, the younger. She marries Frank Cheeryble, the nephew of her brother's benefactor.

—————— *Mrs. :* a well-meaning but weak and loquacious woman, discursive to a degree, and of inaccurate memory.

—————— *Nicholas, the elder :* the father of Nicholas the younger, and Kate.

—————— *Nicholas the younger :* left poor and fatherless at the age of nineteen. Goes as tutor to Dotheboy's Hall whence he rescues Smike. Becomes an actor, then enters the firm of Cheeryble Bros., and finally marries.

—————— *Ralph :* a miserly usurer, uncle of Nicholas the younger, and Kate, and father of Smike [Dickens, *Nicholas Nickleby*].

Nicodemus : the chief character in an old miracle play founded on a book in the apocryphal gospels.

Nigel : *see* Olifaunt, Nigel.

Nina-Thoma : daughter of Tor-Thoma ; she eloped with Uthal, son of Larthmor, who deserted her [Ossian, *Berrathon*].

Nineve : the name of the Lady of the Lake [Mallory, *History of Prince Arthur*].

Nipper, Susan : Florence and Paul's faithful nurse, who marries Mr. Toots. She gives Mr. Dombey a 'piece of her mind' [Dickens, *Dombey and Son*].

Nixon, Christal : Mr. Edward Redgauntlet's agent [Scott, *Redgauntlet*].

'Noddy' : *see* Boffin, Nicodemus.

Noel, Eusebe : the shabby, absent-minded schoolmaster of Bout du Monde [Stirling, *Gold-Mine ; or Miller of Grenoble*].

Noggs, Newman : the honest clerk of Ralph Nickleby [Dickens, *Nicholas Nickleby*].

Nokomis : the grandmother of Hiawatha and daughter of the Moon [Longfellow, *Hiawatha*].

Nonentity, Dr. : thought by most of his acquaintances to be a great scholar and thinker [Goldsmith, *Citizen of the World*].

Noorka, Noorna fin : the betrothed of Shibli Bagaray, who aids him in his adventures by her magic power [George Meredith, *Shaving of Shagpat*].

Norland, Lord : the father of Lady Eleanor Irwin, and Lady Ramble's guardian [Mrs. Inchbald, *Every one has his Fault*].

Norman : the forester of the lord-keeper of Scotland, Sir William Ashton [Scott, *Bride of Lammermoor*].

—— **Captain :** his father having been murdered, Norman was sent to sea as a boy and his mother married again. She wished to make her second son, Percy, her heir. Complications ensued, but in the end Norman obtained his rights [Lytton, *Sea-Captain*].

Norna : a prophetess, whose real name was Ulla Troil [Scott, *Pirate*].

Norris, Black : a swarthy man, whence his soubriquet. He was a wrecker, and wished to marry Marian. She had consented under pressure, but he was had up for murder before Marian was called upon to fulfil her promise [Knowles, *The Daughter*].

—— **Mrs. :** the unamiable, meddling sister of Lady Bertram [Jane Austen, *Mansfield Park*].

North, Lord : one of the judges before whom Geoffrey and Julian Peveril and the dwarf had to appear [Scott, *Peveril of the Peak*].

Norval, Old : an aged shepherd, who finds a deserted infant, and brings it up as his own.

—— **Young :** the infant, who turns out to be the son of Lady Randolph, by her first husband, Lord Douglas [Home, *Douglas*].

Norwynne, William and Henry : two brothers, the very antithesis of one another [Mrs. Inchbald, *Nature and Art*].

Nosebag, Mrs. : the inquisitive wife of a lieutenant of dragoons, and the companion of Waverley on his journey to London [Scott, *Waverley*].

Nottingham, Countess of : she to whom Essex entrusted his ring to convey to Queen Elizabeth when he was imprisoned in the Tower, and who, through jealousy, forebore to deliver it [Jones, *Earl of Essex*].

Nouman, Sidi : husband of the lovely Amine, who turned out to be a ghoul who feasted nightly on the newly dead. He changed Amine into a mare which he daily rode almost to death [*Arabian Nights*].

Noureddin : son of Vizier Khacan of Balsora, whose beautiful Persian slave he possessed himself of. He fled with her to Bagdad [*Arabian Nights*].

—— **Ali :** younger son of the Vizier of Egypt. He quarrelled with his elder brother so went to Basora, where, in due time, he became Vizier [*Arabian Nights*].

Nourmahal : the 'Light of the Harem', Seline's bride [Thomas Moore, *Lalla Rookh*].

Nouronihar : daughter of Fakreddin, a beautiful laughing girl, who married Vathek, and with him descended into Ebliss, whence she never returned [Beckford, *Vathek*].

Nouronnihar : niece of the Sultan of India, and beloved by each of the Sultan's three sons, all of whom had to compete for her possession. She fell to the lot of the youngest [*Arabian Nights*].

Novel : a despicable character. A railer and flatterer, and a craver after novelty in any shape [Wycherley, *Plain Dealer*].

Now-now, Anthony : a wandering fiddler, intended for a skit on Anthony Munday the dramatist [Chettle, *Kindheart's Dream*].

Nubbles, Christopher : always called 'Kit'. Devoted to Little Nell, and acting as odd boy at the Old Curiosity Shop, afterwards servant to Mr. Garland.

—— **Mrs. :** Kit's mother, a poor widow much given to attending 'Little Bethel', a chapel in her neighbourhood [Dickens, *Old Curiosity Shop*].

Nupkins, George, Esq. : the Mayor of Ipswich [Dickens, *Pickwick Papers*].

Nut-brown Maid, The : the heroine of an old ballad. She is wooed by a 'banished man' but in her love for him thinks no hardship too great to endure. He turns out to be a wealthy son of an earl.

Nydia : the blind girl [Lytton, *Last Days of Pompeii*].

Nym : the boon companion of Bardolph and Pistol, and an arrant coward [Shakespeare, *Merry Wives of Windsor*].

Nysa : daughter of Sileno, and sister of Daphne. In love with Apollo, she will have nothing to say to Justice Midas, who loves her [O'Hara, *Midas*].

Oakly, Charles : a nephew of the Major; of a generous spirit but dissipated. He loves Harriot Russet, who reclaims him.

Oakly, Major : called in by his brother, to aid in curing Mrs. Oakly of her jealousy.

——— *Mr. :* an easy-going, merry sort of man, who is unintentionally for ever rousing his wife's jealousy.

——— *Mrs. :* a woman always on the look-out for signs of her husband's infidelity [Colman the Elder, *Jealous Wife*].

Obadiah : a canting Quaker [Mrs. Centlivre, *Bold Stroke for a Wife*].

——— a ' drinking nincompoop' [Howard, *Committee*].

——— clerk to Justice Day. Very foolish and a drunkard [Knight, *Honest Thieves*].

——— a servant employed in the house [Sterne, *Tristram Shandy*].

Oberon : king of the fairies, and the husband of Titania [Shakespeare, *Midsummer Night's Dream*].

Obidah : a young man whose daily actions and travels form a sort of allegorical picture of human life [Dr. Johnson, *Rambler*, No. 65].

Obidicut : one of the five fiends that possessed ' poor Tom ' [Shakespeare, *King Lear*].

O'Brallaghan, Callaghan, Sir : an Irish soldier serving in Prussia. The accepted suitor of Charlotte Goodchild [Macklin, *Love à-la-Mode*].

Obstinate : he dwelt in the City of Destruction, and exhorted Christian to give up his quest and return to the bosom of his family [Bunyan, *Pilgrim's Progress*].

Occasion : the mother of Furor. She was seized and bound hand and foot by Sir Guyon [Spenser, *Faëry Queene*].

Ochiltree, Edie : an old bedesman, good and kind and garrulous [Scott, *Antiquary*].

Octavia : the leading character of a sixteenth century play based on the Latin of Seneca [Nuce, *Octavia*].

Octavian : goes mad because he suspects his lady-love, Floranthe, of loving another [Colman the Younger, *Mountaineers*].

Octavio : the supposed husband of Jacintha [Beaumont and Fletcher, *Spanish Curate*].

——— engaged to Donna Clara [Jephson, *Two Strings to Your Bow*].

O'Cutter, Captain : an Irishman who has a broad brogue and indulges in the language of the sea [Colman the Elder, *Jealous Wife*].

Odoar : the Abbot of St. Felix, who gave shelter to Roderick after his fall [Southey, *Roderick*].

Odoherty, Sir Morgan : one of the interlocutors [Wilson, *Noctes Ambrosianae*].

O'Dowd, Mrs. : a kindly, vain and rather vulgar Irishwoman, wife of the major of Dobbin's regiment [Thackeray, *Vanity Fair*].

Oenone : beloved by Paris, but forsaken by him when Venus promised him the loveliest wife in Greece [Alfred Tennyson, *Oenone*].

O'Ferrall, Trilby : the heroine, the daughter of a sometime clergyman and Fellow of Trinity, ruined by drink. Trilby becomes an artist's model, and afterwards a singer [Du Maurier, *Trilby*].

O'Flaherty, Dennis : an honest and honourable Irishman, known as 'Major O'Flaherty'[Cumberland, *West Indian*].

Og : intended for Thomas Shadwell [Dryden and Tate, *Absalom and Achitophel*, pt. ii.].

Ogier the Dane : the hero of several mediaeval romances. He is probably the same as Oger or Helgi, who appears in the *Edda* and the *Volsunga-Saga*].

Ogle : a man who fancies himself to be irresistibly fascinating to everybody [Mrs. Centliore, *Beau's Duel*].

———— **Miss :** jealous of all junior to herself. She is a friend of Mrs. Racket [Mrs. Cowley, *Belle's Stratagem*].

Ogleby, Lord : an ancient fop, who apes the gaiety and fashions of youth [Colman and Garrick, *Clandestine Marriage*].

Ogniben : the legate who quelled the disturbances at Faenza [R. Browning, *Soul's Tragedy*].

O'Gordon, Edom : *see* Edom O'Gordon.

O'Hara : stories of rebellion, passion and crime, told by two brothers [John and Michael Banim, *Tales of the O'Hara Family*].

Oig M'Combich : a Highland drover who quarrels with an English one, and stabs him, for which crime he is himself condemned to death [Scott, *Two Drovers*].

Oina-Morul : daughter of King Mal-Orchol of Fuarfed [Ossian, *Oina-Morul*].

Oithona : the daughter of Nuath, affianced bride of Gaul, but Fingal sent to him to fight the Britons. In his absence his bride was carried off by Uthal [Ossian, *Oithona*].

Olave : the grandfather of Minna and Brenda Troil [Scott, *Pirate*].

Old Grimes : the subject of a ballad at one time very popular [Albert G. Greene, *Old Grimes*].

———— **Man of the Sea :** a monster whom Sinbad the Sailor encountered when on his fifth voyage [*Arabian Nights*].

———— **Mortality :** a man whose hobby it was to wander about among tombs cleansing them from moss, etc. The character is supposed to have been drawn after a certain Robert Patterson [Scott, *Old Mortality*].

Oldboy, Colonel : a retired officer of sociable habits.
——— *Lady Mary :* his wife ; a lackadaisical, sickly woman [Bickerstaff, *Lionel and Clarissa*].

Oldbuck, Mr. Jonathan : laird of Monkbarns. The antiquary. The house conjectured to have been his is near Arbroath [Scott, *Antiquary*].

Oldcastle, Sir John : the hero of a play the author of which is unknown. The chief character is taken from Sir John Oldcastle, Lord Cobham, who forfeited his life for high treason [*Sir John Oldcastle*].

Oldcraft, Sir Perfidious : a leading character in the play [J. Fletcher and others, *Wit at Several Weapons*].

Oldworth, Squire : a wealthy and a cultured man, who, in the character of guardian, brings up his own daughter [Burgoyne, *Maid of the Oaks*].

Olifaunt, Nigel : the hero, who is so unhappy as to excite the enmity of the Duke of Buckingham [Scott, *Fortunes of Nigel*].

Olimpia : a haughty Roman, who, at the sacking of Rome by the French, took refuge at the high altar of St. Peter's [Byron, *Deformed Transformed*].

Oliphant : the twin-brother of Argante [Spenser, *Faëry Queene*].

Oliver : son of Sir Rowland de Boys, and brother of Orlando. He marries Celia, daughter of the usurping Duke [Shakespeare, *As You Like It*].
——— Twist : *see* Twist, Oliver.

Olivia : the daughter of a peasant, who became the bride of a prince, an event which caused great disturbances in Aragon [Knowles, *Rose of Aragon*].
——— the wealthy lady whose servant was Malvolio. She fell in love with Viola, and married Viola's brother Sebastian [Shakespeare, *Twelfth Night*].
——— in love with Vicentio, who was, however, betrothed to Evadne. Olivia descended to low tricks to gratify her love. but, later, repented [Shiel, *Evadne ; or, The Statue*].
——— a bold and unblushing hypocrite [Wycherley, *Plain Dealer*].
——— de Zuniga : determined to wed Julio de Melessina, she resorts to all sorts of tricks to drive a host of other suitors away [Mrs. Cowley, *Bold Stroke for a Wife*].
——— Primrose : *see* Primrose, Olivia.
——— Woodville : *see* Woodville, Olivia.

Ollapod, Cornet : a country apothecary ; he thinks himself a wit, and sows scandal broad-cast through the countryside [Colman the Younger, *Poor Gentleman*].

Ollomand : an enchanter who was instrumental in raising

an insurrection in the lands under the rule of Misnar Sultan of Delhi [Ridley, *Tales of the Genii*].

Olympia : the Duke of Muscovia's sister [Beaumont and Fletcher, *Loyal Subject*].

O'More, Rory : the hero of a song [Lover, *Rory O'More*].

Omri : intended for Sir Heneage Finch, Lord Chancellor of England [Dryden, *Absalom and Achitophel*].

O'Neill : the hero of a tale in verse [Lord Lytton, *O'Neill ; or, The Rebel*].

Oneiza : she loved Thalaba, and married him, but died on her marriage night [Southey, *Thalaba*].

Ophelia : beloved by and loving Hamlet. Young, beautiful, pure and inexperienced and loving much, she cannot withstand the shock of Hamlet's sudden change towards her, and goes mad [Shakespeare, *Hamlet*].

—— **Miss :** the well-intentioned lady, who does her best to tame and train Topsy [Harriet Beecher Stowe, *Uncle Tom's Cabin*].

Opimian, Rev. Dr. : a kind-hearted, self-satisfied, good living cleric. A peg on which to hang criticisms of his order [Peacock, *Gryll Grange*].

Ople, General : a retired army officer who settles near London with his only daughter. He pays attentions to an eccentric, but aristocratic lady next door, whom he eventually marries. His egoism blinds his eyes to all concerns but his own [George Meredith, *Case of General Ople and Lady Campen*].

Orange, Louise : the heroine [Brougham, *Albert Lunel*].

Ordella : wife of Thierry, King of France. According to Lamb ' a piece of sainted nature ' [J. Fletcher, *Thierry and Theodoret*].

Orelio : the pet charger of Roderick, the last of the Goths [Southey, *Roderick*].

Orestes : the son of Agamemnon affianced to Hermione, daughter of the King of Sparta [Philips, *Distressed Mother*].

—— the hero of a tragedy modelled on the Greek drama [Sotheby, *Orestes*].

Orgarita : the name given to Martha, daughter of Ralph and Louise Lascours, by the Indians who picked her up [Stirling, *Orphan of the Frozen Sea*]. *See also* Lascours, Martha.

Orgilus : the lover of Panthea, but events occurring to prevent their union, Panthea starved herself to death and Orgilus was condemned to death for murder [J. Ford, *Broken Heart*].

Orgoglio : a giant, the personification of pride, who overpowers the Red Cross knight [Spenser, *Faëry Queene*].

Oriana : daughter of King Lisuarte of England, and wife of Amadis of Gaul [*Amadis de Gaul*, a fourteenth century romance].

—— betrothed to the son of her guardian, young Mirabel, who dallies with Lamorce until Oriana, dressed as a page, rescues him from danger of murder [Farquhar, *Inconstant*].

—— the quick-witted and plucky chaser of the ' Wild-goose ',whom she marries [J.Fletcher,*Wild-goose Chase*].

—— the subject of a ballad [Alfred Tennyson, *Oriana*].

Oriel : a fairy who haunted the banks of the Thames in the days when Oberon reigned in Kensington Gardens [Tickell, *Kensington Gardens*].

Orlando : Rosalind's lover, the younger son of Sir Rowland de Boys, and brother of Oliver [Shakespeare, *As You Like It*].

—— the handsome, generous hero and lover of Monimia [Mrs. Smith, *Old Manor House*].

—— **Furioso :** the subject of a tragedy published in 1594 [Greene, *Historie of Orlando Furioso*].

Orleans : desparately in love with Agripynar [Dekker, *Old Fortunatus*].

—— **Gaston, Duke of :** brother of Louis XIII. He heads a conspiracy having for its object the dethronement of Louis and the death of Richelieu [Lytton, *Richelieu*].

Orlick, Dolge : known as ' Old Orlick '. Journeyman to Joe Gargery, he is responsible for the death of Mr. Gargery, and tries to murder Pip [Dickens, *Great Expectations*].

Orme, Victor : a poor man who loves Elsie [Reeve, *Parted*].

Ormond : the hero of the novel [Maria Edgworth, *Ormond*]

Ormont, Lord : a brilliant but badly-used cavalry officer. His efforts to right himself are unsuccessful [George Meredith, *Lord Ormont and His Aminta*].

Oronooko : the hero of a novel. He was an African prince, sold into slavery, and put to death by the authorities. Imoinda, his wife, was also sold into slavery [Mrs. Aphra Behn, *History of Oronooko ; or, Royal Slave*].

—— the same incidents as above, treated in dramatic form [Southern, *Oronooko ; or, Royal Slave*].

Orozembo : a brave Peruvian, who declined to give any information to his Spanish captors [Sheridan, *Pizarro*].

Orpas : sometime Bishop of Seville ; he joined the Moslem faith, and, for the sake of her wealth, tries to win Florinda as his wife [Southey, *Roderick*].

Orraca, Queen : the wife of Alfonso II. She died in accordance with a prophecy of five Moroccan friars [Southey, *Queen Orraca*].

Orsino : the Duke of Illyria, first in love with Olivia, but afterwards with Viola, whom he marries [Shakespeare, *Twelfth Night*].

Orson : twin brother of Valentine and son of Bellisant. Carried off in infancy by a bear, and suckled by it, he was afterwards known as ' the Wild Man of the Forest [*Valentine and Orson*].

—— a worthy Taunton farmer, who disliked the idea of marriage yet liked the society of women. He dallies with Ellen, then neglects her, but after an absence of five years, makes her his wife [Peter Pindar (Dr. Wolcot), *Orson and Ellen*].

Ortheris : a private in the army, a regular ' Tommy Atkins ' [Kipling, *Soldiers Three*].

Orville, Lord : ' handsome, gallant, polite, and ardent ', ' extremely handsome, with an air of mixed politeness and gallantry ' the lover of Evelina [Fanny Burney, *Evelina*].

Osbaldistone, Frank : in love with Diana Vernon, whom he ultimately marries.

—— *Rashleigh :* a deep-dyed villain, the youngest of Sir Hildebrand's six sons.

—— *Sir Hildebrand :* the uncle of Frank, who is his heir [Scott, *Rob Roy*].

Osborne, Capt. George : son of the city merchant, vain, extravagant and selfish, but brave. He wins and marries Amelia Sedley, then neglects her and flirts with Becky Sharp. He fell at Waterloo.

—— *Mr. :* his father, hard and purse-proud, but loving George and furious at his marriage with Amelia, whom he never forgave [Thackeray, *Vanity Fair*].

Oscar : the son of Ossian and grandson of Fingal, slain in battle, in Ulster, fighting against Cairbar [Ossian, *Temora*].

O'Shanter, Tam : the hero of the poem is a farmer of Ayr, who, returning home well primed with drink, sees witches and devils dancing in the Kirk of Alloway [Burns, *Tam O'Shanter*].

O'Shaughnessy, Dennis : the hero of a story replete with autobiographical reminiscences [Carleton, *Dennis O'Shaughnessy, Going to Maynooth*].

Osile : in love with Sir Thierry [*Sir Guy of Warwick*].

Osman : the great sultan who vanquished the Christians. He loved Zara, a Christian captive, daughter of D'Outremer, King of Jerusalem, but stabbed her in a fit of baseless jealousy [Hill, *Zara*], based on the French of Voltaire.

Osmyn : really Alphonso, son of the King of Valentia, and wedded to Almeria. He is shipwrecked and cast on the African coast, but after many tribulations is restored to Almeria [Congreve, *Mourning Bride*].

Osric : a court butterfly and fop, who is appointed umpire in the contest between Hamlet and Laertes [Shakespeare, *Hamlet*].

Osseo : ' son of the Evening Star ' [Longfellow, *Hiawatha*].

Ossian : a bard ; the son of Fingal, King of Morven, and wedded to Roscrana, an Irish princess.

Oswald : Goneril's steward [Shakespeare, *King Lear*].

—— **Prince :** Gondibert's rival for the hand of Rhodalind. Oswald fell, slain by Gondibert in a contest between four chosen representatives [Davenant, *Gondibert*].

Othello : a brave and noble Moor, the victim of jealousy aroused by the evil machinations of others. Under its influence he slays the wife he adores [Shakespeare, *Othello*].

Otho : the host at the banquet where Lara was recognized by Sir Ezzelin, and a duel was arranged. Sir Ezzelin not appearing Otho fought the count in his stead and was wounded [Byron, *Lara*].

O'Todshaw, Tam : a huntsman [Scott, *Guy Mannering*].

O'Trigger, Sir Lucius : a blustering Irishman, always ready for a joke or a fight [Sheridan, *Rivals*].

Ottilia, Princess : the daughter of a German prince, with whom Harry Richmond falls in love. She returns his love, but her royal birth prevents their union [George Meredith, *Adventures of Harry Richmond*].

Otto : Duke of Normandy, who falls a victim to his brother Rollo [Beaumont and Fletcher, *Bloody Brother*].

Otuel, Sir : a Saracen who became a Christian and married a daughter of Charlemagne.

Outalissi : an eagle of the Indian tribe of Oneyda to whom Mrs. Waldegrave entrusted her boy Henry, at the general massacre of the settlers. He carried the child to Albert of Wyoming [Campbell, *Gertrude of Wyoming*].

Averdo, Justice Adam : a justice of the peace [Ben Jonson, *Bartholomew Fair*].

Overreach, Sir Giles : an unscrupulous and grasping man. Said to be a portrait of Sir Giles Mompesson. His desire was to see his daughter wed a peer, but she prefers Allworth, the commoner [Massenger, *New Way to Pay Old Debts*].

Owain, Sir Kyveiliog : an Irish knight, who had to pass through the purgatory of St Patrick as a penance [Henry of Saltrey, *Descent of Owain*].

Oweenee : married to Osseo, who had an ugly exterior,

and no wealth, but was 'most beautiful within'. Oweenee was the youngest of ten lovely sisters [Longfellow, *Hiawatha*].

Owen of Carron : illegitimate son of Lady Ellen, daughter of the Earl of Moray, and the Earl of Nithsdale, the hero of a ballad [Langborne, *Owen of Carron*].

———— **Sir :** in a dream he passed St. Patrick's purgatory, but saved himself from harm by the reiterated cry, 'Lord, Thou canst save' [Southey, *St. Patrick's Purgatory*].

Oxenford, Clerk of : a true scholar, for 'gladly would he learn and gladly teach' [Chaucer, *Canterbury Tales : Clerk of Oxenford's Tale*].

Pacchiarotto : a painter of Siena, who would fain be a reformer too [R. Browning, *Pacchiarotto, and How he Worked in Distemper*].

Pacolet : a dwarf 'full of great sense and subtle ingenuity' [*Valentine and Orson*].

———— the dwarf who attended Norma [Scott, *Pirate*].

Paddington, Harry : 'a poor petty-larceny rascal, without the least genius' [Gay, *Beggar's Opera*].

Paeana : in love with her father's captive, Amias, but he could not return her love. She married Placidas [Spenser, *Faëry Queene*].

Page, Anne : 'sweet Anne Page', in love with Fenton.

———— *Mr.:* her father, who assumed the name of Brock, so as to play a trick on Falstaff.

———— *Mrs. :* Anne's mother. Falstaff made love to her, so she joined her friend, Mrs. Ford, in duping the old reprobate [Shakespeare, *Merry Wives of Windsor*].

Paladore : a Briton serving the King of Lombardy ; he saved the Princess Sophia from the attack of a boar, and altimately married her [Jephson, *Laws of Lombardy*].

Palamedes, Sir : a Saracen who loved Isolde, the same that Sir Tristram loved. The two knights fought and Palamedes was overthrown [*Arthurian Cycle*].

Palamon and Arcite : the heroes of a tale told by 'the Knight' [Chaucer, *Canterbury Tales : The Knight's Tale*].

———— the hero [J. Fletcher, *Two Noble Kinsmen*].

Palemon : in love with the daughter of the ship's commander [Falconer, *Shipwreck*].

———— 'the pride of swains' in love with Lavinia [James Thomson, *Seasons : Autumn*].

Palfrey, Prudence : the fictitious heroine of a novel [Aldrich, *Prudence Palfrey*].

Palinode : a shepherd [Spenser, *Shepheardes Calendar*].

Pallet : a painter quite devoid of all 'reverence for the courtesies of life' [Smollett, *Peregrine Pickle*]

Palliser, Plantagenet : strong, proud and cold, upright and patriotic, but entirely devoid of anything lovable in his personality [Anthony Trollope, *Can You Forgive Her ?*]

Palmira : daughter of Alcanor, Chief of Mecca, she, together with a brother, was taken captive by Mahomet in her babyhood. The brother and sister fell in love with one another [Miller, *Mahomet the Impostor*].

Palomides, Sir : son of Sir Astlabor, always known as 'the Saracen', being unbaptised. After Launcelot, Tristram and Lamorake, the strongest and most valiant of all the knights of the Round Table [Mallory, *History of Prince Arthur*].

Pamela : a simple country girl who goes to service at a wealthy squire's, and her master tries every wile to overcome her virtue, but in vain. He makes her his wife [Richardson, *Pamela*].

——— loved by Musidorus [Sidney, *Arcadia*].

Pamphlet, Dr. : a journalist whose ardent ambition is to be arrested for sedition [Murphy, *Upholsterer*].

Pancks, Mr. : Mr. Casby, the rent-collector's assistant, who loathes his work [Dickens, *Little Dorrit*].

Pangloss, Dr. Peter : a poor pedant, appointed tutor to Dick Dowlas, at a salary of £300 a year. He began life as a muffin maker [Colman the Younger, *Heir at Law*].

Panjandrum, The Grand : the name of a mythical being, now scoffingly applied to local dignitaries convinced of their own importance. First used in some nonsense lines written to test the memory of Macklin the actor [Foote in the *Quarterly Review*, xcv. 516, 527 1854].

Panscope, Mr. : a universal philosopher of the most conceited and worthless description. One of the party at Squire Headlong's [Peacock, *Headlong Hall*].

Panthea : the 'innocent but insipid' heroine [Beaumont and Fletcher, *King and No King*].

Panthino : servant to Anthonio [Shakespeare, *Two Gentlemen of Verona*].

Paracelsus : an earnest student and seeker after truth [R. Browning, *Paracelsus*].

Paradine : son of Astolpho and brother of Dargonet, who like Paradine is a suitor for the hand of Laura. Both brothers were slain in the combat of four [Davenant, *Gondibert*].

Pardiggle, Mrs.: a lady of many committees and many charities, but who made much noise in doing little work [Dickens, *Bleak House*].

Paridel, Sir: a remote descendant of Paris. He eloped with Helinore, the wife of Malbecco, and afterwards deserted her [Spenser, *Faëry Queene*].

Paris: Juliet's rejected suitor [Shakespeare, *Romeo & Juliet*].

Parisina: wife of Azo of Ferrara, the, at one time, betrothed of his son Hugo, whom she continues to love after her marriage. Azo, discovering this, causes his son to be beheaded [Byron, *Parisina*].

Parismenos: the hero of the second part of Parismus. He loved the Princess Angelica [Foord, *Parismenos*].

Parismus: a Bohemian prince, who loved Laurana, daughter of the Thessalian king [Foord, *Parismus*].

Parizade: daughter of the Sultan of Persia. One of three babies who were cast adrift through the cruelty of two aunts [*Arabian Nights: Two Sisters*].

Parolles: 'a notorious liar and fool', the servant of Bertram [Shakespeare, *All's Well that Ends Well*].

Parthenia: the personification of maidenly chastity [Phineas Fletcher, *Purple Island*].

—— the beloved of Argalus [Sidney, *Arcadia*].

Parthenope: beloved by Prince Volscius [Duke of Buckingham, *Rehearsal*].

Partington, Mrs.: an old lady who tried, if we are to credit Sidney Smith, to sweep back the Atlantic with a broom; 'the Altantic was roused, Mrs. Partington's spirit was up, but I need not tell you that the contest was unequal' [Shillaber, *Mrs. Partington*].

Partridge: servant to Tom Jones, and half barber, half schoolmaster [Fielding, *Tom Jones*].

Passebrewell: Sir Tristram's horse [Mallory, *History of Prince Arthur*].

Passelyon: a foundling, reared by Morgan la Fée [*Perceforest*].

Passetreul: *see* Passebriewell.

Pastorella: a shepherdess whom Corydon adored, but she cared 'neither for him nor any other' [Spenser, *Faëry Queene*].

Patch: Isabinda's maid [Mrs. Centlivre, *Busy Body*].

Pathfinder, The: *see* Bumpo, Natty.

Patie: the hero, in love with Patty: supposed to be a shepherd, he is in truth the son of Sir William Worthy [Ramsay, *Gentle Shepherd*].

Patient Griselda or Grissell: *see* Griselda.

Patterne, Crossjay: a delightful boy, who lives at Patterne Hall. A relation of Sir Willoughby Patterne.

Patterne, Sir Willoughby : a rich baronet whose self-love blinds his perception to the true feelings of others. He is in turn engaged to three girls [George Meredith, *The Egoist*].

Pattypan, Mrs. : a widow who lets lodgings and who marries Tim Tartlet [Cobb, *First Floor*].

Pau-Puk-Keewis : a bad man who taught the North American Indians to gamble [Longfellow, *Hiawatha*].

Paul Clifford : *see* Clifford, Paul.

——— **Dombey :** *see* Dombey, Mr. Paul.

——— **Ferroll :** *see* Ferroll, Paul.

——— **Flemming :** *see* Flemming, Paul.

——— **Little :** *see* Dombey, Little Paul.

——— **Monsieur :** the central figure at Mme. Beck's school [Charlotte Brontë. *Vilette* and *The Professor*].

Pauletti, the Lady Erminia : George Heriot's ward [Scott, *Fortunes of Nigel*].

Paulina : wife of Antigonus, and faithful friend of Hermione [Shakespeare, *Winter's Tale*].

Pauline : the subject of a love poem [R. Browning, *Pauline*].

——— the 'Beauty of Lyons' who marries Claud Melnotte [Lytton, *Lady of Lyons*].

Pawkins, Major : an American politician who 'runs a moist pen slick through everything and starts afresh' [Dickens, *Martin Chuzzlewit*].

Paxarett, Sir Telegraph : a good-natured, sensible man, in strong contrast to most of the characters in the book [Peacock, *Melincourt*].

Peachum : a shady character whose house is a meeting-place for thieves.

——— *Mrs. :* his wife, no better than her husband.

——— *Polly :* their daughter, a pretty girl who loved and married Captain Macheath [Gay, *Beggar's Opera*].

Pearl : the child of Hester Prynne, a strange and wayward little creature [Nathaniel Hawthorn, *Scarlet Letter*].

Peckover : the leader of the 'Blue Lambs' [Tom Taylor, *Contested Election*].

Pecksniff, Charity : called 'Cherry', betrothed to Mr. Moddle, but jilted by him on the day appointed for the wedding.

——— *Mercy :* always called 'Merry', Charity's younger sister; like her father a hypocrite and very vain. She marries Jonas Chuzzlewit for his money, and is cruelly treated by him.

——— *Seth :* a Salisbury architect. A self-serving, mean-spirited, canting hypocrite, who becomes a drunkard and dies a beggar [Dickens, *Martin Chuzzlewit*].

Pedrillo : Don Juan's tutor, who is eaten by the men with whom he is shipwrecked [Byron, *Don Juan*].

Pedro, Don : the Prince of Aragon, and the villain who slanders Hero [Shakespeare, *Much Ado About Nothing*].

Peebles, Peter : the drunken pauper who is the litigant in an interminable law suit [Scott, *Redgauntlet*].

Peecher, Miss Emma : a natty little schoolmistress in love with Bradley Headstone, who taught in the boy's department of the same school [Dickens, *Our Mutual Friend*].

Peel, Mr. Solomon : an attorney at the Insolvent Court in Portugal Street [Dickens, *Pickwick Papers*].

Peeping Tom of Coventry : *see* Godiva, Lady.

Peerybingle, John : a 'lumbering, slow, and honest' carrier, 'stolid, but so good'.

—— *Mrs. Mary :* called 'Dot' by her husband, by whom she deserved to be, and was, loved dearly [Dickens, *Cricket on the Hearth*].

Peg-a-Ramsey : the heroine of an old ballad.

Peg of Limavaddy : the heroine of a ballad [Thackeray *Peg of Limavaddy*].

Peggotty, Clara : the faithful servant of Mrs. Copperfield and David's devoted nurse, who marries Barkis, the carrier.

—— *Daniel :* Clara Peggotty's brother. A Yarmouth fisherman.

—— *Emily :* engaged to Ham, but Steerforth lured her away from her home. She was reclaimed, and emigrated to Australia.

—— *Ham :* Daniel's nephew, who lived with him. He loved little 'Em'ly'. An honest, noble fisherman, who lost his life in trying to save his enemy, Steerforth, from drowning [Dickens, *David Copperfield*].

Pegler, Mrs. : Bounderby's mother. He allows her the munificent income of £30 a year to keep out of his way [Dickens, *Hard Times*].

Pekuah : attendant on the Princess Nekayah [Dr. Johnson, *Rasselas*].

Pelagia : a courtesan at Alexandria [Charles Kingsley, *Hypatia*].

Palayo, Prince : his father had founded the Spanish monarchy after the fall of Roderick, and he himself united the royal lines of Spain and of the Goths [Southey, *Roderick*].

Pelham : the hero of the novel [Lytton, *Pelham*].

Pell, Solomon : the attorney who contrives to get Tony Weller sent to the Fleet for debt, in order that he may be near Mr. Pickwick to protect him [Dickens, *Pickwick Papers*].

Pelleas, Sir : 'lord of many a barren isle was he' and he loved the lady Ettarre [Alfred Tennyson, *Idylls of the King : Pelleas and Ettarre*].

Pellenore, Sir : 'knight of the Stranger Beast'. The slayer of King Lot, he lost his own life ten years later at the hand of Lot's son, Sir Gawaine [Mallory, *History of Prince Arthur*].

Pelles, Sir : 'king of the foragn land and nigh cousin of Joseph of Arimathy'. He was the father of the Lady Elaine, who, in her turn, was mother of Sir Galahad, who achieved the quest of the Holy Grail [Mallory, *History of Prince Arthur*].

Pelobates : mud-wader. He is one of the champion frogs [Parnell, *Battle of the Frogs and Mice*].

Pelos=mud. He was the father of Physignathos, the King of the Frogs [Parnell, *Battle of the Frogs and Mice*].

Pendennis, Arthur : a young man with much too good an opinion of himself. With a keen intellect and keen feelings, he is selfish and unattractive, though the hero.

────── *Helen :* the mother of Arthur. Very good and unselfish but rather jealous.

────── *Laura :* the heroine, who, in the end, marries Arthur.

────── *Major :* an old 'buck', and man about town, very worldly, but very fond of Arthur [Thackeray, *Pendennis*].

Pendragon : the title borne by Uther, father of King Arthur [Geoffrey, *Chronicle VI* (1142)].

Penelophon : the name of the beggar maid whom King Cophetua loved and married [Percy, *Reliques : King Cophetua and the Beggar-maid*].

Penfeather, Lady Penelope : the lady patroness of the Spa [Scott, *St. Ronan's Well*].

Penlake, Richard : an easy-going man tied to a shrew [Southey, *St. Michael's Chair*].

Penny, Sir : the subject of a curious old ballad supposed by some to be contemporary with Chaucer, wherein the power of money is described with much wit and satire [*Incipit Narratio de Domine Denario*].

────── *Jock :* a highwayman [Scott, *Guy Mannering*].

Penruddock, Roderick : a recluse and a bookworm. Soured by misfortunes, for his bosom friend came between him and his betrothed : he forgives him in the end and returns good for evil [Cumberland, *Wheel of Fortune*].

Penthea : betrothed to Ithocles, but forced into a hated marriage with Bassanes, she starves herself to death [J. Ford, *Broken Heart*].

Pentweazel, Alderman : a very submissive and obedient husband.

———— *Carel :* son of the alderman ; a schoolboy [Foote, *Taste*].

———— *Mrs. :* his wife. A fearfully vain, ignorant and foolish woman who talks about ' Venus de Medicis, the sister of Mary de Medicis ' [Foote, *Taste*].

———— *Sukey :* daughter of the alderman and married to Mr. Deputy Dripping.

Pepperpot, Sir Peter : a testy old West Indian, very wealthy [Foote, *Patron*].

Peps, Dr Parker : a court physician, who always addressed his patients by a title, that they might think that he only attended those of the very first rank [Dickens, *Dombey and Son*].

Perch, Mr : messenger to the firm of Dombey and Son, who lived at Ball's Pond.

———— *Mrs. :* his wife and the partner of his joys [Dickens, *Dombey and Son*].

Percivale, Sir : third son of Pellinore, King of Wales, and one of the very few knights who ever beheld the Holy Grail [Mallory, *History of Prince Arthur ;* he also figures in Tennyson's *Idylls of the King : Merlin and Vivien ; Launcelot and Elaine*].

Percy : the hero of a tragedy which ran for seventeen nights [Hannah More, *Percy*].

Percyvell : the hero of a romance of the fifteenth century [attrib. Robert de Thomson, *Percyvell of Galles*]

Perdita : the daughter of Leontes and Hermione exposed in infancy, to death, by order of her father, but rescued by a shepherd [Shakespeare, *Winter's Tale*].

Peredur, Sir : son of Evrawe, and a knight of the Round Table [*Mabinogion*].

Peregrine : the hero of the play, who, at the age of fifteen, runs from home, borrowing £30 from a brazier. Nothing is heard of him for thirty years, and then he returns with £100,000, of which he hands £10,000 to the brazier as his honest profit [Colman the Younger, *John Bull*].

Perey, Michael : the ' copper Captain ' who marries a servant, believing her to be a lady of position, she marrying him for money which he does not possess [J. Fletcher, *Rule a Wife and Have a Wife*].

Pericles : a voluntary exile, in order to turn the wrath of the Emperor of Greece, Antiochus, from the Tyrians [Shakespeare, *Pericles, Prince of Tyre*].

Pericles, Antonio : a rich Greek merchant, and partner of Mr. Pole. He has a passion for music and determines to have Sandra Belloni trained in Italy. Clever but unscrupulous [George Meredith, *Sandra Belloni*].

—— **and Aspasia :** the writers of a series of letters [Landor, *Pericles and Aspasia*].

Perigot : in love with Amoret, but beloved by Amarillis who gets herself transformed into the image of Amoret. Perigot discovers the truth and marries Amoret [J. Fletcher, *Faithful Shepherdess*].

Perimones, Sir = the Red Knight. One of those who kept the entrances to Castle Perilous. Gareth vanquishes him. Tennyson calls him ' Noonday Sun ' [Mallory, *History of Prince Arthur*; also Alfred Tennyson, *Idylls of the King : Gareth and Lynette*].

Perissa : the impersonation of extravagance [Spenser, *Faëry Queene*].

Periwinkle, Mr.: ' dotes upon travellers, and believes more of Sir John Mandeville than of the Bible '. He is one of Anne Lovely's four guardians [Mrs. Centlivre, *Bold Stroke for a Wife*].

—— **The Princess :** a character in the comedy [Smart, *Trip to Cambridge ; or, Grateful Fair*].

Perker, Mr.: Mr. Pickwick's attorney in the suit of ' Bardell *v.* Pickwick ' [Dickens, *Pickwick Papers*].

Perkins, Mrs.: the subject of ' a Christmas Book ' [Thackeray, *Mrs. Perkins' Ball*].

Persaunt of India, Sir : the Blue Knight, called by Tennyson, ' Morning Star '. He aided in guarding the approaches to Castle Perilous, but was defeated by Gareth [Mallory, *History of Prince Arthur*; and Alfred Tennyson, *Idylls of the King : Gareth and Lynette*].

Persoun, The Poore : a poor parish priest, who himself walked in the way he pointed out to others [Chaucer, *Canterbury Tales : Prologue*].

Perth, Fair Maid of : *see* Glover, Catherine.

Pertolope, Sir : the ' Evening Star ', or ' Hesperus ', one of the brothers who guarded the approaches to Castle Perilous, overthrown by Gareth [Mallory, *History of Prince Arthur*; and Alfred Tennyson, *Idylls of the King : Gareth and Lynette*].

Pescara : governor of Granada. This part was played by Macready [Sheil, *Apostate*].

' Pet ': *see* Meagles, Minnie.

Petella : attendant on Mantolet's two daughters [J. Fletcher, *Wild-goose Chase*].

Peter, Lord : intended for the Pope of Rome [Swift, *Tale of a Tub* ; also, Arbuthnot, *History of John Bull*].

Peter : the half-idiotic son of Solomon, Count Wintersen's butler [B. Thompson, *The Stranger*].

Peterson : a Swede who goes over from Gustavus Vasa to Christian II [Brooke, *Gustavus Vasa*].

Peto : lieutenant in the regiment where Falstaff was captain, Pistol ensign, and Bardolph corporal [Shakespeare, *King Henry IV*, pt. i. and ii.].

Petowker, Miss Henrietta : an actress who marries Lillyvick, the rate-collector, and then runs away with an officer [Dickens, *Nicholas Nickleby*].

Petruchio : the man who ventures to marry the 'shrew' and succeeds in taming her [Shakespeare, *Taming of the Shrew*].

Petulant : a dreadful person 'without manners or breeding', also without morals or dignity, and full of underhand tricks [Congreve, *Way of the World*].

Peveril, Julian : a Cavalier who falls in love with the daughter of a Roundhead, and, in spite of many difficulties, marries her [Scott, *Peveril of the Peak*].

Phaedra : a waiting woman of very low character [Dryden, *Amphitryon*].

Phaedria : the personification of wantonness [Spenser, *Faëry Queene*].

Phaleg : intended for a Mr. Forbes, at one time tutor to the Duke of Ormond [Dryden and Tate, *Absalom and Achitophel*].

Phaon : in love with Claribel, but believing he had proof of her infidelity he slew her on the spot [Spenser, *Faëry Queene*].

Pharamond : a French king who tried by knightly deeds to win a place at the Round Table [*Arthurian Cycle*].

—— a Spanish prince [Beaumont and Fletcher, *Love Lies Bleeding*].

Pharaoh's Wife=Asia, the daughter of Mozâhem, cruelly tortured by her husband because of her faith in Moses [Sale, *Al Korán*].

Phebe : a shepherdess loved by Silvius, a shepherd [Shakespeare, *As You Like It*].

Philander : a prince of Cyprus who loved the Princess Erota [J. Fletcher, *Laws of Candy*].

—— a counsellor [Norton and Buckhurst, *Gorboduc*].

Philarete : intended for Thomas Manwood, the author's friend [Browne, *Shepherd's Pipe*].

Philargyria : represents Avarice in a moral interlude of the late fifteenth or very early sixteenth century [J. Skelton, *The Nigramansir*].

Philario : an Italian. It is at his house that Posthumus lays his wager with Iachimo [Shakespeare, *Cymbeline*].

Philario: a friend who remained true to the hero through all his troubles [Milman, *Fazio*].

Philaster : loved the Princess Arethusa, whilst Euphrasia was in love with him. Many complications ensue, but the right people marry at last [Beaumont and Fletcher, *Philaster ; or, Love Lies Bleeding*].

Philip : in love with Elspie [Clough, *Bothie of Tober-na-Vuolich*].

—— the hero of the novel ; the story shows ' who robbed him, who helped him, and who passed him by ' [Thackeray, *Adventures of Philip*].

—— Mr. Peregrine Lovel's butler, a dishonest and hypocritical servant [Townley, *High Life Below Stairs*].

—— a dreadful prig, overwhelmed by a sense of his own virtues. He is the hero [Charlotte Yonge, *Heir of Redcliffe*].

—— Van Artevelde : *see* Artevelde, Philip Van.

Philippe : a shrewd though infirm old villain, with a malicious tongue [Knowles, *Provost of Bruges*].

Philipson, Arthur : Sir Arthur de Vere, son of the Earl of Oxford, who accompanies him in his exile.

—— *John, Earl of Oxford :* an exiled Lancastrian [Scott, *Anne of Griestein*].

Philisides=Sir Philip Sidney.

Phillida : *see* Galathea and Phillida.

—— and Corydon : the hero and heroine of ' a pleasant song ' sung before Queen Elizabeth at Elvetham in 1591 [Breton, *Phillida and Corydon*].

Phillips, Jessie : the heroine of a novel written with the object of attacking the poor-law system [Mrs. Trollope, *Jessie Phillips*].

Philoclea=Lady Penelope Devereux, with whom the author was in love [Sidney, *Arcadia*].

Philologus : the hero of a moral play [*Conflict of Conscience*].

Philomelus : a druid bard [James Thomson, *Castle of Indolence*].

Philonides and Menippus : characters in an incomplete Latin play which was probably acted at St. Paul's School [Rightwise, *Philonides and Menippus*].

Philostrate : master of the revels to Theseus [Shakespeare, *Midsummer Night's Dream*].

Philotas : son of Parmenio. By some thought to be intended for the unhappy Earl of Essex [Samuel Daniel, *Philotas*].

Philotine : the Queen of Hell and daughter of Mammon, who offers her to Guyon as wife [Spenser, *Faëry Queene*].

Philotimus : ambition personified [Phineas Fletcher, *Purple Island*].

Philpot [senior] **:** an avaricious, disagreeable old man who shook his head ' like a china mandarin.'

Philpot, George : his son, a young profligate whom every one despises and scoffs at [Murphy, *Citizen*].

Philtra : a wealthy woman whose chief love was money, so, her lover, Bracidas, growing poor, she throws him over for his wealthier brother Amidas [Spenser, *Faëry Queene*].

Phobbs, Captain and Mrs. and Mrs. Major Phobbs : are all characters in the play [J. M. Morton, *Lend me Five Shillings*].

Phocyas : general of the Syrian army, and the hopeless admirer of Eudocia, daughter of the Governor of Damascus [John Hughes, *Siege of Damascus*].

Phoebe, Pyncheon : *see* Pyncheon, Phoebe.

Phosphorus : called by Tennyson ' Morning Star ', the same as Sir Persaunt, q.v.

Phunky, Mr. : assists Sergeant Snubbin in the defence of Mr. Pickwick in the suit ' Bardell *v.* Pickwick '[Dickens, *Pickwick Papers*].

Phyllis=Lady Carey, wife of Sir George Carey [Spenser, *Colin Clout 's Come Home Again*].

—— **and Brunetta :** beauties who vied with each other in the endeavour to shine in the eyes of the world [Addison, *Spectator*, Nos. 1711, 1712, 1714].

Physignathos : the King of the Frogs, who is wounded by Troxartas, the King of the Mice [Parnell, *Battle of the Frogs and Mice*].

Piavens, Laura : a young Italian widow with two children. Her husband was shot by the Austrians and her whole life is devoted to the cause of Italian freedom [George Meredith, *Vittoria*].

Pickle, Peregrine : an ungrateful spendthrift capable of ' base brutality ' and of tormenting others ' by practical jokes, resembling those of a fiend in glee ' [Smollett, *Peregrine Pickle*].

Pickwick, Samuel : the type of all innocence and benevolence, and the founder of the world-famed Pickwick Club [Dickens, *Pickwick Papers*].

Pied Piper of Hamelin : a mysterious piper who, by the power of his flute, could draw, not only rats, but children after him, from out of the town of Hamelin into the Koppenberg [R. Browning, *Pied Piper of Hamelin*].

Pierre : the meddlesome, prying servant of Mon. Darlemont [Holcroft, *Deaf and Dumb*].

Pierre, Peer : takes the leading part in a plot to assassinate the senators of Venice [Otway, *Venice Preserved*].

Piers Plowman : *see* Plowman.

Pigwiggen : a fairy warrior who loves Queen Mab, and fights Oberon [Drayton, *Nymphidia*].

Pinac : a companion of Mirabel on his journeyings [J. Fletcher, *Wild-goose Chase*].

Pinch : a schoolmaster and conjuror [Shakespeare, *Comedy of Errors*].

—— **Ruth :** a governess. The sister of Tom Pinch and his delight. She marries John Westlock.

—— *Tom :* Mr. Pecksniff's clerk and a great lover of the organ, which he sometimes got leave to play in Salisbury Cathedral [Dickens, *Martin Chuzzlewit*].

Pinchbeck, Lady : the lady to whom Don Juan entrusted Leila [Byron, *Don Juan*].

Pinchwife, Mr. : a town-bred man married to an untrained country girl.

—— *Mrs. :* very young and very unsophisticated, and therefore a great anxiety to her husband [Wycherley, *Country Wife*].

Pineapple, Poll : she once went to sea with Lieutenant Belaye, dressed as a sailor, and when he introduced her one day to his crew as Mrs. Belaye, all the crew fainted and then he found out they were all women who had dressed like sailors so as to follow him [Gilbert, *Bab Ballads*].

Pinkerton, The Misses : some most dignified ladies who kept an educational establishment for young ladies on Chiswick Mall. Here Amelia Sedley went to school and Becky Sharp was a pupil teacher [Thackeray, *Vanity Fair*].

Pip : *see* Pirrip, Philip.

Pipchin, Mrs. : the old lady with whom Paul Dombey was sent to board, at Brighton [Dickens, *Dombey and Son*].

Piper, Paddy the : an Irish piper, whom his neighbours thought had been swallowed by a cow [Lover, *Legends and Stories of Ireland*].

—— of Hamelin, The Pied : *see* Pied Piper of Hamelin.

Piperman : a druggist's assistant who prided himself on being 'so handy' [Ware, *Piperman's Predicament*].

Pipes, Tom : a silent old boatswain's mate who lives with Commodore Trunnion and superintends his household for him [Smollett, *Peregrine Pickle*].

Pipkin, Nathaniel : the 'parish Clerk' who falls in love with Marie Lobbs. Good-natured, harmless and lame, with a squint [Dickens, *Pickwick Papers*].

Pippa : a little silk-winder at Asolo, with one holiday a year, and that is New Year's Day. Her innocent gladness has far-reaching influence for good [R. Browning, *Pippa Passes*].

Pirate, The : *see* Troil, Magnus.

Pirrip, Philip : always known as ' Pip ', the brother of Mrs. Joe Gargery, and the teller of the story. Abel Magwitch, the ex-convict, makes him his heir, but he loses all his money again and becomes a clerk and marries Estella [Dickens, *Great Expectations*].

Pisani, Angela : the heroine [Smythe, *Angela Pisani*].

Pisanio : the servant whom Posthumus sends to murder Imogen, his wife, but who instead aids her flight to Milford Haven [Shakespeare, *Cymbeline*].

Pistol : a bragging ale-house bully whom Fluellen forces to eat a leek [Shakespeare, *Henry V*].

Pithyrian : a pagan dwelling in Antioch, with one daughter, a Christian, Marana by name. Upon a dragon infesting the city Marana was chosen as the sacrifice to appease its appetite, but Pithyrian saves his child with the aid of the thumb of a saint [Southey, *Young Dragon*].

Pizarro : a Spanish adventurer who stirred up war in Peru [Sheridan, *Pizarro*].

—— ' the ready tool of fell Velasquez ' crimes ' [Jephson, *Braganza*].

Place, Lord : a candidate for Parliament who employs the aid of bribery [Fielding, *Pasquin*].

Placebo : a brother of January, Baron of Lombardy [Chaucer, *Canterbury Tales : The Merchant's Tale*].

Placid, Mr. : a docile husband, like ' a boiled rabbit without oyster sauce '.

—— **Mrs. :** a wife who had her hsuband as well as her household under absolute command [Mrs. Inchbald, *Every One has His Fault*].

Placidas : the absolute double of his friend Amias [Spenser, *Faëry Queene*].

Plagiary, Sir Fretful : an ineffectual playwright, very conceited too, and impatient of criticism. Said to have been intended for Cumberland [Sheridan, *The Critic*].

Plantagenet, Lady Edith : married to Kenneth, Prince Royal of Scotland, known as David, Earl of Huntingdon, or, the Knight of the Leopard [Scott, *Talisman*].

Plausible : a character in the play [Wycherley, *Plain Dealer*].

—— **Counsellor, and Sergeant Eitherside :** two pleaders [Macklin, *Man of the World*].

Pleydell, Mr. Paulus : an advocate and sheriff [Scott, *Guy Mannering*].

Pliable, Mr. : a friend who went with Christian as far as the Slough of Despond [Bunyan, *Pilgrim's Progress*].

Pliant, Dame : a foolish widow, who marries Lovewit [Ben Jonson, *Alchemist*].

———— **Sir Paul :** a uxorious old man, on whose kindness his wife presumes [Congreve, *Double Dealer*].

Plornish : a plasterer living in Bleeding Heart Yard ; a friend of Little Dorrit.

———— *Mrs. :* his wife, prematurely aged by the cares of poverty and a large family [Dickens, *Little Dorrit*].

Plowden, Kate : an American girl in love with a British sailor, Lieutenant Barnstable [Fitzball, *The Pilot*].

Plowman, Piers : a satirical political poem dated 1370. Piers is at the beginning ' a blameless ploughman and a guide to men who are seeking the shrine of truth ' ; and afterwards 'a blameless carpenter's son who alone can show us the Father '.—*Skeat.* It should be the ' Vision of William concerning Piers Plowman ', [attrib. William Langland, *Vision of Piers Plowman*].

Plume, Captain : in love with the heiress, Sylvia, for whom he resigns his commission [Farquhar, *Recruiting Officer*].

———— **Sir :** intended for Thomas Coke, vice-chamberlain to Queen Anne [Pope, *Rape of the Lock*].

Plummer, Bertha : the blind daughter of Caleb. Secretly in love with Tackleton.

———— *Edward :* Caleb's son who, after a long absence in South America, comes home and marries May Fielding [Dickens, *Cricket on the Hearth*].

———— *Caleb :* a toy-maker, who devotes himself to his blind child.

Pocket, Belinda : Matthew Pocket's wife. A helpless nonentity, and the mother of eight children.

———— *Herbert :* the son of Matthew's, and a great friend of ' Pip's ', who secretly renders him great assistance.

———— *Matthew :* a relative of Miss Havisham's. He is a finished scholar and a Cambridge ' Honours man '. Through force of circumstances he became a literary hack [Dickens, *Great Expectations*].

Podsnap, Georgina : an affectionate, shy and rather foolish girl.

———— *Mr. John :* a self-satisfied, pompous man, swelling with a sense of his own importance and settling all difficulties by a sweep of the arm [Dickens, *Our Mutual Friend*].

Pogram, The Hon. Elijah : an American member of Congress, and ' one of the master minds of our country [Dickens, *Martin Chuzzlewit*].

Poins : one of Falstaff's disreputable boon companions [Shakespeare, *Henry IV*, pts. i. and ii.].

Pole, Arabella, Cornelia and Adela : the daughters of a city merchant, whose great aim is to get into county society. Their efforts to achieve this are full of comedy. Though essentially vulgar, they are super-refined.

———— *Mr. :* a nervous little city merchant, who is forced into expensive living by his three daughters. He has speculated with Mrs. Chump's money and is filled with dread of exposure.

———— *Wilfrid :* his son. He falls partly in love with 'Sandra Belloni, but at the same time proposes to a lady of title, who accepts him. Eventually he loses both [George Meredith, *Sandra Belloni*].

Polish, Mrs. : a character in a comedy [Ben Jonson, *Magnetick Lady*].

Polixenes : the King of Bohemia, and old friend of Leontes, King of Sicily [Shakespeare, *Winter's Tale*].

Poll : *see* Sweedlepipe, Paul.

Pollente : the father of Munera : a Saracen, lord of the Perilous Bridge [Spenser, *Faëry Queene*].

Polonius : a garrulous, self-complaisant old man, chamberlain to the King of Denmark,and the father of Ophelia and Laertes. Full of ' wise saws and modern instances ' [Shakespeare, *Hamlet*].

Polydore : the name used by Prince Guiderius during his concealment in Wales [Shakespeare, *Cymbeline*].

———— beloved by the King of Paphos's sister Calis [Beaumont and Fletcher, *Mad Lover*].

———— son of Lord Acasto, the guardian of Monimia, to whom he behaves in the most wanton and scandalous manner [Otway, *The Orphan*].

Polyglot : tutor of Charles Eustace, and himself master of seventeen languages. His pupil being secretly married, he makes himself the young man's ' scapegoat ' and helps him out of his difficulties [Poole, *Scapegoat*].

Polyxena : the noble wife of Charles Emanuel, King of Sardinia [R. Browning, *King Victor and King Charles*].

Pompilia : a young wife, murdered by her husband Guido Franceschini, who charges her with infidelity [R. Browning, *Ring and the Book*].

Pompey : a clown in the service of Mrs. Overdone [Shakespeare, *Measure for Measure*].

Ponto, Major : a retired officer, who, instigated by his wife, endeavours to mix only with ' county families ' [Thackeray, *Book of Snobs*].

Poole, Mrs. : the woman in charge of the maniac, Mrs. Rochester, and whose carelessness gives the mad woman the opportunity of setting fire to the house [Charlotte Brontë, *Jane Eyre*].

Porcius : like his brother Marcus, in love with Lucie. Marcus falls in battle so Porcius attains his heart's desire [Addison, *Cato*].

Porrex : *see* Gorboduc.

Porsena or Porsenna, Lars : a legendary King of Etruria [Macaulay, *Lays of Ancient Rome*].

Portamour : the officer employed by Cupid to summon lovers who were in disgrace to ' Love's Judgment Hall ' [Spenser, *Faëry Queene*].

Porteous, Captain John : an officer of the Edinburgh City Guard hanged by the mob in the ' Porteous riots ' [Scott, *Heart of Midlothian*].

Portia : the heiress whom Bassanio wins, and who, by disguising herself as a doctor of law and pleading in the judgment hall rescues her husband's friend and benefactor, Antonio, from the hands of Shylock, the Jew [Shakespeare, *Merchant of Venice*].

Posthumus, Leonatus : the unworthy husband of Imogen [Shakespeare, *Cymbeline*].

Pother, Doctor : a great teller of stories and anecdotes [C. J. M. Dibdin, *Farmer's Wife*].

Pots, Tom : occurs in an old ballad, where his valour wins him his heart's desire [*Lover's Quarrel*].

Pott, Mr. and Mrs. : editor of the *Eatanswill Gazette*, and his wife [Dickens, *Pickwick Papers*].

Potterson, Miss Abbey : the owner and manageress of a tavern called ' *The Six Jolly Fellowship-Porters* ' [Dickens, *Our Mutual Friend*].

Pounce, Peter : one of the characters in the novel [Fielding, *Joseph Andrews*].

Poundtext, Peter : a preacher in the army of the Covenanters [Scott, *Old Mortality*].

Poyser, Mrs. : a woman of kind heart and great common sense but caustic tongue, whose sayings and criticisms on life and her neighbours are inimitable [George Eliot, *Adam Bede*].

Pratefast, Peter : ' in all his life he spake no word in waste ' [Hawes, *Passe-tyme of Pleasure*].

Pratt, Miss : a poor relation and hanger-on of the Earl of Rossville. Keen-sighted, prying and impertinent [Susan E. Ferrier, *Inheritance*].

Prattle, Mr. : a general practitioner and inveterate gossip [Colman the Elder, *Deuce is in Him*].

Preciosa : a gipsy girl, the heroine of the poem [Long-fellow, *Spanish Student*].

Prettyman Prince : sometimes disguised as a fisherman, sometimes appearing as a prince, he is in love with Cloris. Said to be meant as a parody on Leonidas, in Dryden's play, *Marriage à-la-Mode* [Duke of Buckingham, *Rehearsal*].

Priamus, Sir : the possessor of a phial of healing waters that came from Paradise. He was a knight of the Round Table [Mallory, *History of Prince Arthur*].

Price, Fanny : the adopted daughter of her rich uncle, Sir Thomas Bertram, and married to his son Edmund.

———— *William :* Fanny Price's sailor brother [Jane Austen *Mansfield Park*].

———— **Matilda :** a friend of Miss Squeers, afterwards Mrs. John Browdie [Dickens, *Nicholas Nickleby*].

Pride, Sir : at one time a drayman, but afterwards a Colonel in Cromwell's army [Butler, *Hudibras*].

Pridwin : King Arthur's shield [Geoffrey, *British History*].

Prig, Betsey : a monthly nurse, the friend, and often the partner of Mrs. Gamp [Dickens, *Martin Chuzzlewit*].

Prim, Obadiah : a Quaker [Mrs. Centilvre, *Bold Stroke for a Wife*].

Prima Donna, Lord : one of the characters in the novel [Lord Beaconsfield, *Vivian Grey*].

Primer, Peter : a country schoolmaster with unbounded faith in himself [Foote, *Mayor of Garrath*].

Primrose, George : went to Amsterdam to teach English, afterwards became a captain in the army and married the heiress, Miss Wilmot.

———— *Moses :* famous for his transaction of selling his father's horse in exchange for a gross of green spectacles.

———— *Mrs. Deborah :* the vicar's comely wife. Proud of her husband, her children, and her gooseberry wine, and very anxious to appear ' genteel '.

———— *Olivia :* elder daughter of the ' vicar '; she eloped with Squire Thornhill.

———— *Rev. Doctor :* charitable, devout, and unworldly, and full of a quiet humour. A very ideal ' vicar.'

———— *Sophia :* the vicar's second daughter,' soft, modest, and alluring '. She marries Sir William Thornhill [Mr. Burchell]. [Goldsmith, *Vicar of Wakefield*].

Prince Ahmed : see Ahmed, Prince.

———— **Alasnam :** see Alasnam, Prince.

———— **Beder :** see Labe, Queen.

———— **Camaralzaman :** see Camaralzaman.

Prince Houssain : *see* Houssain, Prince.

────── **Prettyman :** *see* Prettyman, Prince.

────── **Volscius :** *see* Volscius, Prince.

Pringle, Andrew : son of the Rev. Dr. Pringle, who aims at being a young man of fashion.

────── *Mrs. :* his wife, a very ' managing body ', great in all housewifely arts.

────── *Rachel :* sister to Andrew, who marries Captain Sabre.

────── *the Rev. Dr. :* incumbent of Garnock, the residuary legatee. A benevolent, simple old man [Galt, *Ayreshire Legatees*].

Priory, Lady : Lord Priory's young, beautiful and loving wife, who agreed with him in his old-fashioned ideas.

────── *Lord :* a man with old-fashioned ideas as to the duties and proper conduct of wives [Mrs. Inchbald, *Wives as they Were and Maids as they Are*].

Priscilla : the heroine of the poem [Longfellow, *Courtship of Miles Standish*].

────── of noble birth herself, she fell in love with a poor knight, Sir Aladine [Spenser, *Faëry Queene*].

Prisoner of Chillon : this poem is founded on the experience and sufferings of Bonnivard, the Genevan martyr to independence [Byron, *Prisoner of Chillon*].

Priuli : a member of the Venetian senate, whose daughter Belvidera loved a commoner, Juffier, by name, who had rescued her from a watery grave. Priuli would not consent to their union, and in revenge Juffier formed a plot to murder all the senators, but gave his father-in-law warning in the end [Otway, *Venice Preserved*].

Probe : a surgeon not above magnifying the ailments of his patients that his fees might increase [Sheridan, *Trip to Scarborough*].

Procida, John of : a skilled physician of the thirteenth century, who, after a general rising against the French, was elected King of Sicily [Knowles, *John of Procida*].

Prometheus : the hero of a translation from the Greek of Aeschylus [Elizabeth B. Browning, *Prometheus Bound*].

────── a poem based on the old tradition of how Prometheus stole fire from heaven [Longfellow, *Prometheus ; or, The Poet's Forethought*].

────── steals fire from heaven and is punished by being chained to a rock and pecked at by a vulture [Shelley, *Prometheus Unbound*].

Promos and Cassandra : two characters in a tragedy which is supposed to have suggested some ideas to Shakespeare in *Measure for Measure* [Whetstone, *Promos and Cassandra*].

Prophet of Khorassan, The Veiled : *see* Mokanna.

Prospero : intended as a likeness of Francis Douce [T. F. Dibdin, *Bibliomania*].

―――― through neglect of his office for the sake of the study of magic, he lost the Dukedom of Milan, but he regained it through his mastery of the art. He was the father of Miranda [Shakespeare, *Tempest*].

Pross, Miss : Lucie Manette's maid. An unattractive looking woman with abrupt manners, but very devoted to her mistress [Dickens, *Tale of Two Cities*].

Proteus : one of the two gentlemen of Verona, and in love with Julia [Shakespeare, *Two Gentlemen of Verona*].

Protocol, Mr. Peter : an Edinburgh attorney employed by Mrs. Bertram [Scott, *Guy Mannering*].

Proudie, Bishop : the successor of Bishop Grantley as Bishop of Barchester. A thoroughly henpecked man.

―――― *Mrs. :* his domineering, masculine wife [Anthony Trollope, *Barchester Towers*].

Provis : *see* Magwitch, Abel.

Prudence : the ' noble wyf ' of Melibeus [Chaucer, *Canterbury Tales : Chaucer's Tale of Melibeus*].

―――― **Mistress :** attendant on Violet, Lady Arundel's ward. Not unassailable by bribery so long as the terms were high enough [Lytton, *Sea-Captain*].

Prue, Miss : a precocious and badly brought-up schoolgirl [Congreve, *Love for Love*].

Pry, Kitty : an impertinent and inquisitive waiting-maid, who admires Timothy Sharp, the ' valet ' [Garrick, *Lying Valet*].

―――― **Paul :** ' one of those idle, meddling fellows, who having no employment themselves are perpetually interfering in other people's affairs ' [Poole, *Paul Pry*].

Prynne, Hester : the heroine. A poor woman who having strayed from the path of virtue is compelled thenceforth to wear a large scarlet letter sewn on the front of her dress, that all may know her shame, in accordance with the harsh New England law in force in the early days of the settlement [Nathaniel Hawthorne, *Scarlet Letter*].

Pryor, Mrs. : Shirley Keeldar's governess and companion, who turns out to be Caroline Helstone's mother [Charlotte Brontë, *Shirley*].

Psycarpax=granary-thief ; the name of the son of Troxartas, King of the Mice [Parnell, *Battle of the Frogs and Mice*].

Psyche : the subject of a poem in six cantos [Mrs. Mary Tighe, *Psyche*].

―――― the subject of a poem in twenty-four cantos [Joseph Beaumont, *Psyche ; or, Love's Mystery*].

Publius : son of Horatius. He believed in and acted upon the Roman principle that ' a patriot's soul can feel no ties but duty, and know no voice of kindred ' [Whitehead, *Roman Father*].

Pucel, La Bel : lived in the tower of music, and was loved by Graunde Amoure [Hawes, *Passe-tyme of Pleasure*].

Puck : ' a rough, knurly-limbed, fawn-faced, shock-pated, mischievous little urchin ', often called Robin Goodfellow. Jester to King Oberon [Shakespeare, *Midsummer Night's Dream*].

Puff, Mr. Partenopex : ' a modest wit' who having said a good thing generally tries to father it on to some one else [Beaconsfield, *Vivian Grey*].

―――― a vendor of quack physic [Foote, *The Patron*].

―――― an auctioneer [Foote, *Taste*].

―――― Captain Loveit's servant, married to Tagg [Garrick, *Miss in her Teens*].

―――― ' a practitioner in panegyric. . . a professor of the art of puffing ' [Sheridan, *The Critic*].

Pug : a little hobgoblin, the same as Puck [Ben Jonson, *Devil is an Ass*].

Pullet, Mrs. : Maggie Tulliver's invalid aunt ; a selfish exacting woman [George Eliot, *Mill on the Floss*].

Pumblechook, Uncle : he toadies to wealthy people and bullies the poor. He is a corn-chandler by trade and uncle to Joe Gargery, the blacksmith [Dickens, *Great Expectations*].

Pumpkin, Miss Bridget : sister to Sir Gilbert, who hates the acting, but rather enjoys having to do with love-making [Jackman, *All the World's a Stage*].

―――― *Sir Gilbert :* a country gentleman who is guardian to Kitty Sprightly. His whole household goes mad about acting, and one of the guests, who come to act runs away with Kitty.

Pure, Simon : a Quaker from Pennsylvania, who gets cheated out of a wealthy bride by Colonel Feignwell, who personates him before his arrival in England [Mrs. Centlivre, *Bold Stroke for a Wife*].

Pycroft, Emanuel : a quick-witted and amusing petty naval officer [Kipling, *Their Lawful Occasions*].

Pye, Susie : probably intended for the Saracen girl who fell in love with Gilbert Beckett in the Holy Land, and who followed him to London, just as Lord Beichan is supposed to stand for Gilbert Beckett himself [*Young Beichan*, a ballad].

Pygmalion : the hero of a mythological comedy based on the story of the Athenian sculptor, who prayed to the gods that the statue he had made might really come to life [Gilbert, *Pygmalion and Galatea*].

Pyke and Pluck : satellites of Sir Mulberry Hawk, who do his bidding in all things [Dickens, *Nicholas Nickleby*].

Pyncheon, Clifford : the sometime handsome pleasure-loving heir of the Pyncheons, sacrificed by his brutal cousin, the judge, and wrongly sentenced for a crime he did not commit.

―――― *Hepzibah :* the nervous, near-sighted old maid, reduced in means and striving against heavy odds to keep the old home going against the return of her brother from prison.

―――― *Judge Jaffrey :* a wealthy local magnate, who had risen to distinction at the expense of his innocent cousin Clifford.

―――― *Phoebe :* a bright New England girl, who goes to stay with Miss Hepzibah, and who falls in love with and marries her lodger Holgrave [Nathaniel Hawthorne, *House of the Seven Gables*].

Pyramus : the lover of Thisby who, upon a report of her death, stabbed himself under a mulberry tree [Shakespeare, *Midsummer Night's Dream*].

Pyrocles : one of the sons of Acrates slain by Prince Arthur [Spenser, *Faëry Queene*].

Pythias : a Syracusan noted for his love for Damon. When the latter was condemned to death Pythias offered himself as a hostage whilst Damon went home to bid farewell to wife and child. Damon returned in time. The King of Syracuse was so struck by their friendship that he pardoned Damon [Edwards, *Damon and Pythias*].

Quackleben, Dr. Quentin : a doctor and one of the board of management at the spa [Scott, *St. Ronan's Well*].

Quaint, Timothy : ' an odd fish that loves to swim in troubled waters '. He is in the employ of Governor Heartall [Cherry, *Soldier's Daughter*].

Quale, Mr. : a friend of Mrs. Jellyby's. A loquacious young man, and a philanthropist[Dickens, *Bleak House*].

Quarle, Philip : *see* Hermit, The.

Quaver : a singing-master with a high opinion of the value of his own profession [Fielding, *Virgin Unmasked*].

Quedy, Mr. Mac : a Scotchman with an entirely unromantic and materialistic outlook [Peacock, *Crotchet Castle*].

Queen Labe : *see* Labe, Queen.
———— **Scheherezade :** *see* Scheherezade, Queen.
Quentin Durward : *see* Durward, Quentin.
Quiara : the wife of Monnema. Upon the outbreak of an epidemic of smallpox in Paraguay they migrated to the Mondai woods, where two children were born to them. The father was devoured by a jaguar and the mother and children retreated to St. Joachin, where Quiara soon died [Southey, *Tale of Paraguay*].
Quickly, Mistress Nell : hostess of the *Boar's Head* Tavern in East Cheap, frequented by Falstaff and his boon companions [Shakespeare, *Henry IV* and *Henry V*].
———— **Mistress :** Dr. Caius's factotum and the go-between of Anne Page and her suitors [Shakespeare, *Merry Wives of Windsor*].
Quicksilver : an idle apprentice [Chapman, Marston and Jonson, *Eastward Hoe* !]
———— = Lord Brougham, a caricature [Warren, *Ten Thousand a Year*].
Quidascarpi, Angelo & Rinaldo : two Italians of high birth who join in the revolution [George Meredith, *Vittoria*].
Quidnunc, Abraham : a troublesome, interfering busybody.
———— **Harriet :** his daughter, rescued from a burning house by Belmour.
———— **John :** marries a rich widow under the assumed name of Rovewell, returns to England, pays his father's creditors and arranges his sister's marriage with Belmour [Murphy, *Upholsterer*].
Quidnunkis : a monkey that serves to point a moral in a fable. It climbs higher than its fellows, but falls into a river and is lost [Gay, *Quidnunkis*].
Quilliam, Peter [Pete] : the natural son of Peter Christian. He is the friend of Philip and the husband of Katherine Cregeen. The hero of the story [Hall Caine, *Manxman*].
Quilp, Betsey : the wife of Daniel Quilp, 'a pretty little mild-spoken, blue-eyed woman', who having married a sort of fiend did 'sound practical penance for her folly, every day of her life '.
———— **Daniel :** a hideous dwarf, full of a fiendish admixture of ferocity and cunning, without one redeeming trait [Dickens, *Old Curiosity Shop*].
Quince, Peter : a carpenter who takes the lead in arranging the play to be performed before Theseus and Hippolyta [Shakespeare, *Midsummer Night's Dream*].
Quisara : the heroine of the play [J. Fletcher, *Island Princess*].
Quitam, Mr. : the lawyer at the inn at Darlington [Scott, *Rob Roy*].

Quiverful, Mr. : the father of fourteen children. Rector of Puddingdale [Anthony Trollope, *Barchester Towers*].

Quodling, The Rev. Mr. : chaplain to the Duke of Buckingham [Scott, *Peveril of the Peak*].

Quomodo : a draper and usurer whose ambition it is to become a land-owner [Middleton, *Michaelmas Term*].

Quontem, Caleb : a parish clerk and Jack-of-all-trades [Colman the Younger, *The Review; or, Wags of Windsor*].

Rab : a mastiff, 'as mighty in his own line as Julius Caesar or the Duke of Wellington' [Dr. J. Brown, *Rab and his Friends*].

Rabisson : a tinker and knife-grinder who was in the secret of the gold mine owned by the ' Miller of Grenoble [Stirling, *Gold Mine; or, Miller of Grenoble*].

Rabsheka : intended for Sir Thomas Player [Dryden and Tate, *Absalom and Achitophel*, pt. ii.].

Raby, Aurora : a rich young girl, an orphan and a Roman Catholic, visiting at Lady Amundville's at the same time as Don Juan [Byron, *Don Juan*].

Rachel : a mill-hand in love with Stephen Blackpool [Dickens, *Hard Times*].

Racket, Lady : the daughter of Mr. Drugget, a wealthy London merchant [Murphy, *Three Weeks after Marriage*].

—— *Sir Charles :* quarrels with his young wife over a game of whist and threatens her with a divorce, but thinks better of it afterwards.

—— Widow : a coquette, a wit, and a fine lady [Mrs. Cowley, *Belle's Stratagem*].

Rackrent, Sir Condy : a heedless, good-natured, impecunious Irish landowner, who wastes all the little substance he ever possessed, and is deserted by a wife who had only married him upon a mistaken idea of his position [Maria Edgeworth, *Castle Rackrent*].

Raddle, Mrs. Mary Ann : Mr. Bob Sawyer's shrewish landlady [Dickens, *Pickwick Papers*].

Radigond : Queen of the Amazons [Spenser, *Faëry Queene*].

Radirobanes : intended for Philip II of Spain [Barclay, *Argenis*].

Radnor, Nataly : her irregular marriage with Victor Radnor tinges her whole life with tragedy. She dies suddenly of heart-disease.

—— *Nesta Victoria :* the daughter of Victor and Nataly, who marries Dartrey Fenellan.

—— *Victor :* a wealthy city merchant who is constantly thwarted by the one false step of his life. His end is tragic [George Meredith, *One of our Conquerors*].

Rake, Lord : a gentleman of the type that is fond of drinking, rioting and general 'about town' dissipation, the
friend of Sir John Brute and Colonel Bully [Vanbrugh,
Provoked Wife].

Rakeland, Lord : a libertine [Mrs. Inchbald, *Wedding
Day*].

Ralph : an ignorant bumpkin, jealous of the superior
education of his own sister [Bickerstaff, *Maid of the
Mill*].

—— **Alderman :** the leading character in the story
[Thomas Cooper, *Alderman Ralph*].

—— **Rough :** assistant park-keeper to Sir Geoffrey
Peveril [Scott, *Peveril of the Peak*].

—— **or Ralpho :** squire to Hudibras, and his companion on his adventures [Butler, *Hudibras*].

—— **Roister Doister :** a hare-brained noisy fellow, who
runs fruitlessly after a rich widow of the name of
Custance [Udall, *Ralph Roister Doister*].

Ramble, Lady : wife of Sir Robert, who was the ward of
Lord Norland.

—— *Sir Robert :* a loose liver who so neglects his wife
that she leaves him and returns to her old home and
resumes her maiden name [Mrs. Inchbald, *Every one
Has His Fault*].

Rambone, Parson Jack : a sporting parson who ' held
the belt' for seven years ' for wrestling and boxing '
[Blackmore, *Maid of Sker*].

Ramirez : a monk, father-confessor to the Duke of
Braganza who plots to poison the duke [Jephson,
Braganza].

Ramiro, King : his wife Aldonza eloped with the King of
Gaya. By great ingenuity Ramiro compassed the
death of his enemy and his faithless spouse [Southey,
Ramiro, a ballad from the Portuguese.]

Ramorny, Sir John : master of the horse to Prince Robert
of Scotland [Scott, *Fair Maid of Perth*].

Ramsay, Adam : uncle of Mrs. St. Clair, a man of upright character, shrewd, affectionate, but irascible,
the past and constant lover of Lizzie Lundie. He
leaves his wealth to her daughter, Gertrude, when
she is discarded by the Rossville family [Susan E.
Ferrier, *Inheritance*].

Ramsay, David : a watch-maker near Temple Bar.

—— *Margaret :* his daughter, who becomes the wife
of Lord Nigel [Scott, *Fortunes of Nigel*].

Randolph, Lady : wife of Lord Randolph, and the mother
of Norval by a previous marriage.

—— *Lord :* the nobleman who slew Norval in a fit of

jealousy, believing him to be on too intimate terms with Lady Randolph [Horne, *Douglas*].

Random : a rich, but puffy, gouty old man with a scapegrace son, for whose debts the poor old chap is arrested [Colman the Younger, *Ways and Means*].

────── **Roderick :** a Scottish adventurer. Heartless, mean unscrupulous and sensual [Smollett, *Roderick Random*]

Ranger : one of the characters in a comedy [Wycherley, *Love in a Wood*].

────── the hero, a cousin of Clarinda's [Hoadly, *Suspicious Husband*].

Raphael : an angel that plays a conspicuous part in the epic [Milton, *Paradise Lost*].

Rasni : the King of Nineveh, an 'imperial swaggerer' who marries his own sister [Lodge and Greene, *Lookingglass for London and England*].

Rasselas : Prince of Abyssinia, who sallies forth in search of an earthly paradise but concludes that there is no lot in life free from trials [Dr. Johnson, *Rasselas*].

Rat, Doctor : the curate [attrib. John Still, *Gammer Gurton's Needle*].

Ratcliffe Mr. Hubert : a friend of Sir Edward Manley, the 'Black Dwarf' [Scott, *Black Dwarf*].

Ratcliffe, Charles : a clerk who rescues an old Jew from a London mob, and is left heir to his wealth.

────── *Eliza :* his sister, who had every virtue and was secretly married to the son of her brother's old master, Sir Stephen Bertram [Cumberland, *The Jew*].

Rathmor : the father of Calthon and Colmal, and chief of Clutha [Ossian, *Calthon and Colmal*].

Rattlin, Jack : a sailor [Smollett, *Roderick Random*].

────── the Reefer : the hero of a book at one time wrongly attributed to Marryat [Edward Howard, *Rattlin the Reefer*].

Rattray, Sir Runnion : the friend of Sir Mungo Malagrowther [Scott, *Fortunes of Nigel*].

Ravenshoe, Charles : a high-spirited boy with generous instincts, who, after many tribulations comes into his own [Henry Kingsley, *Ravenshoe*].

Ravenswood, Allan, Lord of : a poor adherent of the Stuart family.

────── *Master Edgar :* son of Allan and hero of the story, who, betrothed to Lucy Ashton, sees her married to another [Scott, *Bride of Lammermoor*].

Rayland, Mrs. : the mistress of the 'Old Manor House, [Mrs. Charlotte Smith, *Old Manor House*].

Raymond, Colonel : son of Sir Charles, who loves his neighbour's daughter, Rosetta Belmont.

Raymond, Harriet : only daughter of Sir Charles, put out to nurse with a woman who sold her at the age of twelve to a man named Villard, who ill-treated her. Her cries of distress were heard by young Belmont, who rescued and married her.

—— *Sir Charles :* a comely gentleman [Edward Moore, *The Foundling*].

Razor : a barber, and the friend of Quidnunc. Together they took a melancholy view of the state and prospects of ' poor old England ' [Murphy, *Upholsterer*].

Ready-to-Halt : a member of Mr. Greatheart's party on the way to the Celestial City. He had to struggle along on crutches [Bunyan, *Pilgrim's Progress*].

Rebecca : the beautiful daughter of Isaac of York [Scott, *Ivanhoe*].

Rebecca and Rowena : the characters in a satirical romance based on Scott's *Ivanhoe* [Thackeray, *Rebecca and Rowena*].

Red-Cap, Mother : an old nurse [Scott, *Fortunes of Nigel*].

Red-Cross Knight=St. George, who in defence of Truth [*Una*], slays the dragon [Spenser, *Faëry Queene*].

Redburn, Jack : ' no man ever lived who could do so many things as Jack ', who was the friend of Master Humphrey and of Mr. Miles [Dickens, *Master Humphrey's Clock*].

Redgauntlet, Sir Edward Hugh : the originater of a conspiracy to bring back the ' Young Pretender '. On the failure of the plot Redgauntlet withdraws to the continent and becomes prior of a monastery [Scott, *Redgauntlet*].

Redgill, Dr. : a vulgar, selfish gourmand, and hanger-on of Lord Courtland [Susan E. Ferrier, *Marriage*].

Redlaw, Mr. : a learned but sorrowful man who in struggling to obliterate the memory of his own sufferings loses, for a time, the power of sympathy for others [Dickens, *Haunted Man*].

Redmond, O'Neale : the hero's page [Scott, *Rokeby*].

Redworth, Thomas : a strong, capable man, who makes a fortune in railways and eventually marries Diana Warwick [George Meredith, *Diana of the Crossways*].

Reece, Captain, R.N. : commander of the *Mantelpiece* who ministered to the creature comforts of all his crew [Gilbert, *Bab Ballads : Captain Reece, R.N.*].

Regan : one of the two fiendish daughters of King Lear [Shakespeare, *King Lear*].

Reginald Dalton : *see* Dalton, Reginald.

Reis, Ada : the heroine of the story who ' is condemned for various misdeeds, to eternal punishment ' [Lady Caroline Lamb, *Ada Reis*].

Reldresal : principal secretary for Private affairs in the Court of Lilliput [Swift, *Gulliver's Travels*].

Remus, Uncle : an old negro fond of recounting all sorts of folk-stories and songs popular amongst his own people, dealing for the most part with animals, ' Brer Rabbit', ' Brer Fox ', etc. [Harris, *Uncle Remus*].

Renault : one of the conspirators against the Venetian senators. He attempted the honour of Belvidera [Otway, *Venice Preserved*].

René, King : of Provence, father of the Queen of Henry VI of England [Scott, *Anne of Grierstein*].

Rentowel, Mr. Jabesh : a Covenanter and a preacher [Scott, *Waverley*].

Restless, Sir John and Lady : a silly couple who are always suspecting one another of infidelity, neither having the remotest grounds for their suspicions [Murphy, *All in the Wrong*].

Reullura : wife of Aodh, a preacher of the gospel in Iona [Campbell, *Reullura*].

Reuthamir : the leading man in the town of Balclutha, whose daughter, Moina, was married to Clessammor, Fingal's uncle [Ossian, *Carthon*].

Reveller, Lady : a lady devoted to cards, but who gives them up for the sake of Lord Worthy [Mrs. Centlivre *Basset Table*].

Rewcastle, Old John : a smuggler, and a Jacobite [Scott, *Black Dwarf*].

Rhadamanth : a justice of the peace [Somerville, *Hobbinol*].

Rhodalind : the daughter of Aribert, King of Lombardy, she loved Gondibert, who did not return her love [Davenant, *Gondibert*].

Rhongomyant : King Arthur's lance [*Mabinogion*].

Riah, Mr. : a generous and noble old Jew who befriends Lizzie Hexam [Dickens, *Our Mutual Friend*].

Ribemont : a brave and noble French soldier [Shirley, *Edward the Black Prince*].

—— **Count :** a character in the play [Colman the Younger, *The Surrender of Calais*].

Ribley, Mr. and Mrs. : the wealthy but unrefined English relatives of Edith Malcolm, with whom she lives for a time, whilst her own fortunes are under a cloud [Susan E. Ferrier, *Destiny*].

Riccabocca, Dr. : ' a soft-hearted cynic, a simple sage whom we recognize chiefly by his pipe, his red umbrella and his Machiavellian proverbs ' [Lytton, *My Novel*].

Richard : a smith. On New Year's Day he marries Meg Veck [Dickens, *Chimes*].

—— **of Almaigne :** the hero of a satirical ballad of the thirteenth century [Harleian MSS. Brit. Museum, 2253, s. 23].

—— **Squire :** an ignorant country lout the son of Sir Francis Wronghead of Bumper Hall [Vanbrugh and Cibber, *Provoked Husband*].

Richelieu, Armand : cardinal and chief minister of France [Lytton, *Richelieu*].

Richland, Miss : marries Mr. Honeywood, the 'good-natured man' [Goldsmith, *Good-Natured Man*].

Richmond Hill, Lass of : Miss I'Anson of Hill House, Richmond, Yorkshire [McNally, *Lass of Richmond Hill*].

—— **Harry :** the son of Richmond Roy and of a daughter of Squire Beltham. His extraordinary adventures bring out the chivalry of his character [George Meredith, *Adventures of Harry Richmond*].

Ridd, John : a Devonian, built in colossal mould and of enormous strength. He is the hero of the tale [Blackmore, *Lorna Doone*].

Riderhood, Pleasant : the daughter of Roger, who marries Mr. Venus [Dickens, *Our Mutual Friend*].

—— **Roger :** known as 'Rogue Riderhood'. A desperate villain who meets his death in a hand-to-hand struggle with Bradley Headstone [Dickens, *Our Mutual Friend*].

Riel, Hervé : a Breton pilot, who saved a French fleet [R. Browning, *Hervé Riel*].

Rienzi : the subject of a tragedy [Mary R. Mitford, *Rienzi*].

—— **Coladi :** the hero of the novel [Lytton, *Reinzi*].

Rigaud, Mons. : imprisoned for the murder of his wife [Dickens, *Little Dorrit*].

Rigby, The Right Hon. Nicholas : 'a fawning, plotting, insolent man of dirty work' [Beaconsfield, *Coningsby*].

Rigdum Funnidos : a character in the burlesque, and the nickname which Scott gave his friend, John Ballantyne [Carey, *Chrononhotonthologos*].

Ringwood : a young Templar [Scott, *Fortunes of Nigel*].

—— **The Earl of :** a cynical nobleman [Thackeray, *Adventures of Philip*].

Rip Van Winkle : a Dutchman who lived in America and who fell asleep among the Kaatskill mountains and did not wake for twenty years. The story is based on an old German legend [Irving, *Rip Van Winkle*].

Risingham, Bertram : egged on by Oswald Wycliffe he

endeavours to shoot Philip of Mortham at Marston Moor [Scott, *Rokeby*].

Risk : a favourite part with Charles Matthews [Colman the Younger, *Love Laughs at Locksmiths*].

Rivella : the heroine of an autobiographical novel [Mrs. Manley, *Adventures of Rivella*].

Rizzo, Barto : a fanatical Italian schemer against the Austrians, who doubts Vittoria's loyalty to the cause and frustrates her with all his power [George Meredith, *Vittoria*].

Roan Barbary : Richard II's favourite charger [Shakespeare, *Richard II*].

Rob Roy, Mac Gregor=Robert Campbell, the outlaw, a Highland freebooter [Scott, *Rob Roy*].

Robarts, Lucy : sister of the vicar of Framley, who marries Lord Lufton.

—— *the Rev. Mr. :* vicar of Framley ; a weak but naturally honest man, who runs into debt [Anthony Trollope, *Framley Parsonage*].

Robert : condemned for a murder he did not commit, and saved by his daughter pledging her hand to Black Norris, the real culprit [Knowles, *The Daughter*].

—— **Earl of Huntington :** the hero of this drama is Robin Hood [Earl of Huntington], though he dies in the first act. His widow, Matilda, daughter of Lord Fitzwalter is wooed by King John [Munday, *Downfall of Robert, Earl of Huntington*].

—— **of Cysille** [Sicily] : the hero of an old English romance, in verse.

—— **of Paris, Count :** a crusading prince who fights in single combat with Hereward [Scott, *Count Robert of Paris*].

—— **of Sicily :** punished for his pride by temporary loss of reason [Longfellow, *Tales of a Wayside Inn*].

Robespierre : the subject of an historical drama [S. T. Coleridge, *Fall of Robespierre*].

Robin : confidential servant of Rovewell [Carey, *Contrivances*].

—— loses his property and emigrates, to return again after only three years [Hoare, *No Song no Supper*].

—— a young gardener, a great frequenter of play houses [Charles Dibdin, *Waterman*].

—— **and Makyne :** 'an ancient Scottish pastoral', Makyne loves Robin, and he scorns her, only in the end to fall at her feet.

—— **Goodfellow :** *see* Goodfellow, Robin.

—— **Gray :** *see* Gray, Auld Robin.

—— **Hood :** *see* Hood, Robin.

Robinson Crusoe : *see* Crusoe, Robinson.

Robsart, Amy : betrothed to Edmund Tressilian, but secretly married to Robert, Earl of Leicester, and put to death by his orders [Scott, *Kenilworth*].

Robson, Sylvia : *see* Sylvia.

Rochdale, Frank : son of Sir Simon who has betrayed a village girl and who, in opposition to his father, marries her.

———— **Sir Simon :** a justice of the peace [Colman the Younger, *John Bull*].

Rochester, Mr. Edward Fairfax : the hero, with a maniac for wife. After her death he marries Jane Eyre [Charlotte Brontë, *Jane Eyre*].

Rock, Dr. Richard : a famous quack, called by his rival, Dr. Franks, ' Dumplin' Dick ' [Goldsmith, *Citizen of the World*].

Roderick Dhu : a Highland chieftain and freebooter [Scott, *Lady of the Lake*].

———— **King :** the hero of this play was thirty-fourth in succession on the Spanish throne. He was slain A.D. 711 [Southey, *Roderick*].

Roderigo : in love with Desdemona and therefore unfriendly towards Othello, and a ready tool in the hands of Iago [Shakespeare, *Othello*].

———— a ruffian who reforms [Middleton, *Spanish Gipsy*].

Rodhaver : beloved by a Persian named Zal, who climbed to her chamber by the aid of a crook [Champion, *Ferdosi*].

Rodmond : chief mate of the *Britannia*, which struck on Cape Colonna, when Rodmond was drowned [Falconer, *Shipwreck*].

Rodogune, King : ' wicked, with a soul that would have been heroic if it had been virtuous ' [Rowe, *Royal Convert*].

Rodrigo : captain of a company of outlaws, and the rival of Pedro [J. Fletcher, *The Pilgrim*].

Roger : the name of the cook who could ' roste, sethe, broille, and frie, make mortreux, and wel bake a pye ' and who tells one of the ' Tales ' [Chaucer, *Canterbury Tales . Cook's Tale*].

———— **Sir :** a curate [Beaumont and Fletcher, *Scornful Lady*].

———— **de Coverley :** *see* Coverley, Roger de.

Rogero : a Sicilian gentleman [Shakespeare, *Winter's Tale*].

———— a character in a play which was written to scoff at the sentimentalism of German plays [Canning, *Rovers*].

Roister Doister, Ralph : *see* Ralph Roister Doister.

Rokesmith, John : *see* Harmon, John.

Roland : the hero of a poem in Anglo Norman, written by an English minstrel in the twelfth century [Turold, *Chanson de Roland*].

—— **and Farragus :** characters in an old English romance which relates to Charlemagne [Early Eng. Romances, *Roland and Farragus*].

—— **de Vaux, Sir :** the Baron of Triermain who rouses Gyneth from her sleep of 500 years' duration [Scott, *Bridal of Triermain*].

Rolando, Signor : a woman-hater vowed to celibacy, who fell in love with Zamora and married her, excusing himself on the ground that she was not a woman ' but an angel ' [Tobin, *Honeymoon*].

Rolla : ' in war a tiger chafed by the hunter's spears ; in peace more gentle than the unweaned lamb '. He was kinsman to Ataliba [Knowles, *Pizarro*].

Rollo : Duke of Normandy, the ' bloody brother ' [J. Fletcher, *Bloody Brother*].

Romano : the monk that sheltered Roderick after his overthrow [Southey, *Roderick*].

Romeo : the son of Montague ; he loved Juliet, of the House of Capulet, his hereditary foes ; they were going to marry secretly, but a series of misadventures ended in their both dying on what should have been their wedding day [Shakespeare, *Romeo and Juliet*].

Romfrey, Everard : the uncle of Nevil Beauchamp. Later on succeeds to the title of Earl of Romfrey. Under the mistaken idea that Dr. Shrapnel has insulted Mrs. Cullin he horsewhips him. This results in a furious quarrel between him and Nevil Beauchamp. Eventually he apologizes to Dr. Shrapnel [George Meredith, *Beauchamp's Career*].

Romola : a youthful Florentine, who loved and married Tito Malema, a subtle and insincere Greek [George Eliot, *Romola*].

Ron : King Arthur's ebony spear [Drayton, *Polyolbion*].

Ronald, Lord : the lover of Lady Clare who remained true to her even when he discovered she was ' not the heiress born ' [Alfred Tennyson, *Lady Clare*].

Rory O'More : *see* O'More, Rory.

Rosa : Lady Dedlock's maid ; a shy village beauty engaged to Walt Rouncewell [Dickens, *Bleak House*].

—— **Rosalynd, and Rosmary :** the heroines of a romance of the very early seventeenth century [Newton, *Rosa, Rosalynd, and Rosmary*].

Rosabelle : Lady Geraldine's maid [Dimond, *Foundling of the Forest*].

—— the subject of a ballad [Scott, *Rosabelle*].

Rosader : the original of Orlando in *As You Like It* [Lodge, *Rosalynde*].

Rosalind : the witty daughter of the banished duke. She falls in love with and marries Orlando [Shakespeare, *As You Like It*].

—— the subject of 'a modern eclogue' [Shelley, *Rosalind and Helen*].

—— the shepherdess who rejected Colin Clout in favour of Menalcas [Spenser, *Shepheardes Calendar*].

Rosaline : 'two pitch balls were stuck in her face for eyes'. She was in attendance on the Princess of France [Shakespeare, *Love's Labour's Lost*].

—— Juliet's cousin with whom Romeo fancied himself in love before he saw Juliet [Shakespeare, *Romeo and Juliet*].

Rosalynde : the heroine of a romance and the prototype of Shakespeare's Rosalind [Lodge, *Euphues' Golden Legacy*].

Rosalura : daughter of Nantolet, whom Belleur loved [J. Fletcher, *Wild-goose Chase*].

Rosamond : the subject of a poetical drama [Swinburne, *Rosamond*].

—— **Fair :** a ballad which tells the story of Jane Clifford, the mistress of Henry II, known to history as 'Fair Rosamond'.

Roscrana : daughter of Cormac, King of Ireland; she married Fingal and was the mother of Ossian [Ossian, *Temora*].

Rose : 'the gardener's daughter' [Alfred Tennyson, *Gardener's Daughter*].

—— **Blanche and Violet :** characters in a novel [George H. Lewes, *Rose, Blanche, and Violet*].

Rosencrantz : a courtier of despicable character [Shakespeare, *Hamlet*].

Rosetta : a young girl, who flies from home to escape a distasteful marriage and takes service at Justice Woodcock's. Here the young man comes, as gardener, he having fled from an uncovered bride. Thus they meet after all and fall in love with one another [Bickerstaff, *Love in a Village*].

Rosiclear : *see* Donzel del Phebo.

Rosiphele : a princess of Armenia, of resplendent beauty but lacking heart, who is worked upon by Cupid [Gower, *Confessio Amantis*].

Rosny, Sabina : a beautiful and virtuous girl, both of

whose parents are dead, and who meets and marries Lord Sensitive [Cumberland, *First Love*].

Rossville, Earl of : the pompous, conceited, dull, and narrow-minded holder of the estates, to which Gertrude was supposed to be the next in succession [Susan E. Ferrier, *Inheritance*].

Rothmar : the chief of Tromlo, who invaded Croma victoriously until Ossian went to the assistance of the blind King of Crothar and defeated the invaders [Ossian, *Croma*].

Roubigné, Julie de : the heroine of the novel [Mackenzie, *Julie de Roubigné*].

Rougedragon, Lady Rachel : the sometime guardian o Lilias Redgauntlet [Scott, *Redgauntlet*].

Rouncewell, Mrs. : Lord and Lady Dedlock's housekeeper [Dickens, *Bleak House*].

Rovewell, Captain : in love with Arethusa, whom he marries, contrary to her father's wishes [Carey, *Contrivances*].

Rowena : the Saxon heroine, the ward of Cedric ; she marries Wilfred of Ivanhoe [Scott, *Ivanhoe*].

Rowland, Childe : the brother of Helen, who, under the guidance of Merlin fetches her back from elf-land [*Ancient Scottish Ballad*].

—— **Mr. :** Mr. Grey's partner, afflicted with a mischief-making, untruthful wife, whose unneighbourly acts he tries to counteract [Harriet Martineau, *Deerbrook*].

Rowley, Master : the past steward of old Mr. Surface and the friend of Charles [Sheridan, *School for Scandal*].

Roxana : in love with Alexander, and therefore jealous of Statira, his wife, whom she slew [Lee, *Alexander the Great ; or, Rival Queens*].

Roy, Richmond : father of Harry Richmond. He claims to be the legitimate son of a royal prince. Halfsincere and half-mountebank. He secretly married one of Squire Beltham's daughters, though loving the other [George Meredith, *Adventures of Harry Richmond*].

Rubi : one of the spirits of wisdom who dwelt with Eve in Paradise [Edward Moore, *Loves of the Angels*].

Rubonax : the man who hanged himself because ot some verses written at his expense [Sidney, *Defence of Poesie*].

Ruby, Lady : a young widow, who upon the death of her husband marries her 'first love' [Cumberland. *First Love*].

Ruddymane : the infant son of Sir Mordant [Spenser, *Faëry Queene*].

Rudge, Mr. : the steward and murderer of Reuben Haredale ; he levied a sort of blackmail upon his wife, and visited her secretly when in want of money.

—— *Mrs. :* mother of Barnaby, and cognisant of her husband's guilt [Dickens, *Barnaby Rudge*].

—— *Barnaby :* the half-witted son of Reuben Haredale's murderer [Dickens, *Barnaby Rudge*].

Rüdiger, Clotilde von : a German girl of good family, with an original mind. She is carried away by the hurricane wooing of Alvan, but fails him in the end [George Meredith, *Tragic Comedians*].

Rudiger : the hero of a ballad. He appeared in a swan-drawn boat to Margaret, who fell in love with, and married him. A baby was born to them, and then one day the swan and boat reappeared and Rudiger was carried off in the arms of a giant [Southey, *Rudiger*].

Rugg, Mr. : a lawyer living at Pentonville, and who revelled in legal difficulties [Dickens, *Little Dorrit*].

Runa : the dog belonging to the sons of the King of Inis-Thorn [Ossian, *War of Inis-Thorn*].

Rupert, Sir : the lover of Catherine [Knowles, *Love*].

Rush, Friar : an evil spirit sent to keep the monks and friars in a state of wickedness. This sort of demon was believed in in the seventeenth century.

Rushworth, Mr. : a wealthy fool, who marries Miss Bertram and is deserted by her.

—— *Mrs. :* the wife of Mr. Rushworth who elopes with Henry Crawford [Jane Austen, *Mansfield Park*].

Rusilla : the mother of Roderick and wife of the rightful heir to the Spanish throne, Theodofred [Southey, *Roderick*].

Rusport, Charlotte : in love with Charles Dudley, whom she marries.

—— *Lady :* Sir Stephen's second wife and step-mother to Charlotte. A vain, mean, and unprincipled woman [Cumberland, *West Indian*].

Russet, Harriot : she loved Mr. Oakly and married him but grew jealous, though needlessly so, and only for a time [Colman the Elder, *Jealous Wife*].

Rust, Martin : an old antiquary, who preferred antique coins to youthful beauty, and resigned the girl he was to have married to another whom she preferred [Foote, *The Patron*].

Rustam : son of Zâl, King of India. The chief of the mythical heroes of Persia [Chardin, *Travels*].

—— on of Tamur, King of Persia, who had a trial of

strength with Rustam, son of Zâl—a kind of 'tug of war', in which neither gained any advantage over the other [Chardin, *Travels*].

Rustum and Sohrab : two heroes who fight, as the chosen representatives of opposing forces. Rustum conquers, only to find he has slain his own son [Matthew Arnold, *Rustum and Sohrab*].

Ruth : the heroine of a lyric [Thomas Hood, *Ruth*].

—— the orphan daughter of Sir Basil Thoroughgood and ward of Justice Day [Knight, *Honest Thieves*].

—— the heroine of two poems [W. Wordsworth, *Ruth* ; also, Sir W. Stirling Maxwell, *Ruth*].

Ruthven, Lord : one of Queen Elizabeth's ambassadors to Mary Queen of Scots [Scott, *The Abbot*].

Ryence, Sir : King of Wales, Ireland, etc., who sent an insulting challenge to King Arthur when King Arthur first mounted the throne. The haughty king was soon reduced to begging mercy of Arthur [Mallory, *History of Prince Arthur*].

Rython : one of the giants whom King Arthur slew. He came from Brittany [*Arthurian Cycle*].

Sabrin, Sabre, or Sabrina : the daughter of Locrine and Estrildis by a guilty love. When his queen, Guendolen, knew of their connexion she caused Estrildis and the child to be thrown into the river, which since then has been called the Severn [Geoffrey, *British History*].

Sabrina : the nymph of the Severn, is petitioned to release the lady from the spell cast over her by Comus [Milton, *Comus*].

Sacharissa=Lady Dorothea Sidney, eldest daughter of the Earl of Leicester, the lady whom the poet, Edmund Waller, loved and courted.

Sadak : a general in the Sultan of Turkey's army, who lived so happily with his wife, Kalasrade, that the Sultan Ammath was envious and had her kidnapped and placed in his seraglio. Ammath was poisoned and Sadak became sultan in his place [Ridley, *Tales of the Genii*].

Saddletree, Mr. Bartoline : 'the learned saddler' [Scott, *Heart of Midlothian*].

Sagan of Jerusalem : intended for Compton, Bishop of London [Dryden, *Absalom and Achitophel*].

Sago, Mr. and Mrs. : a chemist and his wife. She is fond of cards, aims at a superior social standing and carries on an intrigue with Sir James Courtly [Mrs. Centlivre *Basset Table*].

Sagramour le Desirus: a knight of the Round Table [*Launcelot du Lac* and *Morte d'Arthur*; Tennyson, *Idylls of the King: Merlin and Vivian*].

St. Alme, Captain: son of Darlemont the guardian of the Count of Harancourt, a deaf and dumb boy [Holcroft, *Deaf and Dumb*].

St. Cecilia: the patron saint of music [Dryden, *Ode to St. Cecilia's Day*].

St. Clair, Gertrude: the reputed daughter of Thomas St. Clair; really a changeling of obscure birth. She is the heroine of the story and marries the hero, Edward Lyndsay.

—— *Hon. Thomas:* brother to the Earl of Rossville, and reputed father of Gertrude.

—— *Mrs.:* supposed mother of Gertrude the heroine. A scheming, unprincipled and vain, but beautiful woman [Susan E. Ferrier *Inheritance*].

—— *Augustin:* a kind hearted slave-owner, beloved by his slaves.

—— *Evangeline:* his daughter, loved by all the slaves, adored by Uncle Tom.

—— *Ophelia:* a New England Puritan, Mr. Augustin, St. Clare's cousin [Harriet Beecher Stowe, *Uncle Tom's Cabin*].

St. Evrémonde, Charles: *see* Darnay, Charles.

St. Irvyne: a novel of which Megalena di Metastasio is the heroine. The author was in his sixteenth year when he wrote it [Shelley, *St. Irvyne*].

St. John: a clergyman who loves Jane Eyre, but whose offer of marriage she declines [Charlotte Brontë, *Jane Eyre*].

St. Leon: the hero, who knows the secret of the philosopher's stone, and also of the elixir vitae. The story gains additional interest from the likeness of the heroine Marguerite, having been drawn from Mary Wollstonecraft [Godwin, *St. Leon*].

St. Senanus: *see* Senanus, St.

Saladin: the sultan who, disguised as a doctor, visited Richard Coeur de Lion [Scott, *Talisman*].

Salathiel: the wandering Jew [Croly, *Immortal Salathiel*].

Saldar, Countess de: the scheming sister of Evan Harrington, who has married a Portuguese count. She forces her way into society, bringing with her various members of her own family [Meredith, *Evan Harrington*].

Saleh: the brother of Gulnare the Empress of Persia, and the son of Farasche, who ruled over a kingdom under the sea [*Arabian Nights*].

Sally : the heroine of one of the most popular of English ballads [Carey, *Sally in our Alley*].

Salterne, Rose : left to her fate by a jealous husband, Don Guzman, and burnt by the Spanish Inquisition as a heretic and witch [Charles Kingsley, *Westward Ho !*].

Saltire, Lord : a nobleman who concealed great warmth of feeling, and a lasting sorrow, under a cynical and worldly manner [Henry Kingsley, *Ravenshoe*].

Salvage Knight : *see* Artegal.

Sam, Brother : the brother of Lord Dundreary. This play is a kind of sequel to '*Our American Cousin* ' [Oxenford, altered by Sothern and Buckstone, *Brother Sam*].

———— **Slick :** *see* Slick, Sam.

———— **Weller :** *see* Weller, Sam.

Samfit, Mrs. : the cook to the Fleming household, ' very fat and loving . . . whose waist was dimly indicated by her apron strings '. A kind-hearted woman [George Meredith, *Rhoda Fleming*].

Samiasa : a seraph who loved Aholibamah, grand-daughter of Cain, and who bore her away to another planet at the time of the Flood [Byron, *Heaven and Earth*].

Samient : Queen Mercilla's ambassadress to Queen Aldicia who received her with many indignities until Sir Artegal came to her rescue [Spenser, *Faëry Queene*].

Sampson : one of Capulets' servants [Shakespeare, *Romeo and Juliet*].

———— **Dominie Abel :** an honest, ungainly schoolmaster much beloved by his pupils at Ellangowan House [Scott, *Guy Mannering*].

———— **George :** an admirer of Bella Wilfer, who however transfers his affections to her sister, Lavinia, when Bella marries John Harmon [Dickens, *Our Mutual Friend*].

———— **Parson :** the dissipated, wine-bibbing private chaplain of Lord Castlewood [Thackeray, *Esmond and Virginians*].

Samson Agonistes='Samson the Wrestler ', the blind hero of the poem [Milton, *Samson Agonistes*].

Sancho, Don : a foolish old fop, the uncle of Victoria, who wears a light wig to conceal his grey hairs and simulates toothache to convince people his teeth are not false [Mrs. Cowley, *Bold Stroke for a Husband*].

Sandford, Harry : the companion and friend of Tommy Merton [Day, *Sandford and Merton*].

Sanglamore : Braggadochio's sword [Spenser, *Faëry Queene*].

Sanglier, Sir Shan : intended for Shan O'Neil, leader of the Irish insurgents in 1567 [Spenser, *Faëry Queene*].

Sansfoy=Unbelief, a faithless Saracen, the first enemy with whom the Red Cross Knight had an encounter after parting from Una [Truth] [Spenser, *Faëry Queene*].

―――― Brian : *see* Clyomon and Clamydes.

Sansjoy=Joylessness, the brother of Sansfoy. He also fought with the Red Cross Knight, but just as he was about to be overthrown he was rescued and carried off to the infernal regions [Spenser, *Faëry Queene*].

Sansloy=Superstition, brother of Sansfoy and Sansjoy. He carried off Una to a wilderness, and then fled, and left her alone, when fauns and satyrs approached [Spenser, *Faëry Queene*].

Sappho : intended for Lady Worthy Montague [Pope, *Moral Essays*, Ep. iii.].

Sapsea, Mr. Thomas : an auctioneer who came to be Mayor of Cloisterham [Dickens, *Edwin Drood*].

Sapskull : a silly raw Yorkshire lad, the son of a country squire, befooled out of his intended bride by the tricks of Gaylove and Muchworm [Carey, *Honest Yorkshireman*].

Saracinesca : a proud Roman of the old school [Marion Crawford, *Saracinesca*].

Sarchedon : hero of the novel [Melville, *Sarchedon*].

Sardanapalus : the voluptuous King of Nineveh [Byron, *Sardanapalus*].

Satyrane, Sir : the knight who protected Una when Sansloy left her at the mercy of the fauns and satyrs [Spenser, *Faëry Queene*].

Saul : intended for Oliver Cromwell [Dryden, *Absalom and Achitophel*].

Saunders, Clerk : the hero of a popular Scottish ballad ; he was killed in his sweetheart's arms and appeared before her afterwards in ghostly shape [Border Minstrelsy, *Clerk Saunders*].

Savage, Captain : a naval commander [Marryat, *Peter Simple*].

―――― **Harry** : the kidnapped grandson of Sir Phiilp Rampfylde [Blackmore, *Maid of Sker*].

Saville : saves Lady Frances Touchwood from Courtall [Mrs. Cowley, *Belle's Stratagem*].

Sawyer, Bob : a medical student who sets up in practice at Bristol and acts as Mr. Pickwick's host [Dickens, *Pickwick Papers*].

―――― **Mother** : the so-called witch ; a poor, deformed old woman, of whom the villagers stood in awe [Rowley, Dekker and Ford, *Witch of Edmonton*].

Scadder, General Zephaniah : agent of the Eden Land Corporation, who dupes Martin Chuzzlewit into buying

' a little lot of fifty acres ' [Dickens, *Martin Chuzzlewit*].

Scaddock : *see* Scarlet, Will.

Scambister, Eric : the butler of Magnus Troil [Scott, *Pirate*].

Scarlet, Will : one of Robin Hood's company, often mentioned in old English ballads. He is sometimes called Scathelocke or Scadlock.

Scatcherd, Miss : an assistant teacher in the ' Lowood Institution '. Really a portrait of one of the staff who treated little Maria Brontë with great cruelty when she was dying, at the school at Cowan's Bridge [Charlotte Brontë, *Jane Eyre*].

Scathelocke : *see* Scarlet, Will.

Schacabac : the poor, almost starving man whom the wealthy Barmecide invited to a feast [*Arabian Nights*. *see also* Barmecide].

Schahriah : Sultan of Persia. Reasoning from the particular to the general, he believed no women to be faithful to their husbands, and so resolved to marry a fresh wife every night and have her strangled in the morning. Scheherazade taught him better [*Arabian Nights*].

Schahyaman : Sultan of the ' Island of the Children of Khaledan ', and the father of Camaralzaman [*Arabian Nights*].

Schaibar : a grotesque dwarf, brother of the fairy Pari-Banou [*Arabian Nights*].

Schedoni : a monk, a hypocrite, a profligate, an implacable enemy, and the committer of many crimes [Mrs. Radcliffe, *The Italian*].

Scheherazade, Queen : the elder daughter of the Vizier of Persia, who is supposed to be the teller of the stories [*Arabian Nights*].

Schemseddin Mohammed : elder son of the Vizier of Egypt and brother of Noureddin Ali, with whom he quarrelled about their children who were not yet born [*Arabian Nights*].

Schemselnihar : the favourite wife of Haroun-al-Raschid, Caliph of Bagdad, who fell in love with Aboul-hassan Ali ebn Becar, Prince of Persia [*Arabian Nights*].

Scholey, Lawrence : the son of the udaller, Magnus Troil [Scott, *Pirate*].

Sciolto : a Genoese noble, the father of Calista. He was killed in a street-riot [Rowe, *Fair Penitent*].

Scipio : *see* Hannibal and Scipio.

Scott, Joe : Moore's overseer at Hollow's Mill [Charlotte Brontë, *Shirley*].

Scott, Tom : Daniel Quilp's assistant, a boy who entertained an odd sort of liking for his fiendish master [Dickens, *Old Curiosity Shop*].

Scrag, Gosling : intended as a portrait of Lord Lyttelton, against whom the author entertained angry feelings. The character only appears in the first edition of the book [Smollett, *Peregrine Pickle*].

Scribble : an attorney's clerk in love with Polly Honeycombe [Colman the Elder, *Polly Honeycombe*].

Scriever, Jock : Duncan Macwheeble's apprentice [Scott, *Waverley*].

Scroggens, Giles : the hero of a comic ballad, wherein Giles Scroggens, dying before his wedding day, comes in ghostly form to claim his bride, Molly Brown [*A Comic Ballad*].

Scrooge, Ebenezer : converted by some Christmas Eve visions, from hardness into tenderness [Dickens, *Christmas Carol*].

Scrub : Mrs. Sullen's factotum who leads a life of miserable over-work [Farquhar, *Beaux' Stratagem*].

Scrubinda : a scullery maid in Dyot Street, Bloomsbury Square [Rhodes, *Bombastes Furioso*].

Scruple : an honest sort of man in the main, who arranges to elope with Harriet Dunder. His father discovers the plot and frustrates the scheme, but gives his consent to the marriage [Colman the Younger, *Ways and Means*].

Scudamore, Sir='the Shield of Love'. He was beloved by Amoretta [Spenser, *Faëry Queene*].

Seaforth, The Earl of : a royalist and partizan of King Charles I [Scott, *Legend of Montrose*].

Sebastian, Don : King of Portugal, taken prisoner by the Moors, and rescued from death by Dorax, who is a Portuguese, at the court of the Emperor of Barbary [Dryden, *Don Sebastian*].

Sebastian : the father of Valentine and Alice [J. Fletcher, *Mons. Thomas*].

———— **Don :** the hero of a novel [Anna M. Porter, *Don Sebastian*].

———— the brother of Alonzo, King of Naples [Shakespeare, *Tempest*].

————: Viola's brother, to whom Olivia is ultimately married, she mistaking him at first for Viola [Shakespeare, *Twelfth Night*].

Sedley, Amelia : daughter of Mr. and Mrs. Sedley ; an amiable, gentle girl, without much character, but so much in love with shallow, selfish George Osborn that for years she overlooks and underrates the solid worth of Captain Dobbin.

Sedley, Mr. : a wealthy man ruined by the fall in the funds during the Peninsular War.

—— *Mrs.* : a homely, motherly woman embittered by what she feels is unmerited poverty.

—— *Joseph* : Amelia's brother. A fat, self-indulgent and conceited Anglo-Indian, an arrant coward to boot, who falls a prey to the wiles of Becky Sharp [Thackeray, *Vanity Fair*].

Seithenyn : a whimsical eccentricity who plays a conspicuous part in the book [Peacock, *Misfortunes of Elphin*].

Selim : son of the Algerine king, who escaped when his father was slain by the Greek renegade Barbarossa, and who, after a certain lapse of years, recovered his father's throne and married Barbarossa's daughter Irene [Brown, *Barbarossa*].

—— adopted by an uncle who had first murdered Selim's father. Selim fell in love with Zuleika, his cousin, and married her against the wishes of her father, who caused Selim to be shot, and Zuleika killed herself [Byron, *Bride of Abydos*].

—— =Lord Lyttelton, in an ironical poem written to exonerate him [Edward Moore, *Selim the Persian*].

—— married to Nourmahal, the ' Light of the Harem '. She offended him, but won back his affections by her playing on the lute [Thomas Moore, *Lalla Rookh*].

Selima : daughter of the Sultan of Turkey and promised in marriage to Omar, although she loved Axalla. Tamerlane solved the problem by causing both the Sultan and Omar to be killed, thus leaving Selima free to marry Axalla [Rowe, *Tamerlane*].

Selkirk, Alexander : a Scottish sailor who remained for four years alone on Juan Fernandez Island. He is supposed to have been the original of Robinson Crusoe [Cowper, *Verses supposed to be written by Alexander Selkirk*].

Sellock, Cisly : a young girl in the service of Sir Geoffrey and Lady Peveril [Scott, *Peveril of the Peak*].

Selvaggio : the hero, who is the father of Sir Industry [James Thomson, *Castle of Indolence*].

Sempronius : a traitor to Cato and the dishonourable lover of Marcia, Cato's daughter. He tried to carry her off, but his evil designs were frustrated by Juba [Addison, *Cato*].

—— one of Timon's fine weather friends [Shakespeare, *Timon of Athens*].

Senanus, St.: a saint dwelling on the Island of Scattery, who vowed that no woman should ever set foot upon it, so that even when, led by St. Canara, an angel appeared, he refused her admission [Thomas Moore, *St. Senanus and the Lady*].

Senena: a Welsh damsel in love with Caradoc, who followed him to America disguised as a boy, under the name of Mervyn [Southey, *Madoc*].

Sensitive, Lord: a young nobleman who marries a French refugee called Sabina Rosny [Cumberland, *First Love*].

Sentry, Captain: the representative of the army in the club responsible for the publication of the *Spectator* [Addison, *Spectator*, Essay 152, 350, 517, 544, etc.].

Seremenes: brother-in-law of Sardanapalus, who was slain in battle against the insurgents [Byron, *Sardanapalus*].

Serena: whilst gathering flowers in a meadow the Blatant Beast appeared and carried her off in his mouth. She was rescued by Sir Calidore [Spenser, *Faëry Queene*].

Sergeant of Law, The: a busy man who always seemed even more busy than he really was [Chaucer, *Canterbury Tales*].

Sergis, Sir: the attendant on Irena [Spenser, *Faëry Queene*].

Serina: the daughter of Lord Acasto, betrothed to Monimia's brother Chamont [Otway, *Orphan*].

Seyd: Pacha of the Morea, murdered by Gulnare [Byron, *Corsair*].

Seyton, Catherine: daughter of Lord Seyton, a supporter of Mary Queen of Scots, and herself a maid of honour to that queen [Scott, *The Abbot*].

Sforza, Ludovico: the Duke of Milan, surnamed 'the More' because of a mulberry coloured birthstain on his arm [Massinger, *Duke of Milan*].

Shaccabac: *see* Schacabac.

Shaddai, King: fought against Diabolus for the winning back of Mansoul [*Holy War*].

Shadow, Simon: one of Sir John Falstaff's recruits [Shakespeare, *Henry IV* pt. ii].

Shafton, Ned: imprisoned in Newgate gaol with Sir Hildebrand Osbaldistone [Scott, *Rob Roy*].

———— **Sir Piercie:** a cavalier known as the 'Knight of Wilverton' [Scott, *Monastery*].

Shagpat: the merchant on whose head grows 'The Identical'. It is finally shaved off by Shibli Bagaray [George Meredith, *Shaving of Shagpat*].

Shalott, the Lady of: bound to sit and weave, day and night, without ever looking towards Camelot [Alfred Tennyson, *Lady of Shalott*].

Shallow : a foolish, weak-minded country justice [Shakespeare, *Merry Wives of Windsor* and *King Henry IV*, pt. ii.].

Shandon, Captain : a drunken Grub Street hack, kindly and witty ; an inmate of the Fleet Prison [Thackeray, *Pendennis*].

Shandy, Captain : better known as Uncle Toby. A halfpay officer, wounded at Namur, most gallant, modest, brave and simple as a child.

—— *Dinah :* the hero's aunt, who leaves him £1,000.

—— *Mrs. :* a practical nonentity, who let her husband pursue his hobbies uninterrupted but also unadmired by herself.

—— *Tristram :* the son of Walter and Elizabeth Shandy ; he is the nominal hero of the novel, but its real interest does not centre in him but in his father and mother, Uncle Toby, etc.

—— *Walter :* a man of an active and metaphysical, but at the same time, a whimsical cast of mind. Father of the hero [Sterne, *Tristram Shandy*].

Sharp : Major Touchwood's ordinary [Dibdin, *What Next ?*].

—— **Rebecca :** a clever, unprincipled adventuress who wins and abuses the love of Rawdon Crawley [Thackeray, *Vanity Fair*].

—— **Timothy :** valet to Charles Gayless, who tries to pass his penniless master off as a man of wealth [Garrick, *Lying Valet*].

Sharpe, Right Rev. James : Archbishop of St. Andrews, murdered by John Balfour, a Covenanter [Scott, *Old Mortality*].

Shawondasee : King of the South Wind [Longfellow, *Hiawatha*].

She : a mysterious being living in South African wilds [Haggard, *She*].

Shedad : King of Ad who took 500 years to build a splendid palace and then was prevented by the angel of death from entering it [Southey, *Thalaba*].

Shelby, Mr. : Uncle Tom's first master, who became too poor to keep him and had to sell him to a man of the name of Legree, who whipped him to death [Harriet Beecher Stowe, *Uncle Tom's Cabin*].

Shepherd of the Ocean=Sir Walter Raleigh [Spenser, *Colin Clout's Come Home Again*].

Sheppard, Jack : a daring burglar, the son of a Spitalfield's carpenter. He has been made the hero of a romance [Defoe, *Jack Sheppard*].

Sherborne : said to be intended for the author's father, Isaac Disraeli [Beaconsfield, *Vivian Grey*].

Sheva : 'the widow's friend, the orphan's father, the poor man's protector', a noble Jew, who leaves his wealth to Charles Ratcliffe, who had rescued him from the insults of a London mob [Cumberland, *The Jew*].

—— intended for Sir Roger Lestrange, censor of the press, under Charles II [Dryden and Tate, *Absalom and Achitophel*, Pt. ii.].

Shift : one that never was a soldier, yet lives upon lend-ings' [Ben Jonson, *Every Man out of His Humour*].

—— **Samuel :** a mimic, whom Sir William Wealthy employs to aid in saving his son George from ruin [Foote, *The Minor*].

Shimei : intended for Bethel, Lord Mayor of London [Dryden, *Absalom and Achitophel*].

—— intended for Dryden [Pordage, *Azaria and Hushai*].

Shipton, Mother : the heroine of an old tale [Preece, *Strange and Wonderful History and Prophecies of Mother Shipton*].

Shore, Jane : the heroine of a tragedy. The wife of a London merchant, she became the mistress of Edward IV [Rowe, *Jane Shore*].

Shorne, Sir John : he conjured the devil into a boot [*Fantassie of Idolatrie*].

'Short' : *see* Harris, Mr.

Shorthose : a clown in the service of Mrs. Hartwell [J. Fletcher, *Wit Without Money*].

Shrapnel, Dr. : a radical doctor whose talk so influences Nevil Beauchamp that he follows him with enthusiasm. A remarkable and kind-hearted old man [George Meredith, *Beauchamp's Career*].

Shuffleton, The Hon. Tom : a conscienceless borrower of money, who never remembered to repay, and who married Lady Caroline Braymore and her income of £4,000 a year [Colman the Younger, *John Bull*].

Shylock : a wretched old Jew, the victim of his own evil passions and the unrelenting hatred of his race felt by those amongst whom he dwelt [Shakespeare, *Merchant of Venice*].

Siddartha, Prince : the incarnation of Buddha, whose teaching forms the motive of the poem [Edwin Arnold, *Light of Asia*].

Sidney : tutor to Charles Egerton McSycophant, and in love with the girl to whom his pupil is betrothed [Macklin, *Man of the World*].

Sidonia : a strange and fabulously wealthy Spanish Jew, and a philosopher [Beaconsfield, *Coningsby*].

Sidrophel: intended for the astrologer and magician William Lily, who flourished in the seventeenth century [Butler, *Hudibras*].

Sightly, Captain: a young officer who elopes with Priscilla Tomboy [Bickerstaff, *The Romp*].

Sigismunda: the heroine of the tragedy [James Thomson, *Tancred and Sigismunda*].

—— **and Guiscardo:** Guiscardo was the squire of King Tancred, and secretly married Tancred's daughter Sigismunda. Tancred on discovering the truth caused Guiscardo to be strangled, and Segismunda took poison [Dryden, *Sigismunda and Guiscardo*].

Sikes, Bill: a desperate character, one of Fagin's associates; a burglar and the murderer of Nancy, the girl who lived with him [Dickens, *Oliver Twist*].

Silence: a foolish country justice, dull in the extreme when sober, when drunk uproarious in his mirth [Shakespeare, *Henry IV*, pt. ii.].

Sileno: the husband of Mysis, who offers Apollo a home when he is expelled from heaven by Jupiter [O'Hara, *Midas*].

Silva, Don: the Duke of Bedmar, and in love with the gypsy girl Fedalma [George Eliot, *Spanish Gypsy*].

Silvia: daughter of the Duke of Milan, beloved by Valentine [Shakespeare, *Two Gentlemen of Verona*].

Simkin, Simon: the thief who purloined half a bushel of flour and substituted meal in its stead whilst those employed to superintend the filling of it were chasing a runaway horse [Chaucer, *Canterbury Tales : The Reeve's Tale*].

Simon, Margaret: daughter of the miller [Stirling, *Gold Mine ; or, Miller of Grenoble*].

—— a tanner who is elected Mayor of Queenborough [Middleton, *Mayor of Queenborough*].

—— **Lee:** *see* Lee, Simon.

—— **Pure:** *see* Pure, Simon.

Simple: a young man who travels through London and Westminster 'in search of a faithful friend' [Sarah Fielding, *Adventures of David Simple*].

—— the servant of Slender, Justice Shallow's cousin [Shakespeare, *Merry Wives of Windsor*].

—— **Peter:** the hero and title of a novel [Marryat, *Peter Simple*].

Sindall, Sir Thomas: an immoral character in the novel [Mackenzie, *Man of the World*].

Sindbad the Sailor: a rich merchant of Bagdad who made seven voyages teeming with adventures and strange experiences [*Arabian Nights*].

Single Gentleman : the brother of Little Nell's grandfather, who turns out to be Master Humphrey, the teller of the story [Dickens, *Old Curiosity Shop*].

Singleton, Captain : the hero of a novel [Defoe, *Adventures of Captain Singleton*].

Siphax : a soldier. He loved Calis, the sister of the Paphian King, Astorax [Beaumont and Fletcher,] *Mad Lover*].

Siward : the Earl of Northumberland, commanding the English army against Macbeth [Shakespeare, *Macbeth*].

Skeggs, Miss Carolina Wilhelmina Amelia : one of the two fast women introduced to the Primrose family by Squire Thornhill [Goldsmith, *Vicar of Wakefield*].

Skettles, Sir Barnet : an M.P. who lived at Fulham, and whose main object in life was to widen the circle of his acquaintance. His son was at Dr. Blimber's school [Dickens, *Dombey and Son*].

Skewton, The Hon. Mrs. : called '*Cleopatra*' because a sketch of her, published in her youth, was so called. She was the mother of Edith Dombey [Dickens, *Dombey and Son*].

Skiffins, Miss : a lady with some 'portable property' whom Mr. Wemmick marries [Dickens, *Great Expectations*].

Skimpole, Harold : Mr. Jarndyce's protégé—bright and engaging, but altogether selfish. Constantly getting into debt, and as constantly being helped out of his difficulties by friends who are hardly even thanked for their pains [Dickens, *Bleak House*].

Skionar, Mr. : 'the transcendental poet'. A member of the house-party at Crotchet Castle [Peacock, *Crotchet Castle*].

Skyreth Bolgolam : High-Admiral of Lilliput [Swift, *Gulliver's Travels*].

Slackbridge : a 'hand' at Bounderby's mill who wields considerable power over his fellow workmen [Dickens, *Hard Times*].

Slammer, Dr. : of the 'Ninety-Seventh', with whom Mr. Winkle nearly fights a duel [Dickens, *Posthumous Papers of Pickwick Club*].

Slammerkin, Mrs. : 'careless and genteel' and apt to 'affect an undress' [Gay, *Beggar's Opera*].

Slander : an aged crone whose duty it was to abuse goodness, and who was of 'ragged, rude attyre, and filthy lockes' [Spenser, *Faëry Queene*].

Slango : the servant of Gaylove, who passes himself off as Arbella, the wife elect of Sapskull [Carey, *Honest Yorkshireman*].

Slay-good, Giant : one of the giants whom Greatheart slew [Bunyan, *Pilgrim's Progress*].

Sleary : owner of a 'horse-riding' or circus. He had one fixed and one loose eye, and a voice like a broken pair of bellows, and he suffered from asthma.

—— *Josephine :* his daughter, a fair-haired girl of eighteen [Dickens, *Hard Times*].

Sleek, Aminadab : one of the characters in a comedy [Barnett, *Serious Family*].

Slender : Justice Shallow's silly cousin [Shakespeare, *Merry Wives of Windsor*].

Slick, Sam : a Yankee pedlar, and clockmaker of Slickville, full of odd fancies, acuteness and 'pleasant answers' [Haliburton, *Sam Slick*].

Sliderskew, Peg : Arthur Gride's dishonest housekeeper [Dickens, *Nicholas Nickleby*].

Slinkton, Julius : the would-be murderer of Alfred Beckwith, and a suicide [Dickens, *Hunted Down*].

Slip : the scheming valet of young Harlowe [Garrick, *Neck or Nothing*].

Slippery Sam : a highwayman [Gay, *Beggar's Opera*].

Slipslop, Mrs. : an undesirable sort of woman [Fielding, *Joseph Andrews*].

Slop, Dr. : a testy and enthusiastic physician who does his friends grievous bodily harm in experimenting with a pair of new forceps' [Sterne, *Tristram Shandy*].

Slope, The Rev Obadiah : Bishop Proudie's chaplain—a revolting character [Anthony Trollope, *Barchester Towers*].

Sloppy : 'a very long boy with a very little head and an open mouth'; a waif brought up by Betty Higden, whose mangle he turns for her [Dickens, *Our Mutual Friend*].

Slowboy, Tilly : a foundling whom Mrs. Peerybingle employs as nurse to her baby, and as general 'help' [Dickens, *Cricket on the Hearth*].

Sludge : the medium who is detected in the art of cheating [R. Browning, *Mr. Sludge, 'The Medium'*].

Slug, Mr. : a noted statistician with a complexion of 'dark purple' and a 'habit of sighing constantly' [Dickens, *Mudfog Association*].

Slum, Mr. : a writer of poetical advertisements [Dickens, *Old Curiosity Shop*].

Slumkey, Samuel : successful Parliamentary candidate for Eatanswill [Dickens, *Pickwick Papers*].

Sly, Christopher : the tinker, in the 'Induction' [Shakespeare, *Taming of the Shrew*].

Slyme, Chevy : ' an unappreciated genius ' in the opinion
of his friend Montague Tigg ; really a drunken
scoundrel [Dickens, *Martin Chuzzlewit*].

Small, Gilbert : a pin-maker.

—————— *Thomas :* the pin-maker's son, who aims at being
a fashionable man about town and thinks to improve
his position by marriage. After marriage he finds
he has married a cobbler's daughter [Knowles, *Beggar
of Bethnal Green*].

Smallweed Family, The : a dreadful family who have come
down in the world and are paupers by their very
nature [Dickens, *Bleak House*].

Smangle : a fellow-prisoner with Mr. Pickwick in the Fleet
[Dickens, *Pickwick Papers*].

Smart, Tom : the hero of the Bagman's story [Dickens,
Pickwick Papers].

Smauker, Mr. John : Mr. Angelo Cyrus Bantam's footman,
who invites Sam Weller to a ' swarry ' of ' biled
mutton ' in the Crescent at Bath [Dickens, *Pickwick
Papers*].

Smike : the boy rescued by Nicholas Nickleby from Dotheboy's Hall, where Ralph Nickleby, Smike's father,
had placed him [Dickens, *Nicholas Nickleby*].

Smilinda : she who argues with Cordelia as to ' who suffers
most, she who loses at basset, or she who loses her
lover ? ' [Pope, *Eclogue : The Basset Table*].

Smith, Harriet : the rather empty-headed friend and
protégé of Emma, beloved by Robert Martin [Jane
Austen, *Emma*].

—————— **Henry :** *see* Gow, Henry.

—————— **Mr. :** confidential clerk to Messrs. Dornton and
Sulky [Holcroft, *Road to Ruin*].

—————— **Van Diemen :** a colonist who has a passion for
everything English and a great desire to return to
England [George Meredith, *The House on the Beach*].

—————— **Wayland :** a farrier who haunted the Vale of the
White Horse in Berkshire. A more or less historical
character, but overlaid with folk-lore and myth [Scott,
Kenilworth].

Smotherwell, Stephen : the executioner [Scott, *Fair Maid
of Perth*].

Snacks : Lord Lackwit's steward [Allingham, *Fortune's
Frolic*].

Snaggs : drew ' off heads ' and drew ' out teeth '—in other
words he took the likenesses and extracted the teeth
of the villagers [Dibdin, *What Next ?*].

Snagsby, Mr. : a gentle and timid law-stationer in Cook's
Court, Cursitor Street [Dickens, *Bleak House*].

Snake, Mr.: a friend of Lady Sneerwell's, who plays her false [Sheridan, *School for Scandal*].

Snawley Mr.: 'in the oil and colour line'; a low scoundrel, who places two little step-sons at Dotheboy's Hall, with the understanding that they are to have no holidays [Dickens, *Nicholas Nickleby*].

Sneak, Jerry: a pin-maker [Foote, *Mayor of Garratt*].

Sneer: a man that says one thing to authors to their face, and the opposite behind their backs [Sheridan, *The Critic*].

Sneerwell, Lady: in love with Charles Surface, and a member of the Scandal Club [Sheridan, *School for Scandal*].

Snevellicci, Miss: a member of Crummle's Theatrical Company, equal to any part that might fall to her lot. She tried to entrap Nicholas Nickleby, but failed.

—— *Mr.:* also a member of Mr. Crummle's Company, who takes the parts of military swells.

—— *Mrs.:* his wife, who dances [Dickens, *Nicholas Nickleby*].

Snitchey and Craggs: a firm of lawyers [Dickens, *Battle of Life*].

Snodgrass, Augustus: a poet, and a corresponding member of the Pickwick Club, who marries Emily Wardle [Dickens, *Pickwick Papers*].

—— **Charles:** *locum tenens* for Dr. Pringle during his absence from Scotland; Snodgrass marries Isabella Tod [Galt, *Ayreshire Legatees*].

Snout, Tom: the tinker; one of the 'cast' for 'Pyramus and Thisby', in which Peter Quince and Nick Bottom play such important parts [Shakespeare, *Midsummer Night's Dream*].

Snowe, Lucy: the heroine, and also the teller of the story [Charlotte Brontë, *Villette*].

Snubbin, Serjeant: Senior Counsel for Mr. Pickwick in the famous suit of Bardell *v.* Pickwick [Dickens, *Pickwick Papers*].

Snuffim, Sir Tumley: Mrs. Wititterly's doctor [Dickens, *Nicholas Nickleby*].

Snuffle, Simon: the sexton and a member of the Corporation [Foote, *Mayor of Garratt*].

Snug: the joiner, who is cast for the lion's part in the tragedy of Pyramus and Thisbe [Shakespeare, *Midsummer Night's Dream*].

Sohrab: son of Rustum; both are warriors. Ignorant of their relationship, they meet in battle, and Rustum kills Sohrab [Matthew Arnold, *Sohrab and Rustum*].

Soldan, The = Philip II of Spain, who was challenged by Prince Arthur and by him utterly routed [Spenser, *Faëry Queene*].

Soliman and Perseda : a picture of 'Love's constancy, Fortune's inconstancy, and Death's triumphs' [attri-Kyd, *Tragedye of Soliman and Perseda*].

Solinus, Duke of Ephesus : a character in the comedy [Shakespeare, *Comedy of Errors*].

Solomon : a butler ; one of Count Wintersen's household [B. Thompson, *The Stranger*].

—— **and Saturn :** a poem cast in the form of a dialogue [Cynewulf, *Solomon and Saturn*].

Solus : an old bachelor whose wishes sway like a pendulum, between matrimony and a single life [Mrs. Inchbald *Every One Has His Fault*].

Sophia : the mother of the Dukes of Normandy, Rollo and Otto [J. Fletcher, *Bloody Brother*].

—— wife of a Bohemian knight, Mathias by name. During her husband's absence from home Ubaldo and Ricardo tried to attempt her virtue, but in vain [Massinger, *The Picture*].

—— **The Princess :** daughter of the King of Lombardy. Charged with unseemly behaviour, Paladore challanged her accusers. Sophia's innocence was proved and she became the bride of Paladore [Jephson, *Law of Lombardy*].

Sophonisba : daughter of Asdrubal and betrothed to Masinissa, King of the Numidians. This lady has been the subject of so many dramas that it is impossible here to name them all. The two most important are James Thomson, *Sophonisba* ; John Marston, *Wonder of Women ; or, Tragedy of Sophonisba*].

Sophy : 'the dearest girl in the world', who marries Traddles [Dickens, *David Copperfield*].

Sorano : a villain and the brother of Evadne [Beaumont and Fletcher, *Wife for a Month*].

Sordello : an ambitious poet, of the type of the early troubadours, who wishes to influence the world [R. Browning, *Sordello*].

Sorrel, Hetty : the young village girl betrayed by Arthur Donnithorne, who arrives with a reprieve just as she is about to suffer death for child murder [George Eliot, *Adam Bede*].

South, Esquire : intended for the Archduke Charles of Austria [Arbuthnot, *History of John Bull*].

Sowerby, Dudley : the son of a peer, who becomes engaged to Nesta, but on learning the circumstances of her

birth ends it, and tries, too late, to renew it [George
Meredith, *One of Our Conquerors*].

Sowerberry, Mr. : the undertaker to whom Oliver Twist
is apprenticed when he first leaves the workhouse.

—————— *Mrs. :* the wife of the undertaker, who treats Oliver
with great unkindness [Dickens, *Oliver Twist*].

Spado : a mischievous scamp who plays tricks on every one
[O'Keefe, *Castle of Andalusia*].

Spanker, Lady Gay : a telling character in the play [Dion
Boucicault, *London Assurance*].

Sparabella : a shepherdess who loves D'Urfey, who in his
turn loves Clumsilis ; Sparabella determines on suicide,
but cannot decide on the manner [Gay, *Pastoral* iii.].

Sparkish : a coxcomb with a pretence at learning. This
is the character on which Congreve based his ' Tattle '
[Wycherley, *Country Wife*, 1671–2 ; adapted by
Garrick, sub tit. *Country Girl*, 1766, containing the
same character].

Sparkler, Edmund : marries Little Dorrit's sister, Fanny.
He is the son of Mrs. Merdle by her first husband.

—————— *Mrs.:* a pretty, self-willed, determined woman,
who had been a ballet-dancer and ruled her husband
with a firm and steady hand [Dickens, *Little Dorrit*].

Sparowe, Philip : the pet sparrow of Jane Scrope, killed
by a cat [Skelton, *Boke of Phyllyp Sparowe*, c. 1708].

Sparsit, Mrs. : housekeeper to Josiah Bounderby, who
controls the finances of the household, and plays the
spy on her master and mistress [Dickens, *Hard Times*].

Speed : servant to Valentine [Shakespeare, *Two Gentlemen of Verona*].

Spenlow, Dora : the ' child-wife ' of David Copperfield
[Dickens, *David Copperfield*].

—————— *Francis :* of the firm of Spenlow and Jorkins,
Proctors He was the father of Dora, afterwards Mrs.
David Copperfield.

—————— *Lavinia and Clarissa :* his sisters, who brought
Dora up [Dickens, *David Copperfield*].

Spindle, Jack : the son of a wealthy man, who, having
dissipated his fortune, tries to borrow. Some amusing interviews result [Goldsmith, *The Bee*].

Spitfire, Will : Roger Wildrake's boy-servant [Scott, *Woodstock*].

Sprackling, Joseph : a money-lender, not too honest.

—————— *Thomas :* his brother, with about the same standard
of morality [Reeve, *Parted*].

Sprightly, Miss Kitty : a great heiress, the ward of Sir
Gilbert Pumpkin. She falls in love with Charles
Stanley, who has taken part in theatricals at her
guardian's house [Jackman, *All the World's a Stage*].

Sprightly, Sophia: full of fire and spirit, she has a fancy for the Hon. Mr. Daffodil, but learning that he is nothing better than a flirt, rejects him and marries her true lover, Tukely [Garrick, *Male Coquette*].

Spruce, Captain M. C.: one of the characters in the play [J. M. Morton, *Lend Me Five Shillings*].

Spumador: Prince Arthur's charger [Spenser, *Faëry Queene*].

Square, Mr.: a philosopher [Fielding, *Tom Jones*].

Squeamish, Lady: a character in two plays [Wycherley *Country Wife*; and Otway, *Friendship in Fashion*].

Squeers, Miss Fanny: the schoolmaster's daughter, an unattractive and shrewish looking girl of three and twenty.

—— *Mrs.:* a hard-hearted, ill-tempered woman, the schoolmaster's wife.

—— *Wackford:* the proprietor of the school at Dotheboys Hall; a brutal, cowardly bully, who maltreats the boys and steals their pocket-money, The man to whom Nicholas went as assistant master.

—— *Wackford, junr.:* a disagreeable boy, who was dressed in the pupils' best clothes [Dickens, *Nicholas Nickleby*].

Squeeze, Miss: the daughter of a pawnbroker who, having inherited a small fortune: was so afraid of being married for her money that she never married at all [Goldsmith, *Citizen of the World*].

Squint, Lawyer: a public speaker and politician [Goldsmith, *Citizen of the World*].

Squintum, Doctor = George Whitefield, a celebrity of the day (1714-70), whom the dramatist introduced into his farce [Foote, *Minor*].

Squire Meldrum: *see* Meldrum, Squire.

—— **of Dames:** a knight who loved Columbell. She ordained that he should serve for one whole year before she became his bride. This knight proved to be Britomart [Spenser, *Faëry Queene*].

—— **of Low Degree, The:** the hero of a curious old English romance [Ritson, *Ancient Romances*].

—— **Western:** *see* Western, Squire.

Squirt: the apothecary boy [Garth, *Dispensary*].

Squod, Phil: a boy that Mr. George had rescued from the gutter and afterwards employed in his shooting gallery [Dickens, *Bleak House*].

Stagg, Benjamin: the owner of the cellar in the Barbican, where Tappertit and the other 'Prentice Knights' used to meet [Dickens, *Barnaby Rudge*].

Stalky : a troublesome, vulgar schoolboy whose chief object in life was to outwit those set in authority over him [Kipling, *Stalky & Co.*].

Stanchells : head gaoler at the tolbooth, Glasgow [Scott, *Rob Roy*].

Standish, Miles : a New England colonist who had gone out in the *Mayflower*, and who loved Priscilla, but lacked courage to plead his own cause [Longfellow, *Courtship of Miles Standish*].

Stanley, Capt. Charles : the man who acted in private theatricals at Sir Gilbert Pumpkin's, and taking advantage of his position eloped with Sir Gilbert's ward, Kitty Sprightly [Jackman, *All the World's a Stage*].

—— **Sir Hubert :** a poor country squire [Thomas Morton, *Cure for the Heart-Ache*].

Staples, Lawrence : the chief gaoler at Kenilworth Castle [Scott, *Kenilworth*].

Stareleigh, Mr. Justice : the testy and deaf little judge who presided at the trial of Bardell *v.* Pickwick [Dickens, *Pickwick Papers*].

Starno : King of Lochlin, who tried to deal treacherously by Fingal, in return for kindness shown [Ossian, *Fingal*, iii.].

Starveling Robin : a tailor, cast for the part of Thisbe's mother in the tragedy of Pyramus and Thisbe [Shakespeare, *Midsummer Night's Dream*].

Statira : wife of Alexander, and daughter of Darius. A devoted wife, murdered by her husband's mistress, Roxana [Lee, *Alexander the Great*].

Staunton, George : the betrayer of Effie Deans, who afterwards makes her all the reparation he can by marrying her [Scott, *Heart of Midlothian*].

Steel, Sir Gray : *see* Eger, Sir.

Steelyard, Mr. : the housekeeper and mother of Parson Chowne [Blackmore, *Maid of Sker*].

Steenson, Maggie : Willie's wife, also called 'Epps Anslie'.

—— *Steenson :* the Piper, of whom 'Wandering Willie' speaks in his tale.

—— *Willie :* generally known as 'Wandering Willie' [Scott, *Redgauntlet*].

Steerforth, James : David's old schoolfellow, who betrayed Little Em'ly and then proposed to hand her over to his valet. He was drowned off Yarmouth [Dickens, *David Copperfield*].

Steinernherz von Blutsacker, Francis : the executioner [Scott, *Anne of Geierstein*].

Steinfort, The Baron : in love with Mrs. Haller [B. Thompson, *Stranger*].

Stella = Lady Penelope Devereux, the lady whom the poet loved [Sidney, *Astrophel and Stella*].

—— Miss Hester Johnson, the girl whom the author taught, loved, and secretly married [Swift, *Journal to Stella*].

Steno, Michel : one of the chief of the Venetian Council of Forty [Byron, *Marino Faliero, Doge of Venice*].

Stephen : one of Front de Boeuf's train [Scott, *Ivanhoe*].

—— **Master** : a melancholy, stupid countryman [Ben Jonson, *Every Man in His Humour*].

Sterling, Miss : an ill-tempered woman, the elder daughter of the merchant, who fails to marry at all [Garrick, *Clandestine Marriage*].

—— **Miss Fanny** : a beautiful and attractive girl secretly married to Lovewell.

—— *Mr.* : a wealthy city merchant whose ambition it was to see his daughters ' married to titles ' [Garrick, *Clandestine Marriage*].

Steyne, Marquis of : a disreputable though very wealthy old nobleman whose conduct with Becky Sharp scandalized London Society [Thackeray, *Vanity Fair*].

Stiggins, The Reverend Mr. : a dissenting minister much appreciated by Mrs. Weller and known as ' the Shepherd ' [Dickens, *Pickwick Papers*].

Stilgoe, Nanny : a ' wise woman ' living in the village of West Lorraine [Blackmore, *Alice Lorraine.*]

Stitch, Tom : a young and very gallant tailor. A ' *merry history* ' very popular in the seventeenth century.

Stockwell, Nancy : promised by her father to young Harlow, although loving Belford. It turns out that Harlow is already secretly married, so Nancy marries the man she loves [Garrick, *Neck or Nothing*].

Stafford, Earl of : the hero of an historical tragedy [R. Browning, *Stafford*].

Straitlace, Dame Philippa : Blushington's maiden aunt, who had hoped to become his housekeeper [Moncrieff, *Bashful Man*].

Stralenheim, Count of : a mean and grasping nobleman robbed by Werner and murdered by Ulric.

—— *Ida :* his daughter and betrothed to Ulric. When Ulric tells her of his crime they part for ever [Byron, *Werner*].

Strap, Hugh : Roderick Random's faithful follower [Smollett, *Roderick Random*].

Stremon : a shepherd who courts Urania [Sidney, *Arcadia*].

Strickland : an Indian police officer [Kipling, *Life's Handicap*].

—— **Mr.** : the ' suspicious husband ' who suspects

all the women with whom he is connected of reprehensible conduct.

Strickland, Mrs. : his model wife—a world too good for him [Hoadly, *Suspicious Husband*].

Strike, Caroline : The beautiful sister of Evan Harrington, married to an officer in the Marines, who illtreats her. Is introduced into Society by the Countess de Saldar [George Meredith, *Evan Harrington.*

Strong, Doctor : 'the kindest' of men, and the 'idol of the whole school' [Dickens, *David Copperfield*].

Struldbrugs, The : the inhabitants of Luggnagg [Swift, *Gulliver's Travels*].

Strutt, Lord=the 'King of Spain' [Arbuthnot, *History of John Bull.*]

Stryver, Bully : Darnay's counsel at his trial [Dickens, *Tale of Two Cities*].

Stubble, Reuben : Farmer Cornflower's bailiff, 'a plain, upright, and downright man' [C. I. M. Dibden, *Farmer's Wife*].

Stubbs : the Wellingham beadle [Scott, *Heart of Midlothian*].

Stuffy, Matthew : considered that owing to a squint he was peculiarly fitted to act as prompter at a theatre. He could, he said, keep one eye on the actor, the other on his book [Matthews, *At Home*].

Stukely : a dishonest acquaintance of Beverley, and a suitor of Miss Beverley's [Edward Moore, *Gamester*].

—— **Captain Harry** : Sir Gilbert Pumpkin's nephew [Jackman, *All the World's a Stage*].

—— **Will** : one of Little John's boon companions, who was rescued from the sheriff of Nottingham by Robin Hood [*Robin Hood's Rescuing Will Stutly : ballad*].

Sturgeon, Major, J.P. : a Brentford fishmonger who pays court to Mrs. Jerry Sneak [Foote, *Mayor of Garratt*].

Sturmthal, Melchior : a member of the Swiss deputation [Scott, *Anne of Geierstein*].

Stutly, Will : *see* Stukely, Will.

Subtle : a quack who tries to figure as an alchemist [Ben Jonson, *Alchemist*].

—— **Mr. and Mrs.** : a dishonest couple who, dwelling in Paris, live on the weaknesses of Englishmen visiting that city [Foote, *Englishmen in Paris*].

Sulky, Mr. : his repellant exterior belied a kindly nature capable of showing unselfish friendship [Holcroft, *Road to Ruin*].

Sullen, Mrs. : the uncongenial wife of the squire, from whom he was separated at the end of fourteen months.

Sullen, Squire : son of Lady Bountiful by a former marriage. ' He says little, thinks less, and does nothing at all ' [Farquhar, *Beaux' Stratagem*].

Sul-Malla : the daughter of Conmor, King of Inis-Huna [Ossian, *Temora*].

Summerson, Esther : *see* Hawdon, Esther.

Supple : a character in the comedy [Cibber, *Double Gallant*].

———— Squire Western's boon companion [Fielding, *Tom Jones*].

Surface, Charles : a young rake who is possessed of good qualities which in the end prevail.

———— *Joseph :* his brother—a consummate hypocrite, eventually unmasked.

———— *Sir Oliver :* uncle of Charles and Joseph, who assumes the name of Premium Stanley [Sheridan, *School for Scandal*].

Surly : just the opposite of Sir Courtly Nice, and as unattractive as he can possibly be [Crowne, *Sir Courtly Nice*].

———— a gambling friend of Sir Epicure Mammon [Ben Jonson, *Alchemist*].

Surplus, Charles : nephew of Mr. and Mrs. Surplus.

———— *Mr. and Mrs. :* a lawyer and his wife [Morton, *A Regular Fix*].

Surrey, White : the name of King Richard III's charger, ridden by him at Bosworth Field [Shakespeare, *King Richard III*].

Susan, Black-Eyed : the heroine of a ballad [Gay, *Sweet William's Farewell*].

———— Duchess : the young duchess raised from a low position by an old duke. She determines to have a good time and unknowingly causes a tragedy [George Meredith, *Tale of Chloe*].

Susanna : the subject of a poem [Ayleth, *Susanna ; or, the Arraignment of the Two Elders*].

Sutton. Hero : in love with Sir Valentine de Grey. She assumes the dress and manners of a Quakeress in order to win him [*Wit*].

———— *Sir William :* the uncle of Hero [Knowles, *Woman's Wit*].

Suwarrow, Alexander : a Russian general of great brutality, referred to by Campbell in *Pleasures of Hope*, and by Byron in *Don Juan*.

Suzanne : wife of the chemist and druggist, Chalomel [Ware, *Piperman's Predicament*].

Svengali : a Russian hypnotist and musician [Du Maurier, *Trilby*].

Swanne, Knight of the : the hero of an old English tale derived from the French [Copland, *Knight of the Swanne*].

Swanston : a smuggler [Scott, *Redgauntlet*].

Swaran : King of Lochlin (Denmark). who, upon his invasion of Ireland, was defeated by Fingal [Ossian, *Fingal*].

Sweedlepipe, Paul : Mrs. Gamp's landlord. A fashionable hair-dresser, and a bird-fancier [Dickens, *Martin Chuzzlewit*].

Sweepclean, Saunders : a king's messenger [Scott, *Antiquary*].

Sweeting, the Rev. Mr. : curate of Nunnely under Mr. Hall ; a weak but well-intentioned man who marries Dora Sykes [Charlotte Brontë, *Shirley*].

Swidger, Milly : the wife of William and the heroine of the story.

———— *Philip :* custodian of the institution where Mr. Redlaw lectures. A happy old man of eighty-seven [Dickens, *Haunted Man*].

Swiveller, Dick : clerk to Sampson Brass, and friend of Fred Trent. He is nursed through a severe illness by the 'Marchioness', and marries her [Dickens, *Old Curiosity Shop*].

Sybil : the heroine of a novel dealing with political questions [Beaconsfield, *Sybil ; or, Two Nations*].

Sycorax : a witch who confined Ariel in the rift of a pine tree for twelve years. She was Caliban's mother [Shakespeare, *Tempest*].

———— intended to represent Joseph Ritson, the literary critic [T. F. Dibdin, *Bibliomania*].

Sydenham, Charles : the friend of the Woodvilles [Cumberland, *Wheel of Fortune*].

Sylla, Cornelius : his claims were set aside in favour of Marius, as leader in the Mithridatic War. Having ousted Marius from this position, he continued the war with success and caused himself to be appointed 'Perpetual Dictator' [Lodge, *Wounds of Civil War*, etc.].

Syllabub, Tim : a dirty, shabby-genteel man, much given to hymn singing and pot-house wit [Goldsmith, *Citizen of the World*].

Sylli, Signor : a fantastic Italian dandy, in love with Camiola [Massinger, *Maid of Honour*].

Sylvia : the forsaken mistress of Vainlove [Congreve, *Old Bachelor*].

———— the heroine of a pastoral poem [Darley, *Sylvia ; or, May Queen*].

Sylvia, daughter of Justice Balance and in love with Captain Plume. Her father opposing her marriage, she dresses as a man, enlists in Plume's regiment under an assumed name, and finally marries her love [Farquhar, *Recruiting Officer*].

—————— the heroine. The 'Lovers' are Philip Hepburn, a draper of Whitby, and a dashing young sailor, Charlie Kinraid, who is kidnapped by the press-gang [Mrs. Gaskell, *Sylvia's Lovers*; *see also* Robson, Sylvia.

Symkyn, Symond: a miller who dwelt at Trompington, near Cambridge. None too honest and wedded to the stuck-up daughter of a parson [Chaucer, *Canterbury Tales : The Reeves' Tale*].

Symonides the Good: the King of Pentapolis [Shakespeare, *Pericles Prince of Tyre*].

Syntax, Doctor: a wife-ridden, pious, gullible clergyman, who went on three tours—in search of the picturesque, in search of consolation, and in search of a wife, respectively [Coombe, *Three Tours of Dr. Syntax*].

Synteresis: the personification of Conscience [Phineas Fletcher, *Purple Island*].

Syphax: a Numidian soldier in the train of Prince Juba [Addison, *Cato*].

Tachebrune: Ogier the Dane's charger.

Tacket, Martin and Tibb: Julian Avenel's old shepherd and his wife [Scott, *Monastery*].

Tackleton: a toy-maker who disliked children [Dickens, *Cricket on the Hearth*].

Tactus: a character in a curious old play wherein it is asserted that the Tongue is a sixth sense [Brewer, *Combat of the Tongue and Five Senses*].

Tadpole: an electioneering agent [Beaconsfield, *Coningsby*].

Taffril, Lieutenant: in love with Jenny Caxton, a milliner [Scott, *Antiquary*].

Taffy=Talbot Wynne, a Yorkshireman who marries Miss Bagot [Du Maurier, *Trilby*].

Tag: lady's-maid to Biddy Bellair [Garrick, *Miss in Her Teens*].

Talbot, Colonel: an English friend of Waverley's [Scott, *Waverley*].

Taliesin: the chief of the Welsh bards in the days of King Arthur [Drayton, *Polyolbion*].

Tallyho, Sir Toby: a rowdy Englishman [Foote, *Englishman returned from Paris*].

Talus: a brazen man created by Vulcan to guard the Island of Crete ; an attendant upon Artegal [Spenser, *Faëry Queene*].

Tam O'Shanter : *see* O'Shanter, Tam.

—— **O'Todshaw :** *see* O'Todshaw, Tam.

Tamburlaine : the great Tartar conqueror of Central Asia [Marlowe, *Tamberlaine the Great*].

Tamerlane : the hero of a tragedy which achieved great popularity [Rowe, *Tamerlane*].

Tamora : Queen of the Goths [Shakespeare, *Titus Andronicus*].

Tamper : the betrothed of Emily, *q.v.* [Colman the Elder, *Deuce is in Him*].

Tancred : a young nobleman, who goes out to the East to solve 'the Asian Mystery'. His adventures are numerous but futile [Beaconsfield, *Tancred ; or, the New Crusade*].

—— a crusader [Scott, *Count Robert of Paris*].

—— **and Sigismunda :** the hero and heroine of a tragedy founded on a story in *Gil Blas* called ' *Baneful Marriage* ' [James Thomson, *Tancred and Sigismunda*].

Tankard, Squire : Parliamentary candidate who with Sir Harry Foxchase opposes Lord Place and Colonel Promise [Fielding, *Pasquin*].

Taper : an electioneering agent [Beaconsfield, *Coningsby*].

Tapley, Mark : the humble friend and companion of Martin Chuzzlewit when he emigrates to America [Dickens, *Martin Chuzzlewit*].

Tappertit, Simon : Gabriel Varden's apprentice, in love with Dolly Varden, and hence an enemy of Joe Willet [Dickens, *Barnaby Rudge*].

Tapwell, Timothy : Wellborn's butler. He insulted his master when he was under a cloud and fawned upon him when he thought his fortunes were improving [Massinger, *New Way to Pay Old Debts*].

Targe, Duncan : a Highlander who quarrels with his fellow-servant, George Buchanan, upon the subject of Mary, Queen of Scots [Dr. John Moore, *Zeluco*].

Tartlet, Tim : Mrs. Pattypan's servant, who loved ' to see life' because it is 'so agreeable' [Cobb, *First Floor*].

Tasnar : an enchanter who sided with the rebel army against Misnar, Sultan of Delhi [Ridley, *Tales of the Genii*].

Tatlanthe : Queen Fadladinida's favourite [Carey, *Chrononhotonthologos*].

Tattle : a half-witted beau ; made up of ' lying, foppery, vanity, cowardice, brag, licentiousness, and ugliness ' [Congreve, *Love for Love*].

Tattycoram : *see* Beadle, Harriet.

Teague : an Irish servant [Howard, *Committee*].

Teazle, Lady : an innocent country girl who, married to an old man, gets compromised by her relations with Joseph Surface. She sees her folly and repents.

–––––– *Sir Peter :* an uxorious old gentleman with a young wife [Sheridan, *School for Scandal*].

Telemachus : the hero of a musical opera [John Hughes, *Calypso and Telemachus*].

Telfer, Jamie : the hero of an old Scottish ballad.

Tell, William : the subject of a tragedy [Knowles, *William Tell*].

Tempest, Hon. Mr. : late Governor of Senegambia ; contented, testy, hasty, and very poor.

–––––– *Miss Emily :* his daughter ; very lively and very clever, but disinclined to marry the husband selected for her by her father [Cumberland, *Wheel of Fortune*].

–––––– **Lady Betty :** beautiful, wealthy, and of noble birth, she had had her judgment warped by the reading of too many romances [Goldsmith, *Citizen of the World*].

Temple, Henrietta : the heroine of a love-story [Beaconsfield, *Henrietta Temple*].

–––––– **Miss :** one of the teachers at Lowood School. The character is drawn from that of one of the governesses at Cowan's Bridge, who was kind to the little Brontës [Charlotte Brontë, *Jane Eyre*].

Teril, Sir Walter : the bridegroom of Caelistina, who takes a sleeping draught so as to simulate death and thus escape dishonour [Dekker, *Satiromastix*].

Termagant : a woman who uses the most extraordinary language. She is Harriet Quidnunc's maid [Murphy, *Upholsterer*].

Terpin, Sir : a captive of Queen Radigund, who ill-used him shamefully [Spenser, *Faëry Queene*].

Tessa : the girl who loves Tito Melema [George Eliot, *Romola*].

Teste : a clown [Shakespeare, *Twelfth Night*].

Tethys : daughter of Heaven and Earth, and mother of the river-gods, by Ocean, her husband [Milton, *Comus*].

Testy, Timothy : one of the characters in a humorous production [Beresford, *Miseries of Human Life*].

Tetterby, Mr. Adolphus : a vendor of newspapers.

–––––– *Mrs. Sophia :* his wife.

–––––– '*Dolphus :* their eldest son, a railway newspaper-boy [Dickens, *Haunted Man*].

Teufelsdrökh, Herr : an eccentric German philosopher, the enemy of all shams [Carlyle, *Sartor Resartus*].

Texartis : a Scythian soldier, who dies by the hand of Brenhilda [Scott, *Count Robert of Paris*].

Tezozomoc : the chief priest of the Aztecas, who wished to sacrifice 'the White strangers' as a peace offering to the gods [Southey, *Madoc*].

Thaddeus : the hero of a romantic novel which was the cause of the authoress being elected a Canoness of the Teutonic Order of St. Joachim [Jane Porter, *Thaddeus of Warsaw*].

Thaddu : father of Morna, hence the grandfather of Fingal [Ossian, *Fingal*].

Thaïsa : wife of Pericles and daughter of King Simonides [Shakespeare, *Pericles Prince of Tyre*].

Thalaba : the destroyer of evil spirits, a power which he lost by an act of folly [Southey, *Thalaba*].

Thalestris=Mrs. Morley, the sister of Sir George Brown, who also appears in the poem as Sir Pluma [Pope, *Rape of the Lock*].

The Doctor ' : *see* Losberne.

' The Golden Dustman ' : *see* Boffin, Nicodemus.

' The Man from Shropshire ' : *see* Gridley, Mr.

' The Shepherd ' : *see* Stiggins, The Reverend Mr.

' The Zephyr ' : *see* Mivins, Mr.

Thenot : an aged shepherd who tells the fable of the oak and the briar to Cuddy, the herdsman's boy [Spenser, *Shephearde's Calendar*].

———— a shepherd who loved Corin for her fidelity to her lost lover. When she seems about to care for Thenot in his stead her charm for him vanishes [J. Fletcher, *Faithful Shepherdess*].

Theodofred : the father of Roderick [Southey, *Roderick*].

Theodore : the lover of Honoria, and the hero [Dryden, *Theodore and Honoria*].

———— a brave but hasty-spirited soldier, son of General Archas [J. Fletcher, *Loyal Subject*].

———— son of Lord Clarinsal, and grandson of Alphonso [Jephson, *Count of Narbonne*].

Theodoric : the subject of the tale [Campbell, *Theodric*].

Theodorick : the hermit of Engaddi ; an exiled noble [Scott, *Talisman*].

Theodosius : the hero of a tragedy [Lee, *Theodosius*].

Theresa : beloved by Mazeppa, a page at the court of her father, the Count Palatine of Padolia [Byron, *Mazeppa*].

Theron : Roderick's favourite dog [Southey, *Roderick*].

Thersames : in love with the heroine [Suckling, *Aglaura*].

Thersites : ' a deformed and scurrilous Grecian ' [Shakespeare, *Troilus and Cressida*].

Thersytes : an example of how the ' greatest boasters are not the greatest doers ' [*Thersytes : an Interlude*].

Theseus : Duke of Athens [Chaucer, *Canterbury Tales : The Knight's Tale* ; also Shakespeare, *Midsummer Night's Dream*].

Thirsil and Thelgon : two gentle youths, the first a poet, the second a singer [Phineas Fletcher, *Purple Island*].

Thisbe : the heroine of the interlude [Shakespeare, *Midsummer Night's Dream*].

Thomalin : a shepherd [Spenser, *Shephearde's Calendar*].

Thomas : the subject of an old miracle play [*Incredulity of Thomas*].

—— **Evan :** a local bully and farmer, who loses five sons in a sand storm.

—— *Moxy :* wife of Evan Thomas, who takes care of Bardie when she is rescued from the sea.

—— *Watkin :* son of Evan and lover of Bunny Llewellyn [Blackmore, *Maid of Sker*].

—— **Lord :** the hero of an old ballad ; Sir Thomas is about to marry the 'Brown Girl' when Fair Elinor stabs her [Percy, *Reliques : Lord Thomas and Fair Elinor*].

—— **Monsieur :** Valentine's companion, with whom Mary is in love [J. Fletcher, *Mons. Thomas*].

—— **of Reading :** one of the characters in a sixteenth century fiction [Deloney, *Thomas of Reading ; or, the Six Worthy Yeomen of the West*].

—— **Sir :** a foolish and dogmatic country squire [Crabbe, *The Borough*].

Thopas, Sir, or Topas : a sportsman, archer, wrestler and runner ; the subject of a musical burlesque introduced in the Canterbury Tales [Chaucer, *Canterbury Tales : Chaucer's Tale of Sir Thopas*].

Thornberry, Job : a Penzance brazier, honest and direct in his dealings. Intended for a type of the upright English tradesman.

—— *Mary :* his daughter, who marries Frank Rochdale, the son of Sir Simon Rochdale [Colman the Younger, *John Bull*].

Thornburgh, Mrs. : a foolish, matchmaking Westmorland vicar's wife [Mrs. Humphry Ward, *Robert Elsmere*].

Thorne, Dr. : a country practitioner, who gives the title to the book.

—— *Mary :* his daughter, who is subject to many changes of fortune [Anthony Trollope, *Doctor Thorne*].

Thornhill, Sir William : *see* Burchell, Mr.

—— **Squire :** a rake, who induced Olivia Primrose to elope with him, and then discovered that his 'false marriage' was really valid [Goldsmith, *Vicar of Wakefield*].

Thornton, Cyril : the hero of a military novel [Hamilton, *Cyril Thornton*].

Thorpe, Isabella : an acquaintance of Catherine Morland's who flirts with her brother.

———— *John :* a low-class University man much given to horses [Jane Austen, *Northanger Abbey*].

Thoughtless, Miss Betty : a modest and amiable girl, but unconventional and ignorant of the customs of society, therefore frequently blundering [Eliza Haywood, *Miss Betty Thoughtless*].

Thoulouse, Raymond, Count of : a crusader [Scott, *Count Robert of Paris*].

Three Kings of Cologne : the three 'Wise Men' who travelled from the East to pay homage to the Infant Christ. The images shown in the Cathedral of Cologne are called Gaspar, Melchior, and Balthazar.

Thrift, Peggy : Sir Thomas Thrift's orphan child ; her guardian brings her up in the country in absolute seclusion [Garrick, *Country Girl*].

Thrummy-Cap : a Northumberland sprite, a 'queer-looking little auld man'.

Thule, A Princess of : *see* Mackenzie, Sheila.

Thurio : Valentine's rival in Silvia's affections [Shakespeare, *Two Gentlemen of Verona*].

Thwackum : one of the leading characters in the novel [Fielding, *Tom Jones*].

Thyrsis=Arthur Hugh Clough, whom his friend commemorated in a monody or elegiac poem [Matthew Arnold, *Thyrsis*].

———— a herdsman [Milton, *L'Allegro*].

Tibbs, Beau : an impecunious dandy.

———— *Mrs. :* his wife, an untidy, out-at-elbows woman, with remains of beauty and coquettish manners [Goldsmith, *Citizen of the World*].

Tibet Talkapace : waiting-maid to Custance [Udall, *Ralph Roister Doister*].

Tibs : an ungainly, ill-dressed man, with a general knowledge of every subject [Goldsmith, *Citizen of the World*].

Tiburce : an early Christian mentioned in the *Second Nun's Tale* [Chaucer, *Canterbury Tales*].

Tiburzio : the commander of the Pisans who attacked Florence. He was utterly defeated by Luria, the Moor [R. Browning, *Luria*].

Tickell, Mark : a friend of Elsie Lovell's [Reeve, *Parted*].

Tickler, Timothy : intended for Robert Sym, an Edinburgh lawyer [Wilson, *Noctes Ambrosianae*].

Tiddler, Tom : *see* Mopes, Mr. Tom.

Tiffany : maid to Miss Alscrip [Burgoyne, *Heiress*].

Tigg, Montague : murdered by Jonas Chuzzlewit [Dickens, *Martin Chuzzlewit*].

Tighe, Naomi : the heroine of the play [Robertson, *School*, 1869].

Tilburina : daughter of the Governor of Tilbury Fort, in love with Whiskerandos. A character which first occurs in a tragedy [Puff, *Spanish Armada*; afterwards introduced into a burlesque, Sheridan, *The Critic*].

Tilly Slowboy : *see* Slowboy, Tilly.

Tiler, Tom : the subject of a sixteenth century moral play [*Tom Tiler and His Wife*].

Tilney, Eleanor : sister to Henry Tilney, the lover of Catherine.

—————— *Henry :* the hero, who marries Catherine Morland. [Jane Austen, *Northanger Abbey*].

Tim, Tiny : Bob Cratchit's lame child [Dickens, *Christmas Carol*].

Timias (Sir Walter Raleigh) : King Arthur's squire, who whilst pretending to a love for Belphoebe (Queen Elizabeth), carried on an intrigue with Amoret (Elizabeth Throgmorton) [Spenser, *Faëry Queene*].

Timms, Corporal : one of Waverley's non-commissioned officers [Scott, *Waverley*].

Timon : the first Duke of Chandos [Pope, *Moral Essays*, Ep. iv.].

Timurkan the Tartar : Emperor of China, slain, after a usurpation of twenty years, by Zaphimri the 'orphan' [Murphy, *Orphan of China*].

Tinderbox, Miss Jenny : a maiden lady who, having looked too high in the social scale, as regarded a husband, had, in the end, to go through life single [Goldsmith, *Citizen of the World*].

Tinman, Mark : a retired tradesman whose great desire is to have local influence. His dealings with his old friend Smith form the basis of the story [George Meredith, *House on the Beach*].

Tinsel, Lord : a despicable character who ignored all merit but that appertaining to blue blood [Knowles, *Hunchback*].

Tinto, Dick : an artist, the son of a Langdirdum tailor. He occurs in two novels by the same author [Scott, *Bride of Lammermoor ; St. Ronan's Well*].

Tip : *see* Dorrit, Edward.

Tiphany : mother of the three kings of Cologne.

Tipkin, Biddy : the original of Lydia Languish. A sentimental woman who thinks 'it looks so ordinary to go out at a door to be married' [Steele, *Tender Husband*].

Tippins, Lady : a friend of the Veneerings. A nice old lady with a big, ugly face [Dickens, *Our Mutual Friend*].

Tipto, Sir Glorious : an affected and boastful man [Ben Jonson, *New Inn*].

Tiptoe : a footman not above suspicion as regards honesty ; shrewd and lazy [Colman the Younger, *Ways and Means*].

Tirante the White : the hero of a fifteenth century romance of chivalry.

Titania : the heroine [Black, *Strange Adventures of a Phaeton*].

———— Queen of the Faries and wife of Oberon. Under the influence of a magic juice she falls in love with Bottom, the weaver [Shakespeare, *Midsummer Night's Dream*].

Titmarsh, Samuel : the chief character in the story [Thackeray, *Samuel Titmarsh and the Great Hoggarty Diamond*].

Titmouse, Mr. Tittlebat : vulgar, ignorant, and conceited ; a linendraper's assistant who is discovered to be of good birth [Warren, *Ten Thousand a Year*].

Titurel : first King of Graalburg, he founded a temple there, as a shrine for the Holy Grail [*Arthurian Cycle*].

Toby, Uncle : obliged to retire from active service on account of wounds, 'one of the finest compliments ever paid to human nature', according to Hazlitt, and of much greater interest than the nominal hero of the book [Sterne, *Tristram Shandy*] ; *see also* Shandy, Captain.

Titus : according to the poet this was the name of the penitent thief who had attacked Joseph on his flight into Egypt [Longfellow, *Golden Legend*].

Tod, Isabella : the friend and correspondent of Rachel Pringle [Galt, *Ayreshire Legatees*].

Todd, Laurie : the hero of a novel founded on the autobiography of Grant Thorburn [Galt, *Laurie Todd*].

Todgers, Mrs. : the keeper of a commercial boardinghouse, with a hard face but kind heart, who befriends Mercy Chuzzlewit [Dickens, *Martin Chuzzlewit*].

Tom : the 'Portugal Dustman' who took part against France in the war of the Spanish Succession [Arbuthnot, *History of John Bull*].

———— an honest man in the service of Mr. Peregrine Lovel [Townley, *High Life Below Stairs*].

———— Bowling : *see* Bowling, Tom.

———— Brown : *see* Brown, Tom.

———— Corinthian : one of the heroes of the story [Pierce Egan, *Life in London*].

Tom, Jones : *see* Jones, Tom.

―――― **Uncle :** a faithful negro slave. A native of Maryland. One Josiah Henson is said to have been the original of this character [Harriet Beecher Stowe, *Uncle Tom's Cabin*].

―――― **à-Lincoln**=the Red Rose Knight, surnamed the Boar of England [Richard Johnson, *Most Pleasant History of Tom-à-Lincoln*].

―――― **a-Thrum :** a fairy sprite believed in in mediaeval times—a little old man.

Tomahourich, Muhme Janet of : an old sibyl [Scott, *Two Drovers*].

Tomalin : fairy knight related to Oberon. He sided with Pigwiggen in a combat in which Oberon was supported by Tom Thumb [Drayton, *Nymphidia*].

Tomboy, Priscilla : a high-spirited, uneducated hoyden of West Indian birth, sent to London for her education. She elopes with Captan Slightly [Bickerstaff, *The Romp*].

Tomkins, Joseph : Cromwell's secret envoy, at one time secretary to the Parliamentary Captain, Desborough [Scott, *Woodstock*].

Tony Lumpkin : *see* Lumpkin, Tony.

Toobad, Mr. : 'the Manichæan Millevarian. A man who constantly imagines that the devil has come amongst us [Peacock, *Nightmare Abbey*].

Toodle, Mr : an engine-driver, husband of Polly, and father of Robin.

―――― *Mrs. Polly :* the foster-mother of little Paul Dombey.

―――― *Robin :* known as 'Biler' in his family, but generally known as 'Bob the Grinder' [Dickens, *Dombey and Son*].

Toots, Mr. P. : the eldest of Dr. Blimber's pupils. Dull-witted and overworked, and hopelessly in love with Florence Dombey [Dickens, *Dombey and Son*].

Topaz, Sir : *see* Thopas, Sir.

Tophas, Sir : 'an affected, blustering, talkative, cowardly pretender' [Lyly, *Endymion*].

Topsy : a slave-girl, quite ignorant as to her parentage [Harriet Beecher Stowe, *Uncle Tom's Cabin*].

Tormot : youngest son of Torquil of the Oak [Scott, *Fair Maid of Perth*].

Torquil of the Oak : chief of the Quhale Clan and a seer, whose eight sons all took part in the big battle of the Clans Quhale and Chattan [Scott, *Fair Maid of Perth*].

Torre, Sir : brother of Elaine, the 'Lily Maid of Astolat' Alfred Tennyson, *Idylls of the King : Elaine*].

Torrismond : the Spanish general who loves Queen Leonora [Dryden, *Spanish Fryar*].

Totterly, Lord : an antiquated fop who aims at appearing young [Selby, *Unfinished Gentleman*].

Touchstone : court jester full of 'quips and cranks and wanton wiles' [Shakespeare, *As You Like It*].

Touchwood, Clarissa : in love with Colonel Clifford.

—————— *Colonel :* the uncle of Clarissa and Major Touchwood, and father of Sophia.

—————— *Major :* in love with his cousin Sophia.

—————— *Sophia :* the Colonel's sister, in love with Major Touchwood [Dibdin, *What Next ?*].

—————— **Lady :** wife of Lord Touchwood and sister of Paul Pliant. A woman of low morals, in love with her husband's nephew, Mellefont.

—————— *Lord :* Mellefont's uncle [Congreve, *Double Dealer*].

—————— **Lady Frances :** wife of Sir George. An unsophisticated, innocent country girl.

—————— *Sir George :* the devoted husband of Lady Frances, and a perfect gentleman [Mrs. Cowley, *Belle's Stratagem*].

—————— **Peregrine :** an old East Indian, a relative of the Mowbrays [Scott, *St. Ronan's Well*].

Touchy, Tom : fond of 'taking the law of everybody' [Addison, *Spectator*].

'Toughey' : *see* Jo.

Toussaint l'Ouverture : the negro hero of the story, which is founded on the tragic career of this would-be liberator of his country, who had been born a slave [Harriet Martineau, *Hour and the Man*].

Toutrond, Martin : a Frenchman in London in 1844 [Morier, *Martin Toutrond*].

Towlinson, Mr. : a manservant in the Dombey family [Dickens, *Dombey and Son*].

Towneley, Lord and Lady : two characters in the comedy [Vanbrugh and Cibber, *Provoked Husband*].

Townly, Colonel : loving Berinthia, and seeking to win her by exciting her jealousy, he pays attention to her cousin Amanda, who will have nothing to do with him [Sheridan, *Trip to Scarborough*].

Tox, Miss Lucretia : the friend of Mrs. Chick. She at one time hoped to become the second Mrs. Dombey [Dickens, *Dombey and Son*].

Tozer : one of Paul Dombey's school-fellows, who wore very high collars [Dickens, *Dombey and Son*].

Trabb : a prosperous elderly tailor and undertaker [Dickens, *Great Expectations*].

Traddles, Thomas : ' the merriest and most miserable of the boys ' at Salem House [Dickens, *David Copperfield*].

Tradelove : a broker and one of Anne Lovely's guardians [Mrs. Centlivre, *Bold Stroke for a Wife*].

Traffick, Sir Jealous : father of Isabinda, for whom he provides a Spanish husband, but she prefers an English one [Mrs. Centlivre, *Busy-Body*].

Tram, Tom : the hero of a seventeenth century work of fiction, at one time very popular [*Mad Pranks of Tom Tram, Son-in-law to Mother Winter*, etc.].

Tramtrist, Sir : the name assumed by Sir Tristram during his visit to Ireland, whither he went to be healed of the wounds received in his fight with Sir Marhaus [Mallory, *History of Prince Arthur*].

Tranio : servant to Lucentio, Bianca's husband [Shakespeare, *Taming of the Shrew*.]

Transfer : an extortionate usurer of whom Sir George Wealthy borrows money [Foote, *The Minor*].

Transome, Harold : loved Esther Lyon, but she did not return his love.

—— *Mrs. :* mother of Harold, secretly married to the lawyer, Matthew Jermyn [George Eliot, *Felix Holt*].

Trapbois : a miser.

—— *Martha :* the miser's daughter, who marries Richie Moniplies [Scott, *Fortunes of Nigel*].

Travers, Louisa : married to the bigamist, Lord Davenant, whose first wife was Marianne Dormer.

—— *Sir Edmund :* the bachelor uncle and guardian of Lady Davenant. ¡An interfering old man who muddles his niece's matrimonial affairs [Cumberland, *Mysterious Husband*].

Tregarva, Paul : the poetic and radical gamekeeper of Squire Lavington [Charles Kingsley, *Yeast*].

Tremendous, Sir : a character in the farce, intended for the critic, John Dennis [Pope and Gay, *Three Hours after Marriage*] ; see also Appius.

Tremor, Lady : wife of Sir Luke. A woman of plebeian birth, upon which point she was extremely sensitive.

—— *Sir Luke :* a coward who made it a rule never to fight, whatever the provocation [Mrs. Inchbald, *Such Things Are*].

Tremydd ap Tremhidydd : a man possessed of abnormally penetrating sight, who could detect ' a mote in the sunbeam in any of the four quarters of the world ' [*Mabinogion*].

Trenmor : King of Morven and great-grandfather of Fingal [Ossian, *Fingal*].

Trent, Frederick : the dissipated, evil-natured brother of Little Nell.

————— *Nell :* her poor old grandfather's guardian angel, as she wanders with him from place to place, and stands between him and his passion for gambling [Dickens, *Old Curiosity Shop*].

Tresham, Mr. : the elder Osbaldistone's partner [Scott *Rob Roy*].

————— **Richard :** *see* Witherington.

————— **Mildred :** a girl of fourteen living with her brother Thorold. She is betrayed by her lover, the Earl of Mertoun.

————— *Thorold, Lord :* a young man, the sole guardian of a younger sister, who is betrayed by his friend and neighbour [R. Browning, *A Blot on the Scutcheon*].

Tressilian, Edmund : affianced to Amy Robsart, who deserts him for the Earl of Leicester, and is sacrificed to that nobleman's ambition [Scott, *Kenilworth*].

Trevellyn, Mary : the heroine of the poem [Clough, *Amours de Voyage*].

Trevelyan : the hero of a novel [Lady Dacre, *Trevelyan*].

Trevisan, Sir : the knight to whom Despair presented a rope wherewith to hang himself [Spenser, *Faëry Queene*].

Triamond : the son of Agape and husband of Canace [Spenser, *Faëry Queene*].

Triamour, Sir : the hero of an old English romance, probably based on a French one [*Early English Romances*].

Tribulation : a Dutch pastor, the dupe of Subtle and Face [Ben Jonson, *Alchemist*].

Trifle, Miss Penelope : a prim and precise old maid.

————— *Sir Penurious :* Penelope's brother. A teller of stupid, pointless stories.

————— *Sukey :* daughter of Sir Penurious. She marries Mr. Hartop [Foote, *The Knights*].

Trilby : an artist's model, in Paris [Du Maurier, *Trilby*] ; *see also* O'Ferral, Trilby.

Trim, Corporal : Uncle Toby's faithful servant [Sterne, *Tristram Shandy*].

Trinculo : a jester [Shakespeare, *Tempest*].

Trippet, Beau : bound ' never to draw sword in any cause '.

————— *Mrs. :* his wife, a frivolous woman devoted to dancing and cards [Garrick, *Lying Valet*].

Tristan, Sir : *see* Tristram, Sir.

Tristram, Sir : a Knight of the Round Table deputed to fetch Iseult of Brittany home to her affianced husband, Mark of Cornwall, who was Tristram's uncle. They both, in error, drink a love philtre and fall in love with one another [Mallory, *History of Prince Arthur*]. This story has been treated by Alfred Tennyson in *Idylls of the King : Launcelot and Elaine ; Guinevere ;* by Matthew Arnold, *Tristram and Iseult ;* Swinburne, *Sailing of the Swallow*].

Tristram Shandy : *see* Shandy, Tristram.

Troil, Magnus : an old udaller with two beautiful daughters. He is the 'Pirate'.

—————— *Minna and Brenda :* the beautiful daughters of Magnus Troil, the udaller of Zetland [Scott, *Pirate*].

Troilus : in love with Cressida, daughter of Chalchas, a priest. In an exchange of prisoners Cressida becomes the property of Diomed, and preferring him to Troilus forsakes the latter [Chaucer, *Canterbury Tales ;* Shakespeare, *Troilus and Cressida*].

Trompart : Braggadochio's squire, a lazy, cunning fellow [Spenser, *Faëry Queene*].

Troop, Disco : captain of the fishing-boat on which the millionaire's son goes to sea [Kipling, *Captain Courageous*].

Trotley, Sir John : an old-fashioned English gentleman, preferring the high standards of domestic virtue obtaining in his youth to the laxer morals of modern society [Garrick, *Bon Ton*].

Trotter, Job : servant to Mr. Alfred Jingle, too 'cute even for Sam Weller [Dickens, *Pickwick Papers*].

—————— **Nelly :** a fish-wife at old St. Ronan's [Scott, *St. Ronan's Well*].

'Trotters' : *see* Harris, Mr.

Trotty Veck : *see* Veck, Toby.

Trotwood, Miss Betsey : austere, hard-favoured and eccentric, but kindly, and a true friend to David, whose great-aunt she is [Dickens, *David Copperfield*]

Troxartas : King of the mice [Parnell, *Battle of the Frogs and Mice*].

Troy, Sergeant : the villain who married and then deserted Bathsheba Everdene [Hardy, *Far from the Madding Crowd*].

Trueworth : the friend of Fondlove and brother of Lydia [Knowles, *Love-Chase*].

Trull, Dolly : 'so taken up with stealing hearts' she has no time for other thefts [Gay, *Beggar's Opera*].

Trulliber, Parson : a most objectionable parson, the exact opposite to Parson Adams [Fielding, *Joseph Andrews*].

Trundle, Mr. : the young man who marries Isabella Wardle [Dickens, *Pickwick Papers*].

Trunnion, Commodore Hawser : a one-eyed naval officer who, upon retiring from active service, fits his house up like a ship [Smollett, *Peregrine Pickle*].

Trusty, Mrs. : landlady of the *Queen's Arms*, Romford, who sheltered Bess, the beggar's daughter [Knowles, *Beggar of Bethnal Green*].

Tryamour, Sir : a model of chivalry and the hero of an old metrical romance.

Tryanon : heroine of a fifteenth century romance, and the bride of Sir Launfal [Chester, *Sir Launfal*].

Tryphon : the sea-god's doctor [Spenser, *Faëry Queene*].

Tubal : a Jew and the friend of Shylock [Shakespeare, *Merchant of Venice*].

Tuck, Friar : the chaplain and steward of Robin Hood [Scott, *Ivanhoe*].

Tucker, Dan : the subject of a negro song supposed to refer to Captain Daniel Tucker of Virginia.

Tug, Tom : the hero of a musical comedietta [Charles Dibdin, *Waterman*].

Tulkinghorn, Mr. : a solicitor, and the legal adviser of Sir Leicester Dedlock. He is murdered by a French waiting-maid [Dickens, *Bleak House*].

Tulliver, Maggie : the heroine, in love with Wakem and loved by him.

—— *Mr. and Mrs. :* father and mother of the hero and heroine. Mr. Tulliver dies from excitement over a dispute with Wakem, his daughter's lover.

—— *Tom :* Maggie's brother. Both are drowned, swept down by a tidal wave on the Floss [George Eliot, *Mill on the Floss*].

Tupman, Mr. Tracy : a member of the Corresponding Society of the Pickwick Club, who falls in love with every pretty girl he meets [Dickens, *Pickwick Papers*].

Turnbull, Mr. Thomas : a schoolmaster and smuggler, known by the name of Tom Turnpenny [Scott, *Redgauntlet*].

Turnpenny, Tom : *see* Turnbull, Mr. Thomas.

Turpin : a churlish, inhospitable knight who is unknighted by King Arthur for his lack of courtesy [Spenser, *Faëry Queene*].

—— **Dick :** a noted highwayman who is introduced into the novel [Ainsworth, *Rookwood*].

Turquine, Sir : a valorous knight who at one time held sixty-four of King Arthur's knights captive. He was challenged and slain by Sir Launcelot, who set the captives free [Mallory, *History of Prince Arthur*].

Turveydrop, Mr : 'a very gentlemanly man, celebrated almost everywhere for his deportment'. He was a dancing-master.

—— *Prince :* his son, named after the Prince Regent. He married Caddy Jellyby [Dickens, *Bleak House*].

Twangdillo: a one-legged and one-eyed fiddler [Somerville, *Hobbinol*].

Tweedledum=Prince of Wales; **Tweedledee**=Duke of Marlborough [J. Byron, in a satirical squib, c. 1750]. Also twins in 'Lewis Carroll's' *Alice in Wonderland*, 1865.

Twigtythe, The Rev. Mr.: a clergyman living at Fasthwaite Farm [Scott, *Waverley*].

Twineall, The Hon. Mr.: a young man who goes to India, fully expecting to win his way to preferment through his charm of manner, etc., but always saying the wrong things, and offending people in their tenderest spots, ends by finding himself in prison [Mrs. Inchbald, *Such Things Are*].

Twist, Oliver: a nameless orphan, born in a workhouse, he makes his way to London and falls into the hands of thieves. The people whose house he is made to break into rescue him, to discover that they are his relatives and natural protectors [Dickens, *Oliver Twist*].

Twitcher, Jemmy: a character in the play, which the public afterwards allotted to John, Earl of Sandwich [Gay, *Beggar's Opera*].

Tybalt: in love with Laura, Duke Gondibert's niece [Davenant, *Gondibert*].
—— cousin to Juliet. A young and fiery Veronese [Shakespeare, *Romeo and Juliet*].

Tyler, Wat: an honest blacksmith of Essex, whose daughter Alice was insulted by the royal tax-collectors. His story is made the subject of a tragedy [Southey, *Wat Tyler*].

Tylwyth Teg: a family of beneficent fairies whose delight it is to benefit humanity [*Mabinogion*].

Tyrrel, Francis: in love with Miss Aubrey, on whose behalf he fought a duel with Lord Courtland [Cumberland, *Fashionable Lover*].
—— **Frank:** really Martigny, Earl of Etherington, in love with Clara Mowbray [Scott, *St. Ronan's Well*].

Tyson, Kate: in love with and marries Frank Cheeney [Reeve, *Parted*].

Ubaldo and Ricardo: Honoria, Queen of Hungary, wishing to tempt Sophia's virtue, sent Ubaldo and Ricardo to her. Detecting the object of their visit she had them put in confinement [Massinger, *The Picture*].

Udeschini, Cardinal: a snuff-taking ecclesiastic [Harland, *Cardinal's Snuff-box*].

Udolpho: the hero of a romance [Mrs. Radcliffe, *Mysteries of Udolpho*].

Ulfin : a page [Davenant, *Gondibert*].

Ulin : an enchantress who had power over evil doers, but none over the faithful [Ridley, *Tales of the Genii*].

Ullin's Daughter : the subject of a ballad ; she eloped with the chief of Ulva's Isle, and was drowned whilst being rowed over Lochgyle [Campbell, *Lord Ullin's Daughter*].

Ulric : the son of Werner, who saved the Count of Stralenheim from the river Oder only to murder him afterwards in revenge for wrongs received at his hands [Byron, *Werner*].

Ulrica : an old Sybil at Torquilstone; also known as Dame Urfried [Scott, *Ivanhoe*].

—— the mother of Hereward's affianced bride, Bertha. Also known as Martha [Scott, *Count Robert of Paris*].

—— unacknowledged daughter of Ernest of Fridberg, the ' prisoner '. Dressed as a man she aids her father to escape [Stirling, *Prisoner of State*].

Ulysses : King of Ithica. He forms the subject of many literary productions, notably a play [Rowe, *Ulysses*], and a poem [Alfred Tennyson, *Ulysses*].

Umbriel : a sprite who, upon the loss of her lock of hair, supplies Belinda with a large supply of sobs and sighs and lamentations [Pope, *Rape of the Lock*].

Una=' the one true Faith or Truth ', the heroine of the poem, protected throughout her long wanderings by a lion [Spenser, *Faëry Queene*].

Uncas : the son of Chingachcook, surnamed Deer-foot [Cooper, *Last of the Mohicans ; Pathfinder ;* and *Pioneer*].

Uncle Remus : *see* Remus, Uncle.

—— **Toby :** *see* Toby, Uncle ; also Shandy, Captain.

—— **Tom :** *see* Tom, Uncle.

Upland, Jack : the hero of a religious song, popular in the days of Richard II [Wright's *Political Songs*].

Urania=the Countess of Pembroke [Sidney, *Colin Clout 's Come Home Again*].

Urfried, Dame : *see* Ulrica.

Urgan : a human child brought up in elfland and restored to human shape by the sign of the cross being made thrice upon her forehead [Scott, *Lady of the Lake*].

Uriel : the great archangel ' regent of the sun ' [Milton, *Paradise Lost ;* Longfellow, *Golden Legend*].

Urien : the foster-father of Madoc. He followed Madoc to North America [Southey, *Madoc*].

Urre, Sir : a Knight of the Round Table whose wounds were healed by the touch of Sir Launcelot's hands [*Arthurian Cycle*].

Ursula : a foolish old duenna who prided herself upon her dancing [Bickerstaff, *Padlock*].

—— **Sister :** the name by which Lady Margaret Hautlieu was known at St. Bride's [Scott, *Castle Dangerous*].

Utha : the beautiful daughter of Herman, betrothed to Frothal, whose life she saved [Ossian, *Carric-Thura*].

Uthal : son of Larthmor, King of Berrathon. He dethroned his father, but was killed in fight against Ossian and Toscar [Ossian, *Berrathon*].

Uther : father of King Arthur [Geoffrey, *History of Britain*].

Vainlove : a young man about town [Congreve, *Old Bachelor*].

Valantia, Count : an absurd creature, in love with the Marchioness Merida, whom he makes his wife upon condition that she will undertake not to love him [Mrs. Inchbald, *Child of Nature*].

Valdes : one of Dr. Faustus's friends, who induces him to sell his soul to the devil [Marlowe, *Dr. Faustus*].

Valence, Sir Aymer de : Sir John de Walton's lieutenant at Douglas Castle [Scott, *Castle Dangerous*].

Valentine : one of King Pepin's twin nephews [*Valentine and Orson*].

—— eldest son of Sir Sampson Legend, who feigns madness to avoid paying his debts [Congreve, *Love for Love*].

—— in love with Cellide, who does not return his love [J. Fletcher, *Mons. Thomas*].

—— a foolish spendthrift [J. Fletcher, *Wit Without Money*].

—— one of the two gentlemen of Verona [Shakespeare, *Two Gentlemen of Verona*].

—— one of the Duke of Illyria's train [Shakespeare, *Twelfth Night*].

Valentinian : a man of fine temperament ruined by self-indulgence [Beaumont and Fletcher, *Valentinian*].

Valère : betrothed to Angelica, who gives him a picture from which he is never to part. He loses it at the gaming table, Angelica, disguised, being the winner of it. In the end the 'gamster' is cured of his vice [Mrs. Centlivre, *Gamester*].

Valeria : a woman of masculine mind and tastes [Mrs. Centlivre, *Basset-Table*].

—— friend of Horatia and sister of Valerius [Whitehead, *Roman Father*].

Valerio : a young Neapolitan married to Evanthe [J. Fletcher, *Wife for a Month*].

Valerius : a young Roman who is a convert to Christianity [Lockhart, *Valerius*].

—————— the brother of Valeria and in love with his sister's friend Horatia [Whitehead, *Roman Father*].

Valiant-for-Truth : one of Christian's company on his journey to the Celestial City [Bunyan, *Pilgrim's Progress*].

Valirian : the husband of St. Cecilia, executed for his Christianity [Chaucer, *Canterbury Tales : Second Nun's Tale*].

Vallière, The Duchess de la : the heroine of the play [Lytton, *Duchess de la Vallière*].

Valverde : Pizarro's secretary, who is in love with Elvira, and saves her life [Sheridan, *Pizarro*].

Vamp : a bookseller who thought the real merit of a book lay in its 'get up ' [Foote, *Author*].

Van Artevelde, Clara : sister of Philip, the beloved of Walter d'Arlon [Sir Henry Taylor, *Philip Van Artevelde*].

Vanda : wife of Baldric, who appears before the Lady Eveline Berenger in the haunted chamber [Scott, *Betrothed*].

Vanderdecken : a character in the play resuscitated by Sir Henry Irving [Fitzbald, *Flying Dutchman*].

Vandunke : the drunken burgomaster of Bruges [J. Fletcher, *Beggar's Bush*].

Vane, Frank : parliamentary candidate in opposition to Peter Mogg [Sterling, *Election*].

Vanessa=Esther Vanhomrigh [Swift, *Cadenus and Vanessa*].

Vanoc, Sir : one of the Knights of the Round Table, and Merlin's son [*Arthurian Cycle*].

Vanwelt, Ian : supposed to be a suitor for the hand of Rose Flammock [Scott, *Betrothed*].

Vapid : said to be intended by the author for a portrait of himself [Reynolds, *Dramatist*].

Varbel : the hungry squire of Count Floreski [Kemble, *Lodoiska*].

Varden, Dolly : the daughter of Gabriel, who was overwhelmed with lovers. She married Joe Willet.

—————— *Gabriel :* a Clerkenwell locksmith. A frank and kindly man, the father of Dolly, who, during the Gordon riots declined, at the risk of his life, to pick the lock of Newgate Prison.

—————— *Mrs. :* Gabriel's wife ; a lady of uncertain temper [Dickens, *Barnaby Rudge*].

Varley, Lady Helen : sister of Hugh Flaxman and niece of Lady Charlotte Wynnstay [Mrs. Humphry Ward, *Robert Elsmere*].

W.W.F.   U

Varney : Master of the Horse to the Earl of Leicester [Scott, *Kenilworth*].

Vathek : the grandson of Haroun-al-Raschid, and ninth Caliph of his race. In anger ' one of his eyes became so terrible that whoever looked at it either swooned or died ' [Beckford, *Vathek*].

Vaudracour : the hero of a love poem [Wordsworth, *Vaudracour and Julia*].

Vaughan, Cecilia : the heroine [Longfellow, *Kavanagh*].

Vaux, Roland de : the knight who broke the spell which condemned Gyneth, King Arthur's daughter, to an enchanted sleep which lasted 500 years [Scott, *Bridal of Triermain*].

Vavasour : a character in the novel [Beaconsfield, *Tancred*].

Veal, Mrs. : a fictitious person whom Defoe pretended had appeared before Mrs. Bargrave of Canterbury the day following her (Mrs. Veal's) death [prefixed by Defoe to Drelincourt's *Consolations Against the Fear of Death*].

Vecchio, Peter : a teacher of music and of Latin [J. Fletcher, *Chances*].

Veck, Toby : ticket-porter and odd job man known as Trotty [Dickens, *Chimes*].

Velinspeck : the manager of a provincial theatre to whom Stuffy applies for the post of prompter [Matthews, *At Home*].

Velvet, The Rev. Morphine : a preacher who fed ' his audience with milk well sugared ' [Warren, *Ten Thousand a Year*].

Veneering, Mr. and Mrs. : a wealthy parvenu and his wife [Dickens, *Our Mutual Friend*].

Venner, Elsie : the subject of the story. Her mother dies at Elsie's birth, bitten by a rattlesnake, and the virus enters her child's nature, producing most weird results [Holmes, *Elsie Venner*].

Ventidius : Marc Antony's general [Dryden, *All for Love*].

Venus, Mr. : a bird and animal stuffer living in Clerkenwell [Dickens, *Our Mutual Friend*].

Verdant Green : *see* Green, Verdant.

Verdone : Champernal's nephew [J. Fletcher, *Little French Lawyer*].

Verdugo : a captain serving under the Governor of Segovia [J. Fletcher, *Pilgrim*].

Vere, Lady Clara Vere de : the subject o a poem [Alfred Tennyson, *Lady Clara Vere de Vere*].

Verges : a watchman of the old school [Shakespeare, *Much Ado About Nothing*].

Verisopht, Lord Frederick : a dissipated young nobleman, the friend of Sir Mulberry Hawk [Dickens, *Nicholas Nickleby*].

Vernon, Diana : the beautiful mistress of Osbaldistone Hall, who, in secret, favoured the cause of the Stuarts [Scott, *Rob Roy*].

Versatile, Sir George : an amiable man, but weak, so that he varies according to the company he is in. He marries Maria Delaval [Holcroft, *He's Much to Blame*].

Vertaigne : the father of Lamira and Beaupré [J. Fletcher, *Little French Lawyer*].

Vesey, Georgina : pretty, vain, and shallow. Married to Sir Frederick Blount.

—— *Sir John :* a poor and worldly baronet, father of Georgina. He wanted his daughter to marry Alfred Evelyn for his money [Lytton, *Money*].

Vibrate, Lady : the extravagant, frivolous, excitable wife of Lord Vibrate.

—— *Lady Jane :* their daughter ; good and amiable. She marries Delaval.

—— *Lord :* a shilly-shallying, irresolute man. [Holcroft, *He's Much to Blame*].

Vicar of Bray : *see* Bray, Vicar of.

—— **of Wakefield :** *see* Primrose, Rev. Dr.

—— **of Wrexhill :** *see* Wrexhill, Vicar of.

Victor Amadeus : the fierce, unscrupulous King of Sardinia, who abdicated in favour of his son, and then tried to go back on his act [R. Browning, *King Victor and King Charles Emmanuel*].

Victoria, Donna : the wife of Don Carlos [Mrs. Cowley, *Bold Stroke for a Husband*].

Victorian : the hero ; a student of Alcala [Longfellow, *Spanish Student*].

Videna : wife of Gorboduc and the mother of Ferrex and Porrex [Norton and Buckhurst, *Gorboduc*].

Villers, Mr. : a gentleman professing an unbounded contempt for all womankind [Mrs. Cowley, *Belle's Stratagem*].

Villiard : a villain. Charles Belmont rescued Fidelia from his clutches [Edward Moore, *Foundling*].

Vincent, Jenkin : an apprentice known as ' Jin Vin ', in love with Margaret Ramsay [Scott, *Fortunes of Nigel*].

Vincentio : Duke of Vienna, who, assuming the guise of a monk, watches secretly the practices of his various officers and servants [Shakespeare, *Measure for Measure*].

—— betrothed to Evadne. He listens to false tales as to her virtue, and casts her off, but eventually is convinced of his mistake and marries her [Sheil, *Evadne ; or, The Statue*].

Vincentio, Don : a musical devotee who was much irritated by Olivia de Zuniga asserting that of all instruments the Jew's harp was the best [Mrs. Cowley, *Bold Stroke for a Husband*].

Vincy, Frederick : brother of Rosamond, whose character is ruined by the expectation of wealth.

—————— *Rosamond :* the shallow, selfish and obstinate girl who marries Lydgate, the young doctor [George Eliot, *Middlemarch*].

Viola : one of the two daughters of Archas 'the loyal subject' [J. Fletcher, *Loyal Subject*].

—————— one of the poet's most attractive heroines ; unselfish, loyal, brave [Shakespeare, *Twelfth Night*].

Violante : the reputed mother of Pompilia, who is killed by Guido Franceschini [R. Browning, *Ring and the Book*].

—————— **Donna :** intended for a nun, she falls in love with Don Felix and marries him [Mrs. Centlivre, *The Wonder*].

—————— betrothed to Don Alonzo, but forced by the king to marry Henriquey. The latter is killed in battle, so the lovers come together at last [Dryden, *Don Sebastian*].

—————— reputed wife of Don Henrique [J. Fletcher, *Spanish Curate*].

—————— one of the heroines. A combination of grace and nobility, energy and courage [Lytton, *My Novel*].

Violet : the wilful and impulsive but lovable heroine of the novel [Black, *Madcap Violet*].

—————— the ward of Lady Arundel and in love with Norman, a 'sea-captain', who turns out to be her guardian's son by a former marriage [Lytton, *Sea-Captain*].

Violetta : a Portuguese lady married to Belfield, who deserts her. Being shipwrecked and cast ashore near her husband's estate, his villainy is discovered and the husband and wife are reconciled [Cumberland, *Brothers*].

Viper, Dr. : an Irish clergyman of the name of Jackson, against whom the dramatist harboured a grudge for suppressing his play 'The Trip to Calais' [Foote, *Capuchin*].

Vipont : a Knight of St. John [Scott, *Ivanhoe*].

Virgilia : in the play Virgilia is the wife of Coriolanus ; historically this is incorrect, as Volumnia was her name [Shakespeare, *Coriolanus*].

Virginia : *see* Appius and Virginia.

Virginius : father of the Roman maiden Virginia, whom he killed with his own hand rather than have her delivered up to Appius as his slave [Knowles, *Virginius* ;

Macaulay, *Lays of Ancient Rome; Virginia*] and many more.

Virolet : the hero, married to both Juliana and Martia [J. Fletcher, *Double Marriage*].

Vittoria : the *prima donna*, formerly known as Sandra Belloni. She joins in the intrigues of the Italian Revolution of 1848 and marries a noble Italian, Carlo Ammiani, who is killed [George Meredith, *Vittoria*].

Vivian Grey : *see* Grey, Vivian.

Viviane : daughter of Dyonas. Merlin fell in love with her, and she imprisoned him in the forest of Brécéliande. She is generally known as the ' Lady of the Lake ' [*Merlin*].

Vivien : tried unsuccessfully to seduce King Arthur, but induced Merlin to tell her the secret of his power, which, having learnt, she used against himself [Alfred Tennyson, *Idylls of the King : Vivien*].

Voadicia or Boadicea : the British ' warrior Queen ' who defied the Romans, but was at last defeated by Suetonius Paulinus, and took poison [Drayton, *Polyolbion* ; Cowper, *Boadicea*].

Volante : witty and full of life, and in love with Count Montalban [Tobin, *Honeymoon*].

Volpone : a rich Venetian nobleman, by character a crafty hypocrite [Ben Jonson, *Volpone; or, The Fox*].

Volscius, Prince : in love with Parthenope, and in a dispute with Prince Prettyman he champions her beauty as against that of Cloris [Duke of Buckingham, *Rehearsal*].

Voltimand : a courtier at Elsinore [Shakespeare, *Hamlet*].

Volumnia : Shakespeare gives this as the name of the hero's mother; historically it was that of his wife [Shakespeare, *Coriolanus*].

Vortigern and Rowena : the hero and heroine of a drama which the author tried to pass off as the work of Shakespeare [Ireland, *Vortigern and Rowena*].

Vox, Valentine : the ventriloquist hero of the novel [Cockton, *Valentine Vox, the Ventriloquist*].

Vrience, King : a Knight of the Round Table, married to Arthur's half-sister Morgan le Fay [Mallory, *History of Prince Arthur*].

Vyet, Childe : the hero of a tragic ballad printed by Maidment, Buchan and Jamieson.

Wabun : the son of Mudjekeewis [Longfellow, *Hiawatha*].

Wackbairn, Mr. : the schoolmaster at Libberton [Scott, *Heart of Midlothian*].

Wackles, Mrs.: owner of a small day-school for girls at Chelsea.

―――― *The Misses:* her daughters, who assist her in her educational labours [Dickens, *Old Curiosity Shop*].

Waddell, Major: a retired Indian officer who marries Bell Black [Susan E. Ferrier, *Inheritance*].

Wade, Miss: a self-tormenting, unhappy-tempered woman, who entices Tattycoram away from the Meagleses [Dickens, *Little Dorrit*].

Wadman, Widow: sets her cap at Uncle Toby [Sterne, *Tristram Shandy*].

Wagner: servant and friend of Faustus [Marlowe, *Dr. Faustus*].

Waife, Gentleman: an old man who, to screen a worthless son, undergoes a sentence of transportation and the stigma of crime [Lytton, *What Will He Do With It?*].

Waitwell: Edward Mirabell's footman, who makes up as Sir Roland and makes love to Lady Wishfort [Congreve, *Way of the World*].

Wakefield, Harry: the English drover who is killed by Robin Oig [Scott, *Two Drovers*].

―――― Vicar of: *see* Primrose, Rev. Doctor.

Wakem, Philip: in love with Maggie Tulliver [George Eliot, *Mill on the Floss*].

Wakeman, Sir George: physician to Queen Henrietta Maria [Scott, *Peveril of the Peak*].

Waldbourg, Count: married to Adelaide, who after a time eloped. Waldbourg then led a roving life and was only known as 'the stranger'. In his wanderings he met his contrite wife and they were reconciled [B. Thompson, *The Stranger*].

Waldeck, Martin: a miner and the hero of Lovel's story [Scott, *Antiquary*].

Waldegrave, Florinda: the pampered child of Lady Elizabeth Waldegrave and step-daughter to the Chief of Glenroy. Beautiful but unprincipled and pleasure-loving.

―――― *Lady Elizabeth:* an affected, insincere and extravagant woman, who became the second wife of the Chief of Glenroy [Susan E. Ferrier, *Destiny*].

―――― Henry: in command of the British forces who aided in the extirpation of the Snake Indians.

―――― *Henry, the Younger:* handed over to Albert of Wyoming, and afterwards married to Gertrude.

―――― *Julia:* wife of Henry. Bound, together with her child, to a tree, but released and cared for by one of the Indians. She died but her child was saved [Campbell, *Gertrude of Wyoming*].

Walkingshaw, Miss: mistress of Charles Edward, the Young Pretender [Scott, *Redgauntlet*].

Waller: the lover, and afterwards the husband of Widow Green's maid, Lydia [Knowles, *Love Chase*].

Walley, Richard: a regicide [Scott, *Peveril of the Peak*].

Walmers, Master Harry: a little boy of eight, who falls in love with a cousin of six and sets out with her for Gretna Green [Dickens, *Holly Tree*].

Walsingham: betrothed to Helen Mowbray. He believes her faithless and breaks off the connexion, then discovers he has wrongfully accused her, and they marry [Knowles, *Woman's Wit*].

Walter: Marquis of Saluzzo, married to Grisilda, the daughter of a peasant [Chaucer, *Canterbury Tales : The Clerk's Tale*].

—— **Master:** the Earl of Rochdale and father of Julia, to whom he had acted as guardian [Knowles, *Hunchback*].

—— of Varila: a vassal of the Landgrave Lewis [Charles Kingsley, *Saint's Tragedy*].

Waltheof, Father: a grey friar—the Duchess of Rothesay's Confessor [Scott, *Fair Maid of Perth*].

Wamba: Cedric the Saxon's jester [Scott, *Ivanhoe*].

Wandering Jew: *see* Jew, The Wandering.

Warden, Michael: good-looking, thoughtless and extravagant, he loved Marion Jeddler, and married her [Dickens, *Battle of Life*].

—— **Henry:** *alias* Henry Wellwood, a protestant preacher [Scott, *Monastery*].

Wardle, Mr.: of Manor Farm, Dingley Dell. A friend of Mr. Pickwick and Hospitality personified.

—— *Emily :* his daughter, who marries Mr. Trundle.

—— *Isabella :* another daughter, who marries Mr. Snodgrass.

—— *Rachael :* his sister, who elopes with Mr. Jingle [Dickens, *Pickwick Papers*].

Waring = Mr. Alfred Domett, a friend of the poet's [R. Browning, *Waring*].

—— **Sir Walter:** an incompetent Justice of the Peace who was, in his judgments, swayed by his personal leanings [Dudley, *Woodman*].

Warman: Robin Hood's treacherous steward, who gave information against him to his uncle, Prior Gilbert Hood [Skelton, *Downfall of Robert, Earl of Huntington*].

Warner: the steward of Sir Charles Cropland [Colman the Younger, *Poor Gentleman*].

—— **Sybil:** the heroine of the romance [Lytton, *Sybil Warner*].

Warren, Widow : a widow of forty, aping the manners of a girl [Holcroft, *Road to Ruin*].

Warrington, Capt. George : a barrister, the true friend of Arthur Pendennis. [Thackeray, *Pendennis*].

———— **Madam Esmond :** mother of the Virginians, who ruled like a queen on her own estate in Virginia [Thackeray, *Virginians*].

Wart, Thomas : one of Falstaff's recruits [Shakespeare, *Henry IV*, pt. ii.].

Warwick, Diana : a beautiful Irish girl who, married to an unsympathetic husband, is tempted to live her own life apart from him, meddles in politics, and becomes the talk of the town. In the end she finds rest for head and heart in a happy second marriage [George Meredith, *Diana of the Crossways*].

Wasp : a character supposed to have been acted by the author himself [Ben Jonson, *Alchemist*].

Wat Tyler : *see* Tyler, Wat.

Waterproof, Will : the subject of a poem [Alfred Tennyson, *Will Waterproof's Lyrical Monologue*].

Waters, Childe : the subject of an ancient ballad, which tells of a much-wronged woman who follows her betrayer in the guise of a page [Percy, *Reliques : Childe Waters*].

———— **Young :** a ballad supposed to refer to the history of the Earl of Murray, who was murdered by the Earl of Huntley in 1592 [Percy, *Reliques : Young Waters*].

Wattle, Captain : one of the characters in a ballad [Dibdin, *Captain Wattle and Miss Roe*].

Waverley, Capt. Edward : the hero, who entered the service of the young chevalier. He marries Rose Bradwardine.

———— *Richard :* Edward Waverley's father [Scott, *Waverley*].

Wayland, Launcelot = Wayland Smith. A farrier in the vale of Whitehorse [Scott, *Kenilworth*].

Wealthy, Sir George : son of Sir William, who first acts as protector to, and then marries, his cousin Lucy Wealthy.

———— *Sir William :* a city merchant whose only son is a spendthrift [Foote, *The Minor*].

Weazel, Timothy : an attorney who acts as Penruddock's agent [Cumberland, *Wheel of Fortune*].

'Weevle' : *see* Jobling, Tony.

Wegg, Silas : a dishonourable ballad-monger and fruit-seller engaged by Mr. Boffin to read aloud to him [Dickens, *Our Mutual Friend*].

Weir, Major : Sir Robert Redgauntlet's pet baboon [Scott, *Redgauntlet*].

Weisspriess, Captain : a famous duelling captain in the Austrian army. A mixture of many passions, bad and good [George Meredith, *Vittoria*].

Welford : a suitor for the hand of the 'Scornful Lady' [Beaumont and Fletcher, *Scornful Lady*].

Wellborn, Francis : son of Sir John, the much respected and wealthy Northamptonshire landowner. Francis does his best to squander his patrimony, but reforms and enters the army [Massinger, *New Way to Pay Old Debts*].

Weller, Samuel : boots at the *White Hart Inn.* Here he meets Mr. Pickwick, who, liking his looks, engages him as his servant. His subsequent devotion to his master make him invaluable to that gentleman.

———— *Susan :* Sam's step-mother, formerly Mrs. Clarke. Her character made old Tony warn his son to 'beware o' widders all your life'.

———— **Tony :** father of Sam ; a heavy, mottle-faced stage-coachman plying between London and Dorking [Dickens, *Pickwick Papers*].

Wemmuck John : Mr. Jaggers's confidential clerk, noted for his 'castle' at Walworth [Dickens, *Great Expectations*].

Wendover, Roger : the scholarly but cynical squire of Murewell ; first the enemy, afterwards the friend of Robert Elsmere [Mrs. Humphry Ward, *Robert Elsmere*].

Wenlock, Wild : a relative of Sir Hugo de Lacy, constable of Chester. He is beheaded by the rebels [Scott, *Betrothed*].

Wenonah : daughter of Nokomis and mother of Hiawatha [Longfellow, *Hiawatha*].

Wentworth = George Canning, the English statesman [Ward, *De Vere ; or, Man of Independence*].

———— **Captain :** a naval officer. The lover and after-wards husband of Anne Elliot [Jane Austen, *Persuasion*].

———— **Eva :** a pure and noble woman deceived by her lover, De Courcy [Maturin, *Women*].

———— **Cecilia, Dora and Leonora :** the aunts of the Perpetual Curate.

———— *Jack :* the curate's handsome, clever, but un-principled eldest brother.

———— *Rev. Frank C. :* the Perpetual Curate of St. Roques', shocking the old-fashioned inhabitants of Carlingford by his High-Church practices, but winning their respect and affection at last by his unswerving devotion to duty. He becomes rector of Carlingford.

Wentworth, *Rev. Gerald :* the Rector of Wentworth, who goes
over to Rome.

———— *Squire :* the father of the Perpetual Curate [Mrs.
Oliphant, *Chronicles of Carlingford : Perpetual Curate*].

Werner : Count of Siegendorf, and father of Ulric. For
twelve years he wanders the world, a beggar, through
the enmity of Count Stralenheim. At last he robs
his enemy, who is murdered by Ulric the very next
day [Byron, *Werner*].

Western, Sophia : virtuous and beautiful, she is the good
angel of Tom Jones, whom she marries.

———— *Squire :* a jovial, ignorant, fox-hunting country
gentleman, devoted to his daughter Sophia [Fielding,
Tom Jones].

Westlock, John : at one time pupil of Mr. Pecksniff, he
marries Ruth Pinch, Tom's sister [Dickens, *Martin
Chuzzlewit*].

Weston, Mr. : the kindly husband of ' poor Miss Taylor ',
Emma's governess and friend.

———— *Mrs. :* had been Emma's governess and remained
her friend. She was step-mother to Frank Churchill
[Jane Austen, *Emma*].

Wetheral, Stephen : surnamed ' Stephen Steelheart ', a
follower of Lord Waldemar Fitzurse [Scott, *Ivanhoe*].

Weyburn, Matthew : known very commonly as ' Matey '
Weyburn. The private secretary of Lord Ormont,
who elopes with Lady Ormont, with whom he had been
in love when a schoolboy [George Meredith, *Lord
Ormont and His Aminta*].

Whang : a Chinese miller who by constant economy had
amassed considerable wealth. The story tells how
his greed for more resulted in the loss of the whole
[Goldsmith, *Citizen of the World*].

Whiffers, Mr. : a footman who is one of the guests at the
' swarry ' to which Sam Weller is invited at Bath
[Dickens, *Pickwick Papers*].

Whiffle, Captain : a fop adorned in ' silk, lace, and diamond
buckles ' [Smollett, *Roderick Random*].

Whimple, Mrs. : a lodging-house keeper at Mill Pond
Bank, Chinks's Basin [Dickens, *Great Expectations*].

Whimsey : a kind-hearted, funny old man, the father of
Charlotte and ' Young ' Whimsey.

———— *Charlotte :* a pretty girl, in love with Monford
[Cobb, *First Floor*].

Whisker : Mr. Garland's pony [Dickens, *Old Curiosity
Shop*].

Whiskerandos, Don Ferolo : the lover of Tilburina [Puff,
Spanish Armada, embodied by Sheridan in *The Critic*].

White Lady of Avenvel : *see* Avenel.

Whitecraft, Dame : John's pretty wife.

—— *John :* innkeeper at Altringham [Scott, *Peveril of the Peak*].

Whitford, Vernon : a relation of Sir Willoughby Patterne's who lives at Patterne Hall. An athlete, a student, and a keen observer He falls in love with Clara Middleton with happy results [George Meredith, *The Egoist*].

Whittle, Thomas : an old man who courts a young widow of twenty-three, and, in order to achieve his purpose, tries to assume the garb and airs of a young coxcomb [Garrick, *Irish Widow*].

Wickfield, Agnes : the daughter of a Canterbury lawyer, and his housekeeper. A woman of sterling character, who becomes the second Mrs. David Copperfield.

—— *Mr. :* Miss Betsey Trotwood's legal adviser, who is almost ruined by his dishonest clerk, Uriah Heep [Dickens, *David Copperfield*].

Wickham, Mrs. : the wife of a waiter, and one of Paul Dombey's nurses [Dickens, *Dombey and Son*].

Widdrington, Roger : the gallant squire, who, 'when his legs were smitten off, he fought upon his stumps' [*Chevy Chase*].

Wife of Bath : one of the pilgrims who tells one of the 'Tales' [Chaucer, *Canterbury Tales*; also the subject of a comedy, Gay, *Wife of Bath*].

—— **The :** the subject of a tragedy [Knowles, *The Wife*].

Wigalois : the son of one of the Knights of the Round Table [*Wigalois ; or, The Knight of the Wheel*].

Wild Boar of Ardennes = William de la Marck [Scott, *Quentin Durward*].

—— **Jonathan :** a heartless villain who had six wives— both Defoe and Fielding based romances on the story of his life.

Wildair, Sir Harry : a gay young rake that the author twice takes as his hero [Farquhar, *Sir Harry Wildair*, and *The Constant Couple*].

Wildenhaim, Amelia : the baron's daughter.

—— *Baron :* seduces a girl in his youth, then leaves her to starve. Years afterwards their child, grown up, begs of him in the streets. This leads to his marrying the woman he had wronged. [Mrs. Inchbald, *Lover's Vows*].

Wildfire, Madge : the mad daughter of Madge Murdochson [Scott, *Heart of Midlothian*].

Wilding, Jack : a young Oxonian, the hero of the comedy [Foote, *The Liar*].

Wilding, Maria : the clever and sprightly daughter of Sir
Jasper, in love with Beaufort.
———— Sir Jasper : a wealthy fox-hunting squire ; very
ignorant.
———— Young : Sir Jasper's son [Murphy, Citizen].
———— the leading character, often taken by Garrick in
his version of this play, which he called ' The Game-
sters ' [Shirley, The Gamester].
Wildrake : a regular country squire, fond of horses and
dogs, and unconsciously of his old playmate, Constance
Fondlove, whom he   marries   [Knowles, Love-
Chase].
———— Roger : a Royalist, and a ne'er-do-weel [Scott,
Woodstock].
Wilfer, Bella : wayward, wilful and giddy, but cured of her
faults by her love for John Harmon.
———— Lavinia : Bella's younger sister ; a sharp and
saucy girl.
———— Mrs. : Reginald's tall, angular, domineering wife.
———— Reginald : known as ' the cherub ', a spiritless,
hen-pecked clerk [Dickens, Our Mutual Friend].
Wilford : secretary to Sir Edward Mortimer, and in love
with the poacher's daughter, Barbara Rawbold. He
detects a crime committed by Mortimer, years before,
and flies from his presence, only to have his footsteps
dogged from place to place [Colman the Younger, Iron
Chest].
———— in love with his sister's companion, Emily, whom
he marries, against the wishes of his father [Dudley,
Woodman].
———— Lord : son of Lord Woodville, in love with the
Beggar's daughter of Bethnal Green. She proved
to be his cousin [Knowles, Beggar of Bethnal Green].
———— : he desired ' the finest hound, the finest horse, and
the finest wife in the three kingdoms '. He was for
long supposed to be the Earl of Rochdale, but he
proved to be a nobody and the Hunchback was the
Earl [Knowles, Hunchback].
Wilfred : the ' fool ' amongst the six sons of Sir Hildebrand
Osbaldistone [Scott, Rob Roy].
Wilkins, Peter : a mariner cast on a desert shore frequented
by a winged race called glumms and gawreys, whose
wings served them as raiment. Peter marries a
gawrey called Youwarkee [Pultock, Voyage of Peter
Wilkins].
Will and Jean : a touching story of which these two, Willie
Gairlace and Jeanie Miller, are the hero and heroine
[Macneill, Will and Jean].

Willet, Joe : the son of John ; a fine young man, who enlists, and in the end marries Dolly Varden, the locksmith's daughter.

———— *John :* landlord of the *Maypole Inn*, Chigwell, frequented by many of the characters in the story [Dickens, *Barnaby Rudge*].

William : a card-playing footman in the service of Lovemore, who courts Muslin, a lady's-maid [Murphy, *Way to Keep Him*].

———— the hero of an old English romance of which the authorship is unknown. It probably dates from about the middle of the fourteenth century [*William and the Werwolf*].

———— **and Margaret :** the subjects of a ballad [Mallet, *William and Margaret*].

———— **Lord :** the subject of a ballad. He drowns his brother's orphan child that he himself may inherit the property, and is afterwards drawn under the water himself by a mysterious child's hand [Southey, *Lord William*].

———— **of Cloudesley :** an outlaw who dwelt near Carlisle with his wife Alyce and his ' children three '. He was a boon companion of Adam Bell and Clym of the Clough [Percy, *Reliques : Adam Bell, Clym of the Clough*, and *William of Cloudesley*].

———— **of Goldsborough :** a friend and companion of Robin Hood [*see* Grafton, *Olde and Ancient Pamphlet*].

Williams, Caleb : a man of ' insatiable, incessant curiosity ', who discovers that his noble master, Falkland, has committed a murder in the past, and wins his confession from him, but then becomes the victim of the murderer's suspicions [Godwin, *Caleb Williams*].

Willie and May Margaret : the characters in a ballad. Willie gets drowned whilst crossing the Clyde to visit May Margaret [*Drowned Lover*].

———— **Rattlin' Roarin' :** the hero of a Scottish song [*Rattlin' Roarin' Willie*].

———— **Wandering :** the hero of a song [Burns, *Wandering Willie*].

———— **Wandering :** the blind fiddler [Scott, *Redgauntlet*].

Willis, Kitty : a girl of no reputation who at the instigation of Saville impersonates Lady Francis at a masquerade so as to deceive Courtall [Mrs. Cowley, *Belle's Stratagem*].

Willmore : a young rake who finds vice attractive though ' naughty ' ; he is the hero of the play [Mrs. Aphra Behn, *The Rover*].

Willoughby, Mr.: beloved by Marianne Dashwood, but behaving badly to her, she married another (Colonel Brandon), and he married Sophie Grey for her money [Jane Austen, *Sense and Sensibility*].

—— **Sir Clement:** the insolent admirer of Evelina [Fanny Burney, *Evelina*].

Willy: a shepherd in whom Thomalin confides [Spenser, *Shepheard's Calendar*].

Wilmot: there are three characters bearing this name in the tragedy [Lillo, *Fatal Curiosity*].

—— **Arabella:** the beloved of George Primrose, the Vicar's eldest son [Goldsmith, *Vicar of Wakefield*].

Wilsa: a mulatto girl [Scott, *Fortunes of Nigel*].

Wilson, Andrew: a smuggler; the friend of Geordie Robertson [Scott, *Heart of Midlothian*].

Wilton, Ralph de: accepted lover of Lady Clare [Scott, *Marmion*].

Wily Beguilde: the hero of a 'pleasant comedie' [Dodsley's *Old Plays; Wily Beguilde*].

Wimble, Will: 'well versed in the little handicrafts of an idle man' [Addison, *Spectator*, Essays 108, 122, 131, 269, etc.].

Winifreda: the subject of a 'beautiful address to conjugal love' [Percy, *Reliques: Winifreda*].

Winkle, Nathaniel: a thorough cockney in the matter of sports. He marries Arabella Allen.

—— **Mr.:** a Birmingham Wharfinger, father of Nathaniel [Dickens, *Pickwick Papers*].

—— **Rip Van:** see Rip Van Winkle.

Winnie, Annie: one of the two old sibyls present at the death of Alice Gray [Scott, *Bride of Lammermoor*].

Wintersen, Count: brother of Baron Steinfort 'the stranger'.

—— **Countess:** his wife, and Baron Steinfort's confidant [B. Thompson, *The Stranger*].

Winterton, Adam: Sir Edward Mortimer's faithful old steward, who had an unlimited admiration for his master [Colman the Younger, *Iron Chest*].

Winthrop, Dolly: Silas Marner's kindly neighbour, who helps him with little Eppie [George Eliot, *Silas Marner*].

Wishfort, Lady: a witty but vain woman, the widow of Sir Jonathan [Congreve, *Way of the World*].

Witch of Atlas: the heroine of a wild, fanciful and brilliant poem [Shelley, *Witch of Atlas*].

—— **of Edmonton:** see Sawyer, Mother.

—— **of Wokey, The:** the subject of a ballad published in 1756 and afterwards embellished by Shenstone [*Witch of Wokey*].

—— **The:** the heroine of a play [Middleton, *The Witch*].

Witherden, Mr.: a short, active, chubby little notary [Dickens, *Old Curiosity Shop*].

Witherington, General: the real name of Richard Tresham, who also goes under the name of Middlemas.

——— *Richard:* his son [Scott, *Surgeon's Daughter*].

Withrington, Roger: *see* Widdrington, Roger.

Wititterly, Mr. Henry: a man much given to boasting of his grand acquaintances.

——— *Mrs. Julia:* the person with whom Kate Nickleby lives as companion. Underbred but aping the airs of the aristocracy [Dickens, *Nicholas Nickleby*].

Wittol, Sir Joseph: an ignorant, foolish man [Congreve, *Old Bachelor*].

Witwould, Sir Jerry = Jeremy Collier [Thomas Brown, *Stage Beaux Tossed in a Blanket*].

——— *Anthony:* Sir Wilful's half-brother.

——— *Sir Wilful:* a Shropshire man, shy and obstinate, but friendly when in his cups [Congreve, *Way of the World*].

Wobbler, Mr.: a clerk in the secretarial department of the Circumlocution Office [Dickens, *Little Dorrit*].

Wodehouse, Lucy: the heroine, who first acting as sister of Mercy in the curate's parish, afterwards becomes his wife.

——— *Tom:* a disreputable ne'er-do-weel, the brother of Lucy [Mrs. Oliphant, *Chronicles of Carlingford: Perpetual Curate*].

Woodcock, Adam: Lady Mary Avenel's falconer, who takes the part of the 'abbot of Unreason' in the revels [Scott, *The Abbot*].

——— *Justice:* a testy, gouty old country gentleman, who made a point of disagreeing with his sister, Deborah, his housekeeper.

——— *Lucinda:* his merry, lively daughter [Bickerstaff, *Love in a Village*].

Woodcourt, Allan: the doctor who married Esther Summerson [Dickens, *Bleak House*].

Woodhouse, Emma: the heroine, who marries Mr. Knightley.

——— *Mr.:* Emma's father—an amiable, simple hypochondriac, whose hospitable impulses are always checked by fears for his friends' digestions [Jane Austen, *Emma*].

Woodseer, Gower: son of a minister and bootmaker in Whitechapel, who wanders, almost penniless, but thinking 'philosophy', over England and the Continent. The utterer of many wise sayings. A character said to be founded on that of R. L. Stevenson [George Meredith, *The Amazing Marriage*].

Woodvill, John : the hero of the tragedy [Lamb, *John Woodvill*].

Woodville, Harry : a gambler who injured his friend Penruddock by superseding him in the affections of his sweetheart.

—— *Henry :* his son, a captain ; a brave and noble soldier who loved Emily Tempest, and to whom Penruddock makes over all the deeds, bonds, etc., his father had lost in gambling.

—— *Mrs. :* wife of Harry, previously betrothed to Roderick Penruddock [Cumberland, *Wheel of Fortune*].

—— *Lord :* a friend of General Brown's [Scott, *Tapestried Chamber*].

—— *Olivia :* daughter of Sir James. She was left in the guardianship of a man who, to secure her fortune to himself, shut her up in a convent in Paris. Leontine Crocker saves and marries her [Goldsmith, *Good-Natured Man*].

Worldly-Wiseman, Mr. : tries to dissuade Christian from continuing his journey to the Celestial City [Bunyan, *Pilgrim's Progress*].

Worthington, Emily : the lieutenant's lovely daughter, who, after indignantly rejecting dishonourable proposals from Sir Charles Cropland, becomes the wife of Frank Bramble.

—— *Lieutenant :* a poor, disabled and very proud officer on half pay [Colman the Younger, *Poor Gentleman*].

Worthy : he loves Melinda, who after tormenting him for a year consents to become his wife [Farquhar, *Recruiting Officer*].

—— *Lord :* redeems Lady Neveller from her love of play and marries her [Mrs. Centlivre, *Basset-Table*].

Wrangle, Mr. Caleb : a meek young man, very much under the thumb of a fashionable wife.

—— *Mrs. :* daughter of Sir Miles Mowbray. A nagging, shrewish, contradictious woman [Cumberland, *First Love*].

Wray, Enoch : the blind and poor but resigned and pious ' patriarch ' [Crabbe, *Village Patriarch*].

Wrayburne, Eugene : indolent and gloomy, and hating his profession, which is that of a barrister, he is reformed by his love for Lizzie Hexam, whom he marries [Dickens, *Our Mutual Friend*].

Wren, Jenny : *see* Cleaver, Fanny.

Wrexhill, Vicar of : the hero of a novel [Mrs. Trollope, *Vicar of Wrexhill*].

Wronghead, Sir Francis : M.P. for Guzzledown. A blundering country squire who comes to town to attend Parliament, always votes the wrong way, and is nearly ruined by the extravagant follies of his family [Vanbrugh and Cibber, *Provoked Husband*].

Wycliffe, Wilfrid : the son of Sir Oswald, and in love with Matilda [Scott, *Rokeby*].

Wynebgwrthucher : King Arthur's shield [*Mobinogion*].

Wynne, Taffy or Talbot : the Yorkshireman who marries Miss Bagot [Du Maurier, *Trilby*].

Wyoming, Gertrude of : the heroine of the poem. She is the daughter of Albert and marries Henry Waldegrave [Campbell, *Gertrude of Wyoming*].

Xury : a Moresco boy who acts as servant to Crusoe [Defoe, *Robinson Crusoe*].

Yahoos, The : a race who combine the form of man with the nature of brutes and are subject to the Houyhnhnms, a breed of horses endowed with reason [Swift, *Gulliver's Travels*].

Yamen : the lord of Pandalon (hell) [Southey, *Curse of Kehama*].

Yasodhara : the docile bride of Prince Siddartha [Edwin Arnold, *Light of Asia*].

Yellowley, Triptolemus : an experimental farmer of Stourburgh [Scott, *Pirate*].

Yellowplush, Mr. : the hero of a series of humorous sketches purporting to be written by a West-End footman [Thackeray, *Memoirs of Mr. C. J. Yellowplush*].

Yeo, Salvation : a Clovelly sailor who 'sweareth awfully in his talk' [Charles Kingsley, *Westward Ho!*].

Yeruti : the son of Quiara and Monnema, who was born in the Mondai Woods, whither his parents had fled to escape smallpox [Southey, *Tale of Paraguay*].

Ygerne : wife of Gorlois, Lord of Tintagel Castle in Cornwall, who was slain by King Uther. Uther then married Ygerne, and their child was King Arthur [Alfred Tennyson, *Idylls of the King: Coming of Arthur*].

Yniol : the father of Enid. He had fallen upon evil days, when his nephew, Edyrn, came and ousted him from his possessions. Then Geraint came and took the old man's part and overthrew Edyrn and married Enid [Alfred Tennyson, *Idylls of the King: Geraint and Enid*].

Yorick : jester at the Danish Court, 'a fellow of infinite jest and most excellent fancy' [Shakespeare, *Hamlet*].

Yorick: the name assumed by Sterne in *Tristram Shandy*, and also in *A Sentimental Journey through France and Italy*.

Yorke, Mr. Hiram: 'a Yorkshire gentleman he was, *par excellence*, in every point . . . truthful, upright, independent . . . as a rock based below seas; but also . . . harsh, rude, narrow, and merciless'.

———— *Mrs.:* the wife of Hiram. A conscientious, morbid, melancholy and jealous woman.

———— *Jessie and Rose:* the daughters of Hiram Yorke.

———— *Matthew, Mark and Martin:* schoolboys; the sons of Hiram [Charlotte Brontë, *Shirley*].

Young, Maria: a cripple and governess to the Grey and Rowland children [Harriet Martineau, *Deerbrook*].

Youwarkee: the 'Gawrey' whom Peter Wilkins marries [Pultock, *Voyage of Peter Wilkins*]; *see also* Wilkins, Peter.

Ysaie le Triste: son of Tristram and Isold [*Arthurian Cycle*].

Yseult: *see* Iseult.

Yuhidthiton: chief of the Aztecas. Wise in council and mighty in war, he led his people in safety from south of the Missouri to Mexico [Southey, *Madoc*].

Zadoc = Sancroft, Archbishop of Canterbury [Dryden, *Absalom and Achitophel*].

Zaira: the Italian mother of Eva Wentworth [Maturin, *Women: a novel*].

Zamora: the youngest of Balthazar's daughters, in love with a young sailor called Rolando [Tobin, *Honeymoon*].

Zamti: a Chinese Mandarin, the husband of Mandane [Murphy, *Orphan of China*].

Zanga: a revengeful Moor, the servant of Don Alonzo, whom he hates. He is the hero of the tragedy [Young, *The Revenge*].

Zanoni: the hero of the story—an alchemist [Lytton, *Zanoni*].

Zaphimri: the 'orphan' who under the name of Etan is brought up by Zamti [Murphy, *Orphan of China*].

Zaphna: son of Alcanor, the Meccan Chief. Beset by all sorts of untoward circumstances, he falls in love with Palmira, who is his own sister, and slays his own father [Miller, *Mahomet the Imposter*].

Zapolya: the heroine [S. T. Coleridge, *Zapolya: a Christmas Tale*].

Zara: an African Queen, in love with Osmyn [Congreve, *Mourning Bride*].

Zara : the heroine of a play adapted from the French of Voltaire [Hill, *Zara*; based on the French of Voltaire].

Zarah = Sarah, Duchess of Marlborough [Mrs. De la Rivière Manley, *Secret History of Queen Zarah*].

Zaraph : the angel by whom Nama was beloved [Thomas Moore, *The Loves of the Angels*].

Zarca : the gypsy chief, father of Fedalma [George Eliot, *Spanish Gypsy*].

Zeal, Arabella : one of the characters in the comedy [Charles Shadwell, *Fair Quaker of Deal*].

Zeinab : wife of Hodeirah, and the mother of Thelaba [Southey, *Thelaba*].

Zelica : betrothed to Azim, who, mistaking her for the 'Veiled Prophet', slays her [Thomas Moore, *Lalla Rookh*].

Zelis : engaged to be married to a man who forsook her, she travelled to Italy, intending to become a nun in Rome. Captured by Corsairs she was sold as a slave and finally rescued and married by Hingpo, a Chinaman [Goldsmith, *Citizen of the World*].

Zelmane : the name taken by Pyrocles when he passed as a woman [Sidney, *Arcadia*].

Zeluco : the hero of a novel, the scene of which is mostly laid in Italy [Dr. J. Moore, *Zeluco : Various Views of Human Nature*, etc.].

Zenelophon : the beggar-maid who married King Cophetua. Oftener called Penelophon [Shakespeare, *Love's Labour's Lost*].

Zenobia : an excitable, impulsive woman, who drowns herself [Nathaniel Hawthorne, *Blithedale Romance*].

Zenocia : affianced bride of Arnoldo [J. Fletcher, *Custom of the Country*].

Zephon : the cherub who found Satan hiding in the garden of Eden and made him appear before the Archangel Gabriel [Milton, *Paradise Lost*].

Zimmerman, Adam : one of the deputation sent by the Swiss to Charles the Bold [Scott, *Anne of Geierstein*].

Zimri = the second Duke of Buckingham.
'Stiff in opinions, always in the wrong,
Was everything by turns, and nothing long.'
[Dryden, *Absalom and Achitophel*].

Zinebi, Mohammed : the kindly king of Syria, a tributary to the Caliph Haroun-al-Raschid [*Arabian Nights*].

Zobeide : wife of Haroun-al-Raschid [*Arabian Nights*].

Zoleika or Zuleika : sometimes called Raïl, the wife of Potiphar [Sale, *Al Koran*].

Zophiel : ' of cherubim the swiftest wing '. He warns the heavenly host of the approach of the rebels [Milton, *Paradise Lost*].

Zuleika : daughter of the Pasha of Abydos [Byron, *Bride of Abydos*].